DATE DUE

DE 13'98			
AG 5'04			

DEMCO 38-296

Habits of Mind

Habits of Mind

Evidence and Effects
of Ben Jonson's Reading

Robert C. Evans

Lewisburg
Bucknell University Press
London: Associated University Presses

to photocopy items for internal or personal
f specific clients, is granted by the copyright
10.00, plus eight cents per page per copy is
ance Center, 222 Rosewood Drive, Danvers,
387-5301-9/95 $10.00 + 8¢ pp, pc.]

University Presses
orsgate Drive
Cranbury, NJ 08512

Associated University Presses
25 Sicilian Avenue
London WC1A 2QH, England

Associated University Presses
P.O. Box 338, Port Credit
Mississauga, Ontario
Canada L5G 4L8

The paper used in this publication meets the requirements
of the American National Standard for Permanence of Paper
for Printed Library Materials Z39.48-1984.

Library of Congress Cataloging-in-Publication Data

Evans, Robert C.
    Habits of mind : evidence and effects of Ben Jonson's reading /
Robert C. Evans.
        p.   cm.
    Includes bibliographical references (p.   ) and index.
    ISBN 0-8387-5301-9 (alk. paper)
    1. Jonson, Ben, 1573?–1637—Books and reading.   2. Jonson, Ben,
1573?–1637—Knowledge and learning.   3. Books and reading—England—
History—17th century.   4. England—Intellectual life—17th
century.   5. Influence (Literary, artistic, etc.)   I. Title.
PR2642.B6E93   1995
822'.3—dc20   94-45819
                                                                 CIP

PRINTED IN THE UNITED STATES OF AMERICA

for Ruth and my parents

Contents

Preface

Among his many other distinctions, Ben Jonson may be the only great English poet who was directly responsible for two deaths. The first killing occurred when Jonson, still a young man, was serving as a volunteer with English forces in the Netherlands. Years later he would tell his friend William Drummond how, during "his servuce in the Low Countries, he had in the face of both the Campes Killed ane Enimie and taken opima spoila from him."[1] Jonson, that is to say, stripped his vanquished foe of his weapons—an almost Homeric gesture of exaltation in victory. The pugnaciousness later evident in much of his writing was thus also apparent early in his life, and his physical courage and combativeness would display themselves again a few years later. By then he had returned to England, had married, and had begun to establish himself as an actor and playwright. In September 1598 one of his most important plays, *Every Man in His Humour*, was acted at The Curtain theater with Shakespeare in a leading role. Jonson had already begun to make a name and career that would later prove highly distinctive.

Within days, however, he was in trouble with the law. He stood accused of killing a fellow actor, Gabriel Spencer, who, he claimed, had challenged him to fight in an open field. Indicted before a jury, Jonson pleaded guilty that he had,

> with a certain sword of iron and steel called a Rapiour, of the price of three shillings, which he then and there had and held drawn in his right hand, feloniously and wilfully beat and struck the same Gabriel, giving then and there to the same Gabriel Spencer with the aforesaid sword a mortal wound of the depth of six inches and of the breadth of one inch, in and upon the right side of the same Gabriel, of which mortal blow the same Gabriel Spencer at Shordiche aforesaid, in the aforesaid county, in the aforesaid Fields, then and there died instantly.[2]

Jonson himself would later explain that his "adversarie . . . had hurt him in the arm" and that Spencer's "sword was 10 Inches Longer than his," but the jurors nonetheless concluded that the playwright had "feloniously and wilfully killed and slew the aforesaid Gabriel Spencer, against the peace of the said Lady the Queen." Jonson was imprisoned and was "almost at the Gallowes," but he escaped death because of a simple fact: he could read a Bible verse in Latin.

The official record reports how Jonson *"confesses the indictment, asks for the book, reads like a clerk, is marked with the letter T, and is delivered according to the statute."* The statute in question dated from the middle ages and had originally been designed to protect priests from prosecution in the civil courts. By the time Jonson took advantage of this one-time opportunity to plead "benefit of clergy," that opportunity "had become a loophole for educated male felons."[3] The "T" branded in Jonson's thumb stood for Tyburn prison, where he would have been hanged had he been unable to translate the Latin "neck verse." Fittingly enough, Jonson the eventual poet laureate had now himself become a written text, painfully inscribed in the flesh, and anyone who later glimpsed the scarred "T" burnt into his skin would have been able to decipher its significance. Presumably he bore the brand for the rest of his life—a constant reminder to him and to others of his brush with death and of the highly crucial importance his culture often placed on the ability to read.

Never again, perhaps, would the importance of that ability be demonstrated so dramatically in Jonson's life, but reading never had been, and never would be, an unimportant facet of his existence. It was partly thanks to his skill as a reader that Jonson, as a young boy from a family of modest means, had been given the chance to attend the prestigious Westminster School, where he had had his first real taste of the life of the mind, and where the seeds of his later grand ambitions must first have taken root. It was partly thanks to his skill as a reader that Jonson at Westminster so impressed his first important patron, William Camden, the school's headmaster and later one of his most significant intellectual contacts. It was partly thanks to his skill as a reader, and consequently as an author and struggling apprentice playwright, that Jonson was able to support himself and his young family by relying on the fecundity of his brain rather than on the strength of his hands, and it was largely thanks to his skill as a reader that he soon began to carve out for himself a distinctive niche as one of the most learned and sophisticated of English writers. His literary sophistication would soon help him win, for instance, a central place at the court of James I, perhaps one of the most genuinely learned of all the British monarchs. Thus the ability to read not only once saved Jonson's life, but it also, more significantly, allowed him to live the kind of existence that reading itself had largely helped him to conceive.

This, then, is a book about Jonson's reading—which is to say that it is also a book about one of the most important aspects of Jonson's life. More is known about Jonson's biographical activities (where he went; what he did; whom he met; what he said) than about those of most of his great contemporaries, and so it seems fitting that more evidence about his reading should also have survived. Modern catalogues list hundreds of existing books known to have once been owned by Jonson, and many of these books contain markings by the poet that provide extremely interesting evidence of what, literally and precisely, passed through his mind. Source studies have already suggested the impact his reading may have had on the composition of his own works, including his surviving notebook of *Discoveries*, which records and transmutes much of his reading and his reactions to it. However, the marked copies of his surviving books provide a unique and largely untapped source of information about what was quite literally going into (and even on in) Jonson's mind. The poet's marked books allow us to speculate with some confidence about the interior, mental life of one of the most important and influential writers of the English Renaissance.

The value of this study will, I suspect, lie less in my own speculations than in the hard evidence the book provides. I have tried to interpret the significance of Jonson's markings in what I hope and think are plausible ways, but in the final analysis what matters most is the markings themselves. During my work on this project I have developed a system of abbreviations that has allowed me to indicate Jonson's marks with some precision and thoroughness. This book, then, attempts not simply to describe my own interpretations of Jonson's markings but, more importantly, to *report* every passage he marked so that other scholars can speculate for themselves and reach their own conclusions about about the marks' significance.

My central aim has thus been quite simply to provide *new primary evidence* about Jonson's reading—evidence that supplements and is comparable, in some ways, to the data already available in the *Discoveries*. That work has always been considered a prime source of useful information because it gives unequalled insight into what Jonson was reading, what was on his mind. In a more modest way, I hope that my descriptions of the marked passages in some of his books can provide similarly useful information.

His marks offer fairly hard evidence of what actually passed through his thoughts, and while interpreting the marks will always be somewhat speculative, there seems some value in reporting them so that interpretations can be made. The real worth of this project lies less in the particular interpretations I myself have offered than in simply reporting the marked passages to other scholars, who may see many different kinds of significance in them—significance perhaps unsuspected by me. My chief goal, throughout the book, is simply to report Jonson's marks as accurately as I can, even at the expense (sometimes) of rapid narrative flow. I conceive of this book as being as much a reference work as anything else.

The marked books I have selected for discussion are a deliberately mixed lot, and the methods used in discussing them are similarly and intentionally diverse. I have tried to choose works representing differing periods, genres, styles, and thematic concerns. Doing so will, I hope, suggest the impressive range of Jonson's interests as well as the continuities that seem to underlie them. Chapter 1 offers an introduction that surveys the topic of Jonson's reading and that ends by focusing on his response to a surviving copy of the Bible, perhaps the central text of his Christian culture. Chapter 2 then examines his lively reactions to the philosophical writings of Seneca, whose Stoic wisdom had such an impact on Jonson's own life and writings. Chapter 3 discusses the poet's response to another late classical writer, Apuleius, who seems to have been far more intriguing to Jonson than previous scholarship would suggest. Chapter 4 then turns to Jonson's markings in his copy of Chaucer, one of his most significant English and medieval forebears. This chapter is supplemented by photographic reproductions of the actual marked pages of Jonson's Chaucer; these photographs should help give readers a very precise idea of the appearance and methods of some of Jonson's typical styles of marking.

Chapter 5 surveys Jonson's reactions to an important "dramatic" work in Latin prose by Sir Thomas More, one of the most seminal figures of the early English Renaissance. More, along with the Renaissance Christian Stoic Justus Lipsius, is also featured in chapter 6, which examines issues of praise and blame—issues that have always been recognized as central to Jonson's thinking and writing. Finally, chapter 7 focuses on Jonson's responses to Clement Edmondes's responses to the autobiographical writings of Julius Caesar. This highly reflexive topic seemed an appropriate one on which to end: a Christian English writer reacting to a

Christian English writer reacting to a pagan classical writer re-acting to events he helped shape with both sword and pen. Scores of other books marked by Jonson remain to be examined, but this sampling should give some sense of the breadth, depth, and intensity of his responses to several of the most important written texts of his culture.

Perhaps not surprisingly, such a sampling of Jonson's responses to significant works and writers suggests certain broad continuities in his interests. Many of the same themes and concerns that seem to have been central to his own writing seem also to have been central to his reading, and I have tried to suggest these continuities by providing an extensive Topical Index. Jonson seems to have been endlessly interested in certain recurring pre-occupations, and the purpose of the Topical Index is to provide a quick overview of the matters that seem to have most interested him and of where those topics can be located. Literally hundreds of common themes are shared by the marked passages in the handful of books examined here, and the Topical Index can help provide a quick overview of Jonson's interest in a wide range of subjects. Similarly, the Index proper offers a key to the various persons—real or imagined—mentioned in the passages Jonson singled out. I hope that these appendices will help make this book even more useful to other students of Jonson's life, times, and mind.

Acknowledgments

My greatest debt, obviously, is to my parents. My father was himself a great reader, and some of my best memories are of him reading to me as a boy. When he was suddenly no longer there, my mother continued to provide the encouragement and love that sustained my own interest in books. I well remember a shopping expedition, when a twelve-year-old whose parent thought he needed a new suit came home instead with a set of encyclopedias. Since my mother died as this book was being completed, it is especially to her that I wish to express the kind of thanks that cannot finally be expressed.

My wife, my extended family, my friends, my colleagues, and my students have all been involved, in one way or another, in the making of this book. Several students in particular need to be mentioned: Kurt Niland, Mike Crocker, Jullianna Ooi, Hubble Sowards, Neil Probst, Kevin Bowden, Gary Goodson, Joe Csicsila, and Lynn Bryan. Rarely have students taught their teacher so much. Among the many good friends I might thank, I should especially mention Jim Barfoot, Jeff Hyams, Ron Romanoff, Anne Little, Barbara Wiedemann, David Walker, David Brumble, and, above all, my best friend, Ruth Evans. I am particularly grateful for the encouragement provided by my colleagues John Stroupe and Clifford Davidson, who nurtured this project at crucial stages. For many years now, Professor Anthony Low has been exceptionally generous with his time and encouragement.

My debt to the pioneering scholarship of Professor David Mc-Pherson will be evident throughout this book, and I must also thank Professor Henry Woudhuysen for his kindness to a stranger. And, after ten years of professional interest in Ben Jonson, I am now even more aware of the thanks I owe to other Jonsonians. As latter-day sons and daughters of Ben, we share a bond that transcends occasional disagreements.

For fellowships in support of my work, I am extremely grateful to the Auburn University at Montgomery Grant-in-Aid program, the American Council of Learned Societies, the American Philosophical Society, the National Endowment for the Humanities, the Newberry Library, the Huntington Library, and especially the Folger Shakespeare Library. Each of these institutions is, of course, merely an abstraction; it is to the the people who embody these institutions and who pursue their stated missions that I owe my real thanks. Let Laetitia Yeandle of the Folger stand for them all: there could not be a better representative.

Finally, my work on this project will always be associated, in my mind, with happy days spent hunched over old books in libraries throughout Britain and the U.S. Let the library at Emmanuel College, Cambridge, and its wonderful staff, stand for all these. The dedication to this book is meant to express my love and thanks, in particular, to the librarian who has always meant more than words can say.

*　*　*

Several essays included in this book have been published previously in unrevised form. I am grateful to the editors of *English Literary Renaissance* for permission to reprint my article "Ben Jonson's Chaucer," which first appeared in *ELR* 19 (1989): 324–45. I am also grateful to the editors of *Comparative Drama* and to Medieval Institute Publications for permission to reprint my article entitled "More's *Richard III* and Jonson's *Richard Crookback* and *Sejanus*" and also to include a substantially revised version of my article entitled "Jonson's Copy of Seneca." I wish to thank the editors of *The Explicator* for permission to reprint my piece on "Jonson's *Epigrammes I-III*," and I am very grateful to the Folger Shakespeare Library for permission to reproduce pages from Jonson's marked copy of Chaucer.

Abbreviations

Throughout this volume, the following basic abbreviations have been used parenthetically to indicate the kinds of marginal markings Jonson made in the various books he owned. The marks noted below are quite typical, both in their general style and specific appearance, of the markings Jonson made in numerous other books in his possession. Any additional abbreviations used in particular chapters are explained in the appropriate places.

AS = asterisk
BR = bracket
DL = diagonal line
FL = flower or trefoil, often with a stem
CL = curved line
CR = any of several kinds of cross marks; often these resemble
     flowers (FL) not fully formed
CT = circular shape with attached tail
HD = pointing hand; usually the index finger is quite extended
HL = horizontal line
TR = trident-shaped mark
UL = underlining
UM = unusually shaped mark
VL = vertical line

Habits of Mind

1

Introduction

Ben Jonson was one of the best-read and most learned of all the great English poets, and the impact of his reading on his own art was both immediate and strong.[1] Nowhere is this impact more stunningly visible than in the margins of his 1619 copy of Martial's epigrams, presently housed in the Folger Library. Hundreds of poems are underscored, and next to various lines Jonson has drawn flowers, asterisks, swords, or pointing hands. He translates passages, corrects errata, notes connections between works, and uses the margins to comment on contemporary superiors and peers. And, in a tiny hand, he painstakingly translates Book 13's lengthy list of food and beverages—a fact of some relevance to a writer famous not only for his girth but for using copious lists as an effective poetic technique. The Folger volume offers a unique insight into the ways Jonson's mind functioned and into one wellspring of his own creativity. His reading was not a distraction from his own work; it was instead central to his inspiration and artistic development.

Despite the notorious fire that decimated much of his library in the fall of 1623, hundreds of Jonson's books are known to survive, and it seems likely that others remain to be discovered.[2] Fortunately, Jonson was in the habit of marking his books not only with his signature but with his personal motto ("Tanquam explorator"). Moreover, many of the books are full of distinctive marginal markings. All this has helped make individual volumes from his library far easier to track down and identify than is the case with books that belonged to many of his contemporaries. Of course, tracing and describing Jonson's books may at first seem merely a sterile exercise in literary detective work, but to know Jonson is to know differently. He was, after all, the artist who claimed that the spirit gave the body weight (*Ep.* 109), and his own passion for books and learning helped him incorporate his culture's heritage and make it speak anew, both to his present and to ours. For Jonson, reading could be an intense and energetic activity, one evoking maximum responsiveness to stimulating texts. This, no doubt, is how he wanted his own works to be read, and it is fascinating to see him reacting so vigorously to writings that may often have influenced his own. For the insights they can provide into his own thought, works, and intellectual habits, the books from his library seem very much worth studying.

There seems some value simply in describing the passages Jonson marked in various books and in quoting or paraphrasing those passages in detail. Although Jonson's books have often been listed and catalogued, descriptions of the markings they sometimes contain have usually been quite brief. Examining a number of Jonson's marked books can suggest the range of his reading and interests. His responses to other writers, especially to writers from other times and places, suggest his sense of the universality of human experience, of the relevance of the past to the present, and of the apparently foreign to the recognizably familiar. His readings demonstrate his historical and intellectual curiosity, his passion for knowledge and truth, and his sense of his own need—and that of others—for disciplined, responsible learning. His markings show that he often read with the same kind of active thoughtfulness he hoped for as a writer; they show him discharging himself the same obligations he tried to impose on his own audience.[3]

For the most part, it seems best to speak of Jonson's "readings" rather than of anything so abstract as his reading in general. Jonson often owned multiple copies of the same text, and he sometimes seems to have read and marked the same works on more than one occasion. For instance, the Folger Library also owns a 1615 edition of Martial's epigrams that is almost as thoroughly marked as the 1619 version, and, as in other books, the markings have been made sometimes in pencil, sometimes in ink, and sometimes in pencil traced over in ink. Such evidence suggests that Jonson read various authors repeatedly, at different times, and perhaps with different interests in mind. Moreover, the vast majority of Jonson's markings consist not of words but of underlining and of various marginal symbols. Interpreting the significance of such markings is necessarily speculative, and it provides another reason for speaking of Jonson's "readings." Doing so can emphasize his responses to particular, physical *books* rather than his reactions to an author's "corpus" or "texts." Some of Jonson's books, undoubtedly, are lost forever, while others may yet turn up. Our evidence is thus inevitably fragmentary and incomplete, and for that reason, assertions about Jonson's "reading" can only be provisional. Thus it seems best to approach his reading as he did himself—one text, one book, at a time.

This is not to say, however, that generalizations about Jonson's reading are entirely futile. His surviving works, especially the notes preserved in his commonplace book entitled *Timber, or Discoveries*, contain much suggestive evidence about his attitudes toward authors and texts, readers and reading. The diverse contents of Jonson's *Discoveries*, in fact, often grew directly out of his reading; many of the passages quote, translate, or paraphrase other authors, and many portions of the work comment directly or indirectly on the purposes and results of reading. Along with his marked books themselves, Jonson's *Discoveries* help illuminate why and how he read, as well as why and how he hoped to be read.

The topic of reading runs throughout the *Discoveries* and supplies one of its unifying themes. It is already implicit in one of the work's earliest comments, that "very few men are wise by their owne counsell; or learned by their owne teaching" (H&S 8:563), which already suggests Jonson's view that reading is a way of overcoming one's limited, personal perspective and of profiting from the wisdom of others. Of course, the external "counsell" Jonson suggests could be supplied by living contemporaries, but an ensuing comment (indebted to Jonson's own reading of Velleius Paterculus [H&S 11:214]) makes it clear that we tend to "envy the present, and reverence the past; thinking ourselves instructed by the one, and over-laid by the other" (H&S 8:564). For this reason, presumably, we are more likely to take instruction from books than from our immediate contemporaries, who are often necessarily our rivals. We have more autonomy in our dealings with the dead; books pose no immediate sense of threat or of stubborn resistance. A reader can freely choose what to assimilate and what to reject from a book, without feeling under the pressure of an actual living presence. The dead author of an old book poses no insuperable challenge to a reader's self-interests— and, precisely for this reason, a reader can afford to feel less defensive, less self-interested, more open to the counsel a book can provide. Jonson implies that books are often the best teachers because we willingly cooperate in receiving the instruction they provide. Reading, paradoxically, allows one to feel a greater sense of self-control even as it ideally encourages a relaxation of self-defense.

Yet Jonson seems to have felt that the ability to read widely and thoughtfully was not something that could be taken for granted; rather, it required a certain amount of leisure and economic security. In the pithy phrasing of the *Discoveries* (borrowed from Juan Luis Vives), "Learning needs rest: Soveraignty gives it. Soveraignty needs counsell: Learning affords it" (H&S 8:565). Reading and power could thus prove mutually supportive, and learning could prove less an alternative to the world of affairs than a means of entering and engaging it. Of course, even the opportunity to be literate bespoke some social power; in Jonson's culture, literacy was not something that could simply be presumed.[4] Although it had become one of the fundamental avenues to power, to respectability, to being taken seriously, literacy was by no means guaranteed, as Jonson himself had discovered. Precisely because of his own early circumstances, he seems to have regarded the opportunity and ability to read as precious.

The freedom and ability to read undoubtedly meant much to Jonson for the simple reason that he had not been born into a situation in which learning seemed presupposed or assured. His determined self-education was part and parcel of his whole effort at self-assertion; reading was not an escape from the "real world" but a means of self-fashioning and self-preparation for involvement in that world. For Jonson, reading was less a passive behavior than an active effort of the mind and personality, and even his reading of past literature seems not to have been undertaken for pure enjoyment, amusement, or education, but in order to make *use* of it, especially in fashioning his own works and persona. Reading, for him, could prove another means of competition and self-assertion, of establishing a sense of social status and self-worth. As one of England's first professional intellectuals not affiliated with the church, universities, or schools and as one of the first of his countrymen to earn his living almost entirely as a free-lance man of letters, Jonson seems to have considered literacy and wide reading part of his equipment, part of his stock in trade.[5]

Yet he also seems to have considered the impulse to read and to learn irresistible, essential, almost instinctive or compulsive— at least for some people. Following Vives again, the *Discoveries* note that

> *Arts* that respect the mind, were ever reputed nobler, then those that serve the body: though wee lesse can bee without them. As *Tillage, Spinning, Weaving, Building, &c.* without which, wee could scarce sus-

taine life a day. But these were the workes of every hand; the other of the braine only, and those the most generous, and exalted wits, and spirits that cannot rest, or *acquiesce.* The mind of man is still fed with labour: *Opere pascitur.* (H&S 8:568)[6]

This passage suggests that Jonson regarded reading as absolutely vital and necessary—an activity he and others like him could not imagine doing without. Learning was a means to self-worth and social distinction, but it was also driven by an appetite that ordinary people could not truly understand. It thus inevitably made the learned man a bit marginal, a bit different from the mass of humanity, who could never really appreciate learning or the learned in the same ways or for the same reasons as the learned themselves. The "power of liberall studies," Jonson continues, "is not every mans way to hit" (H&S 8:568), yet the learned man benefits everyone. Reading well is like being an explorer, with all the distinction, excitement, hard work, and sacrifice the comparison implies; learned men or wits have "made out their severall expeditions then, for the discovery of *Truth,* to find out great and profitable *Knowledges*" (H&S 8:570). Now, however,

there are certaine *Scioli,* or *smatterers,* that are busie in the skirts, and out-sides of Learning, and have scarce any thing of solide literature to commend them. They may have some edging, or trimming of a Scholler, a welt, or so: but it is no more. (H&S 8:570)

Clearly Jonson wished to distinguish himself from persons such as these, and in fact, reading for him seems never to have been an entirely private act; it was always part of his effort at public self-definition and self-assertion.[7] True learning was "solide" (suggesting strength and permanence); through it, one might be "commend[ed]." It is, in fact, the desire for such commendation that encourages and motivates even the *Scioli,* that makes them want to *seem* learned when they really are not. Whereas commendation is something the learned man wins simply as a by-product of his pursuit of "*Truth*" and "*Knowledge,*" it is the sole motive of the "*smatterers* . . . busie in the skirts, and out-sides of Learning."

Among the qualities such smatterers lack are "*Wit, Industry, Diligence,* and *Iudgement*"; these are traits that Jonson (following Vives) seems to "looke up at, and admire" (H&S 8:567), and they were obviously qualities he hoped others would find admirable in him. Yet his notes also stress that admiration for classic writers is different from acquiescence or complacency, that the very judgment one prizes in the authors one reads is a trait the reader must exercise independently.[8] Judgment itself, however, must be exercised responsibly; it must be prompted by a commitment to truth, not by egotism or pride. It is this grounded judgment that helps distinguish the truly learned from the *Scioli*. Following Vives, Jonson notes that

> *Nothing* can conduce more to letters, then to examine the writings of the *Ancients*, and not to rest in their sole Authority, or take all upon trust from them; provided the plagues of *Iudging*, and *Pronouncing* against them, be away; such as are *enuy, bitterness, precipitation, impudence*, and *scurrile scoffing*. For to all the observations of the *Ancients*, wee have our owne experience: which, if wee will use, and apply, wee have better meanes to pronounce. It is true they open'd the gates, and made the way, that went before us; but as Guides, not Commanders. . . . Truth lyes open to all; it is no mans *severall*. (H&S 8:567)

This passage is crucial, for it suggests the ideal of balance and moderation central to Jonson's concept of reading: a reader's attitude must be critical but not prejudiced, and just as it is important to avoid slavish subservience to other authors, so is it equally important to avoid setting oneself up as an infallible authority:

> If I erre, pardon me: . . . I doe not desire to be equall to those that went before; but to have my reason examin'd with theirs, and so much faith to be given them, or me, as those shall evict. I am neither *Author* or *Fautor* of any sect. I will have no man addict himselfe to mee; but if I have any thing right, defend it as Truth's, not mine (save as it conduceth to a common good). It profits not me to have any man fence, or fight for me, to flourish, or take a side. Stand for *Truth*, and 'tis enough. (H&S 8:567–68)

The *"Scioli"* are capable neither of true self-abnegation nor of legitimate self-assertion; in their dealings with the authors they read, they act either as slaves or as tyrants—either mindlessly following another's lead or ignorantly imposing their own prejudices by indulging in *"envy, bitterness, precipitation, impudence*, and *scurrile scoffing."*

This taste for impudence is one that corrupt writers share with ignorant readers. Following J. J. Scaliger, Jonson later notes that

> nothing is of more credit, or request now, then a petulant paper, or scoffing verses; and it is but convenient to the times and manners wee live with, to have then the worst writings, and studies flourish, when the best begin to be despis'd. *Ill Arts* begin, where good end.
> The time was, when men would learne, and study good things;

not envie those that had them. Then men were had in price for learning: now, letters onely make men vile. Hee is upbraydingly call'd a
Poet, as if it were a most contemptible *Nick-name*. But the *Professors*
(indeed) have made the learning cheape. Rayling, and tinckling *Rimers*, whose Writings the vulgar more greedily reade; as being taken
with the scurrility, and petulancie of such wits. Hee shall not have a
reader now, unlesse hee jeere and lye. It is the food of mens natures:
the diet of the times! (H&S 8:571–72)

Earlier Jonson had suggested that some persons, at least, possessed a natural passion for learning; here he seems to imply that
a passion for reading is indeed shared by most people, but that
most readers are attracted to the worst kinds of materials. For
Jonson, the mere act of reading, in and of itself, was relatively
unimportant, as was the breadth or frequency with which one
read. What mattered above all was the judgment one brought to
one's reading—the intelligence, discrimination, and worthy motives an ideal reader displayed. Proper reading could hone these
qualities, but reading debased materials would not only debase
the reader but also help foster the creation of more such trash.

The same concern with others' opinions that might prompt a
writer to seek public commendation (H&S 8:568) could also make
him fear being "despis'd" for being different or distinct from the
crowd. In the wrong social environment, genuine learning might
actually prove a source of insecurity, isolation, alienation. For Jonson, even reading is in some sense a self-revealing social act, a
performance by which one can be judged. Moreover, he always
seems quite conscious that a writer does not create in isolation,
that in one way or another an author responds constantly to an
external (or internalized) audience, even when he rejects or attacks its values. For Jonson, reading is not a means of escaping
the social world but, as always, of responding to it.

One's audience, unfortunately, is most likely to be composed
of readers interested only in mere excitement, sensation, surprise,
suspense, aggression, malice, and sport, like the patrons of a
bear-pit: "*Nothing* doth more invite a greedy Reader, then an
unlook'd-for subject. And what more unlook'd-for, then to see a
person of unblam'd life, made ridiculous, or odious, by the Artifice of lying?" (H&S 8:572).[9] Crafting such lies does require intelligence, but it is also an abuse of that gift: "It is an Art to have so
much judgement, as to apparell a Lye well, to give it a good
dressing; that though the nakednesse would shew deform'd and
odious, the suiting of it might draw their Readers. Some love any
Strumpet . . . in good clothes" (H&S 8:573). The "judgement"

that should be used in serving truth is here corrupted and debased, and the phrasing implies not only that many readers are deceived, but also (more damningly) that many want to be. Good reading, then, demands not only the ability but the desire to pierce beneath deceptions and superficial appearances.[10]

For Jonson, then, a good reader is mentally active, morally alert, and motivated by a different kind of curiosity than stimulates the masses. The "*Expectation* of the *Vulgar* is more drawne, and held with newnesse, then goodnesse; . . . so it be new, though never so naught, and depraved, they run to it, and are taken" (H&S 8:576). The behavior of such readers displays a strange combination of activity and passivity ("they run to it, and are taken"), so that they cooperate in their own debasement. Ironically, the intellectual laziness of most readers goes hand in hand with an interest in pretentious "difficulty":

> Right and naturall language seeme<s> to have the least of wit in it; that which is writh'd and tortur'd, is counted the more exquisite. . . . Nothing is fashionable, till it bee deform'd; and this is to write like a *Gentleman*. (H&S 8:581)

Yet the difficulty prized in such writing is a difficulty of surface effects, of mere appearance, of superficial jargon and convoluted syntax that becomes a way of obscuring rather than revealing the truth. What is also prized in reading such "writh'd and tortur'd" language is a cheap sense of social distinction derived from being able to follow a jargon that sets one apart from those readers presumably less capable. Jonson ties this preference in writing and reading to a ridiculous social snobbery, and, although his own standards might be termed elitist, the writing he prizes involves a style clear enough to be read and understood by any reasonably educated person. His own *Discoveries* display the kind of style he values, and they also themselves exemplify the kind of active, intelligent responsiveness that ideal reading involves.[11]

In a passage that helps define, by contrast, his own achievement in the *Discoveries*, Jonson condemns the general absence of such discriminating responsiveness. He censures those derivative authors who

> turne over all bookes, and are equally searching in all papers, that write out of what they presently find or meet, without choice; by which meanes it happens, that what they have discredited, and impugned in one worke, they have before, and after, extolled in another. Such are all the *Essayists*, even their Master *Mountaigne*. These, in all

they write, confesse still what bookes they have read last; and therein
their owne folly, so much, that they bring it to the *Stake* raw, and
undigested. (H&S 8:585–86)

Such reader/writers fail to display the judgment, effort, sifting,
analysis, and assimilation that Jonson both prizes and exhibits.[12]
They are little more than plagiarists, and thanks to the "authority,
or, which is lesse, opinion" that they win "by their writings, to
have read much," they even sometimes resort to wholesale invention and fabrication. Jonson, himself following Quintilian, condemns those who "dare presently to faine whole bookes, and
Authors, and lye safely. For what never was, will not easily be
found; not by the most *curious*" (H&S 8:586). In order to expose
such inventions, the readers of these writers would need to display the very qualities of discernment and analysis that the writers themselves lack. If essayists like Montaigne lack consistency,
inventors like the ones Jonson here describes achieve consistency
at the price of wholesale fabrication—which bespeaks a different
kind of laziness.

Equally lazy are the plagiarists, who, "by a cunning protestation against all reading, and false venditation of their owne *naturals*, thinke to divert the *sagacity* of their Readers from themselves,
and coole the sent of their own *fox-like* thefts" (H&S 8:586). All
these kinds of writers—the "*Essayists*," the "faine[rs]," and the
brazen thieves—display equal contempt for their readers' intelligence. Even worse, however, are those writers who genuinely
attempt to rely entirely on their own limited gifts. Such writers
become "obstinate contemners of all helpes, and Arts: such as
presuming on their owne *Naturals* (which perhaps are excellent)
dare deride all diligence, and seeme to mock at the termes, when
they understand not the things; thinking that way to get off wittily, with their Ignorance" (H&S 8:586). To rely wholly on oneself
is even "Wretcheder" than to rely wholly on another (to plagia-
rize); here as in other respects, Jonson seems to have valued the
ideal of balance, of give-and-take, and he clearly implies that both
reading and writing involve not only diligence but also serious
obligations to others. Every writer, but even also every reader,
sets an example: for Jonson, private vice almost always sets a
social precedent, even when the act involved would seem to be
as private as reading a book.[13]

Presented with so many varieties of bad reading, poor writing,
and even poorer judgment, Jonson (following Quintilian) takes
solace in the thought that "An other Age, or juster men, will

acknowledge the virtues of [a good writer's] studies: his wisdome, in dividing: his subtilty, in arguing: with what strength hee doth inspire his Readers" (H&S 8:587). Here as elsewhere in the *Discoveries,* Jonson looks forward to future redemption: just as the learned writers of the past are now appreciated by learned readers like himself, so he and other learned writers of the present will someday be appreciated by the future audience Jonson hopes to help create and fashion.[14] The "strength" he mentions is something the writer both possesses and imparts: good reading is not so much relaxing as refreshing and invigorating. This is not to say that Jonson commends reading that is unrelenting. *"Ease,* and relaxation," he notes, "are profitable to all studies. The mind is like a Bow, the stronger for being unbent." Here as elsewhere, however, achieving proper moderation or "temper" is important (H&S 8:589).

This same ideal is implied again much later in the *Discoveries,* when Jonson suggests the capacity of "diverse studies, at diverse houres" to "delight, when the variety is able alone to refresh, and repaire us . . . As when a man is weary of writing, to reade; and then againe of reading, to write" (H&S 8:619). By following Quintilian closely in these words, Jonson illustrates precisely the interdependence he commends, and indeed the *Discoveries* as a whole indicate how his reading could provide both an alternative and a stimulus to his writing.[15] Although this passage suggests that both reading and writing involve work and can be tiring, it also indicates quite explicitly the sheer pleasure Jonson seems to have taken in such work.

The fact that reading *can* be a delight seems one reason the *Discoveries* caution writers against wearying readers with technical minutiae, as grammarians do. "Many writers perplexe their Readers, and Hearers with meere *Non-sense.* Their writings need sunshine" (H&S 8:620). On the one hand, a reader/writer should not be reluctant to pursue as much knowledge as possible, since he needs to know as much as he can about the subjects of his writing. At the same time, however, he should not burden his readers by displaying every bit of his carefully acquired knowledge. He needs to be exhaustive but not exhausting; the hard work that goes into composing a text should be neither obvious nor taxing to one's readers. Paraphrasing Sir Francis Bacon, Jonson later describes various "distemper[s]" that hamper learning, including the study of mere eloquence, a concern with "Vaine" matter, and "deceit, or the likeness of truth," which is a kind of "Imposture held up by credulity" (H&S 8:627). "Nothing," Jonson contends,

> is more ridiculous, then to make an Author a *Dictator*, as the schooles
> have done *Aristotle*. The damage is infinite, knowledge receives by it.
> For to many things a man should owe but a temporary beliefe, and a
> suspension of his owne Judgement, not an absolute resignation of
> himselfe, or a perpetuall captivity. Let *Aristotle*, and others have their
> dues; but if we can make farther Discoveries of truth and fitnesse
> then they, why are we envied? Let us beware, while wee strive to
> adde, wee doe not diminish, or deface; wee may improve, but not
> augment. By discrediting falsehood, Truth growes in request. (H&S
> 8:627)

Perhaps no other passage better sums up Jonson's attitude toward reading—an attitude not only discussed but also displayed in his own collection of "Discoveries." Both the words just quoted and the larger work containing them illustrate many of Jonson's most typical views of a reader's responsibilities. The ideal reader is active; he reads not merely to absorb but as a preparation to create.[16] He must be independent but not egotistical; he must critically examine everything, including his own motives:

> Wee must not goe about like men anguish'd, and perplex'd, for vitious
> affectation of praise: but calmely study the separation of opinions,
> find the errours have intervened, awake Antiquity, call former times
> into question; but make no parties with the present. (H&S 8:627)

This passage is typical in its rhetorical balance and its ideal of moderation. Active reading requires vigilance, suspicion, and judgment, perhaps especially of oneself; even the most industrious and prolific reader can be lazy if he abdicates his responsibility to read with a critical eye. A reader who is deceived usually cooperates in his own deception; his first obligation is neither to himself nor to the authors he reads but to "knowledge" and "Truth" (H&S 8:627). Just as Jonson repeatedly imagines that the neglected or unappreciated author will find his fit audience in the future, so his words here also suggest his sense of an author/reader's responsibility to the the future—a responsibility that includes rejection of intellectual tyranny or factionalism, whether of the past or of the present. The best readers must achieve a disinterested perspective, an elevated judgment, "For no perfect Discovery can bee made upon a flat or a levell" (H&S 8:628).

*   *   *

Jonson's own *Discoveries; Made Vpon Men and Matter: As They have flow'd out of his daily Readings* . . . show how he attempted to practice the very ideal of creative, disciplined reading that the *Discoveries* themselves endorse. Yet that same ideal is also implied or articulated in many of his other works. This is especially true of some of his masques, those lavish but ephemeral courtly entertainments, usually given only single performances and often tightly tied to specific occasions, particular personalities, and contemporary political or social issues.[17] Jonson chafed at the idea that the poetry of the masques might seem subordinate to their spectacular elements, and he often took care to prepare carefully edited reading texts of these works.[18] The masque texts not only suggest how he wished these works to be read, but they often also imply the kind and quality of reading that went into composing them. The dedications, prefaces, stage directions, descriptions, and marginal comments that often accompany the more obviously "creative" writing in the masques and entertainments show that Jonson viewed these works as texts for reading as much as scripts for performance, and they also show how the poet could use his own reading to craft his writings and defend them against attack. At the same time, however, the very act of printing and publishing the texts of the masques and entertainments made them available to criticism in ways that a single performance was not. Jonson's awareness of this paradox is already visible in a note to the text of his very first entertainment, when he remarks that by having *"suffered* [the work] *to come out,"* he has made it possible for it to *"encounter Censure"* (H&S 7:131n). Ironically, making the masques available to readers could both combat and foment such criticism.

Jonson's thoughts about his masques as texts for reading are suggested in two of his earliest such works—the masques of *Blacknesse* (1605) and of *Beautie* (1608). A preface to the works, which were first published together, begins by announcing that "the splendor of these *spectacles* was such in the performance, as could those houres haue lasted, this of mine, now, had been a most vnprofitable worke" (H&S 7:169). But, of course, "those houres" could not last: the spectacular *"carkasses"* of the masques were destroyed immediately after the events, and their *"spirits"* might also have "perished" if they were not preserved in Jonson's texts (H&S 7:169). In publishing the masques, Jonson attempts to "redeeme them" from "Ignorance" and *"obliuion."* Ironically, however, he again acknowledges that *by* publishing them he opens them to the possibility of "Enuie" and *"censure"* (H&S 7:169)—

which is why he feels the need to offer prefatory remarks. The text designed to preserve the works might cause them to be damned, and so another text—the preface, or "this later hand" (H&S 7:169)—must be added to forestall that possibility.

In a further irony, the defensive tone of the preface might perhaps itself have provoked Jonson's readers to scrutinize his works more carefully; indeed, the elaborate apparatus of the printed text practically compels the kind of sustained attention that the works might otherwise have escaped. The preface's first order of business, after its introductory paragraph, is to begin citing Jonson's sources: "[a]PLINY, [b]SOLINVS, [c]PTOLOMEY, and of late LEO[d] the *African*, remember vnto vs a riuer in *Æthiopia*" (H&S 7:169). Immediately, then, Jonson grounds his invention in authorities, but he also immediately assumes that others may question those authorities by citing others (such as Lucan). An accompanying note anticipates and preempts this possibility, citing *"Plinie"* as a counterwitness to Lucan and also citing Solinus in support of Pliny (H&S 7:169). These notes display Jonson's careful scholarship and responsible learning. They also suggest that part of the purpose of his reading was not only to stimulate his own creativity but also to legitimize and sanction it, to render it less vulnerable to attack. This motive is itself summed up succinctly in a later note, this time to the *Masque of Beautie*, when Jonson again cites Pliny to "giue authoritie to this part of our fiction" (H&S 7:184). Paradoxically, though, Jonson's frequent citation of authorities could itself open him to criticism, so that the very effort to forestall attack might in fact provoke it. Yet Jonson seems to have felt that the risk of seeming ignorant was worse than the danger of seeming pedantic, and a later note heads off criticism on another point by commenting that the "inducing of many *Cupids* wants not defence, with the best and most receiued of the *Ancients*" (H&S 7:188).

Jonson had already suggested some of the motives of his reading, as well as part of the value of reading in general, in his prefatory comments to *Hymenaei*, a masque performed and first printed in early 1606. There he distinguishes clearly between the perishable *"bodies"* of masques and the living *"soules"* preserved in the poetic texts, and he pays the aristocratic masque-participants the significant compliment of claiming that they are thoughtful readers, "curious after the most high, and heartie *inuentions . . .* grounded vpon *antiquitie*, and solide *learnings*" (H&S 7:209). Yet he also admits that some persons

may squemishly crie out, that all endeuour of *learning*, and *sharpnesse*
in these transitorie *deuices* especially, where it steps beyond their little,
or (let me not wrong 'hem) no braine at all, is superfluous; I am
contented, these fastidious *stomachs* should leaue my full tables, and
enioy at home, their cleane emptie trenchers, fittest for such ayrie
tasts. (H&S 7:209–10)

The mockery continues, but the mere fact that Jonson felt the
need to preempt such criticism implies that he feared it, and
if (as various theorists have suggested) literature most basically
embodies the totality of human desires and fears, it also seems
reasonable to assert that Jonson's reading was similarly motivated
not only by the pleasure it gave him but also by the desire to
ward off injury. Of course, some of Jonson's notes suggest a simple
desire to be helpful or explanatory, to provide information his
readers may not have known. Or they call attention to his scholarship and judgment by mentioning alternative possibilities, as
when he notes that the symbol of the golden chain used in *Hymenaei* had been "interpreted diuersely." Although he cites Plato's
explanation, Jonson claims to feel "specially affection in [his] Allusion" to the interpretation offered by Macrobius; he thus points
his readers to a proper understanding of his text, using his personal reading to guide their own. But the note on Macrobius also
ends defensively, claiming that the Latin author's words indicate
that one of Jonson's comparisons has not been made "absurdly"
(H&S 7:221). Typical, too, is the elaborate citation of five classical
authors to explain one debatable reference to a *"pine tree"* (H&S
7:211).

   Thus, in the masques as in his other works, Jonson frequently
relies on his reading to legitimize and defend his writing by appealing to precedents, but the notes and prefaces to the masques
also show how his reading could justify his independence. For
instance, in one note to the *Masque of Queenes* he acknowledges
a departure from his source, yet the very acknowledgment not
only displays his autonomy but also shows that his departure is
deliberate, not the result of simple error (H&S 7:293). Similarly,
a later note to the same masque lays out three possible symbols
of "braue, and masculine *virtue*" authorized by the "Antients";
then it mentions Jonson's choice of one and anchors that choice in
two sources (H&S 7:302). Reading, then, could both help inspire
invention and help defend it; it could suggest alternative possibilities while also legitimizing Jonson's right to choose. For all these
reasons, Jonson seems to have regarded reading less as a means

of constricting his creativity than of unlocking it, and notes from the masques suggest the sheer pleasure he took from his encounters with books. One note, for instance, praises in passing the "admirable height" of Lucan's style (H&S 7:290), while the dedication to the *Masque of Queenes* calls attention not only to Jonson's "labor of annotation" but also to the "zeale" that went into it. Jonson calls his zeal "carefull," and the combination of noun and adjective suggests the disciplined enthusiasm that seems to have motivated and characterized his reading. He anticipates that reading the text of his masque will give the work "life, and authority," but he is also careful to mention that the notes designed to explain and defend the masque were written at royal "command" (H&S 7:279). The notes that defend the masque are thus themselves defended. In any number of ways, then, Jonson seems to have associated his reading with his writing, and to have linked both to issues of real social power.

* * *

Many of the same ideas raised about reading in the *Discoveries* and masques are present, too, in Jonson's plays—particularly in the printed versions, with their dedications and prefaces. Yet the plays were originally written as scripts, and, unlike most of the masques, they were explicitly designed for repeated performances.[19] Although the notes in the standard edition suggest just how much and how frequently Jonson's dramas did derive from his own reading, in the theater they enjoyed a life independent of the page and were not quite as reliant on readers as his works in other genres. Yet Jonson seems to have hoped that even theatrical audiences would approach his plays with the same kind of thoughtful, discerning judgment he expected from the best readers, and the link between intelligent auditors and intelligent readers is implied in another way in the dedication of the folio edition of *Poetaster* to Richard Martin. There Jonson thanks his friend for helping defend and rescue the play from the attacks it initially provoked. He claims that *"posteritie"* owes to Martin its ability to read the work *"without offence,"* since Martin had opposed the *"ignorance, and malice of the times"* which had *"conspir'd to haue supprest"* the work (H&S 4:201). Martin, then, symbolizes the ideal audience member, who not only appreciates a work but actively defends it, thereby aiding both the artist and *"posteritie."* In the *Discoveries,* Jonson often assumes that the judgment of posterity—of later readers—will vindicate worthy writers, but here he also implies that posterity itself initially depends on at

least a few of the author's contemporaries to defend its own right
to read. In cases such as the one presented by *Poetaster*, later
readers may never have the chance to pass true judgment on an
author's work if that work is not first vindicated and preserved
by a few spirited members of its original audience. Just as the
author writes with the future in mind, so his best contemporaries
must also act on behalf of later readers.[20]

Both writer and readers, then, ideally act with posterity in
mind. Although part of Jonson's own distinctiveness depended
on his claim of being a writer who was well read, he also felt that
being a worthy reader was itself a real distinction: an afterword
to *Poetaster* addresses readers who have *"deseru'd that name"* (H&S
4:317), and it also appeals to the judgment of still later readers
(*"Posteritie"*), who themselves *"may make a difference"* (i.e., distinguish) between Jonson and his attackers. Typically, in the course
of defending himself in the play's "apologeticall Dialogue," Jonson
not only cites but quotes his sources (H&S 4:321); here as elsewhere, reading provides protection and functions as self-defense,
allowing other authors to testify on his behalf. By citing the examples of "ARISTOPHANES," "PERSIVS," and "IUVENAL" (H&S
4:323), Jonson appeals to them for precedent and sanction. Yet
he also knew that this appeal depended entirely on the willingness of contemporary readers to acknowledge such authorities
and to admit their relevance to Jonson's case. Whether appealing
to the future for vindication or to the past for sanction, Jonson
could never entirely escape the need to appeal, first and foremost,
to an immediate audience of contemporary readers.

The serious responsibilities of such readers are suggested again
in the famous dedication to *Volpone*, in which Jonson attacks *"inu-
ading interpreters"* who *"professe to haue a key for the decyphering of
euery thing"* and who *"often utter their owne virulent malice, vnder
other mens simplest meanings"* (H&S 5:19). Here he suggests that
reading can sometimes involve misappropriation, including inad-
vertent or deliberate deception. Thus the worthy reader is obliged
not only to suspect the motives of other readers but also to give
an author some benefit of the doubt, to trust his good intentions.
Although readers should not be credulous, they should scrutinize
other interpreters as closely as they examine an author's text.
Everything, again, comes down to judgment: as Jonson succinctly
puts it in dedicating *Epicoene*, *"Read therefore, I pray you, and censure"* (H&S 5:161). This mingled assertiveness and deference, this
simultaneous confidence and humility, suggest a self-assurance
that makes him not just willing but even eager to submit himself

to intelligent judgment, and this posture, in turn, helps encourage the likelihood that such judgment will be favorable.[21]

Thus, in dedicating *Catiline* to the Earl of Pembroke, Jonson *"craue[s] leaue to stand neare"* Pembroke's *"light: and, by that, to bee read."* Pembroke's *"iudgement"* enables him *"to vindicate truth from error"*; he *"dare[s], in these Iig-giuen times, to countenance a legitimate Poeme"* (H&S 5:431). Both Jonson and *"Posteritie"* owe gratitude to Pembroke, and indeed the poet acts on posterity's behalf by paying tribute to the earl, just as the earl acts on posterity's behalf by sanctioning the play. A second dedication, "TO THE READER IN ORDINARIE," sharply distinguishes such a reader from readers like Pembroke. The ordinary reader engages in *"medling,"* in intrusive tampering and misappropriation (H&S 5:432). The same lack of understanding such readers once displayed *"at Schoole"* now emerges once more; true *"knowledge"* is necessary to true judgment (H&S 5:432). Jonson's own *"studies"* have helped make him impervious (or so he claims) to the *"vexation of Censure"* (H&S 5:432). He thus suggests another function of his reading: it not only helps him compose his texts but also helps him to compose himself, to cope with adverse reactions. His reading, then, prepares him both to write and to be read.

* * *

Many of the same ideas about reading implied or articulated in the plays, masques, and *Discoveries* are present as well in Jonson's non-dramatic poems. This is hardly surprising, since the poems—more, perhaps, than any of the other genres—were meant to be read and depended on reading for their full effect. The plays and masques were written to be performed, and the notes printed in the *Discoveries* may or may not have been planned for publication. The poems, however, were obviously written for readers, and indeed this self-consciousness about one's audience is a distinctive trait of Jonson's poetry, which rarely seems completely private or wholly introspective. Jonson was above all a social poet; when he wrote, awareness of readers and concern with reading were never far from his mind. This is immediately obvious from the first three poems of the *Epigrammes* collection; the first, in fact, is addressed explicitly "TO THE READER" (*Ep.* 1). Jonson called the *Epigrammes* "the ripest of [his] studies," and the first three poems exhibit concern that readers may not be equal to his works, either in understanding or in moral sensitivity. They betray his immense self-consciousness, his discomfort with the potential for misinterpretation. Yet they also display his resourcefulness and subtlety in directing and shaping readers' responses.

Jonson seems to have felt that reading and writing were, in the most basic senses, *political* acts, involving the issue of who would have power over a text's meaning. The relation between writer and reader involves not simply exchange or reciprocity but also domination, control, or submission. Jonson's poems are inevitably micropolitical performances designed to assert, maintain, and advertise his own power. Read simply as versified restatements of traditional moral precepts, his poems exert an undeniable appeal; however, read also as frozen maneuvers in his struggle to promote his social and literary authority, his works take on a fascinating complexity of nuance and vibrate with some of their original intensity. Certainly this is true of "TO THE READER." Although the poem seems simple enough, its rich implications stand in inverse proportion to its brevity:

> PRay. thee, take care, that tak'st my booke in hand,
> To reade it well: that is, to vnderstand.

In asking the reader to "take care," Jonson sounds both a warning and a supplication: here as in so many of his works, he blends modesty and pride, making each more potent and effective. The reader must take care, because in reading the book he submits to a challenge; he will judge the book, but his reading will also reveal his quality of mind and thus open *him* to judgment. He must be careful to do the book justice by understanding it well, thereby also doing justice to himself. He must "take care" literally, because only a careful reading—one that scrutinizes his own motives and reactions as closely as the book—will produce true understanding. By referring to "my" book, Jonson emphasizes the intimate relationship between himself and his reader, an intimacy also suggested by the direct address of the poem's title. Mentioning himself helps guarantee the book by asserting the responsible self that stands behind it. This promotes an attractive image of the poet's confidence and integrity, but it also means that failing to read the book properly means failing Jonson as judge. Characteristically, after telling the reader what his responsibility is, Jonson then instructs him how to fulfill it. The poem interprets itself: to read well is "to vnderstand." In a sense, the poem almost preempts the reader's role, making him nearly superfluous except as a witness to its own self-contained performance of the behavior it attempts to elicit. But the assurance this implies is offset by a countervailing sense of vulnerability. The pose of assurance is one way of coping with the vulnerability, but so is the very *exhibition* of the vulnerability itself. By presenting himself and his book as somewhat at the reader's mercy, Jonson makes it much less likely that the reader will abuse the trust invested in him. His guarded expression of trust in the reader thus serves partly as a tactic of intimidation.

The next poem, "TO MY BOOKE" (*Ep.* 2), exhibits similar tactical sophistication and a similar concern with proper reading:

> IT will be look'd for, booke, when some but see
>   Thy title, *Epigrammes*, and nam'd of mee,
> Thou should'st be bold, licentious, full of gall,
>   Wormewood, and sulphure, sharpe, and tooth'd withall;
> Become a petulant thing, hurle inke, and wit,
>   As mad-men stones: not caring whom they hit.
> Deceiue their malice, who could wish it so.
>   And by thy wiser temper, let men know
> Thou are not couetous of least selfe-fame,
>   Made from the hazard of anothers shame:
> Much lesse with lewd, prophane, and beastly phrase,
>   To catch the worlds loose laughter, or vaine gaze.
> He that departs with his owne honesty
>   For vulgar praise, doth it too dearely buy.

In the opening line and throughout the poem, Jonson plays on the equivocation implicit in the phrase "look'd for," which can suggest both hope and expectation. To expect something of another person is to characterize that person; to hope for something from him is to characterize oneself. Jonson's pun implies that what at first seems an expectation is actually a wish, a desire that characterizes the malevolent and superficial reader. Immediately after a poem cautioning his audience to read well, Jonson concedes that many will not. Their shallowness is indicated by the fact that they react to the book without venturing further than its title page; unable to break free of their own preconceptions, they are unable to understand the book or achieve communion with its author. But Jonson turns their expectations back on them: seeking to characterize him, they characterize themselves. Readers who hope he will exhibit malice thereby exhibit their own. By addressing his book, Jonson gives his personal intentions and motives greater objectivity; by personalizing the book, he gives it attributes (such as a "wiser temper" [8]) he could not modestly or openly claim as his own. Characterizing his book, he implicitly characterizes himself. Although he implies that he will not advance his own interests by exploiting others' shame, his poem tacitly satirizes his poetic competitors: low expectations of epigrams exist partly because other authors have abused the genre.[22] Even while defending his own book against the attacks of readers, Jonson implicitly attacks other books and authors. The very statement that he covets no fame won from another's shame functions to shame competing authors and to win fame for Jonson. The closing couplet pulls back from personal defense to ethical generalization, so that this poem can claim to fulfill the ideal of social responsibility it attributes to the whole collection.

Responsibility to higher values is also an implicit concern of the following work, "TO MY BOOKE-SELLER" (*Ep.* 3):

> THou, that mak'st gaine thy end, and wisely well
>   Call'st a booke good, or bad, as it doth sell,
> Vse mine so, too: I giue thee leaue. But craue
>   For the lucks sake, it thus much fauour haue,
> To lye vpon thy stall, till it be sought;
>   Not offer'd, as it made sute to be bought;
> Nor haue my title-leafe on posts, or walls,
>   Or in cleft-sticks, aduanced to make calls
> For termers, or some clarke-like seruing-man,
>   Who scarse can spell th'hard names: whose knight lesse can.
> If, without these vile arts, it will not sell,
>   Send it to *Bucklers-bury*, there 'twill, well.

By referring to the bookseller as one who makes gain his end, Jonson distances himself from similar motives; he presents himself as more concerned with principle than with profit. And yet this very stance was the one most likely to promote his own gain and power; such lofty disinterest would best advance the practical interests he could hardly afford to ignore. Rejecting craven advertising, the poem engages in self-advertisement of a more subtly effective sort; by refusing to beg for readers, Jonson makes himself and his work seem all the more compelling and attractive. The "vile arts" (11) of the bookseller are implicitly contrasted with the nobler art of the poet, but the humor of the closing couplet (at once self-deprecating and assertive) counteracts any sense of arrogant posturing. The book will not make "sute to be bought" (6)—phrasing that wittily blends the language of patronage relations with hints of prostitution. Nevertheless, the poem's explicit disdain for self-promotion becomes one of the most effective means of engaging in it.[23]

Many of the same ideas about reading expressed in the first three epigrams reverberate throughout the collection. Explicitly and implicitly, Jonson frequently instructs his readers in their proper responsibilities—not only to him and to his works but to society at large. *Ep.* 9, for instance, is addressed "TO ALL, TO WHOM I WRITE." Rather than addressing the mass of readers in general, Jonson here focuses particularly on those notables "whose scatter'd names honor my booke," telling them that they should not "For strict degrees of ranke, or title looke" (1–2). He insists that he is a *"Poet,"* not a *"Herald,"* and notes that observing the niceties of rank would be " 'gainst the manners of an *Epigram"* (3). The poem suggests that pride might often motivate reading, even among those readers who are, by definition, most praiseworthy—the ones Jonson chooses to name. In distinguishing himself from a herald, Jonson acknowledges the potential confusion and suggests that even the most virtuous readers can be tainted by self-interest. If the poet apparently violates social manners, it is only to uphold the higher manners of the genre in which he writes: both poet and reader should ideally be distinterested, more concerned with literary achievement and the celebration of impersonal virtue than with private self-aggrandizement. Jonson's title as poet sanctions his relative disinterest in the titles of those he praises; the "manners" of the epigram genre, rather than his own egotism, ignorance, or carelessness, permit his violation of normal social decorum. The poem is cast both as a warning and as a request or plea, and although Jonson disclaims any undue concern with conventional social manners, the poem displays great tact in pressing and defending his interests. It suggests that reading is not merely a private act but a form of social behavior, and this implication lies at the heart of many other poems in the *Epigrammes* volume.

Jonson often attempts to instruct his own readers through praise or blame, by calling attention to various exemplary or unworthy readers. *Ep.* 14, for instance, praises the historian and teacher William Camden for his "sight in searching the most antique springs" (8), implicitly lauding the ideal of alert and active reading that the poet so often extols. The poem's commendation of Camden not only displays personal gratitude to an old mentor but also exemplifies the "pietie" (14)—the almost religious reverence—that intelligent reading of Camden's work should provoke. Camden the active reader becomes Camden the writer worthy to be actively read and then becomes, in turn, the subject of a poem itself worthy of intelligent scrutiny. Such scrutiny is explicitly welcomed in *Ep.* 17, "TO THE LEARNED CRITICK." Here Jonson displays both confidence and humility by submitting his works to the judgment of wise and thoughtful readers; only they can grant his "poemes a legitimate fame" (4), and that, of course, is the only fame that matters. Once again the social consequences of reading are emphasized, and they are imagined as both immediate and permanent: praise offered by intelligent readers will establish a writer's current reputation, but it will also "outliue" the flatteries or censures of readers unworthy to judge.

Although Jonson speaks contemptuously of such readers (the sort depicted in *Ep.* 18, "TO MY MEERE ENGLISH CENSURER"), obviously they bothered him. A certain anxiety often seems to lurk beneath his professed confidence in the enduring judgments of learned critics. In *Ep.* 23, "TO IOHN DONNE," Jonson himself enacts the role of such a critic, praising Donne's "most earely wit" and noting the "example" his works both provided and provide (3–4). Yet by praising Donne as a writer he also calls attention to himself as an exemplary reader, and his praise often seems reflexive in this way. Reading and praising Donne thus become forms of self-display, but not the sort mocked in *Ep.* 28, "ON DON SURLY," which describes how Surly both reads and judges in order to win a reputation for "greatnesse." Jonson's very need to condemn Surly—to read or interpret Surly's acts of reading— suggests that such performances were more threatening than the poem allows. As this and many other poems make clear, reading in Jonson's culture seems very often to have been literally a performance: a social event involving an audience and often competitive self-display. *Ep.* 38, for instance ("TO PERSON GUILTIE"), describes how its subject attempts to hide his personal guilt by fulsomely praising the poet's satire: "long before / Any man else, you clap your hands, and rore, / And crie good! good!" (3–5). Although Jonson claims to be bothered by Guilty's hypocrisy, he also seems to have been offended by such attempts to misappropriate his texts, to use them as an occasions for others' performances.

Many of Jonson's works provide similarly strong evidence of the survival of an essentially oral and public culture, a culture in which print had not yet made reading an entirely private act. *Ep.* 52, for instance, describes how "CENSORIOVS COVRTLING" reacts to a public reading of Jonson's work in a manner apparently the opposite of Guilty's: "When I am read, thou fain'st a weake applause, / As if thou wert my friend, but lack'dst a cause" (3–4).[24] Yet although the responses of Guilty and Courtling superficially differ, at a deeper level they are the same: both readers are more interested in projecting images of themselves than in truly comprehending Jonson's text. As both poems make clear, reading could often prove self-serving. Instead of being an occasion for self-examination, reading could provoke hypocritical accusations against the author, as in the case of Chev'ril, in *Ep.* 54, who condemns Jonson's verses as "libells" (1). Yet such enthusiastic condemnation differs little, in fundamental terms, from the slavish plagiarism described in *Ep.* 56, "TO POET-APE." In both cases reading serves the cause of egotism and self-interest rather than serving the disinterested pursuit of truth. As the poem's title implies, to engage in plagiarism is to betray the faculty of reason, the capacity for judgment, that should distinguish humans from animals.

Plagiarism, in fact, provides a clear contrast to the Jonsonian ideal of true reading. The plagiarist turns reading into a debased form of immediate self-profit, but because he learns nothing through his efforts, his profits are highly superficial. Yet they are hardly immaterial: in fact, they are anything but, since they involve not just prestige but also money. Jonson plays on this sense of the practical rewards of plagiarism when he says that Poet-Ape has grown "To'a little wealth, and credit in the *scene*" (7): the second noun puns, suggesting that thanks to his plagiarism Poet-Ape is not only taken seriously (or "credited") as a writer, but that he can also now expect advance payment for his stolen plays. He may be "Poore" (1) in lacking Jonson's respect, but his thievery has obviously proved rewarding. Here reading becomes quite clearly a means to purely financial profit, and both the genesis and reception of Poet-Ape's texts exemplify an essential laziness. Poet-Ape is successful, after all, because "such crimes / The sluggish gaping auditor deuoures" (9–10). This phrasing is typically ambivalent: the auditors are simultaneously passive and active. On the one hand they are "sluggish," while on the other they gape and devour. The fact that they are merely "auditor[s]" helps explain the apparent contradiction: unlike Jonson's ideal readers, they make no effort, expend no intellectual energy of their own. They simply consume what they are fed, without asking questions or exercising judgment. Here as elsewhere, Jonson counts on the perceptiveness of later *readers* to expose the fraud: his focus shifts from the implied ears of credulous "auditors" to the more perceptive "eyes" of readers who will be able to discern "a fleece / From locks of wooll" (13–14). Once again, however, the poem's

very existence suggests that Jonson was neither certain nor satisfied that posterity would expose the fraud.[25]

The plagiarists Jonson attacks in *Ep.* 56 stand at the opposite
end of the spectrum from those ideal readers celebrated in a number of the later epigrams. Such a reader is Sir Henry Goodyear,
praised in *Ep.* 86 for his "wel-made choise of friends, and bookes"
and for "making thy friends bookes, and thy bookes friends" (2;
4). The heavy repetition of these key words, emphasized by Jonson's use of the rhetorical trope of chiasmus, suggests that he
regarded books almost as living presences, to be approached with
the same intent attention and respect one would devote to a
friend. Friends, by the same token, could be "read," or learned
from, with as much profit as one might read a book. Indeed,
Jonson's epigram turns Goodyear himself into a kind of book that
the poem both reads and interprets, and the poem itself stands
as still another link in the chain: it is a text that interprets and
honors Goodyear as a text who reads and honors texts. Fittingly,
Jonson transforms his "friend" into part of his own book, thus
imitating and encouraging the very behavior he extols.

As the poem to Goodyear makes clear, reading for Jonson is
almost always an act of self-revelation: a person's choice of books,
like his choice of friends, says a great deal about his values and
character. On the one hand reading could be, as it is in *Ep.* 92
("THE NEW CRIE"), a means of satisfying a shallow obsession
with ephemeral current affairs, a way of stimulating a false sense
of excitement and projecting self-importance, of seeming "in the
know." On the other hand, reading could involve, as in *Ep.* 94
("TO LVCY, COVNTESSE OF BEDFORD, WITH Mr DONNES
SATYRES"), self-revelation of a wholly different kind. Lucy's ea-
gerness to read Donne's satirical attacks on corruption becomes
in turn a means of reading *her*; the fact that she approves of such
poems implies her own worthiness. The same is true of Jonson's
willingness to submit his own poems to Donne's judgment (*Ep.*
96). Here Jonson suggests that it is not the number but the quality
of one's readers that matters, yet his submission to Donne becomes itself a means of influencing other readers. Moreover, in
submitting to Donne, Jonson implies that he has already assessed
and affirmed his judge. His own reading of Donne—both the man
and his works—at once precedes and justifies Donne's reading of
the works Jonson submits.

If in these poems to Donne and Lucy the connection between
reading and judgment seems especially clear, that connection is
nonetheless central to nearly all of Jonson's poetry and to nearly

all his thinking about reading. Even when he presents reading as a means of convivial relaxation—as he does, for instance, in the memorable poem "INVITING A FRIEND TO SVPPER" (*Ep.* 101)—Jonson nonetheless never sees it as trivial, as merely a frivolous pastime. Reading is quite literally central to this quintessential Jonsonian poem: the epigram's middle lines invite the titular friend to imagine, amid the feasting and drinking the guests will enjoy, that Jonson's man "Shall reade a piece of VIRGIL, TACITVS, / LIVIE, or of some better booke to vs, / Of which wee'll speake our minds, amidst our meate" (21–23). Physical and intellectual nourishment are juxtaposed; "minds" and "meate" are linked through more than mere alliteration. The words of ancient authors stimulate new thoughts, and the occasion of social reading becomes a spur to individual self-expression. It seems no accident that Jonson so closely associates reading and eating: in the final analysis, each was at once a necessity and a pleasure, a means both of sustenance and of satisfaction.[26]

*   *   *

Jonson's reference in "INVITING A FRIEND" to the prospect that his man will read from "some better booke" of course sets up a joke: the poet immediately disclaims any intention of forcing his guests to listen to a recitation of own works. Yet the reference to "some better booke" can also be read as a tastefully subtle allusion to that best of books in Jonson's culture, the Bible.[27] The allusion—if it is that—would serve to balance the poem's heavy emphasis on classical, "pagan" writers, yet the fact that the allusion is only the merest possibility should not surprise us. Although the Bible is the one book we might safely assume that Jonson knew, we rarely think of him as a religious writer in the same senses or to the same degree as Spenser, Sidney, Herbert, Donne, or even Shakespeare. Of the poets just mentioned, he seems by far the most self-consciously classical, and as "INVITING" implies, he seems to have drawn his inspiration more from the authors of ancient Greece and Rome than from Christian scriptures or Renaissance theologians. The most memorable religious figures in his comedies are Puritan hypocrites, while both of his surviving tragedies are set in pagan Rome. His masques are populated by figures from classical mythology, and most of his few poems on religious subjects seem to have been prompted more by specific occasions than by any deeply personal urge to confront the holy. Even the books that survive from Jonson's li-

brary show a preponderance of the classical over the obviously
Christian.

Yet this view of Jonson's religious stance and circumstances is
seriously incomplete. It overlooks, for instance, his acute awareness that his own father, despite having suffered for his faith,
eventually became a minister.[28] Moreover, religious questions
were important enough to Jonson that he eventually rejected his
father's beliefs, became a Catholic, and thus risked persecution
himself. In fact, in 1606 he *was* officially prosecuted for his beliefs,
but his assertive response suggests how highly he prized a clear
religious conscience (H&S 1:41–43). Jonson seems to have had
contacts with a number of prominent Catholics, yet he also was
friendly with influential Protestants.[29] His eventual reconversion
to Protestantism seems to have been motivated by a sincere
change of mind rather than by any immediate external pressure.
His famous "Execration on Vulcan" (*Und.* 43) indicates that he
had been reading widely on religious topics, but the fire of 1623
lamented in that poem seems to have destroyed (among much
else) various notebook entries on religious matters.[30] In 1628 he
swore, "vppon his christianity & hope of salvation," that he had
not copied verses commending the assassination of Buckingham,
the royal favorite (H&S 1:242), and a friend who visited him in
his final days claimed that the old poet was "much afflicted that
he had profaned the Scriptures in his plays and lamented it with
horror" (H&S 1:115). These data and others indicate that religion
was a more important factor in Jonson's life—and may have been
a more significant influence on his work—than is usually emphasized. As it happens, a small bit of hitherto unreported evidence
from Jonson's library helps bolster this claim.

Jonson owned several copies of the Bible, either in whole or in
part. His copy of an Anglo-Saxon translation of the four gospels
is presently in private hands. The current location of a copy of
the Psalms he supposedly owned is unknown, according to the
standard catalogue. Moreover, the catalogue rejects as "spurious"
a copy of the book of Ecclesiasticus alleged to have belonged to
the poet.[31] This leaves only one other reported biblical text: a
Latin edition of the entire scriptures published in 1599 and presently held at the Pierpont Morgan Library. Fortunately, the playwright's ownership of this book is beyond question, but the
standard catalogue mentions only a few marginal markings and
reports that "None of these marks are especially characteristic of
Jonson."[32] Thus, even the one text whose location and authentic-

ity are beyond doubt seems initially disappointing to the re-searcher interested in tracing Jonson's biblical reading.

However, further examination indicates not only that the mar-ginal markings in the Pierpont Morgan Bible are almost certainly Jonson's, but also that there are many more marginalia than the standard catalogue reports. The Morgan text, in other words, provides valuable evidence of Jonson's detailed interest in the scriptures. Although the poet's markings in the Morgan Bible are confined to the Old Testament (especially to the early chapters of the book of Genesis), these marginalia indicate that Jonson could indeed take a detailed interest in biblical matters, since he marked his text with some care and deliberation. Moreover, many of the passages he highlights share common thematic concerns. Per-haps inevitably in the Hebrew scriptures, many of the marked passages deal with such matters as genealogy, familial strife, God's personal grace, and especially divine punishments for sin. Aside from the topics they highlight, however, the actual mark-ings themselves are also of genuine interest, since they help ex-tend our sense of the styles of marginalia Jonson was capable of using. The markings in the Morgan text help authenticate the unusual markings found in other books that Jonson seems to have owned. The Morgan Bible thus provides important evidence that can help determine whether other texts associated with Jonson's library were really owned and marked by the poet.

According to the standard catalogue, Jonson's most typical mar-ginal markings were distinctively drawn pointing hands and mar-ginal flowers (or trefoils). Several such flowers, drawn in ink, do turn up in the Morgan text, and these are almost surely Jonson's. A pointing hand in Deuteronomy—also ink-drawn—is less cer-tainly his, but it is the other markings, made very faintly in pencil, that are of special interest. Exactly similar marks occur in other books associated with the poet, including his recently discovered copy of the works of Sir Thomas More.[33] The fact that the highly distinctive markings in Jonson's Bible parallel so precisely the kinds of marks also found in the More volume suggests that the marks in both texts were made by the same man, and all the evidence indicates that that man was Jonson. The marginalia in both books are of a sort not emphasized in the standard cata-logue, and so both texts help broaden our knowledge of the range of Jonson's markings. Similar markings have been discovered in other books once owned by the poet, including some listed in the standard catalogue and some others that remain to be de-scribed. Thus, apart from its inherent value as a Bible that happens to contain Jonson's markings, the Morgan text is also of genuine interest for its marginalia alone.

As has already been indicated, most of those marginalia survive as faint pencil markings. Yet the marks are clearly visible on personal inspection, and the vast majority also show up clearly on microfilm and even on photostatic prints. The markings seem designed to highlight specific verses (or parts of verses) in the first twenty chapters of Genesis. The first marks, naturally enough, focus on the creation. For instance, a circle with a curvy tail is drawn next to the first half of Genesis 1:5 ("And he called the light Day, and the darkness Night"), while next to the second part of this verse ("And there was evening and morning one day"), what looks like the numeral "1" has been drawn ("pellaui-taque / ne, dies").[34] Indeed, similar numbers have been penciled next to each of the similar verses marking out the seven days of creation (see chapter appendix). Whether these numerals were drawn by Jonson is less certain than in the case of the more distinctive markings. However, the fact that the numbers are also drawn in pencil and are as faint as the other marks suggests that one person probably drew them both.

Some of Jonson's markings suggest a special interest in the creation (and relations) of the sexes. Thus, a very peculiar diagonal marking occurs next to the last part of 1:27, which explains that "to the image of God he created him. Male and female he created them" ("Dei crea-"). Later, in 2:23, Jonson highlights Adam's reference to Eve as "flesh of my flesh" and the assertion that "she shall be called woman" ("vocabitur"; CT). A similar marking notes that, although Adam and Eve were both naked, they "were not ashamed" ("non eru-"; CT). An earlier, lengthy marking of the last part of 2:5 and all of 2:6 emphasizes that at first "there was not a man to till the earth. But a spring rose out of the earth, watering all the surface of the earth" ("Deus super / superficiem"; CT). An unusual mark picks out the reference in 2:9 to "trees, fair to behold, and pleasant to eat of: the tree of life also" ("lignum / dum suaue"; CT). Another peculiar mark (shaped like a triangle with a tail) occurs next to 3:5, where the serpent tempts Eve by telling her that if she and Adam eat the forbidden fruit, "you shall be as Gods, knowing good and evil" ("scientes bo-"). Several marks detail God's various punishments of the first couple after the sin has been committed, including the cursing of the serpent at 3:14 ("tem / inter"; CT); the decree in 3:15 that enmities will exist between the serpent and the woman's seed ("tuae / insidiaberis"; VL); the declaration in 3:16 that the woman will have pain in childbirth and will be under her husband's domination ("re paries / vero"; VL); the curse of labor and toil laid upon Adam in 3:17 ("praeceparam / comedes"; VL); and the decree in 3:19 that Adam will earn his bread with his own sweat until he returns to the earth ("vultus / quia"; CT). Interestingly, Jonson also marks God's concern at the end of 3:22 that Adam might "take also of the tree of life, and eat, and live forever"; in addition, this mark encompasses God's response to that possibility: "And the Lord God sent [Adam] out of the paradise" ("sumat / eum"; CT). A long line marks the entirety of 3:24, the concluding verse of its chapter: "And he cast out Adam; and placed before the paradise of pleasure Cherubims, and a flaming sword, turning every way, to keep the way of the tree of life" ("sumptus / viam"; VL). Perhaps it is noteworthy that Jonson's most extensive markings in the first three chapters of Genesis deal with the detailed consequences of sin.

This emphasis continues in the markings in chapter 4, where one mark, for instance, highlights God's words to the murderous Cain in 4:10–11: "The voice of thy brother's blood crieth to me from the earth. Now, therefore, cursed shalt thou be upon the earth" ("clamat / male-"; CT). Two of the more interesting of Jonson's jottings (a large, S-shaped mark and a pointing hand) emphasize the end of 4:15, which explains that "the Lord set a mark upon Cain; that whosoever found him should not kill him" ("Cain si- / Cain"). A curious variety of marks picks out verses dealing with Cain's descendants in 4:19–22 (see chapter appendix), and another unusually large mark stresses Lamech's self-recrimination in 4:24: "Sevenfold vengeance shall be taken for Cain: but for Lamech seventy times sevenfold" ("vltio da- / quoque"; CT).

Markings in chapter 5 indicate Jonson's interest in the life-spans of various patriarchs, including Adam, as well as in the ultimate fate of Henoch (or Enoch; see chapter appendix), while the first marked passage in the next chapter (6:5–6) notes that God was so disappointed that man was intent "on evil at all times" that "It repented him that he had made man upon the earth" ("esset ad / Et ta-"; CT). Jonson seems to have taken a detailed interest in the specifications of Noah's (or Noe's) ark given in 6:14–16, including its need to be treated with pitch, its exact dimensions, and the decree that it should have a window ("las / cies"; CT, VL). Finally, a vertical line highlights all of 6:19, in which Noah is instructed to populate the ark with male and female examples of every kind of creature ("ex cunctus / tecum"). Markings in chapter 7 indicate not only Jonson's further interest in prepara-

tions for the flood but also in the deluge itself; he marks, for
instance, parts of 7:11–12: "all the fountains of the great deep
were broken up, and the flood gates of heaven were opened: And
the rain fell upon the earth" ("abyssi / qua-"; CT). Again Jonson's
fascination with specifics reveals itself in his marking of 7:20:
"The water was fifteen cubits higher than the mountains which
it covered" ("Quin- / Consum-"; CT).

Markings in chapter 8 answer those in chapter 7. For instance,
all of 7:2, which describes the closing of the floodgates, is marked
("clausi / calo"; HL). Jonson is careful to note (at 8:4–5) the date
and place where the ark came to rest as well as the receding of
the waters ("simo / crescebant"; CT). He also marks the reappearance, at 8:11, of the dove, "carrying a bough of an olive tree with
green leaves, in her mouth. Noe therefore understood that the
waters were ceased upon the earth" ("speram, / ram"; CT). Another mark highlights God's command to Noe at 8:16: "Go out
of the ark, thou and thy wife, thy sons, and the wives of thy sons
with thee" ("Egredere / Cuncta"; CT). Also marked is the first
part of 8:21: "And the Lord smelled a sweet savour, and said: I
will no more curse the earth for the sake of man" ("ratusque /
ledicam"; CT). The heavy stress on divine punishments noted so
far in Jonson's markings finds a memorable counterpart here—a
counterpart reemphasized by his marking of 9:12–13: "And God
said, This is the sign of the covenant which I give between me
and you, and to every living soul that is with you, for perpetual
generations. I will set my bow in the clouds" ("quod do /
meum"; CT).

Curiously, the longest of any of Jonson's single marks is drawn
next to 9:21–24, verses describing Noe's drunkenness and the
differing reactions of his sons to his nakedness ("est, & / didicis-
set"; VL). The poet's interest in life-spans continues in his marking of 9:29, which reports that Noe lived 950 years ("pleti / rum";
CT). No marks at all occur in chapter 10, but a number dot the
margins of chapter 11, which deals with the building of the Tower
of Babel. 11:1, for instance, notes that at the time of the Tower's
construction, "the earth was of one tongue, and of the same
speech" ("Cumque"; CT). Appropriately enough, Jonson the former bricklayer marks part of 11:3: "Come, let us make brick, and
bake them with fire. And they had brick instead of stones, and
slime instead of mortar" ("Habueruntq; / cae"; CT). He also
marks, in 11:4, the builders' intention to construct a tower "the
top of which may reach to heaven; and let us make our name
famous, before we be scattered abroad into all lands" ("cele- /

di-"; CL). But his focus on divine punishment resumes in 11:6, where God notes that "all have one tongue; and they have begun to do this, neither will they leave off from their designs until they [accomplish] them in deed" ("coepe- / opere"; CL). After God scatters the builders of the city, Jonson notes in 11:9 that "the name thereof [was called] Babel, because there the language of the whole earth was confounded: and from thence the Lord scattered them abroad upon the face of all [countries]" ("men / eos"; CT).

Once again, however, Jonson's emphasis on the wrath of God is juxtaposed with emphasis on God's graciousness. A long mark highlights much of 12:1–3, in which God instructs Abram to go "out of thy father's house, and come into the land which I shall shew thee. And I will make of thee a great nation, and I will bless thee, and magnify thy name; and thou shalt be blessed. I will bless them that bless thee, and curse them that curse thee" ("tui / ti-"; VL). After sojourning in Egypt, Abram and his nephew Lot leave that place, and once again Jonson marks passages depicting strife within families. He highlights, for instance, Abram's attempt in 13:9 to avoid further conflict with Lot: "Behold, the whole land is before thee: depart from me I pray thee. If thou wilt go to the left hand, I will take the right: if thou choose the right hand, I will pass to the left" ("uersa / uatis"; VL). The first of a number of marked passages dealing with Sodom and Gomorrha now occurs in part of 13:10 ("Dominus / sicut"; CT). This is soon followed by the report in 13:12 that Lot "dwelt in Sodom" and by the judgment (in 13:13) that "the men of Sodom were very wicked, and sinners before the face of the Lord, beyond measure" ("danem, / & peccatores"; CT). God's attitude toward Abram, however, remains as positive as ever: "And I will make thy seed as the dust of the earth" ("puluerem / nume-"; CT).

Of the markings in chapter 14, the longest and most interesting deal, respectively, with Abram's effort (in 14:14) to rescue Lot from the pagans who have captured him ("captum / tus est"; CT); with Melchisedech's blessing of Abram in 14:18–19 ("Salem / Deo"; CT); and with Abram's adamant refusal, in 14:23, to take gifts from the king of Sodom ("quod / Abram"; CT). Yet despite his righteousness, Abram is troubled that he has no children of his own; Jonson marks the beginning of 15:3, where the patriarch, having complained to God, "added: But to me thou hast not given seed" ("Eliezer / autem"; CT). When God promises to rectify the problem, "Abram believed God, and it was reputed to him unto justice" ("iustitiam"; CT). Family conflicts arise again, however, after Abram impregnates Agar, the handmaid of Sarai,

Abram's barren wife. In 16:5, Sarai accuses Abram, "Thou dost unjustly with me; I gave my handmaid into thy bosom, and she, perceiving herself to be with child, despiseth me. The Lord judge between me and thee" ("Iniquè / te. Cui"; CT). After Agar flees, an angel tells her that she will give birth to a son named Ismael, who, according to 16:12, "shall be a wild man. His hand will be against all men, and all men's hands against him" ("nem / nium"; CT). Ismael is mentioned again briefly in chapter 17, in a passing reference that Jonson also marks (see chapter appendix).

In 17:5, God tells Abram why he has decided that his name should be changed to "Abraham": "because I have made thee a father of many nations" ("ham"; CL). He also explains, in 17:8, his intention to give to Abraham and his seed "the land of thy sojournment, all the land of Chanaan for a perpetual possession: and I will be their God" ("omnem / ite-"; CT). Moreover, in 17:10–11 he instructs Abraham that "All the male kind of you shall be circumcised. And you shall circumcise the flesh of your foreskin" ("mas- / prae"; CT). Jonson's interest in this issue is reflected as well in his marking of 17:14: "The male, whose flesh of his foreskin shall not be circumcised, that soul shall be destroyed out of his people" ("ca- / delebitur"; CT). Abraham, of course, complies with God's command, and so he proves worthy to be visited by three angels in chapter 18. Greeting them in 18:5, he promises, "I will set a morsel of bread," and he urges them, "strengthen ye your heart; and afterwards you shall pass on: for therefore are ye come aside to your servant. And they said: Do as thou hast spoken" ("namq' / strum"; CT).

But Jonson's—and God's—attention soon shifts again to Sodom and Gomorrha. In 18:20, God announces that "The cry of Sodom and Gomorrha is multiplied" ("Dixit / est"; CT). Abraham, however, attempting to dissuade God from punishing all the inhabitants, protests in 18:25: "Far be it from thee to do this thing, and to slay the just with the wicked, and for the just to be in like case as the wicked. This is not beseeming thee: thou, who judgest all the earth, wilt not make this judgment" ("a te / omnem"; CT). Then follows a series of intriguing marked passages, in which Abraham bargains with God, asking him, for instance, if he will destroy Sodom if forty righteous persons can be found there. To which God responds in 18:29, "I will not destroy it for the sake of forty" ("quadra-"; CT). After more persuasion, God in 18:30–31 reduces the figure again: "I will not do it, if I find thirty there. Seeing, saith [Abraham], I have once begun, I will speak to my Lord" ("Quia / Dominum"; CT). Although God once more drops the relevant total, this time to twenty, Abraham nonetheless persists in 19:32: "I beseech thee, saith he, be not angry, Lord, if I speak yet once more" ("irascaris / semel"; CT). After the figure is reduced to ten, Abraham desists, and so does Jonson's marking. The poet's apparent interest in God's clemency and in Abraham's bold appeals to his superior is itself intriguing.[35]

After two angels enter Sodom and are entertained by Lot, his house is surrounded by men of the city who urge him, in 19:5, to "Bring them out hither that we may know them" ("educ / Egressus"; CT). Oddly enough, however, although Jonson marks this provocative comment and although he has shown some previous interest in the corrupted cities, he marks nothing else concerning the destruction that God soon visits upon Sodom and Gomorrha. Instead, his next marks focus on the plan by Lot's daughters (announced at 19:32) to have sex with him: "Come, let us make him drunk with wine, and let us lie with him, that we may preserve the seed of our father" ("vino / De-"; CT). After the first daughter executes the plan, Lot (at 19:33) "perceived not neither when his daughter lay down, nor when she rose up" ("sen- / nec"; CT). But again nothing more about this incident is marked, and Jonson's final two markings in Genesis switch to another subject entirely. After Abraham moves to Gerara, in 20:2–3 he pretends that Sara, his wife, "is my sister. So Abimelech, the king of Gerara sent, and took her. And God came to Abimelech in a dream by night" ("Soror / autem"; CT). Displeased, God orders the woman returned, and Abimilech speedily complies. Afterward, at 20:17–18, "when Abraham prayed, God healed Abimilech and his wife, and his handmaids: and they bore children: For the Lord had closed up every womb of the house of Abimilech, on account of Sara, Abraham's wife" ("sanauit / Saram"; CT). At this point, Jonson's markings in Genesis suddenly cease.

The remaining marks in Jonson's Bible are strikingly different in style and appearance from the ones just described; all the later marks, for instance, were drawn in ink, while the earlier ones were made with a pencil. Whether the later marks were all made by Jonson is by no means clear. For instance, several heavy dark markings in the book of Exodus (see chapter appendix) bear little resemblance to the marks made in Genesis or to the kinds of marks Jonson usually drew in other books from his library. Nor do the pointing hand and broken marginal lines that flank a passage in Deuteronomy (see chapter appendix) seem especially similar to the kinds of marks Jonson most often makes. However, three of the later ink markings may in fact have been made by Jonson. The first of these occurs at the beginning of the Prologue to the book of Ecclesiasticus. A small Jonsonian flower, flanked by two dots, highlights a passage that asserts that knowledge of "many and great things . . . by the law, and the prophets" has been shown to us ("nobis, & / legem, &").[36] A similar mark emphasizes the famous question that opens Ecclesiasticus 1:2: "Who hath numbered the sand of the sea, and the drops of rain, and the days of the world?" ("per / nam"). After this, however, the markings cease until the Prophecy of Baruch, where a flower similar to the ones just mentioned picks out the part of 1:1 that identifies "Baruch the son of Nerias, the son of Maasias, the son of Sedecias, the son of Sedei, the son of Helcias" ("Maa- / filij"). If (as seems likely) this mark was made by Jonson, it is entirely in keeping with the detailed interest in genealogy indicated by many of his marks in Genesis. The same interest may have dictated the drawing of a fourth (and final) flower next to the opening words of the first book of Machabees, which begins with the words, "Now it came to pass after that Alexander the *son of* Philip the Macedonian, who first reigned in Greece . . ." ("Et / sit"). It seems fitting, somehow, that the final mark in Jonson's Bible should return us to more obviously classical matters. Even when reading Hebrew history, Jonson seems to have retained his interest in the "pagan" culture that proved such a great influence on his own work.

Although the poet's final markings in the Bible deal with matters that might seem disappointingly prosaic, his earlier marks are far more interesting. Many of the marks drawn in Genesis, with their focus on transgressions and punishments, are of the sort one might have expected of a writer so much concerned with depicting and judging immoral behavior. The many marked passages dealing with conflict and deceit within families accord with the emphasis in some of Jonson's own plays on tensions within small groups, while the focus in some of his markings on such matters as incest and sodomy is not surprising in a writer whose own works often ridicule sexual misconduct. The memorable passage in which Abram dickers with God about saving the righteous of Sodom suggests Jonson's enduring concern with clemency and the proper use of power. Finally, the concern for precise historical accuracy that seems reflected in many of the marks is typically Jonsonian, and perhaps it was this concern as much as anything that prompted the poet's apparent fascination with biblical genealogies. It would be extremely interesting to possess a copy of the New Testament filled with Jonson's markings, and perhaps such a text will yet turn up. In the meantime, the Pierpont Morgan Bible, which displays the poet's literally marked interest in the Old Testament and especially in the book of Genesis, provides another piece of the puzzle that was Jonson. It tells us a little more than we knew before about his experiences as a reader, his habits of annotation, and, most importantly, his habits of mind.

APPENDIX

Gen. 1:8 ("mentum"; CT, "2") God called the firmament heaven; second day

Gen. 1:11 ("Germinet / facientiem"; UM) creation of herbs and seeded plants

Gen. 1:13 ("set / mane"; "3") third day

Gen. 1:10–20 ("vespere & / Deus"; "4") fourth day

Gen. 1:23 ("factum / quintus"; "5") fifth day

Gen. 1:31 ("sextus"; "6") sixth day

Gen. 2:3 ("ab omni / vt faceret"; "7") seventh day

Gen. 2:11 ("vbi"; DL) where gold grows

Gen. 2:12 ("bdellium"; CR) bdellium and onyx stone

Gen. 2:14 ("piae / Tygris"; HL) the third river's name is Tygris

Gen. 2:14 ("Fluuius / phrates"; HL) the fourth river is Euphrates

Gen. 3:7–8 ("cum au- / deambu-"; CT) Adam and Eve made themselves aprons; heard God's voice

Gen. 4:3 ("& Cain / post"; DL; this may not be a mark) Cain's offerings to God

Gen. 4:18–19 ("Lemech / Genuitq"; CT) Lamech's wives, Ada and Sella

Gen. 4:20 ("Genuitq / habitantium"; DL) Ada gave birth to Jabel

Gen. 4:21 ("no- / pater"; UM) Jabel's brother was Jubel

Gen. 4:22 ("Sella / fuit"; UM) Sella gave birth to Tubalcain

Gen. 5:4 ("Et facti / filios"; CT) after siring Seth, Adam lived 800 years and begot sons and daughters

Gen. 5:7–8 ("genuit / duodecim"; VL) longevity and children of Seth and Enos

Gen. 5:12 ("anni / que"; CT) Cainan lived seventy years

Gen. 5:24 ("non ap- / Vixi"; CT) Henoch, seen no more, walked with God, who took him

Gen. 7:3–4 ("volatilibus / Adhuc"; CL) male and female fowls for the ark

Gen. 11:28 ("Aran / natiuitatis"; CT) Aran died before his father Thare in Ur

Gen. 11:31 ("Aran, filum"; CT) [Lot was Thare's] son's son [the son of Aran]

Gen. 12:6 ("con- / autem"; CL) [Abram traveled to] Sichem, to the noble vale

Gen. 12:16 ("propter / boues"; CT) Abram had sheep, oxen, asses,
servants

Gen. 13:1–2 ("habebat / plagam"; CT) Abram went south; he was very
rich

Gen. 13:4 ("Hai / ni"; VL) Abram returned to altar he'd made, called
on God

Gen. 13:7 ("& facta"; CT) strife between the herdsmen [of Abram and
Lot]

Gen. 14:3 ("in / seruie-"; CT) kings convened in woodland vale, now
the sea

Gen. 14:10 ("ha- / Itaq"; CT) woodland vale had many pits of slime

Gen. 14:12 ("eius / tabat"; UM) Lot, son of Abram's brother, dwelled
in Sodom

Gen. 15:16 ("quar- / Amorrhaeorum"; CT) Hebrews will return after four
generations; the iniquities of the Amorrhites are not yet at full

Gen. 17:19–20 ("post / exau-"; CT) God's covenant with Isaac's descendants; He also has heard Abraham's words concerning Ismael

Gen. 18:9 ("sub / dixerunt"; CL) after eating, the angels spoke to
Abraham

Exod. 12:27–28 ("domos / Dominus"; CL, dark ink; this mark is not
certainly Jonson's) God punished the Egyptians; the Hebrews adore
and obey

Exod. 12:30–33 ("do- / de"; UM, dark ink; not certainly Jonson's) Egyptian deaths; Pharoah expels the Hebrews

Deut. 17:8–13 ("ain- / cun-"; HD, VL, dark ink; not certainly Jonson's)
submit disputes to judgment by the priests

2

Jonson's Seneca

Jonson has been called "one of the most Senecan of English writers in style and often in temper,"[1] and his numerous allusions to Seneca's writings certainly confirm this claim. The standard edition of his works records scores of echoes from passages in Seneca.[2] The English poet had obviously read and appreciated many writings by the Roman moralist in a wide variety of genres, including plays, epistles, and essays. In fact, even the motto Jonson usually inscribed in copies of books he owned—"tanquam explorator"—derives from an epistle by Seneca.[3] Thus the very motives that guided Jonson's reading were informed by Senecan example. We know that Jonson had access to Seneca's dramatic works in a comprehensive anthology devoted to classical Latin poets, and he probably also read Seneca's works in other collections presently lost or unknown.[4] Surprisingly, however, his ownership of a volume devoted exclusively to Seneca's philosophical prose is not reported in any of the standard descriptions of his library.

As it happens, such a volume does exist. Presently housed at the Glasgow University Library, it is a 1599 edition of Seneca's philosophical writings. It bears all the standard indications of Jonson's ownership, including his distinctive marginalia. His motto appears in its typical location on the title page, as does a recognizable version of his signature.[5] The existence of this book confirms what was already obvious—that Seneca exercised a powerful fascination for Jonson and provided a strong stimulus to the poet's own thinking and writing. Jonson's marginal markings run throughout the book, indicating that he responded with considerable interest to a wide variety of Seneca's thoughts and works. His marks suggest the sorts of ethical and political principles, as well as the kinds of psychological insights and generalizations, that made Seneca an important influence on Jonson's own thinking. The book offers valuable new evidence of the poet's enthusiastic response to a writer who was one of the chief exemplars of what has been called "the Roman frame of mind."[6] A sketch of the philosopher's life may help clarify his signficance for Jonson.

Seneca was born in Cordova, Spain, around 4 B.C., during the reign of Augustus. While he was still a young boy, his wealthy, well established family moved to Rome. His father was a respected rhetor; his mother was a forceful personality in her own right. Physically delicate as a youth, Seneca focused on his studies, developing a strong interest in rhetoric and an even stronger passion for philosophy. He visited Egypt as a young man, and then with the help of family connections he obtained a number of public offices during the reign of Tiberius. His literary and oratorical skills soon brought him renown, although they also earned him the jealousy of the emperor Caligula. During the early reign of Claudius, Seneca was important at court; then the emperor's wife accused him (unjustly, it seems) of an illicit affair with one of her rivals. Although condemned to death, Seneca instead was banished; he spent his next eight years exiled in Corsica. In A.D. 49, however, he was summoned by Agrippina, Claudius's new wife, who made him tutor to her son Nero. She also obtained other offices for him, and in general his wealth grew as his fortunes flourished. When Nero succeeded to the throne, Seneca (along with Burrus, prefect of the imperial guard) helped steer the young emperor along the path of good government for the first five years of his reign. Thereafter Seneca's influence began to decline as Nero began to assume—and abuse—independent power. Following Burrus's death, Seneca began a kind of unofficial retirement, and his relations with Nero were now exceedingly strained. Accused of conspiracy and sedition in the year 65, he was ordered to commit suicide. He left behind numerous dramas as well as the various philosophical works that fill the pages of the hefty folio Jonson owned.[7]

Before discussing in detail Jonson's copy of Seneca and the numerous markings he made in this book, it seems worth asking why he may have reacted to Seneca as strongly as he did. What was it about Seneca's example—as a thinker, writer, and person— that may have resonated with Jonson's own experiences? In their circumstances, attitudes, and styles, and in the varying responses they provoked, the two men had much in common.

Both the parallels and the contrasts between the social circumstances of Seneca and Jonson are immediately striking. Seneca, of course, came from a wealthy and influential family; he owed his early success as much to his connections as to his personal talent. Jonson's background, on the other hand, was much less auspicious, and for this and other reasons his social position was in some ways less secure. Even during his exile, Seneca remained a wealthy man, whereas Jonson never came close to achieving the same measure of financial autonomy. Yet despite this important distinction, the two writers nonetheless shared a number of similar experiences. Both, for instance, depended greatly on court contacts for their social prominence and financial success. Both flourished during times when the role of the court and the power of the monarchy were assuming new significance.[8] Both suffered (or prospered) when new rulers assumed power, and both at times ran afoul of influential figures and endured punishment as a result.

Both Seneca and Jonson sought to use their positions—and their writings—to influence public policy, and both experienced ambivalent relations with superiors. Both felt threatened by the machinations of rivals, and both enjoyed an unusual prominence that also carried with it unusual insecurity. Both addressed the powerful in their writings,[9] and both ran the risk of seeming tainted by their involvements at court. Few writers were more closely exposed to imperial or royal politics than were Seneca and Jonson,[10] and both men sought to use their writings to promote the good of the commonwealth. Seneca, in fact, was one of the few intellectuals in western history to achieve the kind of real influence and proximity to power that Jonson always idealized. He was a writer deeply involved in public life, and his early supervision of Nero gave him the sort of power to do good and discourage evil that Jonson could hope to exercise only in a much less direct and less obvious fashion.

In their political views, public philosophies, and private attitudes, Seneca and Jonson also had much in common. Both celebrated disinterested virtue, yet both had to court the powerful to win influence for their beliefs. Both emphasized the strong connections between private virtues and public morality, and ethics is perhaps the central preoccupation of both men's writings. Both seem more concerned with individual men and morals than with overarching systems or creeds (Griffin 210; Sullivan 120), and both felt great disdain for tyranny while serving under rulers who held strong convictions about their personal prerogatives (Griffin 209). Both writers supported hereditary succession (Griffin 218–19), and both were prepared to endorse a tempered, responsible monarchy (Griffin 137; Sullivan 119, 131). Seneca's penchant for speaking of a single god may have made him attractive to a Christian such as Jonson (Gummere 65), while his persistent concern to balance the claims of the active and contemplative lives probably also struck a resonant chord with a poet who memorized verses celebrating the pleasures of a simple existence (Griffin 315; Motto 97; H&S 1:135). Neither man was particularly original in his thinking; both are famous more for having given memorable expression to widely held views than for formulating any uniquely individual approaches to matters of private behavior or public policy (Griffin 154).

In the styles and features of their writing, in fact, Seneca and Jonson also have much in common. Both share, for instance, a strongly practical and pragmatic emphasis; their works are rarely speculative, theoretical, or high-flown (Gummere 1). Their sources are usually eclectic and their methods syncretic: both men read widely and appropriated what they read (Gummere 60; Motto 103). Both use praise and admonishment to promote their views (Griffin 21, 137; Sullivan 133), and there is sometimes a self-justificatory aspect to their writings (Griffin 140, 294; Sullivan 122, 126, 136–37). Both are skilled at satire, and both have been suspected of lampooning particular targets under the cover of mocking generic types (Griffin 16). In their prose styles, both men showed a preference for brevity, terseness, and clipped sententiousness (Motto 109–10). Their writings are often rooted in particular occasions (Gummere 51), and often they address specific individuals rather than simply the public at large. Both men were capable of mocking themselves (Motto 101), and neither spends much time writing about romantic love.[11] Both were attracted by the ideal of self-possession, yet each was highly self-conscious about his public image and performance (Braden 27). Seneca, like Jonson, could attempt to use "impersonal" moral teachings to promote his personal reputation and to shape an attractive public image (Griffin 21–22), yet reactions to both men, in their own times and since, have often been complicated and ambivalent.

Perhaps this is in part because the lives and writings of both figures were often closely entangled, so that responding to the works has often meant responding to the men who produced them. In both cases their writings have often prompted similar—and similarly complicated—reactions. Like Jonson, for instance, Seneca has often been accused of failing to practice what he preached, of falling short of the lofty standards he endorsed for others. Both men have sometimes been accused of compromising their moral authority, of accommodating themselves too easily to the shortcomings of the court and of particular rulers (Sørenson 158), of serving as apologists and public relations men for monarchs who did not always deserve their support (Griffin 79). The writings of both have sometimes seemed to raise problems involving flattery and sincerity (Sørenson 138, 140), and in general the close involvement of both men with the world of power and the court has raised suspicions about the extent to which they may sometimes have been scarred by the very vices they condemn. On the other hand, of course, each has also been vigorously defended as a sincere exponent (and generally successful exemplar) of a fundamentally moral life. In their own days and ever since, the responses provoked by both Seneca and Jonson have often involved either attack or vindication.

When Jonson read his copy of Seneca, then, he not only read the words of a philosopher who had made interesting observations on important topics; he also responded to a writer whose own circumstances, outlook, aspirations, and reputation must have struck responsive chords. The markings he made in his Seneca suggest the many ways in which what he read resonated with what Jonson himself wrote, felt, and believed. Seneca could not only suggest ways of dealing with the large problems of life that all persons must face (such as illness, death, bad fortune, and insecurity), but he could also offer ways of coping with the specific challenges of a life lived in the orbit of the court and royal power.

As it happens, the first of Jonson's markings occur in one of the Moral Essays by Seneca that must have seemed most immediately relevant to the life of a poet dependent on patronage. It is also an essay on which Jonson drew most heavily in composing one of his own most memorable poems, the "Epistle to Sir Edward Sacvile" (*Und.* 13). Whether Jonson relied on this particular reading of *De Beneficiis* in writing his poem to Sackville is, of course, impossible to say. Several passages from the essay that loosely parallel passages in the poem are also marked in Jonson's copy of the folio, but in only one case does the epistle's phrasing match very closely a marked phrase in the essay. Nonetheless the spirit of the essay is entirely Jonsonian, and in fact *De Beneficiis* served as an inspiration for passages in a number of the poet's other works, including *Poetaster, Sejanus,* and the *Discoveries.* Whether Jonson read and marked this version of the essay before or after writing his lengthy poem, both the poem and the markings testify to his keen interest in the topic the essay discusses.

As its title suggests, *De Beneficiis* deals with what has been

called "the morality of giving and receiving." The extreme length
of the treatise has been explained by pointing to "the necessities
of the ancient social order, in which, by reason of its many relations, benefaction and gratitude were counted, not private graces,
but social virtues."[12] Given Jonson's own interest in the etiquette
of social relations, it hardly seems surprising that he responded
to the essay as he did. More than ten marks appear on the essay's
opening page alone, the first two (a circle-tail and flower) next to
the complaint that we throw our benefits away without discrimination ("Prima / enim"; 1/3). Another flower occurs next to the
claim that by being acknowledged a benefit is repaid and that,
although ingrates deserve blame, so do those who demand gratitude or repayment ("crimen / ingratos"; 1/5). A long bracket and
flower highlight a comic description ("Quis non / non ac") of the
tactics people use to evade others' "pressing needs" ("prop-
erantes necessitates"—a term Jonson underlines; 1/5). Similarly,
an underlined flower picks out the underscored words "iratus
impegit," which Seneca uses to explain that no one will be thank-
ful for benefits pushed at him in wrath; 1/5). Another flower emphasizes the claim that, while kindness is forgotten, injuries are
long remembered ("Satis"; 1/7). Again, a flower marks the advice
that we should make our benefits gifts, not loans; whoever thinks
of repayment is justly deceived ("cogita- / educa-"; 1/7). Also
marked (with a circle-tail, flower, short line, and another circle-
tail) is the advice to persist in giving gifts without seeking return
and to search for a good man even after finding bad. What honor
would there be in doing good if one were never deceived? ("si
quis / magnifici"; 1–2/7–9). A large pointing hand, a curved line,
and a vertical line emphasize the admonition that the prospect
of ingratitude should not deter us from doing good. Whoever fails
to repay a benefit sins more; whoever is stingy sins sooner. Many
benefits must be bestowed before one is placed correctly ("datur /
Perdenda"; 2/9).

These markings, from the first page or so of Seneca's essay, give
a fair flavor of Jonson's concerns. As in many of his other books,
his markings here seem to reflect his interest in summary arguments, memorable phrasing (including wordplay), psychological
generalizations, and sound advice. These and similar concerns
seem to have prompted his markings of other passages in the
early pages of the essay. Thus he marks the assertion that in
benefaction, accounting is simple: anything returned is a profit,
and what fails to return is not lost. One should give with the
intent to give, not enter benefits on a ledger or schedule repay-

ment. A good man forgets what he gives; otherwise his gifts become debts ("computauerat / bonus"; CT, BR, CT, BR; 2/11). Even wild beasts acknowledge good offices ("adiuua"; CT; 2/11). If a man is ungrateful for one benefit, two or three may jog his memory ("cis / oblitus"; VL; 2/13). Surrounded by gifts, he won't dare to look up; gird him with your benefits ("mori / que se"; CT, VL; 2/13).

The first of Jonson's large pointing hands highlights a lengthy digression on the Graces, which is also emphasized by a long vertical line ("miseris / tio cōmendat"; 2/13–15). This passage is particularly interesting, not only because of the various allegorical meanings it suggests for those famous female nudes, but also because of its scepticism about the veracity of allegorical interpretation. Seneca implies that poets and artists alter the names and characteristics of mythical figures at will, merely to suit their private fancies. One wonders how Jonson, whose own scrupulous scholarship is suggested by these very markings, would have reacted to this charge or to the allegation that poets do not consider it pertinent to speak truth; instead, either compelled by necessity or attracted by beauty, they determine names by what fits best into their verses ("aut de- / est, si"; CT; 3/17). Perhaps Jonson was attracted by the idea that writers were not obliged to imitate their predecessors slavishly; after all, even his motto, also derived from Seneca, suggests the freedom an artist could enjoy. Or perhaps a passage such as this merely confirmed his low estimate of the seriousness and responsibility of most of his fellow writers. In any case, his lengthy marking of an admitted digression (which receives by far the longest mark of any passage in the essay) makes for one of the more curious and provocative of his reactions to Seneca's views.

When the main argument resumes, Jonson's next mark suggests why the topic of benefits seemed so important to him: Seneca calls benefaction a practice that greatly nourishes human society ("& or- / specie"; CT; 3/19). Jonson marks Seneca's endorsement of friendly rivalry in the giving of benefits: whoever is obliged to acknowledge a benefit does not requite it unless he exceeds it. Givers should learn not to reckon their debts, but recipients should more than acknowledge them ("consequi-"; CT; 3/19). Seneca rejects arguments for benefaction that are rooted in myths, advising simply that benefactors should forget debts, while debtors should always remember. Jonson marks a passage arguing that mythical frivolities should be left to poets, who intend simply to delight the ear and to fashion a pleasing fable ("ineptiae poë-"; CT, HL; 3/21). Surely Jonson did not regard himself as a poet of this kind, and one of his motives in reading philosophers such as Seneca may have been to ballast his writing with an intellectual weight that would protect it from sarcasm of this sort.

The next marked passage emphasizes that benefits are immaterial and spiritual; the gift itself is less valuable than the giver's goodwill ("interest / Imperiti"; VL; 3/21). Material gifts may be lost or stolen, but the benefits they symbolize endure, for no power can damage a good act ("quod irri-"; CT; 3/21–23). Persons saved from shipwreck or a fire may subsequently be lost, but the benefit still survives ("incendio / illis"; VL; 3/23). As crowns are merely signs of honor, so gifts are merely the symbols of benefits ("Nihil ho- / venit, sed"; CT; 3/23). The gift itself is less important than the intention ("non quid"; VL; 3/23), just as a god is honored not by the sacrifice's victim but by the worshippers' pious motives ("sint, auroque"; VL; 4/25). Even small gifts, gladly given, oblige us ("tem / dum meam"; CT; 4/25), but this is not true of large gifts that are either extorted or tossed away, for (as Jonson notes) a gift is accepted with more gratitude when given with a free rather than a full hand ("ingrata / aut excidunt"; VL; 4/25–27). A flower with a long stem marks out an illustrative anecdote involving Socrates. Aeschines, a poor man, told Socrates that all he could offer was the only thing he possessed—himself. But Socrates was delighted, and by this gift Aeschines surpassed his wealthy rivals ("ei, cui / animum"; 4/27).

Jonson's next few markings are scattered, and concern a wide array of topics. In dealing with suitors, for instance, Seneca advises that one should be careful not to provoke them by being sharp-tongued or grave or by brandishing one's good fortune ("iuturus / uidia"; CT; 4/29). Adultery, he laments in a neatly paradoxical passage marked by Jonson, is now regarded as the most decent or becoming form of betrothal. The unmarried man and widower concur, and no one takes a wife without stealing her ("cant / caelibatus"; VL; 4/29–31). The vicious exhibit undue concern with physical beauty, thus exhibiting an ugly soul ("bit furor / formae"; CR; 4/31). Even drunks and drinking are honored, and in general vices do not stay static ("aliquando"; CT; 4/33). Yet after detailing all these various evils, Seneca concludes that there will always be murderers, tyrants, thieves, adulterers, robbers, sacrilegious persons, and traitors, but the worst of all these is the ungrateful man, except that all these are born from ingratitude, without which scarcely any crime or villainy has arisen. One should beware and avoid this as the greatest crime and should not commit it, but one should forgive it as the least significant thing if it is committed by another ("tores / tas: ignosce"; 4/33).

Signficantly, this passage is marked not only with an extended vertical line but also with only the second pointing hand that Jonson has used thus far. The unusual marking suggests the unusual attention the poet wanted to call to this crucial passage, which memorably explains why both he and Seneca seem to have regarded ingratitude as such an important failing. The marking may also reflect Jonson's concurrence with the view that vice will always be with us, and this sense of pervasive sin may help to illuminate his strong attraction toward satire. Yet the commonness of vice only makes virtuous examples that much more admirable and important, and perhaps that is why Jonson marks Seneca's suggestion that we should offer benefits not only when we judge that the recipients will be ungrateful but when we know them to have been so ("iudicabimus / pericu-"; CR; 5/33).

A pointing hand calls attention to Seneca's shift to another major section of his essay, in which he plans to deal with the kinds of benefits that should be given and the ways they should be given ("vt dica-"; 5/35). Yet Jonson shows little obvious interest in this section, and his markings cease for the rest of book 1. They resume, however, early in book 2, when Seneca declares that we feel no thanks for gifts given reluctantly, as if the giver were depriving himself ("inter / tan-"; CT; 9/51). Many are liberal only from weakness; gifts given freely are the most appreciated, in which the only delay comes from the recipient's modesty. The first thing is to foresee the intended recipient's desire; the next is to grant it ("facit / Il-"; FL; 9/51–53). It is grievous and onerous to have to ask with a downcast look ("mus & / dicendum"; CT; 10/53). Thus we should free a man from this oppressive necessity by foreseeing his desire. Such benefits are remembered. And if we cannot foresee the request, at least let us cut it short ("cuiusque / uenire"; CT; 10/53). Prompt generosity reflects the giver's willingness and joy ("& diu / Itaque"; CT; 10/55). It is best when good works are accompanied by good words; humane and kind language helps commend beneficial behavior ("vultu / humana"; VL; 10/55). If you are freely generous, the recipient will value your spirit more than your gift, and (as Jonson notes) you will be credited with the most manifest virtue and benignity when the recipient goes away saying that he has profited greatly ("quàm / tunc"; FL; 10/55).

No more marks occur in book 2, and none occur at all in book 3. Indeed, only one other mark occurs elsewhere in the entire essay, and that is in book 4. There Seneca argues that some useful services are too minor to be dignified as benefits: "Who ever called a morsel of bread a benefit, or tossing anyone a copper, or enabling him to get a light? And sometimes these are more helpful than very large gifts; yet, for all that, their cheapness detracts from their value even when the necessity of the moment has made them necessities" ("ignis ac- / quod po-"; CT; 37/265). It is intriguing to wonder why this isolated passage received the only other mark Jonson made in his copy of *De Beneficiis*, especially since he had marked the first two books with some consistency. Whatever the reason, the marking suggests some of his usual interests, for with its memorable imagery, clever wordplay, and thematic terseness, this passage typifies many he marked in his copy of Seneca.

Jonson's next marks occur not in an essay but in several *Epistles*—those reflective letters, all addressed to his young friend Lucilius, that were the memorable products of Seneca's final years.[13] Marking does not begin until epistle 30, in which Seneca laments the infirmities of old age. Yet philosophy gives us strength and courage in the sight of death, and Jonson's first mark occurs next to the claim that a great pilot navigates even with torn sails, and if his ship is damaged or impaired, he can still use what is left to stay on course ("stat: in / tamen"; FL; 98/213). Surely the phrasing here caught Jonson's eye, but one wonders, too, whether his interest in this epistle may also have been motivated by his personal circumstances. Did he read this letter, perhaps, during his own old age, when his body had begun to fail him? Markings elsewhere in the lightly marked *Epistles* suggest a recurring interest in mortality, and perhaps it is significant that more marks are made in epistle 30 than in any of the others.

Jonson's next marking highlights Seneca's description of the thoughts his friend Bassus expressed concerning death. Bassus contended that if dying involves any inconvenience or fear, it is the fault not of death but of the person dying; there is no more distress in death itself than in its aftermath. It is as mad to fear what will not be felt as to fear what will not happen ("bis persuadeat / est qui"; CT; 98/215). Yet Jonson's next mark is especially intriguing, coming from a Christian poet responding to a pagan moralist. Seneca assumes that a person would seem more credible and weighty to Lucilius if he returned from death and, having experienced it, said that there was no evil in it ("plus ponderis"; FL; 98/217). Whether Jonson marked this because of some personal discomfort with the merely Stoic consolation Seneca could offer or whether he marked it simply to note a new stage in the progression of Seneca's argument is, of course, impossible to say.

Nonetheless, it seems worth noting that his next mark occurs beside a report that Bassus often said, submitting to the precepts of Epicurus, that he hoped he would have no pain in his last breath ("septimo / primum"; FL; 98/219). Although Seneca's phrasing continues (suggesting that at least a dying man might take solace in the brevity of such pain), it is unclear, from the short stem of Jonson's flower, whether the poet intended to include this consolation in his marking. Even if he did, it seems obvious that the potential pain of death was a topic that caught his interest. His last mark in this epistle, appropriately enough, also deals with the act and moment of dying: Seneca notes that he has seen many people break off from life. Yet those people have more influence with him who come to death without hatred of life, and who admit death but do not drag it toward them ("vidi / admittunt"; FL; 99/221). Jonson's marking of this apparent rejection of suicide suggests that, for him as for Seneca, even the act of expiring was a test of character, a performance to be judged. The marks in epistle 30 are among the most fascinating in the entire folio. Like later marks that also confront issues of death and dying, these suggest an intensely private and introspective aspect to Jonson's thinking—an aspect most memorably expressed in his famous poem on the death of his son, but one that is otherwise rarely voiced in his writing.

Epistle 31, also marked by Jonson, concerns Lucilius's efforts at self-improvement. Seneca counsels him, explaining that he does not desire that Lucilius should make himself greater or better than he already strives to be, since his foundations already occupy a great place ("desidero / occupaue-"; DL; 99/223). He must close his ears to siren songs of the sort that tempted Ulysses, for although the voice that Ulysses feared was enticing, it was not public or all-encompassing. The voice that should be feared is the one that does not come simply from one crag in the sea but that sounds from every part of the earth ("non ta- / terrarum cir-"; FL; 99/223). Lucilius should be deaf to those who love him most. With a good intent, they entreat for what is bad, and, if Lucilius wants to be happy, he should pray to the gods that what his friends wish for him will not befall him ("felix / volunt"; FL; 99/223). The epistle continues in this vein, but Jonson seems to have been interested chiefly in a passage intended to explain, by analogy, that whatever is associated with virtue is good and that whatever is associated with vice is bad. Thus he highlights part of a sentence claiming that, just as nothing is splendid without mixture of light, so nothing is black but that which has darkness in it or draws obscure things into itself. Similarly, without the help of fire nothing is hot ("quod / ignis"; CT; 99/225). The mark drawn next to this passage is highly unusual in appearance (although still recognizably Jonsonian). Why the poet showed such interest in this rather pedestrian series of images is one of the minor mysteries of his markings in this book. Intriguing for different reasons is the one mark made in epistle 54—a small, ink-drawn flower resembling larger ones drawn by Jonson's hand. Seneca explains that he long had tested death. Jonson's flower picks out a passage in which Seneca says that, if asked when he had done this, he would say it was before he was born. Death is simply not to be, and he has known for a long time now what that involves ("sit, iam"; FL; 115/363). If this mark indeed is Jonson's, it seems all the more noteworthy that he focused on this passage while passing over so many of the preceding and subsequent epistles.

In fact, only two more letters are marked, and in the first case the markings are not certainly Jonson's. Next to the opening line of epistle 85 (which the Loeb translator entitles "On Some Vain Syllogisms"), two marks are drawn. The first, an "x" in light brown ink, is flanked by a "#" sign in ink that is somewhat darker ("quasi"; 159/285). Neither mark is especially distinctive or typical of Jonson. This fact, along with the fact that nothing else is marked, disposes of any need to discuss this epistle. The only remaining letter that is marked is epistle 115, entitled "On the Superficial Blessings" by the Loeb translator. Here a Jonsonian mark, unusual only because of its exaggerated size, highlights some of the first few sentences of the letter. Since these comment on questions of style, Jonson's marking is of particular interest:

You should seek what to write, rather than how to write it—and even that not for the purpose of writing but of feeling it, that you may thus make what you have felt more your own and, as it were, set a seal on it. Whenever you notice a style that is too careful and too polished, you may be sure that the mind also is no less absorbed in petty things. The really great man speaks informally and easily; whatever he says, he speaks with assurance rather than with pains. You are familiar with the young dandies, natty as to their beards and locks, fresh from the bandbox; you can never expect from them any strength or any soundness. Style is the garb of thought: if it be trimmed, or dyed, or treated, it shows that there are defects and a certain amount of flaws in the mind. ("scribas, sed / manufa-"; CT; 219/321)

This might serve almost as an epigraph on Jonson's own stylistic ideals; certainly it helps illuminate his well known love for language that is terse, direct, and plain. As the *Discoveries* suggest repeatedly, for Jonson verbal style could provide revealing insights into character.[14]

Given Jonson's famous temper, satiric verve, and fascination with unruly emotions, his next markings—in the essay *De Ira* ("On Anger")—hold a special interest.[15] Like many of the markings in his Seneca, these affect only the essay's first few pages; why his marks so often cease abruptly is an intriguing question. Did Jonson simply stop reading, or did he begin making notes instead in commonplace books now lost to us? Whatever the explanation, his markings in *De Ira*, though brief, are nonetheless suggestive. The first marked passage, for instance, notes the violence and self-destructive passion of anger, which is a kind of brief insanity ("inest / dus. Quidam"; HL, VL; 280/107). It is like ruins that crumble on top of what they crush ("rique inhabilis"; CT; 280/107). An angry man appears dreadful and horrible, distorted and swollen with anger. You cannot tell whether this vice is more detestable or more deformed ("atque intumescentium"; CR; 280/109). No animal is so naturally horrible and pernicious that it does not become even more fierce when possessed by anger, which, like other emotions, is not easily hidden ("tura, vt"; CR; 280/109). Anger's results include burned houses and fire that spreads beyond the city walls, illuminating vast regions with hostile flame ("pita venalia"; HL; 280/111).

Jonson's next mark may have been designed to call attention to a lacuna in Seneca's text; a printed symbol in his copy of the folio alerts readers to the irregularity, and next to this the poet has drawn an unusual symbol of his own. (It resembles a "]" mark, and occurs next to the line beginning "sos"; 280/113). When conventional marking resumes, it is used to call attention to a passage describing the irrational, immature behavior of spectators at gladiatorial contests; like little boys who beat the ground when they fall, such persons are angry without even having been injured, yet still they desire to punish ("Quicquid / ne iniuria"; FL; 280/ 113). Yet Seneca reports (and Jonson marks) a friend's argument that anger is not a desire for revenge since the weakest are often wrathful toward the most powerful; they do not desire a vengeance they cannot hope to enjoy. To this Seneca responds that he had claimed anger was the intent, not the ability, to inflict revenge. Besides, men do desire what they are unable to achieve. Moreover, no one is so socially insignificant that he cannot hope for punishment of the greatest man. Everyone has the power to injure ("cogitatione / potentes"; CR, CR, HL; 280–81/113). This provocative passage—with its careful distinctions, psychological insights, and interesting implications for the relations between superiors and inferiors in a rigidly hierarchical society—is the last one marked in *De Ira*. The essay continues for over thirty further pages, but Jonson's markings cease. When they resume, his new focus is on an essay that deals with the opposite of anger—*De Clementia* ("On Mercy"). His markings here are spread more evenly throughout the piece.[16]

Although the first marking in *De Clementia*—two diagonal lines—is not assuredly Jonson's, its juxtaposition with another mark more certainly his helps raise confidence about the legitimacy of the first. The first mark occurs next to a passage in which Nero is advised to ponder the favor he, of all mortals, has been shown in having been chosen to function on earth in place of the gods ("loqui / funge-"; 315/357). He should consider that his mouth pronounces whatever gift fortune would grant to each mortal. From his responses cities and people take cause for joy. No part of the earth anywhere flourishes unless he is willing and favorably inclined ("nostro / pro-"; CT; 315/357). Such a marking helps suggest why Jonson considered the role of the king—and of those who could influence the king—so important.

The essay's next markings, once again, are less certainly Jonson's, although very probably by him. Next to one sentence, for instance, a diagonal line, crossed twice, has been drawn, and part of the sentence itself has been underlined. Here Seneca proclaims that *that force is pestiferous which is strong for the purpose of injuring. The one man who has a grounded and stable greatness is the one whom all men know to be as much for them as he is above them*, whose care to be vigilant for the welfare of one and all they experience every day ("que sunt / cuius curam"; 316/365–67).[17] Similarly, an oddly shaped cross mark occurs next to another partially underlined sentence declaring that the emperor is *the bond by which the commonwealth is held together or coheres; he is the breath of life which whole thousands* draw, who would be nothing by themselves except a burden and a prey, if the mind of the empire were taken away" ("enim vinculum / nihil"; 316/369). Finally, on the same page two short, nearly vertical lines are drawn in the margin next to the underlined portion of a sentence; this affirms that *"the end of this*

city's [Rome's] *dominion will coincide with the end of its obedience"*
("in partes"; 316/369). Assuming that this mark and the sentiment
it emphasizes belonged to Jonson, we may have new evidence of
his fairly conservative political sympathies.

This emphasis on the prince's centrality is balanced, however,
by the essay's next mark, which is almost certainly Jonson's and
which stresses the prince's need for self-control. The mark flanks
a passage urging him to be merciful, asking, if the placable and
equitable gods do not immediately punish with thunderbolts the
crimes of the powerful, how much more just is it for a man, placed
above other men, to exercise his authority with a gentle mind and
to consider whether the state of the world is more gracious or
pleasing to the eye on a bright and clear day, or when all things
are shaken frequently with crashes of thunder, and when
lightening flashes on this side and that ("potentium / ignes hinc";
CT; 317/377). As this marking suggests, Jonson's interest in memorable language seems to have influenced his habits of annotation,
and this same interest seems reflected in his next marking as well.
Seneca recounts Augustus's merciful words to Cinna, who had
been plotting against him. Jonson notes Augustus's proposal that
he and Cinna should strive with one another to see which might
act in better faith—Augustus in permitting Cinna his life, or
Cinna in acknowledging the debt ("consulatum, que-"; CT; 319/
387). Seneca's admiration for Augustus's forbearance is indicated
again in a passage partially underlined and also marked in the
margin. The emperor, he notes, *appeared to punish himself when
exacting punishment,* because he was so far from killing whomever
he had condemned on account of adultery with his daughter that
as he sent them away he gave them letters of introduction or
passports so that they might be more safe ("quoscumque / essent
di-"; 319/389). Jonson's apparent interest in these passages is itself
interesting, especially in view of his presentation in *Poetaster* of
Augustus and of Julia's flirtations. Yet the only marked passage
from *De Clementia* that is the subject of a direct allusion in one of
Jonson's plays is the next one. There, in a partially underlined
sentence, Seneca declares that he certainly does *not call wearied
cruelty mercy* ("clementia"; 319/391). This phrase, ironically
enough, is echoed by the devious emperor Tiberius in Jonson's
tragedy *Sejanus.* In a letter to the Senate that precipitates the
downfall of his former favorite, Tiberius explains that because of
Sejanus's own *"loyall furie, . . . now our clemencie would be thought
but wearied cruelty, if we should offer to exercise it"* (H&S 4:459).
Assuming that the underlining in Seneca was done by Jonson,

his decision to put the philosopher's words into Tiberius's mouth is a nice example of poetic irony.

Further underlining a little later (again, presumably Jonson's) distinguishes between the cruelty practiced by true princes and that indulged in by tyrants. Seneca explains that *kings* [are cruel] *on account of some cause or necessity* ("causa ac"; 319/391), whereas *a tyrant is cruel at heart* ("non no-"; 319/391–93). The fact that such sentiments are thoroughly Jonsonian increases the likelihood that the underlining is his as well. Surely the next mark is his. It occurs next to a passage that asks whether any father in his right mind disinherits a son for one offence. Only when great and many injuries conquer his patience, and when he fears more than he condemns, does he disinherit ("lent / timet"; CT; 320/399). Less clearly marked (with two short vertical lines and some erratic underlining) is the warning that someone who condemns quickly almost condemns with pleasure, and anyone who punishes excessively comes close to punishing unjustly ("Prope"; 320/401). This, as it happens, is the last of the markings in *De Clementia*.

Jonson's next marks, in the essay *De Vita Beata* ("On the Happy Life"), are surprisingly sparse.[18] They occur more than halfway through the piece, the first one flanking a passage in which Seneca, somewhat defensively, imagines the various charges of inconsistency that could be leveled against a philosopher, and then contemplates his response:

> Add, too, if you like: "Why do you have domains across the sea? Why [do you possess] more than you have seen? And shame to you!—you are either so careless that you do not know your handful of slaves by sight, or so pampered that you have more than your memory can recall to your knowledge!" Later I shall outdo your reproaches and bestow on myself more blame than you think of; for the moment I shall make this reply: "I am not a 'wise man,' nor—to feed your malevolence!—shall I ever be." ("quàm no- / sapie*n*s, &"; CT; 333/143)

The fact that Jonson, who was himself occasionally attacked for hypocrisy, found this passage noteworthy is noteworthy in itself. Interesting for a different reason is the modestly proud and contentious tone of the next highlighted passage, beside which an unusual mark has been drawn, presumably by Jonson. Resembling a large crossed "7," the mark emphasizes the conclusion of Seneca's imagined response to his critic, in which he asserts that

> ". . . It is enough for me if every day I reduce the number of my vices, and blame my mistakes. I have not attained to perfect health,

nor indeed shall I attain it; my gout I contrive to alleviate rather than
to cure, content if it comes more rarely and gives less pain; but when
I compare your feet, crippled though I am, I am a racer!" ("meos /
Vestris qui-"; 333/145)

Later Seneca reports the response of Socrates when he also was
assailed by enemies and ridiculed by his critics. Socrates claimed
that the hardness of flint is known by no men more than by those
who strike at it. He claimed to present himself in no other way
than as a rock somehow destitute in the shoals of the sea, which
waves, which had moved from one source or another, did not
cease to thrash. However, not on that account did they either
move it from its place or, by their repeated strikings through all
the ages, destroy it ("nulli / loco"; CT; 337/177). Ironically, all of
Jonson's markings in the essay "On the Happy Life" highlight
passages dealing with threats to happiness rather than with happiness itself, and this final marked passage is utterly characteristic
in its sense of embattled isolation. For Jonson, Seneca seems to
have provided not only a measure of consolation but also a disqui-
eting sense that other worthy figures had been attacked and persecuted by their contemporaries.

Partly for this reason, the poet's next markings—in the essay *De
Tranquillitate Animi* ("On Tranquillity of Mind")—are of particular
interest.[19] The first marked passage, emphasized in the margin
by a hooked vertical line, presents the self-assessment of Seneca's
interlocutor, Serenus (to whom the treatise is addressed). On the
subject of his moral health, Serenus declares that he finds himself
in a state or condition that is not the worst, yet he is complaining
or morose. He is neither ill nor well. There is no point in Seneca
telling him that in the beginning all virtues are weak, and that
with time they gain in hardness and strength ("positus sum /
labo-"; 343/203). In a long passage, marked first with a diagonal
cross and then with a large wavy sign shaped like a "7," Serenus
lists various of his preferences. He likes simple food that is simply
prepared and is easily acessible and plentiful; it should burden
neither the body nor one's inheritance, and it should stay down.
For a servant, he prefers someone young and unsophisticated,
and he likes a simple table, without intricate workmanship—one
intended for use rather than to please the sight or provoke the
envy of his guests ("parabi- / inuidia"; 343/205-7). If this seems
reminiscent of the simple pleasures celebrated in Jonson's famous
poem "Inviting a Friend to Supper" (*Ep.* 101), the resemblance
seems born of shared fundamental ideals.

The next marked passage is intriguing for its emphasis on an oscillation between the active and contemplative lives, its indication of the alternative attractions of public involvement and private retirement. Serenus reports that sometimes he finds his public duties a waste of time. At these moments he retires, like tired sheep, to his home, intending to live within its walls. He resolves not to be deprived of even one day for unworthy reasons; he intends to contemplate and develop his own mind, focusing it on nothing outside itself. Yet when he reads of great courage or is inspired by noble examples, he wants to burst into the forum and lend his voice to another, attempting to help even if his effort cannot aid ("otium con- / alterius"; CL, VL; 343/209). Surely Jonson was also tugged by such contradictory impulses; surely he recognized the kind of ambivalence Serenus describes.[20]

Whether Jonson recognized himself at all in the next marked passage is an intriguing question; at the very least, he found the passage notable. In this section, Serenus argues that many would already be wise if they did not take their wisdom for granted and if they confronted their own and others' personalities more openly. Self-flattery is no less harmful than flattery from others. Who dares speak the truth to himself? Who, though surrounded by flatterers, does not flatter himself even more? Serenus thus appeals to Seneca to help him halt his fluctuation and achieve tranquillity ("& semper / sistas"; CT; 344/211). When Seneca later responds to Serenus's entire opening address, the first words of his that Jonson marks suggest in part the poet's interest in philology. Seneca tells Serenus that the stability the latter desires is almost divine; he mentions the relevant Greek term for it, even recommending a treatise on it by Democritus, but says that he himself calls this state tranquillity. Imitating or copying the Greek form of words is unnecessary ("& summum / tari &"; CT; 344/213–15).

After disposing of these preliminaries, Seneca next turns to more important matters. He will explain generally how tranquillity may be obtained. Then—and now Jonson's next mark (a curved line) appears—Serenus will be able to take from the public remedy however much he wants. In the interim the whole problem must be exposed, and each person will then recognize his own part in it. At the same time, Serenus will know how much less troubled he is than others ("ramus / gotij"; 344/215). Marking ceases momentarily, and then a long line is drawn next to Seneca's declaration that all are in the same situation, both those who are constantly changing and those who are languid and listless. Add, too, those who are like insomniacs who toss and turn so often that they finally sleep from fatigue. Repeatedly fashioning their lives, such persons finally cease changing not from dislike of change but from the fear of novelty that old age brings. Add, as well, those who are insufficiently fickle not because of constancy but because of inertia—those who live not as they desire but as they started. The aspects of the problem are innumerable, but it has one effect—to be displeased with oneself ("dem causa / fectus"; 344/215–17). After such a long marking, the next is strikingly brief, highlighting a reference to agitated persons who are able neither to command nor to gratify their desires ("nec cupiditatibus"; CT; 344/217).

The passage Jonson marks next must surely have touched a personal chord; the vices it deals with—jealousy and envy—were ones by which he often felt victimized.[21] Seneca declares that inertia produces (among other things) the most inimical envy of the prosperings of others. For their unhappy slothfulness nourishes envy, and they desire to destroy everyone else because they themselves are not able to advance. And next, from this aversion toward the advancement of others and from hopelessness concerning their own, their spirit, becoming wrathful toward fortune and quarreling with the times and withdrawing into corners and incubating its pains, all the while becomes disgusted and annoyed with itself ("incrementis / suorum de-"; CT; 345/219). The human mind, he continues a little later, enjoys being excited, and this is especially true of those who run themselves down with business. Just as some sores yearn for hands to touch and injure them, and just as an itch enjoys being scratched, so these minds, on which desires have erupted like evil ulcers, also delight in labor and vexation ("pessimis in- / quodam"; VL; 345/219). It is a characteristic of the sick to endure nothing for very long, and to employ changes as remedies ("vt reme-"; CT; 345/221). An oddly shaped mark, immediately followed by a curving horizontal line, emphasizes a quote from Lucretius and then Seneca's commentary on it: "In this way each man always flees from himself." But what, Seneca asks, does he profit if he does not get away? He is followed by himself, and the most burdensome companion oppresses him. And thus we ought to realize that the defect we labor under is not external but internal ("fugit / omne to-"; 345/221).

Although Seneca cites Athenodorus's commendation of public service, he also quotes (and Jonson marks at great length) that philosopher's concession that because in this so insane ambition of human beings, when everything is twisted by calumniators from the right and toward the worse, simplicity is by no means safe, and because there will always be more that obstructs than that succeeds, we should retire from the forum and public affairs. Yet a great spirit can display itself even in a private dwelling or at home. The activity of lions and other animals is restrained by their dens, but this is not so with man, who can act from a distance. However, a person should conceal himself in such a way that, wherever he takes his peace, he should be willing to be useful to one and all through his cleverness, his speech, and his counsel. For not only is that person useful to the commonwealth who brings forth candidates and defends the accused and advises for peace or war, but also he who exhorts youth (faced with a great lack of good teachers) and instructs their spirits in virtue, who seizes and restrains those who are hastening on a course toward riches and excess and if nothing else at least delays them; he privately does a public service ("tot calu- / plus prae-"; VL, VL; 345/223–25).

Surely Jonson must have found attractive this ideal reconciliation of public and private, of active and contemplative, of service and retirement. So, too, he must have been attracted by Athenodorus's subsequent comparison of private studies to a soldier's guard duties. He marks a passage claiming that, although the former employments are bloodless, they come under the rank of military services. A person who summons himself to his studies will have escaped all distaste of life; he will not desire the night because of disgust with the light, nor will he be burdensome to himself or useless to others; he will attract many to friendship, and the best persons will flock toward him. For howsoever virtue is obscured, it is never hidden ("stipen- / latet, sed"; CT; 345/225).

Such a passage helps explain Jonson's own passionate devotion to scholarship—a devotion symbolized by his markings themselves. Yet the next marked passage balances this one in its tone and emphasis. For the first time in this essay, Jonson draws in the margin a large hand (pointing toward "ponere"; 346). Although it is difficult to tell from this mark alone what, precisely, he meant to highlight, in the passage that lies just beyond the hand's pointing finger Athenodorus lists various meaningless activities on which time can be wasted (such as erecting certain buildings, demolishing others, turning back the sea, or directing the flow of water to difficult places). We thus dispense badly the time given us by nature. Some use it frugally, some lavishly; some are able to account for it, while others are left with nothing ("ponere / tum, quo"; 346/227). How much of this Jonson intended to single

out is uncertain; all that can be said is that his marginal hand
does flank this entire passage.

The immediately ensuing mark, however, is more precise. It
highlights a passage that stresses the disgracefulness, in Athenodorus's opinion, that often an old man has no argument, other
than his age, to prove that he has lived long. At this point Seneca
himself resumes (and Jonson's mark continues). Seneca contends
that Athenodorus has submitted too readily to the times, retreating too soon. While Seneca would not deny that sometimes
withdrawing is necessary, he insists that any retreat should be
gradual, preserving the standards and the dignity of the soldier
("liquias / dendum"; CT; 346/227). He argues for a more steadfast
response to misfortune than he believes Athenodorus supported,
and Jonson draws a long line next to Seneca's advice that the
unfortunate man, rather than retreating, should involve himself
more moderately with obligations and should with judgment dis-
cover something in which he may be useful to the commonwealth.
Is he not allowed to be a soldier? Let him look to public offices.
Must he live a private life? Let him be an orator. Is he sentenced
to silence? Through silent advocacy let him aid his country. Is it
even dangerous for him to enter the forum? In private homes, at
public spectacles, at banquets let him play the part of a good
companion, a faithful friend, and a temperate guest. If he has
lost the duties of a citizen, let him exercise those of a human
being ("Sed parcius / bus clusimus"; 346/227–29). The final quoted
sentence, with its epigrammatic point, is marked not only by the
vertical line drawn next to the entire passage but also by a
strangely shaped circle-tail, as if Jonson found this pithy summary especially notable.

A judgment similar to that just cited is again offered—and
marked—a number of sentences later. There Seneca argues that
the service of a good citizen is never unprofitable. For by his
hearing, by his sight, by his countenance, by his beckoning or
nod, by his tacit firmness, and even by his manner of walking,
he is helpful ("lis est / prodest"; CT; 346/231). And so, Seneca later
contends (in a passage Jonson marks with two vertical lines—one
short, one long), it is best to mix business with relaxation whenever impediments or civic conditions prohibit an active life; honest
action is always an option. Was any city more miserable than
Athens when the Thirty Tyrants were tearing it in pieces? They
had killed thirteen hundred of the best citizens ("pedimentis /
optimum"; 346/231). Jonson's marking of this passage does not
immediately continue, but it resumes a little later, after Seneca

extols the worthy example Socrates set in face of the tyranny just mentioned. And yet, Seneca continues (in a section Jonson marks), Socrates was the man whom Athens herself killed in prison, unable to bear the freedom of one who had freely insulted the tyrants. Thus the wise man can set a good example when the state is afflicted, while vice may rule when the state is happy and prospers ("tamen / se proferendum"; CT; 346/233).

In another epigrammatic summary that Jonson again seems to have intended to emphasize by drawing a pointing hand, Seneca asserts that to preserve oneself is not the same thing as to bury oneself. He then quotes Curius Dentatus as having said that he would prefer to be dead than to live dead. The worst of evils is to exit from the number of the living before you die. But if you fall upon a time when you cannot involve yourself in the commonwealth without trouble, you should lay claim to more time for leisure and letters ("tutem / vt plus"; CT; 346/233–35). And, with this sense of partial resolution, Jonson's markings in the essay *De Tranquillitate Animi* now cease.

His next marks occur in the essay *Ad Marciam De Consolatione* ("To Marcia on Consolation"), one of a number of Seneca's efforts to comfort friends or relatives in mourning.[22] Here the problem of death—the focus of a number of markings elsewhere—becomes central. In attempting to console Marcia for her son's death, Seneca notes (and Jonson marks) her strength in bearing the loss of her father, whom she loved no less than her children, except that she did not want him to survive her. And yet she may have desired even that, for great devotion sometimes conflicts with proper mores ("patris / rem magna"; CT; 380/3). Her duty to her father, the historian Cordus (celebrated in Jonson's *Sejanus*), was all the more remarkable in an age in which it was considered great piety merely to do nothing impiously ("hil impie"; CL; 380/5). After her father's suicide, Marcia delivered him from true death by restoring as public monuments those books which that most courageous man had written with his own blood ("casti morte"; CT; 380/5). Thanks to Marcia, her father's memory will now live for as long as there will be anyone who may wish to turn to the acts of his forefathers, for as long as there is anyone who may wish to know what it is to be a courageous Roman who, when the necks of all are bowed and burdened with the yoke of Sejanus, may be an indomitable man, free in character, spirit, and fist ("scire / iugum ad-"; CT; 381/5). She thus rescued a man who died for two of the most beautiful pursuits, eloquence and liberty. Now he is read, he flourishes, accepted into men's hands and hearts ("eloquen- / receptus"; VL; 381/5–7). The same admiration for Cordus expressed in Jonson's play seems reflected in his markings. In both cases one suspects that Jonson strongly identified with this writer-hero.

Jonson next marks Seneca's comment that he has reminded Marcia of old evils; to prove that her latest wound will heal he has shown her the scar of an old one equally great. Let others treat her gently and speak soothing words ("vulneris"; CT; 381/7). Other consolations have failed, and Jonson marks the claim that even that natural remedy, time itself, which smooths the greatest hardships, has wasted its force on Marcia alone ("in te vna"; CT; 381/7). Seneca knows that those wishing to advise another begin with precepts and conclude with examples, but sometimes it is useful to change this order ("desi- / Quosdam"; 381/9). A particularly odd mark is drawn next to a passage in which Seneca says that he intends to present Marcia with two examples, the greatest of her sex and era. One was a woman carried away by sorrow, the other a woman who was afflicted with a similar calamity and an even greater injury but who quickly recovered her mental balance. Octavia and Livia, the sister and wife respectively of Augustus, lost their sons, each of them possible future emperors ("quae / auun-"; CR; 381/9). Jonson, however, marks no more concerning these enlightening examples.

When his marking resumes, Seneca is denying any intention to draw Marcia toward stronger precepts, as if to command her to bear a human fate in an inhuman fashion or as if on the funeral day itself to dry the eyes of a mother. He will come to her as an arbitrator. This will be the issue between them: whether sorrow ought to be great or perpetual ("re humana / veniam"; CT; 382/17). Later Jonson marks words spoken by the philosopher Areus to the mourning Livia; he charged her with neglecting to remember her good fortune and with focusing instead on the bad ("aud-ire / qua deterior"; CT; 382/19). Livia, according to Areus, should reflect that the art of a pilot is not exhibited by a tranquil sea or favorable wind. It is necessary that he may encounter something adverse that may test his spirit. Therefore she should not submit, but rather stand firm, and sustain whatever burden may fall from above, terrified initially only by the rumbling. Nothing may be a greater reproach to fortune than a contented spirit. After saying this, Areus showed to her her uninjured son, and he showed her the children left by her dead son ("Nec gubernatoris / incolu-mem"; CT, DL; 382/21).

Seneca himself soon picks up the naval metaphor, and Jonson

marks the passage twice. We should control our vessel, not allowing the force of grief to divert it. Only a poor helmsman submits to the sea's fury and jumps ship, but he is praiseworthy, even in shipwreck, whom the sea buries while he still grasps the helm, resolute ("Turpis est / tenentem &"; VL, CT; 383/21–23). Of the animals, only man suffers an extended grief for dead off-spring; man indulges his sorrow and is afflicted less by what he feels than by what he resolves to feel ("dolori / non esse"; FL; 383/23). In order that Marcia may know that such grief is not dictated by nature, she should note that women grieve more greatly than men, barbarians more than the peaceful and cul-tured, the uneducated more than the learned ("non esse / Atqui"; VL; 383/23).

Excessive grief comes from taking our fortune for granted. Jon-son marks a passage in which Seneca claims that so many rich persons fall into sudden poverty in our sight, but it never enters our mind that our own resources also stand in an equally slippery position ("nobis num- / itaque"; VL; 383/27). We stand exposed to all the spears striking others. As if besieging some city or fortified position, anticipate injury; assume that all the missiles are aimed at you. When others fall, declare that fortune will not trick you, attacking you while sure and negligent. Proclaim that you know her intentions and that, though she strikes another, she aims at you. Who looks at his property expecting to perish? Who dares to think about exile, indigence, sorrow? ("fixerunt / nostrum de"; VL; 383/27). Nothing truly belongs to us. The use and enjoyment are ours, but the duration is set by the giver. It behooves us to have ready at hand those things which were given to us for an uncertain day and, when they are called for, to give them back without complaint. It is very wrong for a debtor to reproach his creditor ("tanquam inter / sunt, &"; CT, DL; 384/29–31). The rele-vance of sentiments like these to a poem such as Jonson's elegy on his own son (*Ep.* 45) is immediately clear. However, the poet's last marking in the essay to Marcia deals less with personal mourning than with the public consequences of a single death. The relevant passage deals with the demise of Julia, the wife of Pompey and the daughter of Julius Caesar, whose death helped break the link between those men and unleash the civil war. Jon-son marks Seneca's claim that Caius Caesar, while he traveled through Britain and was not able to have his felicity contained by the ocean, heard that his daughter had died, drawing the fate of the republic with her ("Britan- / filiam"; CT; 385/45). After noting this, Jonson marks nothing else in the essay.

His markings resume, however, in another treatise on grieving—the essay *Ad Helviam Matrem De Consolatione* ("To Helvia His Mother on Consolation").[23] This is the last of the works that Jonson marked in his copy of Seneca. The essay to Helvia, however, deals not with mourning caused by death but with Helvia's aggrieved response to Seneca's own exile. This is clear from the first marked passage, in which Seneca explains his decision to write to his mother, saying that he did not doubt that he would have more influence to arouse her if he had first aroused himself ("interim / dubitabam"; CT; 392/417). Yet he hesitated to write to her too early, just as in sickness nothing is more dangerous and pernicious than untimely medication ("derent / matura"; CT; 392/ 417). Now that he is writing, however, he does not doubt that he will have greater power over her than her sorrow has, although nothing is more powerful among the miserable ("qua*m* / concurram"; CT; 393/419). He will not minimize her distress; he will burn and cut ("Hoc erit non"; CT; 393/421). Let those people weep and groan the longer whose delicate minds have been enervated by long felicity and who begin to totter at the motion of the lightest injuries. But those whose years have all been spent going through calamities bear the most burdensome blows with strong and immoveable constancy ("diutius, & ge- / forti"; VL; 393/421).

Helvia is one of these: fortune has given her no vacation from the gravest sorrows, not even on the day she was born ("luctibus: ne"; CT; 393/421), when her mother died. A strangely shaped mark (two curved lines, narrowly separated but joined at the bottom) is drawn next to the passage explaining that Helvia was brought up by a stepmother, whom Helvia indeed by all submission and piety, as great as scarcely could be seen in a daughter, compelled to become a mother. Yet there is no one who has not paid greatly even for a good stepmother ("obsequio / non ma-"; 393/421). Whether Jonson (who was himself a stepchild and who had also lost a parent at the earliest possible age) found these remarks personally relevant is, of course, uncertain, although the possibility is tantalizing. In any case, he continues to mark the listing of Helvia's misfortunes. Thus, not only did she lose her uncle, but then her husband died shortly thereafter. Jonson marks Seneca's observation that Helvia was told this while she was lamenting, indeed while all her children were absent, as if her ills were purposely thrown together into that time so that there might be nothing on which her sorrow might recline ("industria / tot pe-"; CT; 393/423). But now into that same lap from which she had let loose three grandchildren she has received again three sets of bones. Within twenty days of having solemnly buried Seneca's son, who died in Helvia's arms and with her kisses, she heard that Seneca had been ripped away. This was something hitherto denied her: to mourn for the living ("sinum / in cor-"; CT; 393/423). Now, with Seneca's exile, even that bit of good fortune has been stripped away.

Yet, just as fresh soldiers exclaim because of light injuries and fear the physician more than the sword (while veterans, although stabbed through, patiently and silently endure the cutting of their bodies), so Helvia should courageously dare to submit herself to be cured ("manus me- / cura-"; VL; 393/423). The first of several large marginal hands, followed immediately by a curved horizontal line, now points to a passage in which Seneca asks his mother whether he has dealt too fearfully with her. He has concealed to her nothing of her misfortunes, but rather has placed all of them, heaped up, before her. He has done this with a great spirit, for he has resolved to conquer her sorrow, not to contain or deceive it ("tecum / Vincam"; 393/423). As the first part of his cure, Seneca will prove to his mother that he is enduring no evil. However, she will not be able to believe this, yet he will please himself the more because he will be happy among those things that are wont to make people miserable ("at ego / Non est"; CT; 393/425).

Four closely linked marks—the first very peculiar, the second a brief vertical line, the last two a pair of short brackets—highlight a passage in which Seneca reflects upon how people sacrifice their original advantages. We are born, he says, in a good condition, if only we did not forsake it. It accords with the nature of things that living well should take no great preparation of work. Everyone is able to make himself happy. There is slight importance in external things, which have great force in neither direction. Successful events do not lift up the wise man, nor do adverse ones cast him down, for he always has striven that he might depend most on himself and might seek all of his joy from himself. What, then? Does Seneca claim to be a wise man himself? Not at all. For indeed if he were able to profess that, he would not only deny that he is miserable, but would proclaim that he is the most fortunate of all and is brought to nearness with god. At present, he has devoted himself to wise men (an act which is enough to alleviate all miseries). Although not yet strong enough to give assistance to himself, he has taken refuge in the camp of others, namely of those who easily protect themselves and their own ("Bona con- / confugi, eorum"; 393/425–27). All this is soon followed by a marginal hand, pointing to Seneca's claim that he is obligated to look for all the efforts of fortune and all its attacks long before they occur ("incurrant. Illis"; 393/427). Those who are prepared for war, well composed and equipped, easily endure the first blow, which is the most tumultuous. Never has Seneca credited fortune, even if it seemed to be making peace ("facile / illa quae"; CT; 393/427). He has kept his distance from the temptations of prosperity, so that fortune has simply taken them rather than tearing them away. No one is broken by adverse fortune whom good fortune did not deceive ("ea sine / la, non"; CT, VL; 394/427).

Seneca finds nothing so terrible and hard about the things commonly feared as evils ("circumlita"; CT; 394/429). Thus, rejecting the judgment of the many, who are deceived by initial appearances, we can see that exile is simply a shift of place ("Remoto / deamus"; CR; 394/429). People move to Rome, for instance, for many reasons: in pursuit of ambition, public duties, embassies, opportunities for vice and luxuries, liberal studies, spectacles, friendship, the chance to exhibit industry, and the opportunity to sell beauty or eloquence. All kinds of people have flocked to the city that greatly rewards both virtues and vices ("adducit / non hominum"; VL; 394/429–31). Some say there is an innate impulse to change residences and shift homes; man was given a changing and restless mind that maintains itself in no single place; it scatters itself, dispatching its thoughts in all directions, known and unknown. It is rambling and impatient with rest and rejoices most in the novelty of things ("dicant / uitate" ; VL; 394/431–33). An oddly shaped mark is drawn next to the declaration that all the heavenly bodies revolve. They are always in transit, as natural law ordains, carried from one place to another ("Semper"; 394/433).

The nature of god is delighted with or even preserved by constant and most rapid alteration. Yet if Marcia turns from heavenly doings to those of humans, she will see that entire tribes and peoples have changed homes ("mutatione / Videbis"; CT; 394/433). A large mark, shaped like a "7" with a circle at the left tip of its crossbeam, highlights a passage explaining that some nations, driven by long wandering, have not judiciously chosen a place but rather, fatigued, have occupied the first possible location. Others have used arms to impose their justice in alien lands. Some peoples, pursuing the unknown, were consumed by the sea; some settled where scarce provisions deposited them ("elegerunt / illas re-"; 395/435). Another motive summoned others from their homes. And so this is evident: nothing has remained in the same place where it was born ("Alios alia / quo ge-"; CL; 395/ 437). Rome itself has established many colonies; Jonson marks the observation that wherever a Roman conquers, he inhabits ("locorum"; HL; 395/437). Even Corsica, the place of Seneca's exile, has seen many inhabitants; a vertical line highlights the comment that the Ligurians went over into Corsica, and the Spaniards came over as well—which is apparent from the similarity of manners, for the coverings on their heads and feet are of the same kind as the Cantabrians wear, as are certain words ("Transierunt / verba quae-"; 395/439). In sum, all people are thoroughly mixed and engrafted. One group has succeeded another. One group eagerly desires what is loathed by another. A group that expelled others has been ejected in turn from the same place. And so it has pleased fate that nothing should always stand still in the same fortune ("Hic con- / certis in-"; CT; 395/439).

Therefore, because change is so normal for humans, exile is not to be greatly feared. A vertical line marks Seneca's claim that whatever is best for a man lies outside the power of other men; it can neither be given nor snatched away. This world, than which there is nothing greater or more adorned of the things nature has begotten, along with the most magnificent part of it (the human spirit, the contemplator and admirer of the world), belong to us perpetually and will remain with us for so long as we ourselves shall remain. And so, lively and upright, wherever circumstance will lead, let us hasten with intrepid step ("est, id / quamdiu ipsi"; 395/441). Jonson uses two marks—including a pointing hand—to highlight a passage in which Seneca responds to the imagined objection about Corsica that no precious stone is hewn there, no veins of gold or silver are dug up. To this Seneca replies that it is a narrow mind or spirit that delights in earthly things ("ruunter"; HD, CT; 396/443). Moral conduct can be practiced anywhere. A circle-tail marks the claim that no place is narrow which contains a gathering of great virtues; no exile is burdensome in which one is permitted to go with this companionship. Brutus, in the book he composed concerning virtue, says that he saw Marcellus, banished to Mitylene, living most happily insofar as is in the power of human nature ("hanc tam / nis exulantem"; 396/445). Marcellus undoubtedly steeled himself by thinking that he had so imbued himself with instruction that he knew that to the wise man every place is a homeland ("plinis imbuisti"; CT; 396/447). Nor did Marcellus's change of place provoke any change in his spirit, although he was followed by poverty, in which there is no evil ("tauit loci"; CT; 396/447).

Bodily needs are easily met, but not by gluttons. Jonson marks a passage claiming that such persons vomit so that they may eat; they eat so that they may vomit. They do not consider the feasts for which they seek throughout the entire world worthy to digest. If anyone despises such things, what injury may poverty do to him? If anyone eagerly desires such things, poverty is even advantageous to him. For he is cured against his will, and if he does not take his remedy even when compelled, for a time certainly, his inability can appear to be a refusal ("vltimo / dem recipit"; CT, VL; 396/449). Oh, miserable men, whose taste is not excited except by costly foods!—costly, however, not from exceptional taste or some sweetness to the tongue, but from rarity and the difficulty of obtaining them ("prouinciarum / raritas"; CT; 396/449–51). If our desires were moderate, we could live more simply than we do today. Seneca sardonically contrasts the supposed unhappiness of the ancient Romans with their extravagant descendants.

For instance, he contrasts the venerable Manius Curius with the more recent Apicius. The former, while meeting with ambassadors from a defeated tribe, cooked inexpensive food with the very hand that had slain enemies and had carried the symbol of triumph. However, Apicius (at the very time the philosophers were expelled from Rome for corrupting youth) poisoned the age with the science of the cook-shop. After he had bestowed vast monies on his kitchen and had consumed huge sums in feasting, he was finally forced to inspect his accounts. Although still left with a sizable sum, he found it insufficient to support his lifestyle and then with poison killed himself ("viuebat di- / centies vi-"; VL; 397/453). He dreaded his vast wealth and with poison fled what others pray for. For a man so mentally depraved, his last drink was the most beneficial ("exti- / vltima po-"; CT; 397/453).

Nature makes troublesome nothing that man truly needs. However, if the exile desires cloth deeply dyed with purple, interwoven with gold, and adorned with various colors and designs, it is not fortune's fault but his own that he is a pauper. Even if you restore to him whatever he has lost, you will do nothing ("non fortunae"; CT; 397/455). For places of exile supply necessary things, while not even kingdoms furnish things that are superfluous. It is the spirit that makes people rich. This follows one into exile; in the roughest solitudes, when one discovers what is enough for sustaining the body, the spirit abounds and delights in its own goods ("Animus est / satis est"; VL; 397/457). Money does not pertain to the mind—no more than material things,

valued by the ignorant and those addicted to their bodies, pertain
to the immortal gods ("animum per- / nimis cor-"; CT; 397/457).
Punishments, robberies, and sicknesses vex the body, but the
mind or soul itself is sacred and eternal and cannot be touched
("Ani- / putes ad"; CT; 397/459). However, so that Seneca will not
seem to be using philosophy to make light of poverty (which is
serious only to those who think it so), we should first consider
how many poor there are; yet they are not more sorrowful or
distressed than the wealthy. In fact, they may be happier, because
fewer things perplex their minds ("putes ad / pauciora"; VL;
397–98/459). Referring to the rich who occasionally pretend to be
poor, Seneca laments the ignorance and mental darkness of those
who normally flee what, for the sake of enjoyment, they sometimes imitate ("semper / giunt"; CT; 398/459).

Jonson's interest in historical details sometimes seems to have
influenced his markings. He highlights, for instance, Seneca's reference to two men of little wealth who nonetheless contributed
to the public welfare. Menenius Agrippa, who helped bring civil
peace to Rome, was nevertheless sufficiently poor that his funeral
had to be funded by public contributions. Similarly, Atilus Regu-
lus, while he was vanquishing the Carthaginians, reported that
his hired servant had deserted his farm, which the senate ordered
to be cared for at public expense during his absence ("bus vi-
deatur? / psit, mercenarium"; VL; 398/461). The example of such
men shows that poverty itself is no disgrace. Yet someone may
object that, while isolated ills are tolerable, aggregated ills are
not. Jonson marks Seneca's response that, when virtue has once
hardened the spirit, it keeps it invulnerable on all sides ("nerabi-
lem"; CT; 398/463). Even disgrace cannot afflict a wise man. Jonson highlights the claim that worse even than ignominy is an
ignominious death ("secessit?"; HL; 398/463). However, Socrates
entered prison with that same countenance with which he had
once by himself brought the thirty tyrants into order and thus
was able to remove ignominy even from that place, for indeed a
place that contained Socrates could hardly seem a prison ("secessit? / miniam"; VL; 398/463–65). From this and other examples
Seneca concludes that no one is disdained by another unless he
is first disdained by himself. A shallow and abject spirit may be
exposed to this contumely, but a person who truly lifts himself
up against the most raging mishaps and overturns the evils by
which others are oppressed has replaced his miseries with a holy
crown, since we have been influenced in such a way that nothing
before us fills us with greater admiration than a man who is

bravely miserable. At Athens Aristides was being led to execution; whoever ran to meet him cast down his eyes and groaned, not as if a just man but as if justice itself might be executed. Nonetheless, one person was found who spat in his face. Aristides was entitled to be vexed because of this, because he knew that no one with a clean mouth would have dared it. But he wiped his face and, smiling, said to the magistrate accompanying him, "admonish that man that he might not afterward open his mouth so impudently." This was to affront effrontery itself ("contemptus est / tam improbe"; VL, VL; 398/465). A great man who falls is no more condemned than the ruins of a holy temple are trampled, which the religious still venerate as if it were standing ("illum putes / ac stantes"; CT; 398/465–67).

Since Helvia thus has no reason to weep for Seneca, she must grieve for two other reasons. Jonson marks Seneca's reasoning that she is moved either because she seems to have lost some protection or because she is not able to bear the desire to see him. Seneca will touch very lightly upon the first possibility, for he has known that her spirit loves nothing in her children beside themselves ("ipsum per / nihil"; CT; 399/467). Helvia is unlike other mothers, who both exhaust and catch at their sons' patrimonies and who fatigue their eloquence in loaning it out to others. But she has rejoiced a great deal in the goods her children possess and very little in her use of them. She has always imposed a limit on their liberality, but she imposes none on her own ("aliis / locupletibus"; VL, CT; 399/467). It is fortunate that Seneca and Helvia had been separated before the exile, fortunate that an absence of several years had prepared her for such a calamity. By returning to Rome she was not only unable to take pleasure in her now-exiled son, but also lost the habit of separation.[24] If she had been absent long before, she would have borne his exile with greater strength, the interval itself dampening the longing. If she had not departed, she would have had the final enjoyment of seeing him for two more days. Yet cruel fate disposed things so that she would neither be present during his ill fortune nor become accustomed to his absence ("diui- / meae in-"; CT, DL; 399/469).

On this note, Jonson's markings end—not only in the essay *Ad Helviam* but in his volume of Seneca's works as a whole. In none of the works he marks is the marking carried through till the text's very end; Jonson's jottings always conclude before Seneca finishes. Why this should be so is a curious—but unfortunately unanswerable—question. Yet the markings that do exist are fascinating in their possible resonances and implications. They provide a wealth of new information about the poet's interests, and they suggest a great deal about his responses to a number of significant issues. The sheer range and variety of the topics that Seneca covers and that Jonson highlights are noteworthy in themselves. These include (to recollect just a few) the ideal of the writer as national hero; the celebration of liberty; the goal of immortality through writing; the need for self-examination; the dangers of self-flattery; the right to creative adaptation (rather than slavish imitation) of literary sources; the importance of moral and emotional centeredness; the competing attractions of the active and contemplative lives; the public responsibilities of a scholar; the ideal of devotion to study; the liabilities of having stepparents; the ways misfortunes test character; the obsession of most people with mere appearances and with satisfying their appetites; the problem of anger; the need for self-defense; the sense of being embattled and under siege; the complexities of relations between superiors and inferiors; the ideal of kingship; the legitimacy of literary allegory; the ideal of accuracy; the etiquette of gift-giving; the problem of death; issues of self-presentation; stylistic motives and goals; and, above all, the demands of virtue in all its manifestations and ramifications. In a more concentrated, focused, and explicit manner than is perhaps true of any other surviving source, Jonson's markings in his copy of Seneca give us rich new insights into his reaction to the Stoicism that was such an important influence on his thinking.[25] In general terms, the markings provide new data about his responsiveness to "the Roman frame of mind." More specifically, they provide valuable evidence about the mind of the writer who created them.

3

Jonson's Apuleius: The *Apology* and *Florida*

Apuleius is remembered today chiefly as the author of the *Metamorphoses* or *Golden Ass*, one of the most famous of ancient novels and one of the most lively and fantastic works of fiction ever written. Jonson's markings in his copy of Apuleius indicate that he read parts of the *Metamorphoses*, and the detailed (if limited) nature of the marks suggests that he responded to the work with some enthusiasm. However, far more interesting and suggestive are the markings he made in two of Apuleius's lesser-known writings, the *Apology* and the *Florida*. These were among the works that helped to establish their author's contemporary reputation as a serious thinker, and it is these works that seem to have attracted most of Jonson's attention. His markings in them reveal a great deal about the specifics of his interest in this important Latin writer.

The life of Apuleius can be recounted quickly. He was born in Madaura, a Roman colony in Africa, around A.D. 124 or 125. "His father was the leading citizen of the town";[1] at his death he "left his sons the considerable fortune of two million sesterces."[2] After receiving the beginnings of his education in Madaura, Apuleius studied further at Carthage, Athens, and Rome. His course of study was as varied as his interests; among other subjects, "he studied philosophy, rhetoric, geometry, music, and poetry" (Hadas 340). He traveled widely in pursuit of knowledge and experience, but during a stay in Rome he achieved success as a public speaker, particularly in the courts. Back in Africa, he married a rich widow—an act that prompted a legal suit which in turn produced the *Apology*, in which he defends himself against the charge (among many others) of having used magic to seduce his wealthy bride. He lived out the rest of his life in Carthage, where he was memorialized with a statue and where he "was appointed to the chief priesthood of the province, the highest honor it could bestow" (Hadas 341). He wrote (or is reputed to have written) many works on a wide variety of scholarly and philosophical topics and in a wide variety of genres (Hadas 349–50). When he died, probably sometime between 170 and 180 (Hadas 341), he was one of the most prominent and respected intellectuals of his day.

Apuleius's fame endured, in one form or another, throughout the middle ages and the Renaissance. "References to his writings appear in both grammarians and historians, and in the Christian fathers" (Haight 92). Lactantius, in the early fourth century, considered him a magician, and his life or works are mentioned by such other figures as Macrobius, Priscianus, Cassiodurus, Apollonaris Sidonius, and Saint Jerome (Haight 94–95). It was Saint Augustine, however, who probably ensured his notoreity. *The City of God* contains numerous passages alluding to (and disputing) Apuleius's discussion of demons, and one of Augustine's letters indicates the mingled admiration and disdain he felt for his pagan countryman. He calls Apuleius "a man of superior education and great eloquence," but he also accuses him of ambition, self-promotion, and hunger for fame.[3] He concedes that Apuleius "defended himself with brilliant eloquence against some who imputed to him the crime of practicising magical arts; which makes me wonder at his panegyrists, who, in affirming that by these arts he wrought some miracles, attempt to bring evidence contradicting his own defence of himself from the charge" (487–88). Augustine considered "simply ridiculous" anyone who would "attempt to compare with Christ, or rather to put in a higher place, Apollonius and Apuleius, and others who were most skilful in magical arts" (487). The vigor of Augustine's language, and the enormous respect he enjoyed among later Christians, would both have ensured that Apuleius's reputation would survive throughout the middle ages and the Renaissance—although not, perhaps, in quite the way that Apuleius himself might have hoped. Jonson, who claimed to have read widely in the writings of the early church fathers,[4] may well have known about Augustine's reaction to Apuleius the miracle-worker and writer on demons.

At one point Augustine calls Apuleius "the Platonist of Madaura,"[5] and in fact Elizabeth Haight offers evidence suggesting that in the early middle ages he was chiefly known as a philosopher. She notes that the "catalogues of [French] libraries previous to 1300 do not mention the *Metamorphoses*, although they do list Apuleius' philosophical writings" (106). By the time of the Renaissance, however, Apuleius's fame as a writer of fiction had begun to grow. "It was Poggio who first discovered a manuscript of Apuleius' novel, but Boccaccio is the one who did most in making it known. There is a copy of the *Metamorphoses* written in Boccaccio's own hand and he was soon re-telling Apuleius' stories in Italian to the delight of his readers" (Haight 112). Cervantes, Machiavelli, Giordano Bruno, and Cornelius Agrippa all seem to have read and been influenced by *The Golden Ass* (Haight 114–17), and the impact of Apuleius's highly distinctive prose style began to be felt. In an extremely valuable article, John F. D'Amico has argued that a style he calls "Apuleianism" was one of three major options available to writers of sixteenth century Latin.[6] Like the clipped Tacitean and Senecan prose to which Jonson himself was so attracted, Apuleianism allowed its practitioners to distinguish themselves from the orthodox Ciceronian style of the day. "The Latin writers of the Golden Age, and above all Cicero, had perfected the balanced, periodic sentence and had standardized Latin vocabulary to such an extent that their followers felt there was little left to do but imitate them" (D'Amico 383). Imitating Seneca was one way out of this confinement; imitating Apuleius was another. Jonson's interest in one alternative style may help explain his interest in another.

D'Amico shows that "the use of archaic words from early writers was basic to Apuleianism, [and] it also included writers who used uncommon words from late classical sources, words with a Greek base, and a convoluted syntax which could impress a reader" (361). Renaissance commentators either rebuked or praised Apuleius's style for its *"curiositas,"* a term that in its negative sense implied "excessive interest in the unknown and useless or the dangerous" (D'Amico 388). "However, there was also a positive side to this *curiositas;* it was a logical complement to erudition. To find the word which was uncommon but effective in a literary context required both artistic knowledge and a desire to investigate and experiment" (D'Amico 388–89). The learning and wide reading demanded by this style might well have appealed to a man like Jonson, but D'Amico argues that the "very qualities which made Apuleianism appealing to some, especially its emphasis on searching the past artistically, made it ultimately a small and doomed movement" that inspired imitation mainly among the literary elite (391).

Jonson's emphasis on clear sense and plain speech may have checked his enthusiasm for the ornate ornamentation of Apuleius's style, but the African's public stance and encyclopedic learning seem to have impressed him. His markings suggest as much, and several quotations and allusions also suggest his interest in the substance of Apuleius's writings. Annotations to the *Masque of Queens*, for instance, several times refer to *The Golden Ass*, particularly to its comments on the powers of witches and magicians. Interestingly, in phrasing that might just as easily have come from St. Augustine, Jonson at one point comments that such powers "are mere arts of *Sathan*, when eyther himselfe will delude them wth a fallse forme, or, troubling a dead body, make them imagine these vanities the meanes" (H&S 7:297). Such words show the extent to which Jonson could distance himself from the thoughts of a pagan writer, but several allusions to Apuleius in the *Discoveries* suggest a more favorable view, and even a measure of empathy and identification. Twice Jonson borrows from the *Apology* in ways that suggest he saw parallels between his own circumstances and those of Apuleius, and elsewhere he seems to recall bits of Apuleian phrasing (H&S 11:616).

Far more interesting than such scattered allusions, however, are the intense and enthusiatic markings he made in his personal copy of Apuleius's works.[7] Most of these marks occur not in the *Metamorphoses*, the novel for which Apuleius is best known today, but in the *Apology* and the *Florida*, writings that grew directly from their author's experience as a public speaker. The *Apology*, his lengthy and witty self-defense, not only answers allegations that he had practiced magic, but also ranges so widely over his life and interests that it has been justly called "an *apologia pro vita sua* rather than an *apologia de magia*."[8] Refuting the main charge was important, since practicing magic was a crime punishable by death,[9] but Apuleius turned the occasion into an opportunity to defend his values as well as his personal conduct. As James Tatum has written, "Apuleius transforms a debate on the issues of a civil suit into an encomium of the philosopher's life. He becomes an African Socrates"[10]—a point made by a number of scholars, who note Apuleius's efforts to play up the similarities between his own trial and that of the Athenian sage.[11]

The larger issues raised by this effort would probably have made the *Apology* more intriguing to Jonson, but other aspects of the speech may also have heightened his interest in it. Haight, for instance, observes that the speech "gives an amazing revelation of private life in the period" (61). Similarly, Moses Hadas considers the *Apology* "our best introduction to second century Latinity as well as very valuable for the abundant light it throws on the private life and intellectual atmosphere" of its era (342). He notes that the work is "the only forensic speech surviving from imperial times" (341) and suggests that because the "speech as we have it is too long to have been delivered, . . . it was probably enlarged for publication" (342).[12] This very expansiveness would have enhanced the work's appeal for Jonson because of the range of topics it covers, but he seems also to have responded to its emphasis on unjust accusations.[13] Perhaps he was also attracted by its confident tone, its rhetorical expertise,[14] its mingled humor and seriousness, and the stinging pungency of its satire.

Of course, the best way to assess his interest in the work is to examine his numerous markings. The topics they cover are almost as varied as the speech itself. These include such issues as the proper interpretation of conduct and writings; the usefulness of precedents; the nature of innocence and guilt; the difference between love and desire; the function and features of philosophy; the proper response to poverty; the use and abuse of language; the connection between style and character; the problems of envy and calumny; the traits of philosophers and friends; the rendering of moral judgments; the reputation of actors; the corruption of family relations; the opposition of morality and money; the distinction between appearance and reality; the techniques of satire; the nature of justice; the traits of women; the characteristics of effeminate conduct; the ideal of marriage; the country versus the city; gratitude versus ingratitude; freedom of thought; clemency; deceit and self-deception; the purpose of poetry; poetic naming; the attractions of being learned; and many, many others. Jonson's markings also suggest his interest in effective insults, memorable phrasing, secondary sources, sententiae, facts of all kinds, crucial distinctions, specialized phrasing, odd details, mythological data, Platonic philosophy, ancient customs, psychological generalizations, esoteric knowledge, and lists, catalogues, and rhetorical series of every sort. His detailed reaction to the *Apology* implies an intense response to both its matter and its manner—to the issues it treats and to the ways they are treated.

The specific allegations to which the *Apology* responds may be worth mentioning, since, as James Tatum has wittily remarked, "the personalities and issues of the trial itself are complicated— a sure sign that a good lawyer has been at work."[15] These, briefly, are the facts (at least as Apuleius presents them): on a trip to Alexandria, Apuleius became sick at Oea (on the African coast) and was persuaded by a friend, Pontianus, to come and recuperate in the house of the latter's wealthy mother, a middle-aged widow named Pudentilla. Pontianus encouraged his young friend to marry Pudentilla, but then had second thoughts. He changed his mind again, however, but he died shortly after the marriage took place. Pudentilla's relatives, including her young son Pudens and Pudens's uncle and step-father, accused Apuleius of having murdered Pontianus and of using magic to attract Pudentilla. The first charge was soon dropped, but the charge of magic—and a host of other attacks on his character—prompted him to defend himself in a trial conducted before the proconsul Claudius Maximus in A.D 158–59.

The very proliferation of Jonson's markings in the *Apology* makes them fairly difficult to describe briefly; in addition to his typical marginal marks, the speech is also heavily underlined, and there is every reason to think that the underlining is Jonson's. Such underscoring often allows him to pick out only a few words of phrasing, while in other cases lengthy passages are similarly marked. Marking begins with the very first sentence, two thirds of which is underlined. Addressing the judges, Apuleius alleges that one of his accusers has merely abused him rather than making substantial charges. Any innocent person can be accused, but only the guilty can be convicted ("mei / potest:"; UL, FL; 303/ 247).[16] Apuleius notes that his chief accuser, after dropping the charge of murder, accused him of practicing magic—an accusation easier to make than to prove. Jonson picks out the last comment with a marginal cross and underlines the entire passage discussing the accuser's maneuverings ("est de / tur"; UL; 304/ 248). The general moral significance of these matters is literally underscored in a passage in which Apuleius claims that "one who is evil-disposed repeats his offence with increased audacity," so that "the more frequently he offends, the more undisguisedly he does so. For it is with shame as with a garment—the more it is worn, the less it is cared for." In addition to his underlining, Jonson highlights this whole passage with a large pencilled cross ("iam de / habetur"; 305/249).

Apuleius insists that he is defending not only himself but also Philosophy, whose "high character spurns the least slur as though it were the weightiest of charges" ("Philosophiae / reprehensio"; UL; 305/249). Besides, he remarks, "according to my way of thinking, it is the part of a modest and honorable spirit to be incensed even by a false accusation" ("puden / con-"; UL, CR; 305/249). If Jonson shared this view, this would help explain why he so often chose to respond so vigorously to attacks from his own critics.[17] Even those who know they are guilty hate to be reproached, "although from the very moment that they began to do wrong, they may have been accustomed to hear themselves ill-spoken of " ("con- / malefacere"; UL, CR; 305/249–50). However, the virtu-

ous man is used to praise, not reproach ("laudis as-"; UL; 305/
250). Apuleius's accusers are disgraced by their charges, whereas
he should not be blamed, but honored, for refuting them ("etiam /
erit"; UL; 306/250).

Apuleius begins his refutation by recounting the more ridiculous charges first. Thus, they accuse him of the "monstrous"
crimes of being a handsome philosopher who is eloquent in both
Greek and Latin ("nefas"; UL; 306/250). Apuleius responds that
one of his accusers is certainly not eloquent himself, and he continues by wishing that the accuser had "had good grounds for
making such weighty charges against me—of being possessed of
good looks and of eloquence," for then "I should have had no
difficulty in answering him, as Paris does Hector, in Homer: 'Man
may not reject / The glorious bounty by the Gods bestowed, /
Nor follows their beneficence our choice'" ("cusationem / Mun-
era"; UM, UL; 306/250). He further notes that "Pythagoras, who
was the first to call himself a philosopher, was the handsomest
person of his age" ("ram / culi"; UL, CR; 306/250). However, in
his own case, "unremitting application to learned labours has
effaced from me all comeliness, has made me thin, dried up my
natural juices, expunged my healthy colour, and impaired my
vigour" ("litterati / rem"; UL, UM; 306/251). Jonson's marking of
this passage may suggest his interest in Apuleius's own biography
as well as in the practical sacrifices that a life of study entails,
while the rhetorical series with which the sentence ends may also
have attracted his attention. In any event, he marks Apuleius's
detailed description of his tangled hair ("amoenus / Sa-"; UL,
CR; 306–7/251), and he highlights another reference to the young
Apuleius's constant devotion to learning ("viribus"; UL; 307/251).

In a marking that is brief but significant, Jonson underlines the
already emphasized claim that "*Innocence is eloquence*" (307/251);
in this respect, Apuleius admits, he is indeed eloquent, since he
has "never so much as entertained a thought to which I did not
dare give utterance." He is most truly eloquent, "for all guiltiness
I have ever esteemed as a thing not to be named" ("cogitaui /
diser-"; UL; 307/251–52). Turning to specific allegations against
his writings, he refers to verses of his "which they put forward
as compositions of mine, of which I ought to be ashamed" and
notes that "you saw me smiling at them in scorn, because they
delivered them in so uncouth and illiterate a manner" ("cum /
quòd"; UL, CR; 307/252). This sense of superiority to one's antagonists is recognizably Jonsonian, so it seems fitting that the
writings criticized were a poem.[18] Apuleius's antagonists objected

particularly to an epistle he wrote about dentrifices ("scriptum"; UL; 307/252), which he had sent to his friend Calpurnianus, who "had asked me for something to be used for the purpose of cleaning his teeth" ("ver-"; UL; 307/252). Jonson underlines the opening phrase of the poem in question ("In hurried verse, I bid Calpurnian hail" ["versibus"; 307/252]), then underscores as well Apuleius's ironic concession that he may have deserved rebuke "for sending to Calpurnianus a powder made of Arabian drugs, seeing that he was a person who might have with much more propriety, after the filthy manner of the Iberians, 'With his own [urine] washed his teeth and rusty gums,' as Catullus says" ("Calphurniano / Dentem"; UL, CR; 307–8/252). However, whereas modern editions end the quotation from Catullus at this point, Jonson's text provides additional lines that seem in fact to come from the poem over which Apuleius stood accused. Jonson underlines a few essential phrases, including "the dentrifice, / . . . A fine choice powder, a rare whitener, / A soother of the swollen tender gums" ("Tenuem / Complanatorem"; 307–8/252). The absurdity of this entire episode could hardly have been lost on him, just as it was not lost on Apuleius, who has great fun at his opponents' expense.[19]

However, Apuleius manages as well to wring some serious reflections from this matter, and Jonson (not surprisingly) responds. Apuleius concedes, for instance, the importance of a clean mouth, since "it is the vestibule of the mind, the gateway of speech, and the outer court of the thoughts" ("quòd / tationum"; UL; 308/253). Calumniators needn't worry about cleaning their mouths with fine powders; charcoal will do. Of one of his accusers, Apuleius suggests that he should "let his malignant tongue, the caterer of falsehoods and of bitter abuse, for ever lie amid the stench and foulness which so well become it." Does it make sense "that one should have a clean and purified tongue, and at the same time a loathsome and offensive voice," or "that he should, like the viper, instil black venom from teeth white as snow?" ("laua- / Cete-"; UL, CR, VL, VL; 309/254). Here the imagery and satiric fury no doubt caught Jonson's attention, but the moral righteousness is also recognizably his own. Apuleius transforms what had seemed simply a matter of humor into a question of virtue opposing vice.

Vice, in fact, is the charge he must refute in connection with some love poems his enemies have attacked. His opponents have read these "in such harsh and uncouth tones, as . . . to provoke hatred" ("odium mo-"; UL, CR; 309/254). The issue of misinterpretation, always an important one to Jonson, now comes clearly to the fore.[20] So, too, does the moral status of amorous verse.[21] Apuleius quotes (and Jonson underlines) a lascivious line from Solon in order to justify his own ("Desirous of her thighs and honeyed mouth"; UL; 310/255). He recites some lines of his and claims not to be ashamed of them ("denuo"; UL; 310/255) The lines are from a poem celebrating his love for the boys Critias and Charinus; Jonson marks the last three of these ("*Hasce / Hoc*"; UL, VL; 310/255). He also marks the entirety of another love poem to Critias ("*Florea / Cedent*"; UL, VL, CR; 310/255–56), and he underscores Apuleius's ironic comment that "the charge against me [is] founded upon garlands and songs" ("Habes / ris"; UL; 310/256). In a marked passage with definite implications for Jonson's own practice as a poet, Apuleius defends the appropriateness of using pseudonyms in writing about others, citing the precedent of other poets ("Eadem / Plania in"; UL, DL, DL, DL; 311/256). He condemns the poet C. Lucilius "because he openly defamed the youths Gentilis and Macedo in his lines under their own names" ("Gentilem & / prosti-"; UL, DL; 311/256). The first of Jonson's pointing hands highlights a passage stressing Virgil's use of pseudonyms and mocking the churlish rigidity of Apuleius's accuser ("Corydonem / Ser-"; UL, HD; 311/256). Apuleius justifies his love poems by noting that even Plato wrote such verses ("Platonis ip- / nisi"; UL; 311/256), and he mocks his opponent's ignorance of literature ("litteras"; UL; 311/256). He then quotes (and Jonson marks with underlining and various marginal symbols) several verses ascribed to Plato that celebrate different youths (311–12/257).

All this emphasis on the practice of such exemplary figures as Plato and Virgil helps support Apuleius's attempt to distinguish between art and life—a distinction in which Jonson seems to have been interested. He marks, for example, the sentence in which Apuleius asks the plaintiffs, "are you not rather acting the part of calumniators, even to produce these matters as the grounds of your accusation against me? just as though, forsooth, it were any proof of a man's mode of life, that he writes wanton lines" ("potius / lum"; UL, CR; 312/257). Apuleius quotes Catullus, who wrote that "'Tis fit the worthy poet should be chaste—/ There's no need that his verses should be so'" ("*Nam / Ipsum*"; UL, FL; 312/257). He also quotes the emperor Hadrian, who wrote of the poet Voconius, "'Wanton thou wast in verse, but chaste in mind'" ("*Lasciuus*"; UL, CR; 312/257). Even Hadrian himself wrote such verses, and Apuleius dares his opponent to assert "that it is evil to do that which the divine [Hadrian], our emperor and censor, has done, and has handed down to memory as having been done by him. [Besides,] do you suppose that Maximus is likely to censure anything that he knows I have done after the example of Plato?" ("Aemiliane / sciat"; UL, CR; 312/257–58).

These markings are intriguing for what they suggest about the importance of appealing to poetic and royal precedent. However, they are also fascinating in their possible implications for Jonson's own conception of the rights of writers; they recall, for instance, his defence of himself against similar charges of wantonness in the elegy beginning "Let me be what I am" (*Und.* 42; H&S 8:199–202). His interest in the proper way to deal with wanton themes is suggested again by his marking of a passage in which Apuleius declares that "to dissemble and to conceal these and all such matters, is the part of an offender, while, to discourse of them openly and without disguise, is the part of him who speaks but in jest; for so it is, that by nature the power of utterance has been given to innocence, while silence has been allotted to criminality" ("que & / dicere"; UL, CR; 312–13/258). An endorsement of forthrightness more Jonsonian in tone could hardly be imagined.[22] However, Apuleius's defence against the charge of having written lascivious poetry also leads him to make (and Jonson to mark) a number of interesting assertions about the distinction between lust and love. He notes, for instance, "that Venus is a twofold goddess" ("Venerem"; UL, CR; 313). After describing the vulgar Venus, who stimulates animal passion, he asserts that "the other is the 'Heavenly' Venus, who presides over the purest love, who cares for men alone and but few of them, and who influences her devotees by no stimulants or allurements to base desire" ("opti- / per-"; UL, CR; 313/258). Jonson's marking of this passage helps shed, perhaps, new light on his own attitudes toward love, as does his marking of a line of verse attributed to Afranius claiming that "'Where wise men love, all others will desire'" ("*ceteri*"; UL, CR; 313/258). This is one of many similar distinctions between the true and the merely bogus that typify Jonson's markings of Apuleius.[23]

Having now disposed of the charge of wantonness, Apuleius turns next to the allegation that he owned a mirror and was vain about his appearance. Jonson marks a number of retorts to this charge (see Appendix), but the most lengthy and most interesting passage raises larger issues of representation that may have been particularly fascinating to a writer. Apuleius notes that

in the mirror is to be seen the image wonderfully reflected, not only
with the resemblance traced out, but endowed, too, with motion, and
obedient to every gesture of the person whom it represents. Then,
besides, it is always of the same age with the beholder, from the
earliest boyhood down to the very close of old age: so many aspects
of life does it assume, of such varied conditions of the body does
it partake, such numerous changes of the same features, whether
influenced by joy or by grief, does it imitate. ("dinem / quòd"; UL,
VL; 314–15/260)

One wonders what Jonson, in an age accustomed to describing
drama as a mirror held up to life, might have thought of such a
passage. That it may have prompted him to think of distinctions
among the various arts is suggested by his next marking, of a
passage that contrasts mirror images with such arts as sculpture
and engraving. Art of this kind "always preserves the same rigid
unmoved features, just like a corpse. To such a degree then, does
the highly-wrought smoothness of its polished surface, and artificial brightness of the mirror, surpass all art in reflecting the
likeness of the person" ("im- / splen-"; UL, CR; 315/260–61). That
Jonson may have shared Apuleius's sense of the limits of the visual arts is suggested, for instance, by an epigram he wrote late
in life to Richard Weston (*Und.* 77; H&S 8:260–61).[24]

Typically, Apuleius soon turns this discussion in a moral direction, and Jonson just as typically follows. He marks, for instance,
the claim that Socrates urged his followers "to view themselves
repeatedly in a mirror, so that he among them who was smitten
with his own good looks, might be the more scrupulously careful
not to disgrace the beauty of his person by bad manners" ("crebrò
vt / minus"; UL; 315/261). "And thus," Apuleius concludes, "did
a man, who was wiser than all others, make use of the mirror for
the purpose even of improving moral cultivation" ("sa- / vteba-
tur"; UL, CR; 315/261). Yet in addition to highlighting this ethical
emphasis, Jonson's markings also suggest some genuine curiosity
about the physics associated with mirrors ("est, cur / fectiora";
UL, CR; "aduersum / litudine"; UL, VL; 316/262). Here as in other
respects, his interests seem genuinely encyclopedic.[25]

Jonson's next markings are particularly interesting, especially
since the passages marked lie behind an important section of his
own *Discoveries* volume (see H&S 8; 605; 11:254). In these passages Apuleius confronts another charge leveled against him—
the charge of poverty. Jonson's markings are significant not only
for what they suggest about his social sympathies but also for
what they reveal about how he digested his reading and incorpo-

rated it into his own writing. In one of the most lengthy markings in the entire *Apology*, he highlights a passage in which Apuleius notes that his opponent

> has even gone so far as to reproach me with my poverty, a charge truly acceptable to a philosopher, and one to which I plead guilty. For Poverty has long been the handmaid of Philosophy, frugal, temperate, contented with little, eager for praise, averse from the things sought by wealth, safe in her ways, simple in her requirements, in her counsels a promoter of what is right. No one has she ever puffed up with pride, no one has she corrupted by the enjoyment of power, no one has she maddened with tyrannical ambition; for no pampering of the appetite or of the passions does she sigh, nor can she indulge it.

However, he continues, these faults and others like them are nurtured by wealth ("pertatem / test"; UL, CR, VL; 318/265). Even more emphatically, he insists that when the worst crimes of human history are reviewed, "you will not find a single poor man among the perpetrators" ("censeas"; UL; 318/265). In addition, two large pointing hands call attention to the opening and conclusion of the following string of assertions, which are also underlined and marked with a vertical line:

> Poverty, I say, she who in former ages was the foundress of all cities, the inventress of all arts, she who is guiltless of all offence, who is lavish of all glory, who has been honoured with every praise among all nations. For this same Poverty it was that among the Greeks showed herself just in Aristides, humane in Phocion, resolute in Epaminondas, wise in Socrates, and eloquent in Homer. It was this same Poverty, too, that for the Roman people laid the very earliest foundations of their sway, and that offers sacrifice to the immortal Gods in their behalf with the ladle and the dish of clay, even to this day. ("nabulis / immorta-"; 318–19/265)

A long line drops from the wrist of the second pointing hand and encompasses a lengthy passage in which Apuleius cites many examples of great Romans who were not wealthy ("iudi / Phi-"; 319/265–66). Imagining how they would react if they were present at his trial, he turns to his antagonists and asks, "would you then have dared to reproach a philosopher for his poverty, in the presence of so many consuls distinguished for theirs?" ("Phi- / tibi"; UL; 319/266). Surely Jonson was struck by the rhetorical brilliance of these passages, with their overpowering catalogues. Just as surely, however, he was sympathetic to the basic sentiments that Apuleius expresses.[26]

A further indication of his sympathy is the fact that his mark-ings on this topic continue at some length. He marks, for instance, a passage in which Apuleius claims that his accusers are mistaken if they suppose that the judge in this case,

> a man of such rigid morals and so long used to warfare, is not better disposed towards circumscribed moderation than fastidious opu-lence; if you suppose that he does not approve of wealth on the same principles that he does a garment, rather when it suits the person than when it is remarkable for its length. For wealth, too, if it is not conveniently carried, becomes an impediment to us, and trips us up, no less than a draggling garment. ("diu- / prae-"; UL, CR; 319/266)

Similarly, Apuleius contends that "every thing that steps beyond becoming moderation is superfluous, and is rather a burden to us than useful." Thus, "immoderate wealth, just like a large and disproportioned rudder, is more apt to sink than to guide" ("supergradi- / mer-"; UL, UM; 319/266). The rich, Apuleius notes, often pretend to be poorer than they are; when then should the poor be ashamed? ("miles / tenuiores"; UL, CR; 320/266). In fact, however, "none of us are poor who do not wish for super-fluities, and who possess the things that are necessary" ("minem / poscit"; UL; 320/267). Therefore, "he who wants but little, is most likely to have as much as he wants" ("quantum"; UL, CR; 320/ 267). In a passage intermittently underlined but marked in the margin, Apuleius claims that riches are determined not by prop-erty but according to a man's mind; an avaricious man will never be satisfied, not even with gold, and will always be begging. "And this is the real exposition of poverty. For all desire of acquiring, arises from the opinion which each man entertains as to what is poverty. And it matters not how great is the amount of which you are in want" ("lius / minus"; UL, VL, CR; 320/267). Consider Crassus the Rich: "although he surpassed all in wealth, he himself was surpassed by his own avarice, and seemed to be rich in the eyes of all others rather than in his own" ("lebat / tus"; UL, CR; 320/267).

From all this, Apuleius concludes that "you become poor through the want of acquisition, and rich through having no wants to satisfy" ("petendi"; UL; 320/267). Therefore, if his ac-cusers "wish me to be accounted poor, you must of necessity first show that I am avaricious" ("liane / necesse"; UL; 320/267). The mind is like the body: "in a healthy state it is lightly clad, but in sickness it is wrapped in cumbrous clothing; and it is a sure sign of infirmity to have many wants. It is with life just as with swimming; that man is the most expert who is the most disengaged from all encumbrances," since "that which is light tends to our buoyancy, that which is heavy, to sink us" ("cer- / didi-"; UL, CR, CR; 321/268). For this reason, "him among us who has the fewest possible necessities, I consider most strongly to resemble a God" ("minimis"; UL; 321/268). Apuleius was pleased by the charge of poverty; "I only wish that I had such perfect control over my mind, that I required nothing whatever beyond" the few articles his accusers alleged that he possessed ("habi- / sed"; UL, CR; 321/268). He notes that Hercules, "shortly before he was summoned to heaven for his virtues, had no better clothing than a single hide, . . . and no other attendants than a single staff" ("caelum / neque"; UL, VL; 322/269). External attributes such as wealth and national origin are unimportant, "For the proper subject of enquiry is not where a man is born, but what are his manners" ("sed vt"; UL, CR; 323/270)—a thoroughly Jonsonian sentiment.[27]

Having now disposed of the more trivial charges against him, Apuleius turns to one of the more serious—the allegation that he is a magician. If a magician, he asks, "means, in the language of the Persians, the same thing that the word 'priest' does in ours, what is the crime, pray, in being a magician? what is the crime in properly knowing, and understanding, and being versed in the laws of ceremonials, the solemn order of sacred rites, and religious ordinances?" ("lego / atq"; UL, CR; 324/272). Plato, he notes, calls magic "the service of the Gods" ("Si quidem"; UL; 324/272), and he quotes a long passage in Greek in which Plato describes how the Persians prepare a boy for the throne, including teaching him magic (324–25/272; UL, VL). If a magician is a kind of priest, what is wrong with understanding magic? But if, as is commonly thought, a magician possesses extraordinary powers (Apuleius asks), why are his accusers unafraid to attack him? ("bona / Neque"; UL, CR; 325/273). After elaborating on this contradiction, Apuleius notes that the ignorant often allege magic against philosophers, so that "such of them as make enquiry into the pure and primary causes of matter, they look upon as irreligious" ("simpliceis ri-"; UL; 325/273). However, he wants "all this vast multitude" to "fully understand" that "not only nothing can be truthfully alleged against philosophers, but that nothing even can be falsely devised against them, which they would not prefer to rebut, although they could deny it, in full reliance on their innocence" ("de atque / igi-"; UL; 326–27/275). Apuleius intends to show that he is not a magician, and that even if he were, he is guilty of no malpractice ("igi- / de"; UL, VL; 327/275). The forthright, confident tone of this defence must surely have appealed to Jonson.

In the course of his defence, Apuleius manages to touch on a wide variety of topics. For instance, while refuting his accusers' charge that he purchased fish for use in magic, he mocks his opponent's reluctance to mention two fish whose names were synonymns for the sex organs ("genitalia in- / libro"; UL, CR; 331/ 281). Jonson's marking may suggest not only an interest in precise terminology but also an attraction for plain speaking and a disdain for circumlocution.[28] Thus he also marks a passage in which Apuleius mocks his accuser, who "babbles shamefully even about things that are proper to be mentioned, and often, when speaking about subjects that present not the slightest difficulty, either hems and haws or comes to a dead stop altogether" ("quentiae / fringultiat"; UL; 332/282). On a more substantive note, Jonson marks a passage in which Apuleius, after mentioning that Aristotle and other ancient philosophers studied animal life, asks, "If it was honorable and praiseworthy in them to write on these particulars which had been investigated with such scrupulous care, why should it be disgraceful for me to try to do the same?" ("honestum / experiri?"; UL, CR; 333/284). This and other markings suggest Jonson's interest in scientific matters and in freedom of intellectual exploration.[29]

In a fascinating digression—delivered while one of his friends searches for a book he has mentioned—Apuleius says that Sophocles once

> was accused by his own son of madness, as having, through extreme old age, fallen into a state of dotage. On this, it is said he produced his OEdipus Coloneus, the most excellent of his Tragedies, and which he happened just then to be writing, and having read it to the judges, he added not a word in his defence, except that he requested them, without hesitation, to pronounce him mad if the lines written by him in his old age should show him to be so. ("senectam: / dementiae"; UL, CR; 334/284)

Instead, however, "all the judges arose to pay all due respect to a great poet"; they praised the skill and features of his play, "and it all but turned out that, on the contrary, they pronounced the accuser mad" ("ego / satorem"; UL, VL; 334/285). This anecdote, presented almost as an afterthought, seems to have caught Jonson's attention; his combined markings here are among the most extensive he made in the entire book. The story of the embattled poet triumphing through the sheer force of his artistic skills and winning public respect as a result may have resonated deeply with a writer who was so often embattled himself.[30]

It is not long after Apuleius reports this story that Jonson's markings cease for a while; he marks little else in the rest of book 1, and most of what he does mark has to do with matters that are literally fishy. However, here as in other books he owned, the markings stop abruptly, for no apparent reason; why Jonson chose to ignore the many topics covered in the rest of book 1, especially in view of his plentiful markings in its first section, is unfortunately unknown. What is clear is that when his markings do resume, at the start of book 2, they are just as detailed and painstaking as they had been earlier.

Two brief underlinings at the very beginning of book 2 indicate the new focus of Apuleius's speech and of Jonson's markings: "matrimonium . . . inimicum" ("an alliance . . . disastrous" [357/ 314]). Attention now shifts, in other words, to the disputed marriage itself. Apuleius begins his defence by attacking once more the character of Aemilianus, his chief accuser. He speculates about Aemilianus's motives, contrasting him with great orators of the past who used court trials to enhance their public reputations. Such men, "in the prime of life, made these their first efforts in the forensic art for the sake of gaining renown; and their object was, that by engaging in some celebrated cause they might become known to their fellow-citizens" ("hoc / iudi-"; UL, CR; 357/ 314). Jonson's marking of this passage is interesting for what it suggests about his understanding of the personal advantages of public rhetoric, while his next marking sheds further light on the traits ascribed to rhetoric by Apuleius. He continues his attack on Aemilianus, arguing that "neither would the boasts of eloquence have become a person so rude and so unlearned, the desire for glory one so clownish and so uncouth, nor the practice of pleading causes an aged man with one foot in the grave" ("osten- / ro"; UL, CR; 357–58/314). Yet Apuleius expresses an interest not only in what suits aged men but also in the risks to celibate women. He reports that one of his wife's motives for getting married was that,

> although she might have been able to endure the tediousness of celibacy, she was quite unable to bear up against bodily ailment. A woman of inviolable chastity, who had lived so many years in a state of widowhood, without a blemish, without an aspersion on her character, with her system torpid from her prolonged disuse of the married state, afflicted with a protracted inactivity of the vital parts, the

interior of her womb disordered—she was often brought by her sufferings to extreme peril of her life. ("posset / do-"; UL, VL; 359/316)

Jonson further marks professional opinions that Pudentilla's illness had arisen "through disuse of the married state" ("malum"; UL; 359/316–17). His interest in these passages is in line with his interest elsewhere in scientific matters and in the traits of women.[31]

Many of Jonson's markings in this section of the book indicate his concern with properly understanding the complex details of the events leading up to the trial (see Appendix), but these hardly seem worth describing here. Far more interesting is his enthusiastic marking of several lengthy passages full of vigorous satirical abuse. In these, Apuleius lambastes Herennius Rufinus, the father-in-law of Pudens and, according to Apuleius, the driving force behind the suit ("insti- / postula-"; UL, VL; 363/321). Jonson may have been intrigued by such attacks purely as pieces of rhetoric, as examples of the effective use of catalogues. However, it is easy to imagine that he also enjoyed the sheer comic inventiveness of the vituperation. Apuleius condemns Rufinus, for instance, as

> the base contractor of all litigation, the inventor of all falsehoods, the framer of all pretences, the hotbed of all mischiefs; he, too, is a very haunt, a den, a brothel for lusts and debaucheries; from his very earliest age he has been universally notorious for his disgraceful vices. Formerly, in his boyhood, before he was disfigured by that baldness of his, he was subservient to his corruptors in the perpetration of every infamous crime; after that, in his youth, as a dancer on the stage, he was so pliant in body as to seem to be utterly without bones and nerves; but, from what I hear, he was remarkable for a coarse and uncouth effeminacy. Indeed, he is said to have had nothing whatever of the actor, except the immodesty. ("enim / enim"; UL, CR; 363–64/321–22).

After a brief pause, Jonson's marking resumes, with a huge pointing hand drawn in the margin next to the following passage:

> . . . his whole house is a brothel, his entire household a mass of corruption, himself devoid of all shame, his wife a prostitute, his sons just like himself. His door, a sport, day and night, for the young men of the place, is battered by their heels, his windows serenaded by their ditties, his dining-room kept in an uproar by revellers, and his bed-chamber a common thoroughfare for adulterers; nor, in fact, has any one the least fear to enter it, with the exception of him who has

brought no admission-fee to the husband. In this way is the dishonor of his bed a source of income to him. Formerly he used to earn money by his own person; now he earns it by letting out the person of his wife. ("lenonia / ipso"; UL, HD; 364/322)

Similar charges follow and are marked ("virum / quàm"; UL, VL; 364/322), including one reminiscent of Jonson's mockery of the alleged cowardice of Inigo Jones, who (Jonson said) would rather see his sister naked than a sword (*Ep.* 115, 22). Likewise, Apuleius tells Rufinus that "such is the effeminacy of your disposition, such is your dread of steel, that you are afraid to dance with the mimic sword" ("quas / ferri"; UL; 366/325). Jonson's marking of this passage is not surprising considering his own pride in his physical prowess.[32]

Jonson's interest in the traits of women is suggested once more by his marking of a passage in which Apuleius argues that, even if Pudentilla had lied about her attraction to him, "Is not this a common artifice with all females, to try to make it appear that they act by compulsion when they have once set their minds upon anything of this nature?" Besides, even if Pudentilla had claimed he was a magician, this would hardly make him one ("amore / Vos"; UL, CR; 367/325). The mere fact that a charge is in writing hardly proves it, as Apuleius shows by pushing the argument to absurd conclusions ("cuius- / aliquid"; UL, CR; 367/325). He has great fun illustrating the illogic of his opponents' thinking ("scriberet? / se"; UL, VL; 367/326), and surely Jonson must have enjoyed this display of superior wit and intelligence. In the end, however, Apuleius is able to show that the main charge against him depends on selective quotation from a letter Pudentilla once wrote defending him (*"Magus / amplius?"*; UL, CR; 369/328). In a long marked passage that resonates with some of the same thinking Jonson himself expresses in his *Discoveries*, Apuleius notes that there was no one to take his part and say,

'Have the goodness to give me the whole of the letter. Allow me to see every part of it, and to read it from beginning to end. There are many things, which when produced in an unconnected form, may seem amenable to accusation. Any person's language may afford ground for a charge, if words which are connected with preceding ones are to be curtailed of their beginning; if certain parts in the current order of what has been written are to be suppressed at pleasure; if what has been asserted ironically, is to be read rather in the tone of a person who admits, than of one who indignantly expostulates.' ("Totam / genus"; UL, VL; 369/328)

Fortunately, Maximus, the wise judge, ensured that the trial would take place as soon as possible so that the evidence could not easily be tampered with ("sed / subneruasti"; UL, VL; 370/ 330). Apuleius pretends to marvel that Rufinus would persuade Pudens to defame his own mother, but then he claims that he is a fool "to expect that you should be observant of the fair name of another, seeing that you have lost your own" ("conser- / conqueror"; UL, CR; 371/330). He is astonished at Rufinus's manipulation of the boy before such a pious judge ("mi- / quin"; UL, VL; 371/330). And, in one of the longest, most excited, and and most image-filled of the marked passages, he cries out:

> Alas! unhappy was thy womb, Pudentilla! Oh, barrenness, how far preferable to progeny! Oh, ten months productive of what unhappiness! Oh, fourteen years of widowhood thus ill repaid! The viper, I have heard say, eats through the womb of its mother, and crawls forth to light, and so owes its birth to parricide. But upon thee, while living, are inflicted wounds still deeper, those, too, by a son who has already arrived at years of maturity. Thy state of solitude is lacerated, they fair name is mangled, thy breast is stabbed, thy inmost vitals are torn away!

All of Jonson's own ideals about proper family relations seem reflected in his marking of this passage dealing with their unnatural corruption.[33] The passage continues ("Pudentilla! / similes"; UL, VL; 331/371), descending for a moment into the particulars of the case before resuming with its earlier, more general fury:

> when he beholds him, like a sort of monster, full grown up in crime before he is mature in years, venomous before he is come to his strength, green in boyhood, in villainy hoary, and even more baneful because he is sure of impunity, and while he is abundantly able to inflict injuries, he is not liable to pains and penalties. ("atque / nae"; UL, CR; 371–72/331)

Perversions or unnatural behaviors of all sorts seem to have interested Jonson, and his marking here seems to reflect that interest.[34] Similarly, Apuleius notes that the Athenians, when at war with Philip of Macedon, refused to publish captured letters from his wife because they held that "universal right ought to be regarded rather than private vengeance" ("rent"; UL, CR; 372/332). Pudentilla's son has violated even this basic standard of decency. Apuleius charges that during the time Pudens was apparently allied with his mother, "even then you were acting a fox-like and unnatural part" ("tamen"; UL; 372/332). As further evidence of this he points to a counterfeit letter, full of blandishments, that Apuleius supposedly wrote to Pudentilla. What bothers him almost as much as the counterfeiting itself is its shoddy quality: "why should I write in expressions so ungrammatical, in language so barbarous," he asks, especially when he has also been accused of knowing Greek ("iidem"; UL; 373/332). "Why, too, should I solicit her with compliments so absurd, so pot-house like, when they say that I am able to express myself elegantly in the wanton numbers of amatory verse?" ("autem / Sic"; UL, CR; 373/333). Apuleius's pride as a stylist and his cleverness in argument must both have been traits Jonson could appreciate.

But Apuleius's defence depends on more than just wit and skillful logic. Like Jonson himself when he was accused of misdeeds, Apuleius returns repeatedly to assertions of his basic innocence.[35] He notes, for example, that many a person charged with a crime has successfully defended himself by showing that "his whole course of life has been utterly averse to misdeeds of such a nature; and that it ought not to prove to his detriment if there seemed to exist some inducements to the perpetration of the crime. For not every thing which possibly may have happened, ought to be considered as really having happened" ("suam / potue-"; UL, CR; 375/336). In a very Jonsonian tactic, he offers, as proof of his innocence, his vehement conviction of his innocence: consider, he suggests, "what a degree of confidence in my own innocence I display, and what supreme contempt" for his accusers ("fiducia / quam-"; UL; 375/336).[36] Similarly, in another marked passage with broad implications, he defends his knowledge of magicians' names, arguing that "it is one thing to be acquainted with their names, but quite another to have been initiated into the art itself," and he urges the judge to consider "that the appliances of learning, and the recollections of erudition, are not to be held to be a confession of criminality" ("scriptores / pro"; UL, CR; 376/337). In this marking as in others, Jonson seems to show an interest in important distinctions and in the defense of freedom of thought.

Later markings suggest once more his interests in the traits of women. At one point Apuleius comments, for instance, that "a beauteous virgin, even though she may chance to be utterly destitute, is still provided with an ample marriage portion" ("pauper / nouum"; CR, UL; 377/338). Interestingly, Jonson does not mark the immediately subsequent assertion that such a bride "brings to her new husband the winning nature of her disposition," but he does mark the succeeding list of endowments, including

> the charms of her beauty, the first fruits of her maidenhood. The very recommendation itself of virginity is rightly and deservedly most highly esteemed by all husbands. For whatever else you gain by way of portion, you may, whenever you please, return the whole of it, so as to remain under no obligation whatever. Money you may repay in full, slaves you may restore, a house you may quit, an estate you may leave. Virginity alone [a large hand points to this], when once it has been bestowed, can never be returned; of the things that form a marriage portion, that alone must of necessity remain with the husband. ("rudimentum / ve-"; UL, HD; 377/338)

Although such a passage might easily today be construed as sexist for describing a woman's body as a kind of property, in a certain sense it can be seen as emphasizing the importance of respecting the special value of a woman's unique possession.

Jonson's interest in matters of style is a frequent concern of his markings. In one particularly intriguing passage Apuleius describes a letter written by Lollianus Avitus, former proconsul, who commented on Pontianus's retraction of his original accusations against Apuleius. Apuleius notes that the proconsul,

> in conformity with his usual extreme kindness of disposition, . . . commended Pontianus for having so readily made amends for his error, and wrote back to me, by him, good Gods! what a letter! what a style, what wit, what grace and sweetness of expression! He wrote, in fact, just as a good man, and one skilled in the arts of eloquence ought to write. ("te / auditurum"; UL; 379/340)

Apuleius's own stylistic skills are amply demonstrated throughout the treatise, but perhaps nowhere more effectively than in his closing arguments. After sarcastically refuting the numerous charges made against him, he ticks off some of those charges, and some of his responses, in a series of rapid-fire oscillations that Jonson highlights:

> 'You clean your teeth'—Pardon my cleanliness. 'You look in a mirror'—A philosopher ought. 'You compose verses'—'Tis not unlawful to do so. 'You examine fishes'—Aristotle teaches me. 'You make Gods of wood'—Plato advises it. 'You marry a wife'—The laws enjoin it. 'She is older than you'—No uncommon thing. 'You have sought to advantage yourself'—Take up the deed of settlement, recollect the

gifts you have received, read over [Pudentilla's] will. ("Den- / testa-mentum"; UL, CR; 385–86/349)

Jonson's last markings transform a series of broken phrases into an emphatic final plea. Addressing Maximus, Apuleius argues that

> if . . . I have kept philosophy aloof from censure; if I have in no way blemished the honour of philosophy, which is dearer to me than my own well-being, . . . then I may more securely afford to respect your good opinion than to dread your power, seeing, I deem it less griev-ous and less to be dreaded by me, to be condemned by a proconsul, than to incur the censure of a man so good and so virtuous as your-self. ("nias / improber"; UL, CR; 386/349)

This passage, exhibiting Jonson's last markings in the *Apology* and Apuleius's literal last words in his own defense, seems fittingly typical of many of the passages he marked. His marking here suggests his interest in the larger issues involved in the *Apology*, the larger principles that Apuleius claims to vindicate. The pas-sage expresses a typically Jonsonian distinction between the office and the man who fills it—between Maximus as a Roman bureau-crat and Maximus as a moral man, with ethical obligations to discharge. The mixture of deference and moral pressure that Apu-leius uses in appealing to Maximus is not unlike Jonson's own tactics in his relations with superiors, and this passage, like many of the others cited, must have had an interest for Jonson that went beyond the narrowly antiquarian.[37]

If Jonson's interest in the *Apology* seems understandable, his interest in Apuleius's *Florida* may at first seem less easy to explain. Whereas the *Apology*, for all its apparent digressions, nonetheless possesses a unifying theme and serious purpose, the *Florida*—a collection of snippets from Apuleius's speeches—can seem, in the words of Moses Hadas, "essentially trivial" (343). Similarly, another standard source contends that the *Florida* "contains little of intrinsic interest," even though it does offer "useful documen-tation on the activities and status of Apuleius after his return to Carthage."[38] Given these assessments, Jonson's evident fascina-tion with the work may seem hard to fathom, but to dismiss the *Florida* too quickly would be a mistake. James Tatum, for instance, argues that in the *Florida* Apuleius acts as a "transmitter of Greek wisdom to a Roman world evidently unacquainted with it,"[39] and elsewhere he suggests that the work "amply supports Apuleius' claim to be a polymath—an accomplishment . . . he takes no pains to conceal in the *Apology.*"⁴⁰ Both of these factors may have contributed to Jonson's interest in the *Florida*, in which, as in the *Golden Ass*, "the didactic urge competes equally with the desire to entertain."⁴¹ Reading the *Florida*, Tatum contends, is "the quickest way for any reader to become acquainted with the novelties of Apuleius' literary style,"⁴² and surely an interest in the stylistic qualities of the work must have been part of Jonson's reaction to it. Even Hadas, noting the "inordinate care lavished on the artistic structure of these pieces," concedes "the mesmerizing effect their chanting must have had on their auditors" (343).

Whatever their precise effect on Jonson, his detailed marking of these pieces indicates a genuine interest in the work. Marking begins with the very first words, in which Apuleius comments on the customs of religious travellers ("est / ita"; UL; 217/374). The first really intriguing marking, however, is the next one, of a passage in which Socrates is said to have "thought that men were to be considered not with the eyes, but with the rays of the intellect and the gaze of the soul" ("oculo- / Nec"; UL; 217/374). Socrates is said to have argued that "'One earwitness is worth more than ten eye-witnesses.' But if the judgments formed by the eyes were more valued than those of the mind, the palm of wisdom would be due to the eagle" (*"decem* / Homines"; UL, CR; 217/374). Our physical vision is dull: a great poet has said that "there is a mist, as it were, before our eyes, and that we cannot see clearly beyond a stone's throw" ("profectò / valere"; UL, CR; 218/375). In this we are unlike the eagle, whose piercing vision Apuleius describes in highly evocative language ("gitur / inanimatum"; VL; 218/375). Jonson's interest in these passages may have some relevance for his own view of poetry's status vis-à-vis the visual arts.⁴³

Also intriguing is his interest in Apuleius's remarks on the Indian "Gymnosophists," who "cultivate wisdom, both the aged professors and the young students" ("senes / tau"; UL; 221/378). Before being allowed to eat, the students are quizzed about the good things they have done that day:

Thereupon one relates that having been chosen arbitrator between two, he has allayed their quarrel, restored good will, cleared up suspicion, and changed them from enemies to friends. Another states that he has obeyed some command or another of his parents; and another, that he has found out something by his own reflection, or from another's teaching. . . . He who has no cause to offer why he should dine, is turned out of doors, and sent about his business without a dinner. ("duos / extruditur"; UL, CR, CR, CR; 221/378)

The ideal that learning and virtue could be incorporated so fully into the affairs of everyday life must surely have appealed to Jonson.[44] This ideal may also lie behind his marking of a passage in which Apuleius wishes that psuedophilosophers would not "disgrace that royal science which was devised both for speaking well and living well, by talking ill and living no better." For what can be easier "than rabidness of tongue and baseness of conduct, the former from contempt of others, the latter from self-contempt? For to conduct oneself basely is self-contempt; to vilify others barbarously, is insolence towards one's hearers" ("ti / contumelia"; UL, CR, VL; 222/379).

Apuleius imagines that he himself might become the victim of such vilification, for at one point he comments that "in a great city that kind of men is also found who like rather to rail at their betters than to imitate them, and who affect enmity towards those whom they cannot hope to resemble; men whose own names being obscure, wish to become known through mine" ("ge- / meo"; UL; 223/380). He warns such carpers about the risks involved in public speaking ("conseruandae / cum"; UL, VL; 223/380) and notes that such risks are particularly great for him, whom public expectations "suffer not to utter any thing negligently, and without deep reflection" ("non / hiscere"; UL, VL; 223/380). He lists various oratorical faults that his audience would find unforgivable in his case, "[y]et these faults you easily and very justly pardon in others" ("& / di-"; UL; 223/380). If he utters a phrase, they "test it by the file and the rule, and again compare it with the lathe and the buskin" ("& / iterum"; UL; 223/380). He notes that in public speaking, "dignity is difficult" ("quantum / dignitas"; UL, CR; 223–24/380), and he reports that any speech of his is immediately repeated, "nor is it free to me to recall any part of it, or to change or correct it in any respect" ("ctum / re"; UL, CR; 224/381). Alluding to the sophist Hippias, he reports that the latter was "superior to all in the number of the arts he knew, inferior to none in eloquence" ("Et / quentia"; UL; 224/381), and he also notes of Hippias that "his studies [were] various, his rivals many" ("varia"; UL; 224/381). All these passages, taken together, suggest Apuleius's sense of the ways in which he was implicated in the various social networks of his day, the ways in which he had to be highly conscious of his audience. Jonson's markings demonstrate, if nothing else, his awareness of this Apuleian self-consciousness.[45]

In describing Hippias, Apuleius relates his wide-ranging craftsmanship, calling him "a Daedalus in the use of so many tools."

But he immediately balances this by saying that "I would rather rival the fecundity of his genius in matters of learning, than in multitudinous appliances for personal use" ("vtensilium / qui-"; UL; 225/382). Apuleius reports that he prefers to compose, "with a writing reed, poems of all kinds adapted to the laurel branch, the lyre, the sock, the buskin; likewise satires and enigmas" ("nosse / cothurno"; UL; 226/382). His goal, he says, is to compose "with two-fold study, with equal diligence and in similar style" ("Graecè / sed"; UL, CR; 226/382). He seeks the approval of the proconsul he addresses, because

> by no one am I more desirous of being esteemed than by him which I justly esteem above all others. For it is a law of nature that whom you praise, him you also love; and moreover, whom you love, by him you wish to be praised. . . . [Apuleius feels] bound to you [the proconsul] by no private, but by all manner of public favours. I have, indeed, obtained nothing from you, for nothing have I asked. ("uata / stulaui"; UL, CR, VL; 226/382–83)

Philosophy, he claims, has taught him "to prefer public expediency to my own. Hence, whilst the majority love the beneficial effects of your goodness, I love its principle" ("quàm / que"; UL, CR; 226/383). The proconsul has "benefitted many individually, and all by your example" ("beneficium / multis"; UL, CR; 226/383). "Never . . . did the province of Africa ever revere more, and fear less" any proconsul; under no other administration "had shame more power than fear towards restraining offences" ("lum / pudor"; UL, CR; 226/383). For the interest they reveal in Apuleius's conception of his own functions and those of his superiors, Jonson's markings of these passages are quite intriguing. Apuleius's emphasis on mutual duty to the public good is exactly what we might have expected Jonson to highlight.[46]

Not all of his markings, however, pick out passages so essentially serious. His interests in the *Florida* seem to have been as wide-ranging as the work itself. One marked passage, for instance, comments on the intermediate powers of the gods, "which we can feel, but which it is not given us to see; as of Love and the like, whose form is unseen, their force known" ("datur / forma"; UL, VL; 227/384). Such power "levelled the expanse of plains" and "everywhere defined the courses of rivers, the green vigour of the meadows, and gave flight to birds, gliding folds to serpents, swift feet to wild beasts, and upright gait to men" ("ex- / feris"; VL, UL; 227/384). Surely Jonson's interest in this passage was as much in its language as in its subject matter, but the genuine breadth of his curiosity is indicated by the many widely scattered markings he makes in a section in which Apuleius describes parrots, focusing on their size and colors, the hardness and use of their beaks, their maturation, their traits when aged, their capacity to learn speech, their vocal apparatus, and their ability to mimic men's voices ("Indiae / tur"; UL, CR, CR, CR, CR; 228/ 384–85). Apuleius warns that "If you teach a parrot ribaldry, he will be a ribald" ("tiant"; UL; 228/385), and he concludes that "If you would be free from its ribaldry, you must cut out its tongue, or at once send it back to its woods" ("repetit / excidenda"; UL; 228/385).

A more serious note seems reflected in Jonson's scattered markings in an extended discussion of the philosopher Pythagoras, whom Apuleius describes as having been "deeply versed in minstrelsy and all kinds of music" ("Samius / ficaeq'"; UL; 230/388). He notes, however, that "the philosopher was by no means a favourite with the tyrant" who ruled the island of Samos, his native land ("ty- / orso"; UL; 231/388). Thus "Pythagoras fled privily from the island" ("Mnesarcho"; UL; 231/388) and may have been taught by Persian magi, especially Zoroaster; by Gillus of Crotona; and by Egyptian priests, who instructed him in "the incredible powers of ceremonies, the wonderful commutations of numbers, and the most ingenious figures of geometry" ("doctores / expletum"; UL, DL; 231/388). Later he studied with the Chaldeans, Brahmins, and Gymnosophists, from whom he learned such things as "the definite orbits of the planets, and the various effects of both kinds of stars upon the nativity of men; as also, for much money, the remedies for human use derived from the earth, and the air, and the sea" ("viri / conquisita"; UL, HD; 231/388). But the Brahmins taught him the most, including "how many are the faculties of the soul, how many the mutations of life; what torments or rewards devolve upon the souls of the dead according to their respective deserts" ("contulerant / Phe-"; HD, UL; 231/388–89). Because of his wide training, Pythagoras became a "man of surpassingly mighty genius, and of more than human grandeur of soul," a philosopher who "taught his disciples nothing in the first place but to be silent," advising any future sage that "as for the words which poets call winged, to pluck their plumes and shut them up within the walls of his white teeth" ("vir / premere"; UL, VL, VL; 232/389). In this respect, Apuleius's master, Plato, "imitates Pythagoras" ("paululum"; UL; 232/389), and Apuleius himself was taught "to speak with all my might when speech is required; and when silence is required, to hold my tongue willingly" ("tionibus / ratione"; UL, CR; 232/ 389). All of these reflections on Pythagoras seem naturally to have interested Jonson, for, in their praise of wide learning and measured speech, their spirit seems recognizably Jonsonian.[47]

Jonson seems also to have taken an interest in Apuleius's anecdote concerning "the comic writer, Philemon" ("nostis"; UL; 233/ 390), who "was a writer of the middle comedy. He produced pieces for the stage along with Menander, and contended with him, being perhaps inferior to him, but at all events his rival"; the fact that he was often victorious over Menander is "a shameful thing to tell" ("scriptor / mul-"; UL, CR; 233/390). Yet his writings exhibited such features as "personages suited to the matter; phrases appropriate to each character; gaieties not beneath the sock; gravities not quite up to the buskin. Impurities are rare in his works, and amours are admitted as errors" ("congruen- / amores"; UL; 233/390).

> Nevertheless, you find in him the perjured pimp, the hot lover, the cunning slave, the wheedling mistress, the peremptory wife, the indulgent mother, the scolding uncle, the helpful friend, and the fighting soldier, together with various parasites, and stingy parents. ("ser- / te-"; VL; 233/390)

Once, as Philemon was reciting from a play he had recently written, "when he had come to the third act, and was exciting . . . pleasant emotions," a sudden storm caused him to cancel his reading ("cens / ri"; UL, CR; 234/390). The next day, a large audience assembled to hear another performance; Jonson marks most of a lengthy passage describing the behavior of this crowd. When at length Philemon did not appear, it was discovered that he had died in his sleep ("num / in suo"; UL, VL, CR; 234/390–91). "His hand was still inserted in the scroll; his face was turned toward the book which he held straight before him; but he was already senseless, unconscious of the book, and regardless of his audience," who marvelled at "so beautiful a death" ("gitanti / tam"; VL; 234/391). Thus it was announced that Philemon,

> who was expected to finish his fictitious plot in the theatre, had concluded the real comedy at home. He had said to human affairs, 'Farewell and applaud,' but to his friends, lament and wail; . . . his comedy had arrived sooner at the funeral than the nuptial torch. And since this excellent poet had made his exit from life, it was meet that the audience should proceed straightway to his obsequies; that his

bones should now be collected, and by and by his poems." ("qui /
eius"; UL, CR, CR; 234/391)

For their suggestions not only about the genre of comedy but also
about the relations between art and life, these passages must
surely have been of genuine interest to Jonson.

Of similar interest must have been several marked passages in
which Apuleius discusses the nature of gifts and benefits. Expressing gratitude to Carthaginian nobles for erecting a statue in
his honor, Apuleius says that he hastened to the city "that I might
return you many thanks for that honour for which I had not
petitioned you" ("dice- / magnitudo"; UL, HD; 235/392). The fact
that he did not ask makes the gift greater, "for neither does he
who prays buy the object of his prayers for a cheap consideration,
nor does he who is solicited accept a small price, so that you
would rather buy all kinds of commodities than beg for them"
("mer- / rogare"; UL, DL; 235/392). Anyone "who has received [a
benefit] without the trouble of a canvass, owes a double debt of
gratitude to the grantors; both because he has not sought, and
he has obtained" ("duplam / quòd"; UL, CR; 235/392). Apuleius
promises that the thanks he owes the Carthaginians "I shall always and everywhere declare" ("uerò"; UL; 236/392). Such sentiments, like those expressed in so many of the marked passages,
could have come as easily from Jonson as from Apuleius.[48]

So, too, could Apuleius's description of his relations with rivals
and superiors.[49] Thus, although grateful for the recognition he
has received, he also anticipates envious criticism for being honored by the great men of Carthage, particularly Strabo ("hon-
orem / etiam"; UL, VL; 236/393). Apuleius describes his
friendship with and his own support of Strabo ("laudator / Iam";
UL, VL; 236–37/393), and he notes his pleasure "that a man of
his eminence declares that he is beloved reciprocally by me" ("se
ex"; UL, CR; 237/393).[50] Strabo's greatest favor is "that he, a most
influential witness, commends me to you even by his own suf-
frage" and has promised "that he will erect a statue to me in
Carthage" ("quòd me / &"; UL, CR; 237/393). Strabo, "soon by
universal consent to be proconsul, pronounced his opinion concerning the honours to be paid to me in the senate of the Carthaginians: all followed his lead" ("procon- / vi-"; UL, CR; 237/394).
Apuleius thanks the Carthaginians for honoring him in their senate house ("decorauê- / honor"; UL; 237/394). Their action has
made it possible for Apuleius "to be pleasing to the people, ac-
ceptable to the order, and approved by the magistrates and chief

men . . . fascination apart" ("nobis / probari"; UL, CR; 238/394).[51]
He notes that to the Carthaginians, expense is no object; they are
accustomed rather "to decree than to compute the cost" ("etiam /
putare"; UL; 237/394). In reciprocation, he promises to express
his thanks in a book that will "publish abroad the praises of your
bounty throughout the whole world, in all time to come, among
all nations, throughout all years" ("Quin / semper"; UL, VL; 238/
394–95). These passages must surely have intrigued Jonson for
what they suggest about Apuleius's role as a public intellectual,
honored by his city and capable of bringing it honor, promoted by
the influential and envied because of this promotion. Considering
Jonson's own aspirations, achievements, and social circumstances,
these passages may have had some real personal relevance.[52]

Jonson may also have considered relevant Apuleius's address
to another superior, Scipio Orfitus. Apuleius claims not to need
the latter's friendship in order to promote the fame of his genius,
since "it is already in its degree too well known to the world to
need new commendation; and I desire more than I boast of your
good-will and that of men like you; since no one can desire a
thing unless he thinks it really desirable; but anyone may boast
falsely. Moreover, I have always thus studiously applied myself
to good morals from the outset of my life" ("iampridem / semper";
UL, CR; 238/395). Apuleius further contends "that my friendship
is not less worthy of your acceptance than yours of being sought
by me" ("locupletissimus / capessenda"; UL; 238/395). This tone
of self-respect in dealing with superiors was one, of course, that
Jonson himself expressed, while Apuleius's emphasis on the ideal
of friendship is also typically Jonsonian. Jonson underlines, for
instance, another passage in which Apuleius claims that "it is a
great proof of friendship to delight in the frequent presence of
friends, to be angry with them when they stay away, to praise
him who is constant in his attendance, to feel the loss of him who
stays away; for it is certain that he must be liked whose absence
gives pain" ("eius / silentio"; UL; 238–39/395). This stress on the
importance of friendship no doubt struck a resonant chord in
Jonson's mind.[53]

The importance of art and learning in human society is also
stressed by Apuleius and is highlighted by Jonson's markings. At
one point, for instance, Apuleius describes how Orpheus and
Arion played musical instruments for beasts, then comments, "I
would admire them more if they had delighted men rather than
brutes" ("nitebantur / tius"; UL, CR; 240/396). Similarly, Apuleius
proclaims that "whoso has a song to sing that is good for youth,

and adults, and seniors, let him sing in the midst of thousands of men" ("qui / rus"; UL, CR; 240/396). Later he remarks that "I must rather congratulate Carthage that it counts in it so many friends of learning" ("uenistis / amicos"; UL; 240/397), and then, after listing numerous superficial attractions that might draw people to a public performance ("paui- / popu-"; UL, VL; 241/397), he insists that "nothing else ought to be considered but the understanding of the audience and the language of the speaker" ("nihil / di-"; UL, CR; 241/397). He asks that "if I utter words worthy of the senate, think of them as though you heard me in the senate itself; if the things that I deliver are learned, accept them as though they were read in the library" ("si / vtinam"; UL, CR; 241/397–98). What matters, in other words, is the matter and content of a speech, not the site of its delivery.

Apuleius frequently indicates—and Jonson frequently marks—self-consciousness about his potential reception, repeating at one point, for instance, the old saying that "'Nothing has been granted to man by the gods so fortunate but that some difficulty is nevertheless attached to it'" ("Nihil / am-"; UL, CR; 241/398). Similarly, he speaks of the "combination of honey and gall. Where there is a breast of milk there is a tuberosity" ("tu-"; UL, CR; 242/ 398). Apuleius applies these reflections to his own situation as a public speaker, noting that "the more suffrages I seem to have among you in my favour, the more timid I am in addressing you, from the exceeding respect I bear you" ("ad / saepenu-"; UL, CR; 241/398). He says that he "now hesitate[s] among my own countrymen, and, strange to say, I am deterred by what should allure, curbed by what should spur me, restrained by what should incite me" ("mero / frenor"; UL, CR; 242/398). Addressing the Carthaginians, he notes that "my books . . . nowhere receive a higher honour than that they are approved by your judgment" ("sexennium / bantur"; UL, CR; 242/398), but his very popularity in Carthage constrains him from praising Carthage as freely as he might like, since "a man's modesty stands in his way among his own people, but before foreigners truth is free" ("quàm / adeò"; UL, VL; 242/398). All these comments suggest Apuleius's—and Jonson's—awareness of the ambiguous circumstances of anyone who faces an audience.[54]

While facing his own audience, Apuleius tells a pair of tales about two wise men, Protagoras and Thales. His comments about the former suggest his disdain for mere sophistry (see Appendix), whereas his assessment of Thales indicates his respect for genuine intellectual achievement. In a long marked passage, Apuleius details Thales' scientific discoveries ("Thales / Thales"; UL, VL; 243–44/399–400), and Jonson draws a large flower next to a passage describing the scientist's response when he was asked what reward he desired for communicating his most recent discovery. "'I shall be sufficiently paid [he said] if, when you have begun to unfold to others what you have learned from me, you do not attribute it to yourself, but declare that it was I, and no one else, who discovered it'" ("iussit / alium"; UL, FL; 244/400). Apuleius declares that "tribute will be paid to Thales by all of us who are truly acquainted with his celestial studies" ("dehinc / bis"; UL; 244/400). These passages, like others Jonson marked, suggest the value of fame as a stimulus and reward for the pursuit of knowledge.[55]

The pursuit of knowledge is also emphasized in a section of the *Florida* that is among the last passages that Jonson marked in this work. Apuleuis notes the saying of a wise man who once remarked that in drinking wine, "the first cup is for thirst, the second for mirth, the third for delight, the fourth for madness" ("mensam / quarta"; UL, DL; 246/402). "The goblet of the Muses, on the contrary, the oftener it is drained and the more unmixed it is, the more it conduces to soundness of mind" ("quarta / pior"; DL; 246/402).

> The first cup, that of the reading master, takes away ignorance; the second, of the grammarian, instructs in science; the third, the rhetorician's, arms with eloquence. Thus far most people drink. But I have drunk other cups at Athens; the cup of poetry, the inventive; of geometry, the limpid; of music, the sweet; of dialectics, the roughish; and of universal philosophy, the never-satiating nectareous cup. For Empedocles gives us verses; Plato, dialogues; Socrates, hymns; Epicharmus, modulations; Xenophon, histories; Xenocrates, satires; your Apuleius all these together; and he has cultivated the nine Muses with equal assiduity, that is to say, with more good-will than capacity. ("pior / cultate"; UL, VL, HD; 246/402)

The ideal of encyclopedic knowledge, alluded to a number of times in the passages Jonson marked in Apuleius, is given one of its most memorable statements here. Although Apuleius modestly concedes that his desire for knowledge may outstrip his ability, he also suggests that perhaps he is "the more to be praised for this, since in all good things the attempt is laudable," and that "crimes that are but designed, not accomplished, are punished; the mind being blood-stained, the hands pure" ("bus / adhuc"; UL; 246/402). Intent, in other words, is as important as accom-

plishment, and surely Jonson shared Apuleius's respect for anyone sincerely intent on pursuing knowledge. In fact, precisely for
this reason Apuleius celebrates the citizens of Carthage, "among
whom, boys learn all they know, adults exhibit it, and old men
teach it."[56] Carthage is thus "the venerable mistress of our province" ("mi / magistra"; UL, CR; 246/402). This ideal of an entire
city devoted to learning must surely have appealed to Jonson.
After all, one of the very last statements he marked in the *Florida*
is the assertion that "all the riches under the sky avail nothing
towards a happy life" ("se / uendum"; UL; CR; 248/386). What
mattered, to Apuleius no less than to Jonson, were riches of the
mind rather than of the body.[57]

Jonson seems to have felt that Apuleius's own writings could
provide such riches in abundance. His markings in his copy of
the *Apology* and *Florida* are among the most extensive and most
interesting he made in any of the books he owned. His response
to Apuleius, as measured by the sheer volume of his marks, was
vigorous and intense. The marks he made in any of his books
can tell us much about the subjects of his attention and reflection,
but few volumes are as full of this kind of information as his copy
of Apuleius. It clearly ranks as one of the most valuable of Jonson's
surviving books.

Appendix

Apologia

303/247: UL; "incessere ma- / necis"; the major charges against A
304/247–48: UL, FL; "ta; vltrò / dentia"; A's challenge; his accusers'
  response
304/248: UL; "est de / nis"; the accuser drops the charge of murder
304/248: UL, CR; "maciter"; chief accuser even maligns the judge
304/248: UL; "qualis / for &"; nature of accusation reflects on the accuser
304/248: UL; "stamentum"; a will known to be genuine denounced as
  false
304–5/249: UL; "contra / vocem"; the accuser swore the will was a forgery
305/249: UL; "futi-"; A's accusers' "mercenary loquacity"
305/249: UL; "rabulis / dolori"; the venomous tongues of professsional
  accusers
307/251: UL; "Sanè qui-"; A hopes more to acquire eloquence than to
  display it
308/252–53: UL, VL; "Quaeso / nihil"; philosophers and toothpaste
308/253: UL; "patulo"; man makes frequent and conspicuous use of
  the mouth

308/253: UL, CR; "quippe / puus"; words precede acts and proceed from the mouth

308/253: UL, VL; "vsu / asperatis"; human mouths, unlike animals', are exposed

309/253–54: UL, CR; "laua- / qui"; shouldn't teeth be as clean as feet?

309/254: UL, VL; "suum / olenticetis"; slanderers don't need clean mouths

309/254: UL, CR; "Cete- / poculum"; a clean mouth befits good expressions

309/254: UL, CR; "Belua im- / Nam"; the crocodile allows its teeth to be cleaned

309/254: UL, CR; "fluuiali- / exsculpit"; river birds clean crocodile teeth

309/254: UL; "Magus"; does being a poet make A a magician?

309/254: UL; "est, nec / At"; bad verses? blame the poet, not the philosopher

310/255: UL; "meris / mendet"; Sappho's sweetness commends her strange dialect

313/259: UL; "neces- / superest"; a few phrases; e.g., "appendages to my defence"

314/259: UL; "speculum"; charge against A: "A philosopher has a looking-glass!"

314/259: UL, VL: "credas / contrà"; A's dress differs from that of actors

314/259: UL, CR: "inspectio / praesentibus"; they must show how A used the mirror

314/260: UL; "fateor"; what's the crime of knowing one's own image?

314/260: UL; "lacrum"; statues allow honored man to see his merit rewarded

315/261: UL, CR; "senten / omnium"; Agesilaus forbade portraits, busts of himself

315/261: UL, CR; "suam / Phi-"; why is a mirror disgraceful and scuplture isn't?

315/261: UL; "est / magistrum"; Demosthenes practiced oratory before a mirror

315/261: UL, CR; "ar- / con-"; Demosthenes used a mirror to strive for perfection

316/261: UL; "bet"; why shouldn't a philosopher look into a mirror?

316/261–62: VL; "oportet / trà"; philosophers' theories of how mirrors work

316/262: UL; "tilitate / morandus"; Archimedes consulted the mirror often

316/263: UL; "istud"; the "extremely ugly features" of A's accuser

317/263: UL; "mirarêere / boni"; the accuser's wrinkled face

317/263: UL, CR; "boni / praeter-"; his manners more repulsive than his looks

317/263: UL; "satis no-"; A unsure whether his accuser is white or black

317/263: UL, CR; "peccata / te"; A seeks to veil his faults, not expose others'

317/263: UL, HD, VL; "conlustra- / ser-"; A is exposed, his accuser is obscured

317/263: UL; "laboro. At"; A's accuser's exchange of labor with his neighbors

317/264: UL; "Tantámne / manumisit"; the accuser contradicts himself

317/264: UL; "Nescis / causa"; A attacked for the scantiness of his retinue

318/264: UL; "sularem / triumphos"; other important men have had few servants

318/264–65: UL, VL; "se, / quinque"; M. Cato had few servants

320–21/267–68: UL; "me ideo / pra-"; poverty is no shame in animals; why in man?

321/268: UL, CR; "ego con-"; A is lightly clothed and spends little on food

321/268: UL; "Aemi- / sese re-"; Crates, a rich man, gave away his property

321/269: UL; "πόντω / περίρρυτος"; punning description of Crete; from Homer

322/269: UL, CR; "Iam / phantibus"; lists attributes it would be foolish to envy

322/269: UL, HD; "quidem / guribus"; scrip and staff: insignia of the Cynics

322/269: UL; "gno / riabatur"; Diogenes boasted that his staff was his sceptre

322/269: UL; "vt quaedam"; A cites Hercules as example rather than mendicants

322/269: UL, CR; "tamen / plurimis"; A's inheritance, expenses, and donations

322/270: UL, CR; "ctum / in trunco"; barren tree valuable only for its timber

322–23/270: UL, CR; "quem / teterri-"; the accuser's own poverty and inheritances

323/270: UL, CR; "Seminumidam"; A admits he is a Semi-Numidian and a Semi-Getulian

323/270: UL, CR; "Se- / vt"; Cyrus's parentage also mixed; Median and Persian

323/270: UL; "Quip-"; the wine of Thasos and the vegetables of Phlius

323/270–71: UL, CR, CR; "prouenere? / hoc"; national traits; individual exceptions

323/271: UL; "in quae / cunctis"; A's pride in his region; his father's status

323/271: UL; "pari / protuli?"; A enjoys the same honor and status as his father

323/271: UL; "potiusq"; A mentions his status to prevent accuser's attacks

324/271: VL; "puditum / barbaram?"; A summarizes the charges against him

324/272: UL, CR; "nefandas?"; A's accusers offer weak arguments, strong outcries

324/272: UL, CR; "quandóne / sententiam"; the charges are like a brief blaze

324/272: UL; "gum / uocatis"; A asks his accusers what a magician is

324/273: UL, CR: "venit / ineuitabi-"; how can accusers prevent harm from A's magic?

325/274: UL; "autem, qui"; Democritus and other "advocates of natural causes"

326/274: UL; "Prouidentia*m* / etiam"; other philosophers accused of magic

326/274: UL, CR; "ἀγαθόν / ris"; A proud to be added to this list of the great

326/274: UL, CR; "ideo"; A fears the charge may be believed because it was made

326/274: UL; "gratia / causa"; a philosopher may study the fish a glutton eats

326/274: UL; "*tredecim* / quòd"; it's a wonder the widow didn't marry sooner

326/274: UL; "*ta* / niori"; no magic needed to make widow marry a young man

326/274: UL; "*mi* / quod"; it would be a true crime to worship nothing

326/274–75: UL, CR; "quod / psus?"; what if an old man or a boy fell near A?

326/275: UL; "psus / matrimonio"; summary of some trivial charges against A

327/275: UL, VL; "Aemi- / dilucide"; A's marriage provoked rage, accusations

327/275: UL; "diem / effe-"; Pontianus and Pudens; the latter manipulated

327/276: UL, CR; "similem / Aemilia-"; Aemilianus, the accuser, characterized

327/276: UL, CR; "er- / piscator"; A ridicules the charges concerning fish

328/276: UL, CR; "& pomum / tur"; were all A's foodstuffs purchased for magic?

328/276: UL; "respondeat / sationem"; A asks the grounds of the accusation

328/277: UL, CR, CR; "lo / quod nescis"; does buying fish make one a magician?

328/277: UL; "nium / tis"; the improbable nature of the charges

328/277: UL, CR; "pelago / quòd"; Venus is said to have arisen from the sea

328/277: UL; "tas / ceram"; lists numerous items Virgil says are used in magic

328–29/277: UL; "Pubentes / amor"; last two-and-a-half lines of Virgil poem marked

329/278: UL, CR; "pulmen- / pra-"; contrasts Virgil and the accuser on magic

329/278: DL, UL; "eruunt / dulcedines"; lines from a poem on magic ingredients

329/278: UL; "cete / adiuta-"; cook captured fish; magic is of no avail

329–30/279; "pisces / profundo"; Pythagoras returned fish to the sea

330/279: UL; "ctus / vim"; all-knowing Homer linked drugs' power to earth, not sea

330/279: UL, CR; "nec / nec"; alludes to Homeric episodes involving Circe, Venus

330/279–80: UL, VL; "suatis / transferentur"; classical deities linked to magic

330/280: UL, CR; "go / & qui"; examples of absurdity of linking fish to magic

330/280: UL, VL; "nem / medicamento"; commodities have more than one use

331/280: UL, VL; "suis / er"; is anyone linked with fish a magician?

331/280: UL, CR; "emissem / ge-"; abusing drug does not mean drug is a poison

331/281: UL; "lepo / fuit"; accusers even misidentified one of the fish

331/281: UL; "quaerere"; A's servant hasn't even managed yet to find a sea-hare

331/281: UL, CR; "incide- / Quamobrem"; A *is* interested in examining fish

332/281: UL, CR; "legit / *palmae*"; quotation from A on the vagina

332/282: UL, CR: "Veneris / stultitiae"; A's accuser borrows a term from A

332/282: UL; "marina"; underscores the terms "Veretillam, & Virginal"

332/282: UL, CR; "re, / cem"; absurdity of linking animals' names with their use

332–33: UL; "impenso / expuuntur"; other sea life A could have been accused over

333/283: UL; "fascina, pro-"; sea creatures and venereal matters

333/283: UL; "cancer / ni-"; mocks facile links between names and functions

333/283: UL, CR; "diceren- / mirabar"; A laughed at his accusers' trivial charges

333/283: UL; "veterum"; instruction for accuser, however late and posthumous

333/283–84: UL; "Ari- / ge"; Aristotle, Plato, others studied animal habits

333/284: UL; "ςο- / innumera"; lists works by Aristotle dealing with animals

333–34/284: UL; "Graecè & / quàm"; A's project and books on natural science

334/284: UL; "liq"; underlines phrase "Naturalium Quaestionum"

334/285: UL, DL; "membris / ouiparos"; viviparous and oviparous fish
334/285: UL, DL; "mis, scitu"; fish facts necessary, but irrelevant in court
334–35/285: UL, CR; "nentibus / aqua-"; terms used in A's research about fish
335/286: UL; "cla- / percen-"; A anticipates being charged with using jargon
335/286: UL; "nescire? ne-"; is it worse to know or to be ignorant?
335/286–87: UL; "marina / echini"; marks phrases in some lines by Ennius on fish
335/287: UL; "quisque / lentus"; Ennius not censured for his remarks on fish
358/315: UL, VL; "Herennium / prouarit"; A's envious enemies, including H. Rufinus
358/315: UL, CR; "se nubere / Nouissima"; summary of charges about the marriage
358/315: UL, CR; "gebantur / tam"; charge that A extorted money after marriage
358/315: UL; "estis / rem"; A, confident, fears seeming in collusion with accusers
359/316: UL; "diligen-"; A asks judges to consider origin and grounds of the trial
359/316: UL, HD; "mihi / memo-"; A begins recounting the facts of the case
359/316: UL; "inuitam / bonis"; attempted forced marriage for Pudentilla
359/316: UL; "tabulas / verùm"; Pudentilla was contracted to Sicinius Clarus
359/316: UL, CR; "ita / esset"; Pontianus named guardian of his brother Pudens
359/317: UL, CR; "aliquid / foret"; accuser first approved, then disputed, marriage
360/317: UL; "dacem"; a liar ought to have a good memory
360/317: UL, CR; "nit / tum"; the accuser had recommended that the widow marry
360/317: UL; "festam"; Pudentilla was aware of the accuser's malignity
360/317: UL, CR; "filio / te eam"; no charge of magic if accuser's man chosen
360/318: UL, CR; "testimonio / maluit"; Pudentilla kept accuser's letter
361/318: UL, CR; "ali- / agritudini"; her sons, grown, agree to her marriage
361/318: UL, CR; "prae"; Pudentilla perchance preferred A to the rest
361/318: UL, VL; "iudicium / praelatum"; other suitors accept this, but not accusers
361/319: UL; "esset / sollici-"; Pontianus feared a greedy man would marry Pudentilla
361/319: UL; "aequum / timorem"; Pudentilla owed some money to her sons

361/319: UL, VL; "numquam / an-"; A almost wishes none of this had happened

361–62/319: "Pon- / arto"; A recounts his friendship with Pontianus

362/319: UL, CR; "maritum / fortunam"; Pontianus felt A suitable for his mother

362/319–20: UL; "infirmitas / ferat"; Pontianus entreated A to move to his mother's

362/320: UL; "mihi / adiuuantur"; A assisted the brothers in their studies

362/320: UL; "fieremq"; A was requested to become a citizen of Oëa

362/320: UL; "eo / cum"; Pontianus desires A to marry the sought-after Pudentilla

362/320: UL; "considere / mihi"; A was offered no pretty maiden but a mother

362/320: UL, CR; "tia / neque"; A no friend or philosopher [if he rejects her]

363/320: UL, CR; "perpetim / ta-"; A admired Pudentilla but wanted to travel

363/321: UL, CR; "errorem / leuitatem"; A doesn't mean to make Pontianus seem fickle

363/321: UL, VL; "festi- / facere"; Pontianus changed his mind about the marriage

363/321: UL; "vitio / aut"; Rufinus should really be blamed; no one more vile

364/322: UL, DL; "ex / defoeneratus"; Rufinus's father preferred money to honor

364/323: UL, DL; "dissoluere / miliaris"; the father's financial maneuvers

365/323: UL, VL; "pau- / gu-"; Rufinus's gluttony, waste, ambition, and appetite

365/323: UL; "vi- / mul-"; Rufinus's old-maid daughter married Pontianus

365/323: UL, CR; "quàm / fue-"; she had been deserted by her former fiance

365/323: UL; "nomen / octopho-"; she was an unblemished maid in name only

365/324: UL; "erat / postulabat"; her dowry was seized the day before the wedding

365–66/324: UL, VL; "Pon- / referat"; Rufinus tried to turn Pontianus against A

366/324: UL; "adulescentulo"; Rufinus threatened to take his daughter from Pontianus

366/324: UL; "matrem"; Pontianus, alarmed, went straight to his mother

366/324–25: UL; "oratione / riti"; Pudentilla was now all the more set on marrying

366/325: UL, CR; "Hisce / sua"; Rufinus, enraged, attacked Pudentilla and A

366/325: UL, CR; "quibus / rem"; Pudentilla's letter "admitting" she was bewitched

366/325: UL; "omnia"; in every point the letter supports A, not his accusers

367/325: UL; "suam"; Pudentilla could have blamed magic falsely if she'd wanted

367/326: UL; "non / *te*"; the illogic of their charges; one charge quoted

368/326–37: UL, CR; "sanus / non"; contradictions in their thinking about sanity

368/327: UL; "petiuit / est"; Pudentilla's letter tells the same story A has told

368/327: UL, CR; "sium / medes"; A says judge must concede the accusers' treachery

368/327: UL, CR; "fini / &"; Rufinus's craft is incomparable, worthy of prison

368/328: UL, DL; "le / de"; Pontianus, at Rufinus's dictation, called A a magician

369/328: UL, CR; "legendas / con-"; Rufinus quoted Pudentilla's letter selectively

369/328: UL; "scripta / con-"; Pudentilla's words defending A used against him

369/329: UL; "ἀιτίας /σο-"; the full text of Pudentilla's letter supporting A

370/329: UL, VL; "mùm / rae"; wouldn't the suppressed parts of the letter cry out?

370/329: UL, CR; "tius / detectum"; Rufinus's falsehoods are exposed to daylight

370/329: UL, VL; "teras / extremam"; A conquers by Pudentilla's letter

370/329: UL; "cors / εἱμαρμέϊ"; Pudentilla's letter denies she's been enchanted

370/330: UL; "dentilla / praeconio"; the letter defends her sanity from calumny

370/330: UL, CR; "Igitur / sed"; Pudentilla denies A is a magician and denies magic

372/332: UL, CR; "rêre / tuam"; A mocks Pudens for reading his mother's letters

372/332: UL; "direr"; why would A need blandishments if he could use magic?

373/333: UL, VL; "eam / inuolu"; charges against Pudens; reasons for country wedding

373/333: UL; "me / suburbana"; why the marriage contract was signed in the country

374/333: UL, CR; "rum / terno"; reasons for marrying in the country vs. the city

374/334: UL; "sulatus"; in the Roman past, high offices were bestowed in the country

374/334: UL; "tam sibi"; her father declared Pudentilla his daughter at her birth

374/334–35: UL; "gnum / assignabat"; let documents showing her age be examined

374–75/335: UL, HD, VL; "multo / anni"; methods and mistakes in finger counting

376/337: UL, VL; "Formam / vberem"; the accusers insulted Pudentilla and A

376/337: UL, CR; "des / posteriori"; Pudentilla's financial legacy explained

376–77/338: UL, VL; "Pudeat / ponentem"; Pudentilla's generosity; A's true love

377/338–39: UL; "ve- / sed"; a widow, marrying, brings nothing she can't reclaim

377/339: UL; "coniu-"; a woman whose husband has died should be avoided as unlucky

377–78/339: UL, CR, CR; "mulierem / artius"; tactics A could have used if greedy

378/339–40: UL; "uoraram / uitate"; A's efforts on behalf of Pudentilla's sons

378/340: UL; "nerat / nium"; Pontianus asked forgiveness from A and Pudentilla

378/340: UL; "postea"; Pontianus asked to be excused to proconsul Lollianus Avitus

379/340: UL, CR; "tu / fluere"; A asks for Avitus's letter, his source of safety

379/340–41: UL, CR; "laudato- / Multos"; what better advocate/witness than Avitus?

379/341: VL; "inuidia / amico"; Avitus combines the talents of many great stylists

379/341: UL; "& / fero"; A will postpone further praise of Avitus

380/342: UL, CR; "nem / ficij"; will A's accusers still pursue their charges?

380/342–43: UL, CR; "Puta"; suppose A had not read Avitus's letter

380/342: UL; "se / ctionibus"; Pontianus himself acknowledged A's beneficence

380/342: UL; "nam / egisset"; if only Rufinus hadn't obstructed Pontianus's intent!

380/342: VL; "paulisper / memoriae"; Pudens contrasted with Pontianus

380/342: UL, CR; "tianus / tempore"; Pontianus called A parent, master, instructor

380/342: UL; "ctum / honestissimè"; Pontianus's will commends A highly

380/342: UL; "hereditatis / tiani"; Rufinus's valuation of Pontianus's property

381/342: UL, CR; "caeca / ma-"; Rufinus, like a blind beast, gaped and got nothing

381/343: UL; "ho- / oblitus"; Pontianus disinherited his wife, Rufinus's daughter

381/343: UL, DL; "Rufino / animam"; Rufinus is enticing Pudens with his daughter

381/343: UL, CR; "Rufino / admo-"; Rufinus is favored by Aemilianus

381/343: UL, CR; "suspi- / Planè"; A's moderation keeps him from airing suspicions

381/343–44: UL, VL; "re- / facie"; mockery of Aemilianus's new interest in Pudens

381/344: UL; "accepisti / ma-"; Aemilianus now treats Pudens differently

382/344: UL; "gistros / inter"; Aemilianus's bad influence on Pudens

382/344: UL; "uiuio"; Pudens now frequents the gladiatorial contests

382/344: UL; "honestè / neque"; Pudens's lack of learning in languages

382/344: UL; "damna / illi"; Pudens's corruption due to Rufinus, Aemilianus

382/344: UL, HD, VL; "paenissimè / leret"; A kept Pudens from being disinherited

382/345: VL, UL; "leret / liberaret"; A persuaded Pudentilla to be kind to Pudens

382/345: UL; "enim / tumeliis"; Aemilianus did not expect A to be so gracious

382–83/345: UL, CR; "quoque / accusationem"; A could have taken revenge on Pudens

383/345: UL, CR; "ex / proli-"; A's freedom from avarice; his efforts for Pudens

383/345: UL; "precibus"; the accusers call A a robber

383/345–46: UL, VL; "lega- / testa-"; Pudentilla's will shows A is left little

383/346: UL; "& / testa-"; A urges Pudens to read the will, not private letters

383/346: UL, CR; "FI- / in"; Pudentilla's "insanity": her generosity to Pudens

383/346: VL; "in / ibi"; a summary of Pudens's despicable behavior to Pudentilla

383–84/346: UL; "ventila- / ipse"; more instances of Pudens's misconduct

384/346: UL, CR; "testamento / reliquit"; let Pudens now deal with Pudentilla

384/346: UL; "matri / exorare"; since Pudens can harangue, let him plead his case

384/347: UL; "iecta / est"; envy because of property was the reason for the trial

384/347: UL; "sò / lieris"; A allegedly spent Pudentilla's money on an estate

384/347: VL, UL; "guum / mihi"; A refutes this charge; introduces a witness

384/347: UL; "est?"; is the price paid for this little property ground for complaints?

384–85/347: UL; "reperisti? / an vt"; why should A use incantations on Pudentilla?

385/347–48: UL; "fa- / quid-"; Pudentilla had previously left nothing to her sons

385/348: UL; "diffi-"; A mockingly says he used his magic to help Pudens

385/348: UL; "substituite / ei"; traits of a corrupt judge, unlike Maximus

385/348: UL, CR; "cur se- / suae"; summary of charges and refutations

385/348: UL; "do- / igi"; A mimics Pudens's accusation against him

385/348: UL; "maleficiorum / du-"; more mimicry of Pudens's accusations

Florida

218/375: UL; "tiforatili"; a pipe of so many holes

218/375: UL; "nare. Primus"; Hyagnis first "separated the hands" in flute playing

219/376: UL, CR; "specimen / deliramen-"; Marsyas's competition with Apollo

219/376: UL, VL; "& / tenuis"; Marsyas describes Apollo's handsome appearance

219/376: UL, VL; "inquit / maximam"; Marsyas links Apollo with luxury, not virtue

220/376: UL, CR; "peritus / primè"; modes of flute-playing characterized

220/377: UL, VL; "praesidere / phos"; various uses of togas and covers

220/377: UL; "mis / diuites"; various peoples characterized

220–21/377–78: UL, CR, CR; "men / am-"; how elephants fight with dragons in India

221/378: UL; "Gymnosophistae vo-"; a race among the Indians called Gymnosophists

221–22/378–79: UL, CR; "maior / rare"; the unique greatness of Alexander

222/379: UL; "merè"; Alexander forbade brass, paint, engraved depictions of himself

222/379: UL, CR; "sanctissimi / eum"; inferior artists punished for depicting him

223/379–80: UL, CR, VL; "baiulis / li-"; insults; rarity of virtue and learning

224/381: UL, CR; "legit / consulis"; different speech styles of crier and proconsul

224/381: UL; "recitata"; proconsul's sentence is inserted in provincial registry

224/381: CR; "ribus / ratius"; A will explain his reference to Hippias

225/381: UL; "eme- / va-"; a description of Hippias's self-made clothing

225/382: UL, CR; "commemora- / coe-"; A tells what Hippias wasn't ashamed to display

225/382: UL; "baxeas / gestare"; A buys his garments and his shoes

225/382: UL; "nec / vti"; A knows how to use the loom, the awl, the file, the lathe

227/383: UL; "manen- / Prorsus"; the proconsul's son exhibits his father's virtues

227/383: UL, DL; "Prorsus / frui!"; more on the son's virtue; long may it last!

227/383–84: UL, CR; "Hono- / pro-"; the son's imminent promotions

229/385: UL, VL, VL; "est / per-"; various kinds of birdsong

229/386: UL; "Dio- / magis"; Crates threw down his wealth like a load of dung

229/386: UL, CR; "beatè / in-"; Crates then lived happily; a noble virgin chose him

229/386: UL; "fu- / quam"; Crates reveals his "shortcomings" to the virgin

229/386–87: UL; "Iamdudum / posse"; the virtuous virgin accepts Crates

229/387: UL, VL; "por- / mari"; Crates's plan to make love to his bride in public

229–30/387: UL; "mari / aratro"; location and traits of the island of Samos

230/387: UL, CR; "scalpitur / rum"; agriculture on Samos; its natives and visitors

230/387: UL, VL; "abest / cognouisse"; description of the temple of Juno on Samos

230/387–88: UL, CR, VL; "canenti / ctus"; description of a statue in the temple

231/388: UL, CR; "artifices / opem"; Pythagoras's father was a gem engraver

231/389: UL, CR, CR; "Phe- / &"; scattered marks; men Pythagoras studied under

232/389: UL, FL; "totum / rocis"; Pythagoras's followers' attempts at silence

233/389–90: UL; "statuam / volo"; A thanks African nobles for a statue in his honor

233/390: UL; "& / institui"; Persian waters are pleasant and curative

233/390: UL, CR; "fa- / Quid"; A will submit all his actions to their judgment

235/391: UL, CR; "propin- / corpore"; A's recitation interrupted; his injury

235/392: UL; "abire / igitur"; A's sickness almost ended his life

235/392: UL; "quàm / in-"; he recovered through the warmth of Persian waters

236/392: UL, CR; "eum / praenobilior"; praise of the genius of Strabo

236/392–93: UL; "inter / vtrosque"; Strabo is best and most learned

236/393: UL; "*Dum memor*"; several words from a line of Virgil underscored

236/393: UL, CR; "sed prae"; A wants to appear grateful, but his joy hinders him

237/394: UL; "aderant / sci-"; Carthage's senate approved a place for A's statue

237/394: UL; "sed se- / per-"; the senate didn't want to seem to rival Strabo

239/395: UL, CR; "coarten- / boan"; the importance of using one's voice

239/396: VL, UL; "Si- / Mitto"; sounds of instruments contrasted with human voice

239/396: UL, CR; "mu- / rabies"; different animal sounds characterized

239/396: UL; "vtilitatem / celebra-"; human voice more useful than pleasing

239/396: CR; "fi- / conse-"; A would seek crowded audiences as a lute player

239/396: UL, CR; "*Arion* / tores"; the legends of Orpheus and Arion

240/397: UL; "frenes / cundia"; Scipio's "generous modesty"; A's "bashfulness"

240/397: UL; "admiramur"; A will touch on at least a few of Scipio's many virtues

241/397: UL, CR; "loci / conferat"; lines from Plautus quoted

242/398: UL; "vtrumque / multiscius"; Protagoras was a sophist of varied knowledge

242/399: UL, CR, CR; "doctrina / dis"; Protagoras's arrangement with Euathlus

243/399: UL, VL; "ego / damnationem"; Protagoras's reasoning about the bargain

243/399: UL, VL; "verterato- / viden-"; Euathlus's opposite reasoning triumphs

243/399: UL; "spi- / praestat"; sophisms stick to each other like burs

244/400: UL, CR, CR; "disciplinis / sius"; A expresses gratitude to Carthage

244/400: UL, CR; "nunc / buntur"; A alludes to a dialogue of his in Greek and Latin

244/400: UL; "doctrina / clariores"; admirable qualities of S. Severus and J. Persius

244/401: UL, CR; "gis / contendunt"; their rivalry in their love for Carthage

245/401: UL, CR, CR; "per- / &"; scattered markings of comments on the dialogue

245/401: UL, CR; "Atti- / cuius"; Asclepiades first used wine as a remedy

245/401: UL, VL; "loca- / ingenij"; Asclepiades's curiosity about a funeral

245/401: UL; "perspersa / pollin-"; the body was anointed with perfumes and ointment

245/401: UL, CR; "pertra- / faces"; Asclepiades found life in the "dead" body

245/401: UL, CR; "Murmur"; Asclepiades: take funeral banquet from tomb to table

245/401-2: UL, CR; "partim / At-"; over relatives' resistance, the body preserved

246/402: UL, CR; "confestimque / mensam"; Asclepiades medically re-
vived the corpse

246–47/403: UL: "est / collium"; inconveniences of travel by cart

247/403: UL, CR; "fortitudi- / peruo-"; advantages of horse travel; Lucilius quoted

247/403: UL, CR; "cohibent / ille"; scattered UL: travel delayed out of
courtesy

247/386: UL, CR; "ille / clausa"; Crates adored by Athenians; no door
shut to him

247/386: UL, CR; "omnium & / Quod"; Crates made peace within
families

247/386: UL, CR; "omneis / Igitur"; Crates was like Hercules in appearance, acts

247/386: UL; "nu- / praediatus"; Crates's originally prosperous
circumstances

248/403: VL, UL; "ctam / rint"; extended simile: pilot must guide good
ship well

248/403: UL, HD; "lectum / uitium"; conduct of physician with sick
wealthy patient

4

Ben Jonson's Chaucer

Chaucer's possible influence on Jonson has not received much scholarly attention, partly because those scholars who *have* been interested in Chaucer's legacy to the Renaissance have quite naturally focused on more obvious heirs such as Spenser and Shakespeare.[1] Jonson never claimed Chaucer as a literary father quite so enthusiastically or convincingly as Spenser did, nor did he ever model any of his own works on Chaucer's writings quite so obviously as Shakespeare. His own poetic style—with its famous emphasis on plain diction and clear sense—seems little indebted to Chaucer's medieval English, which by the Renaissance, at least, was so distant from current usage that for many it had become synonymous with archaism and required extensive glossing to be understood. Indeed, Jonson himself in the *Discoveries* warns against allowing callow youth to "taste *Gower* or *Chaucer* at first, lest falling too much in love with Antiquity, and not apprehending the weight, they grow rough and barren in language onely" (H&S 8:618). A little later he objects again to contemporary writers' enthusiasm for "*Chaucerismes* . . . , which were better expung'd and banish'd" (H&S 8:622). The adoption of a Chaucerian style was precisely part of his complaint against Spenser, and it is the main reason for his opinion that "in affecting the Ancients, [Spenser] writ no Language" (H&S 8:618). Yet Chaucer is one of the authors cited most frequently in Jonson's *Grammar* (only Gower surpasses him), and Chaucer, Gower, and Spenser are three of the four exemplary English poets honored by being presented (along with Lydgate) as characters in *The Golden Age Restor'd*. Chaucer's works are frequently echoed in Jonson's own writings; some served him as sources, while others offer analogues; and Jonson's personal copy of Chaucer suggests that in some instances, at least, he read his predecessor with careful thoroughness.[2] Indeed, his markings of two very peculiar poems—both dealing with the rather un-Jonsonian topic of romantic love—suggest an intriguingly enthusiastic and detailed interest. The very complexity of Jonson's response to these poems can help define the complexity of his own conception of poetry and of the poetic vocation.

It is, in fact, in connection with the *vocation* of poetry, with the idea of a literary *career*, that Jonson's reaction to Chaucer can seem particularly intriguing. Richard Helgerson has shown how Spenser's attempt to fashion a "laureate" role for himself helped prepare for—and helped legitimize—Jonson's own efforts to do the same.[3] But before Spenser there was Chaucer, who had by Jonson's day attained unequalled eminence as an *English* poet of lasting historical significance. Chaucer was widely honored as the "English Homer," and his Renaissance admirers admired him all the more for having achieved so much at a time when (they believed) so little else of genuine literary consequence had been accomplished. Jonson, of course, had other models to emulate in attempting to fashion a literary career and a lasting reputation. Spenser had recently helped pave the way—although his way (as Helgerson so convincingly shows) could not be Jonson's. The great Roman poets—especially Horace and Martial—provided models more to his tastes, although their examples would need to be tailored to fit his own circumstances and historical moment. What, if anything, could Chaucer's example provide? What lessons could Jonson learn from Chaucer's career? Which aspects of that career could Jonson emulate or appropriate, and which were irrelevant to his own situation? In attempting to answer such questions, it is helpful to turn to Jonson's marked copy of Chaucer, presently housed in the Folger Library.

Jonson owned the 1602 edition of Chaucer's works, edited by Thomas Speght.[4] In his extremely valuable annotated catalogue of Jonson's surviving books, David McPherson discusses Jonson's Chaucer briefly. However, the catalogue's note describes the book incorrectly in several respects. First, McPherson writes that "flower symbols and hands in the margin, probably Jonson's, run all the way through the text, but the only pattern I can discern is that they point out *sententiae* not indicated by the editor."[5] If this report were true, it would be of potentially great significance to Jonson scholars, since such markings would provide fascinatingly detailed evidence of Jonson's response to a great (and native) forbear. Even if no other pattern existed, this would still tell us something about Jonson's habits of mind and ways of reading poetry and might therefore suggest something about the ways he himself not only wrote but expected to be read. The markings would be especially interesting because many of them call attention to passages relevant to some of Jonson's own obsessive interests (such as the problem of flattery). Unfortunately, however, the scores of marginal hands that run throughout the book, pointing fingers at significant passages, were not drawn by Jonson. Rather, they are printed in the text and were added by Speght to the 1602 edition as a convenience to the reader and as a selling point designed to appeal to those interested in Chaucer's wisdom.[6] The example of a marked passage that McPherson cites ("For pitie renneth soone in gentle hert," [fol. 5ʳ]) is also marked by an identical printed hand in other copies of the 1602 edition available at the Folger.

However, numerous unreported markings clearly *are* by Jonson and give the book an interest independent of the inauthentic hands. These markings are bunched in three different sections of the book: in the address "To the Readers"; in the poem "The Remedie of Loue"; and in another poem also concerned with love, "Of the Cuckow and the Nightingale." In addition, throughout the book (as McPherson does note), Jonson marks and rectifies typographical errors, usually by writing the correct words in the margins. This practice is typical of him and is not unimportant, considering the great significance he attached to print as a means of establishing (in several senses of that word) a poetic reputation. It is this concern with the accuracy of the printed word and with the vagaries of literary transmission that Jonson shared with Chaucer. According to Speght, one of the Chaucerian passages quoted in the address "To the Readers" testifies to Chaucer's fear of having his works "miswritten, or his verse mismeasured":

> And for there is so great diuersitie
> In English, and in writing of our tounge,
> So pray I God, that none miswrite thee,
> Ne thee mismetre for defaut of tongue, &c.

Significantly, Jonson marks this quotation (from *Troilus and Cressida*) by drawing a large bracket in the margin next to it. The same concern about printed inaccuracies, the same worry about the possible misapprehension and misappropriation of an author's works that seems indicated by this marked passage pervades, of course, Jonson's own work in any number of ways. The care he demonstrated in preparing his own folio *Workes* for publication is only one of the means by which he attempted to impose his own literal *authority* on the transmission and reception of his writings.

His markings in his copy of Chaucer provide explicit evidence of his real interest in this problem. Thus it seems all the more ironic that the two Chaucerian poems mentioned above, which Jonson marked so carefully and enthusiastically, have since been excluded from the Chaucer canon as inauthentic. They themselves paradoxically exemplify Chaucer's own inability, at least, to impose complete control over the shape and body of his work. The extent to which Jonson or his contemporaries recognized these poems as inauthentic is unclear, but Jonson certainly realized the advantage he possessed over medieval authors precisely because of the development of print and (even more significantly) because of his ability to supervise the printing of much of his writing.[7] Because of print, Jonson's ability to impose control over the transmission of his works and thus over the development of his historical reputation was much greater than Chaucer's. Ironically, the problem with the Jonson canon is not that inauthentic works have crept in, but that genuine works—especially certain crucial early writings of which Jonson seems to have been ashamed—have been suppressed by the author himself. In his copy of Chaucer, Jonson marks with a marginal line Speght's contention that many of the corruptions of Chaucer's meter are the fault of *"Adam Scriuener"* ("To the Readers"). He was thus fully aware of the hazards of manuscript transmission, and his own careful attention to the printing of his works seems to be one response to that awareness.[8]

But Jonson's markings also suggest another kind of awareness— a recognition that, however much an author might impose control over his own works, he could not control the historical evolution of the language in which he wrote. Many of the passages marked in the address "To the Readers" concern the peculiarities of Chaucer's style, and indeed one of the great selling points of the Speght edition was the claim that its glossaries and notes helped make Chaucer's works more comprehensible to a native audience no longer conversant with his archaic English. Jonson marks passages in which Speght discusses Chaucer's use of double negatives (as in, "I ne said none ill"), abbreviated word forms (as in *"gon* for *begon"*), and contracted verbs (as in *"I not what men him call"* instead of *"I know not"*). In addition, he marks passages that discuss Chaucer's use of names in his works ("as, *Argonauticon* for *Apollonius Rhodius* . . .") and that comment upon Chaucer's use of *"Metaplasmus"* in translating proper names from Latin and Greek, "as *Atheon* for *Acteon: Adriane* for *Ariadne"* ("To the Readers"). All of these markings suggest his genuine interest in understanding Chaucer's style as precisely as possible, in appreciating it on its own terms. At the same time, such markings may also be relevant to Jonson's own cultivation of a "plain style." The clarity he strove to achieve in much of his own writing may have been partly born from recognizing that the language of writers like Chaucer had ceased, to a great degree, to be a *living* language (in a way, for instance, that Martial's or Horace's, despite being Latin, had not). Jonson's markings in his copy of Chaucer square with the concerns about stylistic archaism expressed in the *Discoveries*. It seems likely that the main reasons Chaucer was not a great or more obvious influence on Jonson are related precisely to this question of style. To echo Chaucer too directly would have been to embrace a kind of linguistic archaism that would have inhibited the clear expression Jonson so highly prized. And, no less important, it would have undermined his effort to distinguish himself from Spenser and from Spenser's imitators—an effort that, as Helgerson shows, was central to Jonson's enterprise of self-definition and self-display. Chaucer could not be an explicit and obvious influence on Jonson in part because he had so recently been used by Spenser in just that way.

Nonetheless, the similarities between the artistic *projects* of Jonson and Chaucer are numerous, and there is some evidence to suggest that Jonson pondered certain of these parallels. His interest in Chaucer must have been fed in part by his recognition that Chaucer was a great English predecessor whose fame depended significantly on his skills as a *comic* writer, as a humorous satirist of social vices and individual foibles. Unlike Spenser, whose writings were not notoriously funny, Chaucer offered Jonson the example of a great English poet who had won preeminent fame through close attention to the comic details of daily life. Like Jonson, he was a poet especially skilled in depicting a wide variety of contemporary character types and mocking their humors and pretensions. Also like Jonson, Chaucer often cultivated a "middle" style, and, just as many of Jonson's plays effectively bring together a strange and conflicting assortment of character types, so of course does Chaucer's greatest work. It hardly seems surprising that Francis Beaumont (in his prefatory letter commending Speght's labors) should praise Chaucer in terms that recall Jonson's own technique in his "humour" plays (which were then very much in vogue). "*Chaucer's* deuice of his Canterbury pilgrimage," Beaumont remarks, "is meerely his owne : His drifte is to touch all sortes of men, and to discouer all vices of that age, which he doth so feelingly, and with so true an ayme, as he neuer failes to hit whatsoeuer mark he leuels at."[9]

In fact, Chaucer's position as a kind of unofficial poet laureate—a writer moving comfortably in the corridors of power, honored and rewarded at court—may have particularly caught Jonson's interest, and it is intriguing to know that Jonson's own position at court was eventually formalized not only through the granting of an annuity, but later also through the awarding of a yearly tierce of canary wine from the royal cellars. Since Speght's edition indicated that Chaucer had also received the very same mark of royal favor ([bvi^v]; see also H&S 1:248), perhaps Jonson's patrons chose it deliberately to emphasize the parallels between this great English poet and his respected medieval predecessor. Certainly by the height of his career, Jonson had achieved a kind of literary prominence and a proximity to power unlike those of any English poet before him except Chaucer. It is hard to imagine that he could have been unaware of this.

Jonson could have known the details of Chaucer's life (at least as they were understood in 1602) by consulting the biographical introduction to Speght's edition. Unfortunately, this section of the book bears none of his markings, so it is impossible to use the introduction to speculate securely about his attitudes concerning many aspects of Chaucer's career or to guess with any assurance about which of those aspects he found most interesting or relevant to his own circumstances. If he read the biographical section at all, or if he knew of the same information from other sources, he may have been struck by several facets of Chaucer's biography that bore comparison with his own situation and aspirations. But he may also have noticed the important ways in which their careers were not (and for very practical reasons could not be) alike.[10] Both poets were probably born in London (bij^r), and both were closely associated with the city for much of their lives. Like Jonson, Chaucer was "descended not of any great house" (bij^r). But unlike Jonson, in his youth he had the advantages of wealth and was brought up in such a way as to prepare him for royal service (bij^r). He was educated at both Oxford and Cambridge (biij^r), whereas Jonson's chances for a university education were of course undermined by his family's lack of funds. Chaucer's time at the university, combined with his extensive foreign travels as a young man, allowed him to attain "great perfection in all kind of learning" (biij^r), and after returning to London he frequented not only the Court but "the Colleges of Lawyers" (biij^r). His connections in both places, plus his marriage into one of the kingdom's most prominent families, helped him win and maintain social prominence and literary renown, although his security was threatened when he favored "some rashe attempt of the common people" (biij^r—ci^r). Still, in financial terms Chaucer was quite comfortable: "hee had lands and reuenues in diuers places, and that to the yearely value, as some say, almost of a thousand pounds" ([bvi^r]).

If Jonson knew these data, he may have noticed especially the extent to which Chaucer's prominence depended on his connections with the socially influential—whether it was the King, his brother-in-law John of Gaunt, the various other "Nobility both Lords and Ladies, which fauoured him greatly" ([bvi^v]), or his friends at the Inns of Court. Jonson possessed none of the early advantages Chaucer had, nor did he ever win quite the same kind of financial fortune that Speght ascribed to Chaucer. Moreover, his role as a writer was much more professional than Chaucer's, who was essentially a courtly amateur (in Helgerson's sense of the term). Perhaps partly for all these reasons, Jonson's own desire to win a secure and recognized place at court and to cultivate contacts with the socially powerful was all the more pressing.[11] Chaucer's example may have reinforced Jonson's sense of the importance of winning aristocratic patronage as a means of achieving and maintaining literary renown. Like the fame won by the Roman poets Jonson especially admired, Chaucer's literary success was part and parcel of his social success, of his acceptance and encouragement by the socially powerful. This lesson could hardly have been lost on Jonson.

Perhaps the most important theme that runs throughout the preliminary matter of Speght's edition is the emphasis on Chaucer's remarkable learning: the biographical introduction stresses that it was this intellectual prowess that won him the affection and admiration of his contemporaries. The edition itself testifies in numerous ways that Chaucer's learning continued to command the reverent respect of his Elizabethan audience, and Jonson's markings of the address "To the Readers" suggest that he was himself particularly interested in this aspect of Chaucer's accomplishment. For a poet who began life with far fewer advantages than Chaucer enjoyed, the importance of learning and knowledge as ladders to social advancement must have seemed all the greater. Jonson's assiduous cultivation of his own learning was no doubt due in part to his native curiosity and in-born disposition, but he was hardly ignorant of its usefulness as a weapon of ambition. The only passage in Speght's address that Jonson both marks in the margin *and* underlines is the comment that Chaucer was "a man of great reading, & deep judgement," and it is clear that

these were the qualities in Chaucer that resonated most power-
fully with Jonson's own most cherished aspirations. This is the
image Jonson repeatedly tried to construct for himself in his own
works and, most especially, in his own folio *Workes;* this is the
kind of historical fame to which he himself aspired. Moreover, if
Chaucer offered Jonson the example of a great English comic poet,
he also provided him with the model of a comic poet whose
fundamental *seriousness* was essential to his social respectability.
Indeed, Speght emphasizes Chaucer's learning partly to defend
him against the attitudes of the "diuers [who] haue thought him
vnlearned, and his writings meere trifles." As a comic poet who
was also serious, Chaucer provided a precedent in many ways
for the kind of career Jonson hoped to achieve and for the kind
of writing Jonson did best.[12]

Other markings suggest Jonson's identification with Chaucer's
career. At one point in his address, Speght suggests that "It were
a labor worth commendation, if some scholler, that hath skil and
leisure, would confer *Chaucer* with those learned Authors, both
in Greek and Latin, from whom he hath drawn many excellent
things" (Jonson marks this passage lightly in the margin).
Whether or not Jonson had any ambitions to undertake such a
project cannot be said, but what does seem clear is that he recognized in Chaucer a poet who had done what he himself aspired
to do: to draw on and "english" the writings of important classical
authors, to make them so much his own that it would require
scholarly labors to record all the echoes. Chaucer provided an
important model for Jonson because he was an English poet who
had deliberately opened himself to Continental influences, who
had seen and had helped perpetuate the fundamental continuity
of the classical and the Christian, of the European and the more
narrowly English. Jonson's markings in the "Address to the Readers" suggest that he valued Chaucer not simply as a poet who
happened to write in English but as a poet who could infuse
into the native poetic tradition the results of his own extensive
investigations of non-native sources. Chaucer's work provided an
important (because prominent) precedent for his own practice
of *imitatio.*[13]

But Jonson's markings of his Chaucer extend far beyond the
opening pages; in fact, they run through much of the volume and
suggest that he may have read Chaucer with deliberation and in
detail. Because most of the markings are simply corrections of
errata, and because most of these corrections follow changes suggested by the errata sheet Speght appended to the rear of the

volume, they tell us little about Jonson's specific responses to important works. It would be fascinating to know, for instance, how the author of *Volpone* read *The Miller's Tale* or how the creator of Ursula the pig woman reacted to the Wife of Bath. But the corrections of errata do not provide this kind of information, although they do imply that Chaucer's writings were important enough to Jonson for him to take the time to locate and make the scores of corrections Speght suggested.[14]

By far the most interesting markings in the entire book, however, are the ones found in two poems ("The Remedie of Loue" and "Of the Cuckow and the Nightingale") we now know were not even written by Chaucer. There is no evidence to suggest that Jonson suspected the poems' authenticity, although it is always possible that he did. In any case, it seems more than a little ironic that the works which bear the most obvious marks of his interest made their way into Speght's edition through the very process of textual corruption that is the subject of such concern in the "Address to the Readers." But what is most intriguing about Jonson's interest is the subject matter the two poems share: romantic love. In a famous poem ("Why I Write Not of Love" [*For.* 1]), Jonson himself commented on his relative neglect of a topic central to Renaissance poetics, and this neglect has not gone unremarked.[15] Lawrence Venuti, for instance, has recently attempted to explain Jonson's poetic inattention to love in terms of his philosophies of art and language. Whatever the reasons, love is certainly a far less common concern in the poems of Jonson than in those of his contemporaries.[16] This fact makes his close and careful reading of the apocryphal Chaucerian love poems all the more worthy of investigation. What do Jonson's markings suggest about his response to these poems? What might they imply about his attitudes toward love as a subject for poetic expression? How do his markings square with what we know about his own aesthetic and philosophical concerns?

While none of these questions can be answered absolutely, Jonson's markings do provide ample evidence for sound speculation. Some of the marks, to be sure, are interesting in only a very limited sense: these are the ones that correct errata, that call attention to unfamiliar words or phrases, that literally underscore important characters or plot developments, or that seem designed mainly to note some particularly striking passage or expression. Some of Jonson's markings of the two poems undoubtedly fall into these categories, but many more seem instead to indicate a real interest in the moral or philosophical issues the poems raise.

Before discussing the implications of the latter kinds of markings, however, it may be helpful to summarize briefly the plots of both poems and to indicate the more important of Jonson's marks.

"The Remedie of Loue" opens with a long prologue addressed mainly to prosperous youths, warning them about the dangers of taking their current good fortune for granted and of risking their mental and physical welfare through the entanglements of "loue encombrous" (fol. 305ᵛ). Jonson marks none of this prologue. The poem itself is preceded by a brief summary in prose: "This booke drawn for the most part out of the Prouerbes of Salomon, is a warning to take heed of the deceitfull companie of women" (fol. 306ᵛ). Jonson's markings of the poem proper begin in the very first stanza and continue intermittently for more than a page. The poem begins by reiterating the Prologue's claim that its intended audience is young men. It advises them to avoid the physical and spoken charms of deceitful women, and it illustrates this warning by telling the story of three lovers who all desired the same woman. "Ech of them knew others maladie, / Wherefore was all their daily labour, / Who could approch next in her fauour" (fol. 306ᵛ). Although they usually visited her at different times, it once happened that they all arrived simultaneously. After sitting them all down to supper,

> Her one louer first friendly she eied,
> The second she offred the cup courtesly,
> The third she gaue token secretly,
> Underneath the bord she trade on his foot,
> Through his entrailes tikled the hartroot
>
> (fol.307ʳ;UL, FL)

At this point the poem's narrator interrupts to ask if his readers can anticipate which one of the three won this contest of love. He then says that no one can answer the question better than he, confessing that he was himself one of the contestants. None of them, it turns out, won the woman's affection, "But Wattes packe bare we all by and by" (fol. 306ᵛ; UL, AS, HD). The narrator then expresses sorrow for his transgressions and vows his determination to seek God's forgiveness. If all the earth were parchment, he says, and all the trees pens and all the seas ink, not even a perfect scribe could detail "The cursednesse yet and deceit of women" (fol. 307ʳ; Jonson underlines this entire stanza, marks it with a line in the left margin, and in a note calls attention to the use of the same metaphor in another poem later in the book).

Women are like a "stinking rose" (fol. 307^r; UL) or like deceitful poison; "Wine and women into apostasie / Cause wisemen to fall, what is that to say, / Of wisedom cause them to forget the way" (fol. 307^r; UL, VL). For these reasons, readers are advised,

> With the straunger to sit in no wise,
> Which is not thy wife, fall not in clipping
> With her, but beware eke of her kissing,
> Keepe with her in wine no altercation
>   (fol. 307^r; UL, FL, CR)

Although the poem continues on for more than two pages, Jonson's markings stop at this point; his special interest in the poem seems to have been confined to this first story.

"Of the Cuckow and the Nightingale" is a shorter poem than "The Remedie," but Jonson's concern with it seems to have been more sustained: it is marked intermittently from beginning to end. The opening stanza emphasizes the mighty power of the God of Love: "he can make of low herts hie, / And of high low, and like for to die, / And hard harts he can maken free" (fol. 316^v; UL; AS next to the final two lines). "[A]ll that euer he woll he may, . . . For he can glad and greue whom him liketh, / And who that he woll, he lougheth or siketh, / And most his might he shedeth euer in May" (fol. 316^v; UL).[17] Like "The Remedie," this poem also has a narrator; he tells how, on "the third night of May" (UL, AS), he went to a brook in the woods, where he came to an enchanting place: "The ground was greene, ypoudred with daisie / The floures and the greues like hie, / All greene and white, was nothing els seene" (fol. 316^v; UL, FL). Sitting down here, he listened to the birds as "They began of May for to done houres" (UL, FL). But as he listened in delight, his pleasure was interrupted by the sound of a "leaud cuckow" (UL, AS). The narrator called on Christ to punish the bird, but as "I with the cuckow thus gan chide, / I heard in the next bush beside, / A nightingale so lustely sing" (fol. 317^r; UL, FL). The nightingale and the narrator both began to upbraid the cuckow, but the conflict soon erupted into a debate between the two birds on the merits of love and on the worth of their respective songs. The cuckow condemned love's yoke, claiming that it caused those subjected to it "disease," misfortune, and unhappiness (fol. 317^r; most of this passage is underlined and is marked with a marginal flower). To this the nightingale responded passionately in defense of love:

> . . . in this world is none so good seruise
> To euery wight that gentle is of kind.
>   For thereof truly commeth all goodnesse,
> All honour, and all gentlenesse,
> Worship, ease, and all hearts lust,
> Parfite ioy, and full assured trust,
> Jolitie, pleasaunce, and freshnesse,
>   Lowlyhed, largesse, and curtesie,
> Semelyhead, and true companie,
> Drede of shame for to done amis:
> For he that truly loues seruant is,
> Were lother be shamed than to die.
>   [fol. 317ʳ; UL, FL]

But the cuckow is not easily dissuaded, responding with equally firm assertiveness:

> . . . loue is in yong folke but rage,
> And in old folke a great dotage,
> Who most it useth, most shall enpaire.
>   For thereof commeth disease and heuinesse,
> So sorow & care, and many a great sicknesse,
> Despite, debate, anger, and enuie,
> Deprauing, shame, untrust, and ielousie,
> Pride, mischeefe, pouertie, and woodnesse.
>   Louing is an office of despaire,
> And one thing is therein that is not faire,
> For who that getteth of loue a little blisse,
> But if he be alway therewith iwis,
> He may full soone of age haue his haire.
>   (fol. 317ᵛ;UL, VL, VL, VL)

The debate continues in similar terms for several more stanzas, a number of them heavily marked by Jonson. Shortly after the cuckow alleges that "loue hath no reason, but it is will" (UL) and that often "untrue folk he easeth, / And true folke . . . bitterly he displeaseth" (fol. 317ᵛ; UL), the nightingale heaves a sigh and bursts into tears. At this point the cuckow takes his leave, contemptuously scorning the narrator as a "Popingay" (fol. 317ᵛ). But the nightingale promises to sing to him, urges him not to believe what the cuckow has said, tells him to look on daisies to help ease the pains love causes, and instructs him to "looke alway that thou be good and trew" (fol. 317ᵛ; Jonson underlines and marginally marks many of these details, including the quoted phrase). She tells him that she "shrew[s] all hem that been of loue untrue" (fol. 317ᵛ; UL, FL) and invokes the god of love to send the narrator joy (UL, FL). As she returns to the other birds, the narrator prays that God will always be with her and that He will "shilde us from the Cuckow and his lore, / For there is not so false a bird as he" (fol. 317ᵛ; UL, FL). After the nightingale recounts to the other birds the day's frustrating events, one of them proposes holding a parliament, and the poem proper concludes with two underlined and marginally marked stanzas detailing this meeting's time ("The morrow after saint Valentines day") and place and describing the Nightingale singing and the narrator awaking from his dream (fol. 318ʳ).

The interest Jonson showed in marking up these poems (especially the second one) recalls in some respects his baroquely annotated copies of Martial. But surely these poems did not have the same significance or importance for him as Martial's did. Why, then, might they have provoked his intense reaction? A careful reading of the first poem might prompt the reply that Jonson marked it for the same reasons teachers write "Awkward" on student compositions. But the second poem is aesthetically far more effective, and in neither case does it really seem likely that Jonson's marks are meant to express ridicule. In fact, there are many plausible connections between the subjects, stances, and techniques of these poems and Jonson's own art and attitudes.

Perhaps the most important of these connections is moral: in these poems as in Jonson's art generally, love is very much an *ethical* issue. His concern is usually less with love in its strictly physical or emotional aspects than with the questions of right or wrong, of proper or improper behavior, it can pose. Jonson does not often celebrate love through simple lyricism; he neither elevates it to central social importance nor treats it as a merely amusing game. Instead he usually treats love in a context defined by a pervasive concern with what it means to be good, to do right, to behave responsibly to oneself, to others, and (implicitly) to God. Perhaps his most memorable treatment of the theme—Volpone's attempted seduction of Celia—best exemplifies this moral emphasis, but it does so indirectly, ironically. However, Lovel's eloquent defense of proper love in the third act of *The New Inn* illustrates the same point in more positive terms. Juxtaposing these two examples allows one to stress a crucial distinction that seems to lie at the heart of all of Jonson's thinking about "love"— a distinction between true, charitable love and selfish, cupidinous desire. Volpone speaks of loving Celia, but clearly his first love is himself. His deceiving (perhaps even self-deceptive) seduction speech reeks of a pungent irony highlighted by the beauty of its words. Both of the poems in Jonson's Chaucer raise explicitly many of the same ethical concerns that characterize Jonson's own thinking about love; it is little wonder that they appealed to him.

Like many of Jonson's own works, these Chaucerian poems raise the possibility of people falling victim to their passions, being driven by irrational desires they seem powerless—or at least unwilling—to control. Both poems (the first directly, the second more obliquely) suggest how capitulating to irrational desire can mean abdicating self-command and thus allowing someone else to manipulate one's thinking and behavior. The alluring lady in the first poem and the glib nightingale in the second both enjoy a power over their devotees they could hardly exercise had it not been freely relinquished. Jonson's works, of course, are full of similar characters who allow themselves to be exploited through their own desire to exploit. Indeed, the situation in the first poem—three visitors converging on a central location to pay court to a fourth character who strokes their desires while deceiving them—is remarkably similar to the kind of plots Jonson mastered in *Volpone* and *The Alchemist.* In both Chaucerian poems, the idea that uncontrolled passions can animalize human beings is strongly suggested. In the first, women are referred to as "allectiue bait" (fol. 306ᵛ; part of a passage underlined and marked by Jonson), while in the second, much of the humor stems from the narrator's eager willingness to submit so readily to the nightingale's tutelage. The woman in the first poem plays on the pride and self-love of her "lovers," while the nightingale arguably exploits the naive narrator's desire to pursue desire at any cost. As in Jonson's dramas, we witness the complex interplay of gullers and gulled.

In both poems the female seductresses enjoy their power as much through their alluring speech as through their other charms. The young men addressed in "The Remedie of Loue" are warned to "Ware the straungers bland eloquence" (fol. 306ᵛ; part of a passage underlined and marked), while in the second poem the cuckow contrasts his own "plaine" truth-telling with the nightingale's seductive singing: "I cannot crakel so in vaine," he mockingly tells her (UL, AS; fol. 317ʳ). This opposition between plain speaking and "bland eloquence" probably appealed to Jonson, who saw his own role in terms remarkably similar to that of the first poem's caustic narrator and the second's sarcastic cuckow. The now wise and wizened old narrator of the first poem opens his work by comparing himself to a physician who must seek out his patients' sickness before applying a remedy (fol. 306^v; Jonson underlines and marks part of this passage). This metaphor undoubtedly appealed to Jonson; clearly he conceived of his own function in much the same fashion. The purpose of *his* art was to strip away the world's illusions, to shock his audience into a clear sense of the idiocy of irrational, passionate behavior. To the extent that erotic desire was either immoral or amoral, to the extent that it could give the body control of the spirit, promote emotional discord, create deceiving appearances, and contaminate language with falsehood, Jonson suspected and censured it. Little wonder that he found these two poems so much worth his time.

But his presumptive interest in their moral implications should not obscure other aspects that probably also appealed to him, including their humor, their comic complications, and their artistic techniques. The awkward dinner party in the first poem, with the competing lovers glaring at each other around a common table (while the hostess "plays footsie" with one of them underneath), is one of the few moments of truly Chaucerian wit in a poem otherwise too heavy-handed for its own good. And the deft ironies and clever characterizations in the second poem must have been as amusing to Jonson as they still are today. Both the point and the humor of the second poem are more subtle than those of the first, and indeed the movement from the first to the second is not unlike the transition from Jonson's early "humour" plays, with their somewhat obvious satire and their blatantly moralistic spokesmen, to the more subtle, more ambiguous comedies of his great middle period. Surely this resemblance is coincidental, but it seems likely that in some ways Jonson did find these poems interesting as much for their *techniques* as for their messages. The effective use of the debate format in the second poem, for instance, would have had an obvious interest for a playwright like Jonson, who showed (especially in *Epicoene* and *The Alchemist*) a real talent for comically dramatizing conflicting points of view.[18]

In both of the poems as in many of Jonson's works, there is a heavy emphasis on comic *irony*; the reader is encouraged to distance himself from the participants' perspectives, to attempt to achieve a vantage point from which their actions and spoken rationales can be *judged*. In the second poem such judgment is more difficult—but for that reason more challenging—than in the first (just as judgment becomes more complicated in Jonson's great comedies than in his early ones). Part of the difficulty arises from a simple fact. In the first poem, the narrator himself eventually

mocks his earlier perspective; he explicitly rejects his earlier behavior. In the second poem, however, no such self-realization occurs: the deluded narrator (if indeed he *is* deluded) awakes from
his dream but not from his delusions. The second poem is more
provocative and demanding than the first; its moral—if it has
one—is not so clearly pointed. The nightingale is more alluring
to the reader than is the obviously deceptive woman of the first
poem; it is harder to dismiss the bird's appeal, because, for all her
irrationality and vindictiveness, many of her arguments seem at
least superficially plausible. Perhaps for this reason, the reaction
the second poem provokes (even more intensively than the first)
is a taut moral *alertness*, an inquisitive, even inquisitorial stance
that is far more active and invigorating that the simple, passive
acquiescence the first poem seems to require. In the second poem
(as, for instance, in the closing moments of *The Alchemist*, in the
trial scene in *Volpone*, or in the surprising denouement of *Epicoene*), the audience becomes uncomfortably aware of its own potential for being taken in, for being deluded and deceived. The
first poem encourages mere acceptance of a straightforward
moral; the second encourages personal moral vigilance and
thoughtful contemplation.

As in so many of Jonson's works (especially *Volpone*), part of
the humor of the first poem comes from the fact that none of the
gulls triumphs, that their expectations end in self-defeat and their
comic competition comes to nothing. Although the mature self-
realization that dawns on the narrator of the first poem is rare in
Jonson's works, the stinging humiliation he feels is not. And to
the extent that some of Jonson's gulls *do* eventually awake from
their folly, social humiliation (not conscience) is usually the chief
reason. But what are we to make—and, more importantly, what
did *Jonson* make—of the intense satire on women in this poem?
Doesn't this satire conflict with and undermine the narrator's acceptance of his own responsibility and foolishness? Doesn't it
make women scapegoats for the immorality of men? These are
difficult questions, but the poem does suggest an answer that
Jonson seems literally to have noted. Although the poem casti-
gates women in very harsh terms as temptresses and deceivers,
its real satire seems aimed not at women *in general* but at the
temptations of the world that women could be (and often in Western literature have been) conveniently used to symbolize. The
poem distinguishes between proper love (for one's wife) and for-
nication and adultery. It endorses the first and condemns the
latter. Jonson underlined and marked with a flower a section of

the poem advising youths "With the straunger to sit in no wise, /
Which is not thy wife" (fol. 307ʳ), and earlier he had underlined
and marked with an asterisk a passage defining a "straunger" as
"her that is not thy wife" (fol. 306ᵛ). To modern ears the poem
might sound misogynistic; perhaps in some deep sense it is. But
it seems likely that Jonson read it not as an attack on women per
se but as an indictment of strumpets and of adultery and other
forms of illicit sex.

Even more intriguing than the poem's attitude toward women
are its explicit religious orientation and Jonson's markings of the
passages in which this orientation is expressed. After realizing
his folly, for instance, the narrator at one point worries that he
has not only wasted his time, but that "my fiue fold talent, / That
my lord committed me, I cannot recompence" (fol. 307ʳ; UL).[19] But
he comforts himself by recalling that

> Despiseth not God the meeke contrite hart
> Of the cock crow, alas yt I would not retch,
> And yet it is not late in the second wetch,
> Mercy shall I purchase by incessaunt crying,
> The mer[c]ies of our lord euer shall I sing.

(fol. 307ʳ)

(The first three lines are underlined; the first two are also marked
with a line in the margin; "meries" is corrected to "mercies" in
the margin and by adding a "c" to the text.) That Jonson found
such piety worth noting is suggestive about the religious values
that seem to underlie much of his own work, but that in his work
are more often implied that openly expressed (see, for instance,
Volpone's first speech). Interestingly, in "The Cuckow and the
Nightingale," religious values are likewise insinuated ironically
rather than insisted upon in any blatant way.

Other aspects of Jonson's notes in his Chaucer could be discussed, but the main point is by now sufficiently clear: although
at first it might surprise us that these were the poems he marked,
in the final analysis his interest in them seems both comprehensible and complex. His markings, by suggesting how he reacted
to another's works, imply much about his own. They provide
fascinating evidence about his habits of mind and about his response to a poetic tradition he both extended and transformed.
Although Jonson is often regarded as in many ways a "classical"
writer and although the impact of the classics on his thinking
and his works is everywhere visible, the markings in his Chaucer

indicate his connections to, and his interest in, the rich poetic traditions of his native land.[20] Chaucer's works, Chaucer's concerns, Chaucer's career—all these might provide Jonson with valuable models he could choose to emulate, modify, or avoid. Given Chaucer's great prestige in Tudor-Stuart England, Jonson could hardly avoid some confrontation with his predecessor's legacy, some reaction to Chaucer's influence and art. His markings in Speght's edition provide the concrete evidence of that confrontation and suggest the complex nature of his response.

🙵 To the Readers.

*Fter this booke was laſt printed, J vnderſtood, that
M. Francis Thynn had a purpoſe, as indeed he
hath when time ſhall ſerue, to ſet out Chaucer with
a Coment in our tongue, as the Italians haue Petrarke
and others in their language. Whereupon I purpoſed
not to meddle any further in this work, although ſome promiſe made to
the contrarie, but to referre all to him; being a Gentleman for that purpoſe inferior to none, both in regard of his own skill, as alſo of thoſe helps
left to him by his father. Yet notwithſtanding, Chaucer now being
printed againe, I was willing not only to helpe ſome imperfeſtions, but
alſo to adde ſome things: whereunto he did not only perſuade me, but
moſt kindly lent me his helpe and direſtion. By this meanes moſt of his
old words are reſtored: Prouerbes and Sentences marked: Such
Notes as were colleſted, drawne into better order: And the text by old
Copies correſted.*

*But of ſome things I muſt aduertiſe the Readers; as firſt, that in
Chaucer they ſhall find the proper names oftentimes much differing
from the Latin and Greeke, from whence they are drawne: which they
muſt not condemne in him as a fault. For both he, and other Poets, in
tranſlating ſuch words from one language into another, doe vſe, as the
Latins and Greeks do, the ſundry Species of* Metaplaſmus: *as* Cam-
paneus *for* Capaneus: Atheon *for* Aſteon: Adriane *for* Ariadne.
Which Chaucer *doth in other words alſo: as* gon *for* begon: leue *for*
beleue: peraunter *for* peraduenture: loueden *for* did loue: wone-
den *for* did won, &c.*

*Jt is his manner likewiſe, imitating the Greekes, by two negatiues
to cauſe a greater negation: as,* I ne ſaid none ill.

Alſo many times to vnderſtand his verbe: as, I not *what men
him call, for,* I know not, &c.

And, for the Author, to name ſome part of his worke: as, Argonauticon *for* Apollonius Rhodius. *And that ſometime in the genitiue
caſe a former ſubſtantiue being vnderſtood: as, read* Æneidos: Meta-
morphoſeos: *for the Authors of thoſe workes.*

And

Marked pages of Jonson's copy of Chaucer.

And for his verses, although in diuers places they may seeme to vs to stand of vnequall measures: yet a skilfull Reader, that can scan them in their nature, shall find it otherwise. And if a verse here and there fal out a sillable shorter or longer than another, I rather aret it to the negligence and rape of Adam Scriuener, *that I may speake as* Chaucer *doth, than to any vnconning or ouersight in the Author: For how fearfull he was to haue his works miswritten, or his verse mismeasured, may appeare in the end of his fift booke of* Troylus and Creseide, *where he writeth thus:*

And for there is so great diuersitie
In English, and in writing of our tongue,
So pray I God, that none miswrite thee,
Ne thee mismetre for defaut of tongue, &c.

Moreouer, whereas in the explanation of the old words, sundry of their significations by me giuen, may to some seeme coniectural: yet such as vnderstand the Dialects of our tongue, especially in the North, *and haue knowledge in some other languages, will iudge otherwise: and for the satisfying of others, which want such skill, I haue by these Caracters* a.g.l.i.f.d.b. *notified to them from what tong or Dialect such words are deriued.*

It were a labor worth commendation, if some scholler, that hath skil and leisure, would confer Chaucer *with those learned Authors, both in* Greek *and* Latin, *from whom he hath drawn many excellent things; and at large report such Hystories, as in his workes are very frequent, and many of them hard to be found: which would so grace this auncient Poet, that wheras diuers haue thought him vnlearned, and his writings meere trifles, it should appeare, that besides the knowledge of sundrie tongues, he was a man of great reading, & deep iudgement. This course I began in the former impression, but here of purpose haue left it off; as also the description of Persons and Places, except some few of more worthie note; as a labour rather for a Commentor, for that it concerneth matter, than for him, that intendeth only the explaning of words. And thus to conclude, I commit to your wonted fauor this our Poet, and what here is done, for the Poets sake.*

Graunt mercie lord,sith it thee doeth like
To license me,now I woll and dare boldly
Assaile my purpose,with scriptures autentike,
My werke woll I ground,vnderset,& fortesie,
Aspire my beginning,O thou wood furie,
Alecto,with thy sisters,and in especiall
To the mother of ielousie Iuno I call.

Explicit Prologus.

The Remedie of Loue.

This booke drawn for the most part out of the Prouerbes of Salomon,is a warning to take heed of
the deceitfull companie of women.

 His werke who so shall see or
rede,
Of any incongruitie doe mee
not impeche,
Ordinately behoueth me first
to procede
In deduction thereof,in manner as the leche
His patients sicknesse oweth first for to seeke,
The which known,medicin he should applie,
And shortly as he can,then shape a remedie.

Right so by counsaile,willing thee to exhort,
O yong man prosperous,which doth abound
In thy floures of lust belongeth on thee sort,
Me first to consider what is root and ground
Of thy mischeefe,which is plainly found,
Woman farced with fraud and deceit,
To thy confusion most allectiue bait.

Flie the miswoman,least she thee deceiue,
Thus saith Salomon,which taught was fully
The falshed of wome in his daies to conceiue,
The lips of a strumpet ben sweeter than hony,
Her throte he saith soupled with oile of flatery,
Howbeit,the end and effect of all
Bitterer is than any wormwood or gall.

Flie the miswoman,louing thy life,
Ware the straungers bland eloquence,
Straunge I call her that is not thy wife,
Of her beautie haue no concupiscence,
Her countenaunce pretending beneuolence,
Beware her signes,and eye so amiable,
Hold it for ferme,they ben deceiuable.

Lo an ensample what women be
In their signes and countenaunce shortly,
I woll shew thee how louers three
Loued one woman right entirely,
Ech of them knew others maladie,
Wherefore was all their daily labour,
Who coud approch next in her fauour.

At sundry seasons,as fortune requireth,
Seuerally they came to see her welfare,
But ones it happened,loue them so fireth,
To see their Lady,they all would not spare,
Of others comming none of them were ware,
Till all they mette,whereas they in place,
Of her Lady saw the desired face.

To supper set,full smally they eat,
Full sober and demure in countenaunce,
For there taried none of hem for any meat,
But on his Lady to giue attendaunce,
And in secret wise some signifiaunce
Of loue to haue,which pretending she,
Fetely executed thus her propertie.

In due season,as she alway espied
Euery thing to execute conueniently,
Her one louer first friendly she eied,
The second she offerd the cup courtesly,
The third she gaue token secretly,
Underneath the bord she trade on his foot,
Through his entrailes tikled the hart root.

By your leaue,might I here aske a question
Of you my maisters,that sewe loues trace,
To you likely belongeth the solution,
Which of these three stood now in grace,
Clerely to answere ye would aske long space,
The matter is doubtfull and opinable,
To acertaine you I woll my selfe enable.

Of the foresaied three my selfe was one,
No man can answere it better than I,
Hartely of vs beloued was there none,
But Wlattes packe we bare all by and by,
Which at last I my selfe gan aspie,
In time as me thought then I left the daunce,
O thoughtfull hart,great is thy greuaunce.

Hence fro me hence,that me for to endite,
Halpe aye here afore,O ye muses nine,
Whilom ye were wont to be mine aid & light,
My penne to direct,my braine to illumine,
No lenger alas may I sewe your doctrine,
The fresh lustie metres,that I wont to make
Haue been here afore,I vtterly forsake.

Come hither thou Hermes,& ye furies all,
Which fer ben vnder vs,nigh the nether pole,
Where

Where Pluto reigneth,O king infernall,
Send out thine arpies,send anguish and dole,
Miserie and wo,leaue ye me not sole,
Of right be present must paine & eke turment,
The pale death beseemeth not to be absent.

To me now I call all this lothsome sort,
My paines teincrease,my sorows to augment,
For worthie I am to be bare of all comfort,
Thus sith I haue consumed and mispent
Not onely my daies,but my fiue fold talent,
That my lord committed me,I cannot recompence,
I may not too derely abie my negligence.

By the path of penaunce yet woll I reuert
To the well of grace,mercy there to fetch,
Despisest not God the meeke contrite hart
Of the cock crow,alas y I would not retch,
And yet it is not late in the second wretch,
Mercy shall I purchase by incessaunt crying,
The mercies of our lord euer shall I sing.

But well maist thou waile wicked woman,
That thou shuldest deceiue thus any innocent,
And in recompence of my sinne,so as I can,
To all men wol I make & leue this monument,
In shewing part of thy falshed is mine entent,
For all were too much,I cannot well I wote,
The cause sheweth plainly he y thus wrote,

If all the yearth were parchment scribable,
Speedie for the hand,and all manner wood
Wer hewed and proportioned to pennes able,
All water inke,in damme or in flood,
Euery man being a parfit Scribe and good,
The cursednesse yet and deceit of women
Coud not be shewed by the meane of pen.

I lie all odious resemblaunces,
The deuils brond call women I might,
Whereby man is encensed to mischaunces,
Or a stinking rose that faire is in sight,
Or deadly empoyson,like the sugar white,
Which by his sweetnesse causeth man to tast,
And sodainly sleeth & bringeth him to his last.

It is not my manner to vse such language,
But this my doctrine,as I may lawfully,
I woll holly ground with authoritie sage,
Willing both wisedome,and vertue edifie,
Wine and women into apostasie,
Cause wisemen to fall,what is that to say,
Of wisedome cause them to forget the way.

Wherefore the wiseman doeth thee aduise,
In whose words can be found no leasing,
With the straunger to sit in no wise,
Which is not thy wife,fall not in clipping

With her,but beware eke of her killing,
Keepe with her in wine no altercation,
Least that thine hart fall by inclination.

May a man thinkest hide and safe lay
Fire in his bosome,without empairement,
And brenning of his clothes or whider he may
Walke on hote coles,his feet not brent?
As who saieth nay,and whereby is ment
This foresaied prouerbe and similitude,
But that thou ridde thee plainly to denude

From the flatterers forgetting her gide,
The gide of her youth,I meane shamefastnes,
Which should cause her maidenhead to abide,
Her gods behest eke she full recheles,
Not retching,committeth it to forgetfulnes,
Neither God ne shame in her hauing place,
Needs must such a woman lacke grace,

And all that neigh her in way of sinne
To tourne,of grace shall lacke the influence,
The pathes of life no more to come in,
Wherefore first friend thee with Sapience,
Remembring God,and after with Prudence,
To thine owne weale that they thee keepe,
Unto thine hart least her words creepe.

In his booke where I take my most ground,
And in his prouerbes,sage Salomon
Telleth a tale,which is plainly found
In the fifth chapiter,whider in deed don,
Or meekely fetned to our instruction,
Let clerkes determine,but this am I sure,
Much like thing I haue had in vre,

At my window (saieth he) I looked out,
Fair yong people,where I saw many,
Among hem all,as I looked about,
To a yong man fortuned I lent mine eye,
Estraunged from his mind it was likely,
By the street at a corner nigh his own hous,
He went about with eye right curious,

When that the day his light gan withdraw,
And the night approched in the twilight,
How a woman came and met him I saw,
Talking with him vnder shade of the night,
Now blessed be God (qd.she)of his might,
Which hath fulfilled mine hearts desire,
Islaked my paines,which were hote as fire,

And yet mine authour,as it is skill
To follow,I must tell her arrayment,
She was full nice,soules like to spill,
As nice in countenaunce yet as in garment,
For ianglyng she was of rest impatient,
Wandring still,in no place she stode,

Ggg.iii.　　　　　　But

Make wise men fallen in dotage,
Wherefore by counsaile of Philosophers sage,
In great honour learne this of me,
With thine estate haue humilite.

Balade de bon consail.

IF it befall that God thee list visite
With any tourment or aduersite,
Thanke first the lord, and thy selfe to quite,
Upon suffraunce and humilite
Found thou thy quarell, what euer that it be:
Make thy defence, & thou shalt haue no losse,
The remembrance of Christ and of his crosse.

Explicit.

Of the Cuckow and the Nightingale.

Chaucer dreameth that hee heareth the Cuckow
and the Nightingale contend for excellencie in
singing.

THE God of loue, and benedi=
cite,
How mightie and howe great
a lord is he,
For he can make of low herts
hie,
And of high low, and like for to die,
And hard harts he can maken free.

He can make within a little stound
Of sicke folke hole, fresh, and sound,
And of hole he can make seeke,
He can bind and vnbinden eke
That he woll haue bounden or vnbound.

To tell his might my wit may not suffice,
For he can make of wise folke full nice,
For he map do all that he woll deuice,
And lithy folke to distropen vice,
And proud herts he can make agrise.

Shortly all that euer he woll he may,
Against him dare no wight say nap,
For he can glad and greue whom him liketh,
And who that he woll, he lougheth or siketh,
And most his might he shedeth euer in May.

For euery true gentle heart free,
That with him is or thinketh for to be,
Againe May now shall haue some stering,
Or to ioy or els to some mourning,
In no season so much, as thinketh me,

For when they map here the birds sing,
And see the floures and the leaues spring,
That bringeth into her remembraunce
A manner ease, medled with greuaunce,
And lustie thoughts full of great longing.

And of that longing commeth heuinesse,
And thereof groweth oft great sicknesse,
And for lacke of that that they desire,
And thus in May ben harts set on fire,
So that they brennen forth in great distresse.

I speake this of feeling truly,
If I be old and vnlusty,
yet I haue felt of the sicknesse through May
Both hote and cold, and axes euery day,
How sore twis there wote no wight but I.

I am so shaken with the feuers white,
Of all this May sleepe I but a lite,
And also it is not like to me,
That any heart should sleepie be,
In whom that loue his fierie dart woll smite.

But as I lay this other night waking,
I thought how louers had a tokening,
And among hem it was a commune tale,
That it were good to here the Nightingale,
Rather than the leud Cuckow sing.

And then I thought anon as it was day,
I would go some where to assay
If that I might a Nightingale here,
For yet had I none heard of all that yere,
And it was tho the third night of May.

And anone as I the day aspide,
No lenger would I in my bed abide,
But vnto a wood that was fast by,
I went forth alone boldely,
And held the way downe by a brooke side.

Till I came to a laund of white and greene,
So faire one had I neuer in been,
The ground was green, ypoudred with daisie
The floures and the greues like hie,
All greene and white, was nothing els seene.

There sate I downe among the faire floures,
And saw the birds trip out of her boures,
There as they rested hem all the night,
They were so topfull of the dayes light,
They began of May for to done houres.

They coud that seruice all by rote,
There was many a louely note,
Some song loud as they had plained,
And some in other manner voice pfained,

And

And some all out with the full throte.

They proyned hem, & made hem right gay,
And daunceden and lepten on the spray,
And euermore two and two in fere,
Right so as they had chosen hem to yere
In Feuerere vpon saint Ualentines day.

And the riuer that I sate vpon,
It made such a noise as it ron,
Accordaunt with the birds armony,
Me thought it was the best melody
That might ben yheard of any mon.

And for delite, I wote neuer how,
I fell in such a slomber and a swow,
Nat all asleepe,ne fully waking,
And in that swow me thought I heard sing
The sorie bird the leaud cuckow.

And that was on a tree right fast by,
But who was then euill apaid but I:
Now God(qd.I)that died on the crois,
Eue sorrow on thee,and on thy leaud vois,
Full little ioy haue I now of thy crie.

And as I with the cuckow thus gan chide,
I heard in the next bush beside,
A nightingale so lustely sing,
That with her clere voice she made ring
Through all the greene wood wide.

Ah,good nightingale(qd.I then)
I little hast thou ben too long hen,
For here hath ben the leaud cuckow,
And songen songs rather than hast thou,
I pray to God euill fire her bren.

But now I woll you tell a wonder thing,
As long as I lay in that swouning,
Me thought I wist what the birds ment,
And what they said,& what was her entent,
And of her speech I had good knowing.

There heard I the nightingale say,
Now good cuckow go somewhere away,
And let vs that can singen dwellen here,
For euery wight escheueth thee to here,
Thy songs be so elenge in good fay.

What(qd.she)what may thee aylen now,
It thinketh me, I sing as well as thou,
For my song is both true and plaine,
And though I cannot crakell so in vaine,
As thou dost in thy throte,I wot neuer how.

And euery wight may vnderstand me,
But nightingale so may they not done thee,

For thou hast many a nice queint cry,
I haue thee heard saine,ocy,ocy,
How might I know what that should be?

Ah foole(qd.she)wost thou not what it is,
When that I say,ocy,ocy,ywis,
Then meane I that I would wonder faine,
That all they were shamefully yslaine,
That meanen ought againe loue amis.

And also I would that all tho were dede,
That thinke not in loue her life to lede,
For who so y wol not the God of loue serue,
I dare well say he is worthy to sterue,
And for that skill,ocy,ocy,I grede.

Eye(qd.the cuckow)this is a queint law,
That euery wight shall loue or be to draw,
But I forsake all such companie,
For mine entent is not for to die,
Ne neuer while I liue on loues yoke to draw.

For louers ben the folke that ben on liue,
That most disease haue,and most vnthriue,
And most endure sorrow,wo,and care,
And least feelen of welfare,
What needeth it ayenst trouth to striue.

What(qd.she)thou art out of thy mind,
How might thou in thy churlenesse find
To speake of loues seruaunts in this wise,
For in this world is none so good seruise
To euery wight that gentle is of kind.

For thereof truly commeth all goodnesse,
All honour,and all gentlenesse,
Worship,ease,and all hearts lust,
Parfite ioy,and full assured trust,
Iolitie,pleasaunce,and freshnesse,

Lowlyhead,largesse,and curtesie,
Semelyhead,and true companie,
Drede of shame for to done amis:
For he that truly loues seruaunt is,
Were lother be shamed than to die.

And that this is sooth that I sey,
In that beleeue I will liue and dey,
And cuckow so I rede that thou do ywis:
Then(qd.he)let me neuer haue blisse,
If euer I vnto that counsaile obey.

Nightingale thou speakest wonder faire,
But for all that is the sooth contraire,
For loue is in yong folke butrage,
And in old folke a great dotage,
Who most it vseth,most shall enpaire,

¶ For thereof commeth disease and heuinesse,
So sorow & care, and many a great sicknesse,
Despite, debate, anger, and enuie,
Depraving, shame, vntrust, and ielousie,
Pride, mischeese, pouertie, and woodnesse.

¶ Louing is an office of despaire,
And one thing is therein that is not faire,
For who that getteth of loue a little blisse,
But if he be alway therewith iwis,
He may full soone of age haue his haire.

And Nightingale therefore hold thee nie,
For leue me well, for all thy queint crie,
If thou be ferre or long fro thy make,
Thou shalt be as other that been forsake,
And then thou shalt hoten as doe I.

Fie (qd. she) on thy name and on thee,
The god of Loue ne let thee neuer ithee,
For thou art worse a thousandfold thã wood,
For many one is full worthy and full good,
That had be naught ne had loue thee.

For euermore loue his seruants amendeth,
And from all euill taches hem defendeth,
And maketh hem to brenne right in a fire,
In trouth and in worshipfull desire,
And whe him liketh, ioy inough hem sendeth.

Thou Nightingale he saied, be still,
For loue hath no reason, but it is will,
For oft tune vntrue folke he caseth,
And true folke so bitterly he displeaseth,
That for defaut of courage he let hem spill.

Then tooke I of the Nightingale keepe,
How she cast a sigh out of her deepe,
And saied, alas that euer I was bore,
I can for tene not say one word more,
And right with y word she brast out to weepe.

Alas (qd. she) my hart woll to breake,
To heare thus this leaud bird speake
Of loue, and of his worshipfull seruise,
Now God of loue thou helpe me in some wise,
That I may on this Cuckow been awreake.

We thought then he stert vp anone,
And glad was I that he was agone,
And euermore the Cuckow as he flay,
Saied farewell, farewell Popingay,
As though he had scorned me alone.

And then came the Nightingale to mee,
And saied friend forsooth I thanke thee,
That thou hast liked me to rescow,
And one auow to loue make I now,

That all this May I woll thy singer be.

I thanked her, and was right well apaied:
Ye (qd. she) and be thou not dismayed,
Tho thou haue herd the Cuckow erst thã me,
For if I liue, it shall amended be
The next May, if I be not affraied.

And one thing I woll rede thee also,
Ne leue thou not the Cuckow, ne his loues so,
For all that he hath saied is strong leasing:
Nay (qd. I) thereto shall nothing me bring,
For loue and it hath doe me much wo.

Ye, vse (qd. she) this medicine
Euery day this May or thou dine,
Go looke vpon the fresh Daisie,
And though thou be for wo in point to die,
That shall full greatly lessen thee of thy pine.

And looke alway that thou be good and trew,
And I woll sing one of the songs new
For loue of thee, as loud as I may crie:
And then she began this song full hie,
I shrew all hem that been of loue vntrue.

And when she had song it to the end,
Now farewell (qd. she) for I mote wend,
And god of loue, that can right well, and may,
As much ioy send thee this day,
As any yet louer he euer send,

Thus taketh ÿ Nightingale her leaue of me,
I pray to God alway with her be,
And ioy of loue he send her euermore,
And shilde vs fro the Cuckow and his lore,
For there is not so false a bird as he.

Forth she flew the gentle Nightingale
To all the birds that were in that dale,
And gate hem all into a place in fere,
And besoughten hem that they would here
Her disease, and thus began her tale.

The Cuckow, well it is not for to hide
How the Cuckow and I fast haue chide,
Euer sithen it was day light,
I pray you all that ye doe me right
On that foule false vnkind bridde.

Then spake o bird for all, by one assent,
This matter asketh good auisement,
For we been birdes here in fere,
And sooth it is, the Cuckow is not here,
And therefore we woll haue a parliment.

And thereat shall the Egle be, our Lord,
And other peres that been of record,

And

And the Cuckow shall be after sent,
There shall be yeue the iudgement,
Oz els we shall finally make accozd.

And this shall be without nay
The mozrow after saint Valentines day,
Under a Maple that is faire and grene,
Befoze the chamber window of the quene,
It woodstocke vpon the grene lay.

She thanked hem, and then her leaue toke
And into an Hauthozne by that bzoke,
And there she sate and song vpon that tree,
Terme of life loue hath withhold me,
So loud that I with that song awoke.

Explicit.

Lend book with thy foule
rudenesse,
Sith thou haste neyther
beautie ne eloquence,
Who hath thee caused oz
yeue thee hardinesse,
Foz to appeare in my La-
dies pzesence,
I am full siker thou knowest her beneuolence,
Full agreeable to all her abying,
Foz of all good she is the best liuing.

Alas that thou ne haddest wozthinesse,
To shew to her some pleasaunt sentence,
Sith that she hath thzough her gentillesse
Accepted the seruaunt to her digne reuerence,
O, me repenteth that I ne had science
And letter als, to make thee moze flourishing,
Foz of all good she is the best liuing.

Beseech her meekely with all lowlinesse,
Though I be ferre from her in absence,
To thinke on my trouth to her a stedfastnesse,
And to abzidge of my sozrowes the violence,
which caused is, whereof knoweth your sapi-
She like emong to notific me her liking (ence,
Foz of all good she is the best liuing.

Lenuoye.

Uroze of gladnesse, and day of Lusti-
nesse,
Lucerne a night with heauenly influ-
ence
Illumined, root of beautie and goodnesse,
Suspires which I estunde in silence,
Of grace I beseech alledge let your wziting,
Now of all good, sith ye be best liuing.

Explicit.

In the written copies the title hereof is thus: Here
followeth a morall ballade to the Prince, the
Duke of Clarence, the Duke of Bedford, the
Duke of Glocester, the kings sonnes, by Henry
Scogan, at a supper among the Marchants in
the Vintry at London, in the house of Lewis
Iohn.

Y noble sonnes and eke my
lozds dere,
I your father called vnwooz-
thely,
Send vnto you this litle trea-
tise here,
Wzitten with mine owne hand full rudely,
Although it be that I not reuerently
Haue wzitten to your estates. I you pzay
Mine vnconning taketh benignely
Foz Gods sake, and herken what I say.

I complain me soze when I remember me
The suddaine age that is vpon me fall,
But moze I complain my mispent inuentute,
The which is impossible ayen foz to call,
But certainly the most complaint of all,
Is to thinke, that I haue be so nice,
That I ne would vertues to me call
In all my youth, but vices aye cherice.

Of which I aske mercy of the Lozd,
That art almightie God in maiestie,
Beseking to make so euen accozd
Betwirt thee and my soule, that vanitie,
Wozldly lust, ne blind pzosperitie,
Haue no lozdship ouer my flesh so frele,
Thou Lozd of rest and parfite vnitie,
Put fro me vice, and kepe my soule hele.

And yeue me might while I haue life a space,
Me to confirme fully to thy pleasaunce,
Shew to me the abundaunce of thy grace,
And in good werks graunt me perseueraunce,
Of all my youth forget the ignozaunce,
Yeue me good will to serue thee aye to queme,
Set all my life after thine ozdinaunce,
And able me to mercy oz thou deme.

My lozds dere, why I this complaint wzite
To you, whom I loue most entirely,
Is foz to warne you as I can endite,
That time lost in youth folily,
Greueth a wight bodily and ghostly.

Fii, ii.   I

5

More's *Richard III* and Jonson's *Richard Crookback* and *Sejanus*

One of the most tantalizing of all the surviving data about Jonson's life is Philip Henslowe's record that in June 1602 he paid the playwright not only for additions to Kyd's *Spanish Tragedy* but also "in earnest of a Boocke called Richard crockbacke." The sum listed—£10—was substantial, suggesting either that the additions were extensive or that Jonson's play on King Richard III was nearly complete.[1] Yet no other unambiguous record of the play survives, and most catalogues list it simply as "lost." However, the possibility that the play was not lost but was deliberately suppressed, as Jonson seems to have suppressed other early works, has also been raised. Various explanations have been offered for why Jonson may have chosen not to publish this play. Perhaps he rejected it as not wholly his; after all, *Sejanus* survives only in a rewritten version designed to eliminate the work of an anonymous collaborator. Or perhaps Jonson, dissatisfied with the work, withdrew it from posterity's judgment. Despite his early reputation as a competent writer of tragedies and despite surviving records of his other works in this genre, *Sejanus* and *Catiline* are the only two tragedies he chose to print. Still another possibility is that he felt his work could not rival its most obvious competitor, Shakespeare's *King Richard III*. If *Sejanus* was written partly in response to *Julius Caesar*, perhaps *Richard Crookback* was meant to reply to *Richard III*, and perhaps Jonson was disappointed in his own performance.[2] It would be fascinating to know how he would have handled a subject so effectively handled by Shakespeare; it would be intriguing to see how he might have responded not only to Shakespeare but to one of the most enigmatic and compelling figures in English political history; and it would be interesting to know how he might have dealt with the themes and problems raised by Richard's reign.

As it happens, newly discovered evidence—the playwright's marked copy of the Latin version of Sir Thomas More's *History of King Richard III*—allows us to speculate with much more assurance about the possible nature of Jonson's play and his response to Richard. The marked book suggests not only the shape the play may have taken but also the kinds of political issues and concerns that Richard's life may have raised for Jonson. Jonson's markings imply that he saw More's *Historia* not only as a source of useful information and dramatic techniques, but also as a valuable warning about the dangers of tyranny and of unbridled ambition and selfishness. Moreover, the markings suggest much about the kinds of historians—and historiographical principles—that Jonson found important. In short, the newly discovered book implies a great deal, not simply about one of Jonson's most important "lost" works, but also about the political and historical concerns that seem to have motivated his early thinking. As an immediate predecessor to *Sejanus* and as a play with clear political implications, *Richard Crookback* would be a valuable work to possess. Lacking that, we at least now have what is arguably the next best thing—probably the major source of Jonson's missing drama, complete with his own marginal markings.

Jonson's 1566 Louvain edition of More's Latin works is presently housed at the Library at Canterbury Cathedral.[3] Its existence seems to have been unknown to all previous cataloguers of Jonson's books, and in fact it seems to have been discovered only recently, during preparation of an extensive new computerized listing of the Cathedral's holdings. Everything points to the legitimacy of the book's Jonsonian markings. Not only does the title page bear Jonson's usual motto and signature in their typical places and handwriting, but that page also bears a note in Jonson's hand presenting the book to William Dakins ("Amicissimo, et eruditissimo / viro Guil. Dakinsio. / Ben. Jonson / D. D. D."). Jonson's friendship with Dakins has not been previously noted, and so the book provides some further information about the poet's early biography. Like Jonson, Dakins was educated at Westminster school—a fact that may have led to their apparently close friendship. Yet whereas Jonson's schooling stopped after Westminster, Dakins went on to Cambridge, receiving various degrees before being elected Greek lecturer at Trinity College in 1602, the year Jonson was at work on his play. In 1603 Dakins became a vicar in Cambridgeshire, and in 1604 he was chosen a professor of divinity at Gresham College in London (with which Jonson himself was later affiliated). He was recommended to Gresham not only by various academics and nobles but also by King James, and he was also chosen to help prepare the authorized translation of the Bible. In 1606 he became junior dean at Trinity, but he died in February 1606–7.[4]

From these facts about Dakins, certain inferences can be drawn about Jonson. First, the poet obviously must have owned and read his copy of More no later than early 1607, when Dakins died; this increases the likelihood that he used it for his play. Indeed, another note on the title page, in Dakins' hand, shows that Dakins himself presented the book to still another friend, Johann [or John] Blumfeild ("Joanni Blumfeild doctiss°, amiciss° / dono dedi amoris causa hunc libru<m>"). Perhaps Jonson presented the book to Dakins sometime in or after 1602, after his work on *Richard Crookback* was substantially complete, and perhaps Dakins then later presented it to Blumfeild. Secondly, Jonson's connection with the learned and increasingly influential Dakins suggests something about his own intellectual aspirations and the kinds of circles in which he was moving at this time. Thirdly, Jonson's friendship with the presumably Protestant Dakins shows that the poet's Catholicism did not prevent links with (or acceptance by) significant members of the established Church.[5]

To turn from the title page to the book itself is initially disappointing, for More's *Utopia* is nearly unmarked. Some peculiar marginal lines occur next to one small passage, but it is not clear whether these were made by a reader, and even if they were, they are not distinctively Jonsonian.[6] There is another tantalizingly brief mark, but whether this is Jonson's is again uncertain.[7] Otherwise, More's greatest prose work is left untouched. The heavy concentration of Jonson's obvious markings in the *Historia* suggests, once again, that his main interest at the time was in More's views of Richard's reign. Jonson, like Shakespeare, seems to have used More's account as one of the chief sources for his play about the allegedly tyrannical king.

Other marks that precede those in the *Historia* seem more likely to be Jonson's. For instance, More's panegyric on Henry VIII's coronation is fairly heavily marked in pencil (D ij^v.2—D iij^v.1), and these markings strongly resemble marks (also in pencil) more certainly made by Jonson in the margins of the *Historia*. Jonson himself would one day write a coronation panegyric that may have been influenced by More's poem (H&S 7:111–17; see next chapter). Yet the markings in More's coronation poem assume an additional interest when studied alongside the markings in the *Historia;* the poem celebrates a good king who comes to power with acclamations of his people's love, determined to rectify injustices, whereas the *Historia* details the rise of an ambitious tyrant who exploits his people and rules without their consent. Whether Jonson read the two works at roughly the same time is unknown. Certainly, however, his markings in the panegyric reflect his enduring interest in such issues as right rule, proper kingship, and sound ethical values. This last topic also seems to have prompted the marking of two of More's brief Latin epigrams, although in these instances the marks are much less assuredly Jonson's. One of the poems, "De luxu immodico" (D jᵛ), emphasizes the self-defeating nature of extravagance; the other, "De luxu & libidine" (D jᵛ), warns about the consequences of self-indulgence. Both poems are marked in brown ink, with short, slanted marginal lines. In neither case is the marking distinctively Jonson's.

Fortunately, the numerous marginal pencil marks in the *Historia* are almost certainly his. They exhibit many typical characteristics, and anyone who has looked at many of his marked books will immediately recognize the markings here. One has only to compare the flowers and hands in More's *Historia* with those in a dozen other books once owned by Jonson to realize that they were all drawn by the same hand. In addition, various markings in the *Historia* that are less easy to describe also seem reminiscent of marks found in his other books. Unfortunately, no words have been written, but Jonson used words less commonly than the kinds of markings already mentioned. The absence of words is thus no reason to doubt that these marginalia were genuinely made by the poet.

However, before describing Jonson's markings in the *Historia*, it seems worth asking why he may have turned to it. What might have made More's work seem valuable to Jonson? What themes, techniques, issues, sources, values, historiographical principles, and other features of the work would have prompted the intense interest displayed by Jonson's markings? Aside from its simple value as a repository of information, what other aspects of More's *Historia* is Jonson likely to have appreciated?

For one thing, he may have valued it as an important model of how history could and should be written. Although some today are reluctant to call More's book a history in the modern sense, most Renaissance Englishmen regarded it as a fine example of historical writing. It fulfilled many aspirations of Renaissance humanist historiography, which was less concerned with accumulating data than with teaching moral lessons. The moralistic emphasis in Jonson's own history plays has recently been

stressed,[8] and More's similar concern to promote virtue and repre-
hend vice surely helped encourage Jonson's interest. More's study
has been called "the first true work of Renaissance historiography
done by an Englishman,"[9] and More himself has been termed
England's earliest native humanist historian of note.[10] Surely Jonson, well connected with other prominent historians (his teacher
had been William Camden), would have appreciated More's book
as an important precedent, as an internationally respected model
of historiography. More was the sort of intellectual Jonson aspired
to be: well read, well regarded, eloquent, responsible, and concerned above all to promote civic virtue. The various factors that
help make More's work a recognizable humanist history—its focus on human motives and causes, the strict limitation of its subject matter, its rhetorical eloquence, its close attention to political
events, its emphasis on long invented speeches, and its concern
with an important recent chapter of specifically national history
(Harris 43, 48, 96, 105, 109)—could all have been expected to
appeal to Jonson's own humanist instincts, especially his deep
respect for classical precedent and his deep interest in appropri-
ating classical models and sources.

Indeed, Jonson probably recognized how indebted More's work
was to many of the very same Roman historians the playwright
himself admired. Reading More, in fact, may have helped stoke
his interest in those historians and may thus have helped suggest
the topic of his next work, *Sejanus*, his first play set in Rome and
the first of his two surviving tragedies. Just as *Sejanus* is obviously
indebted to the great historians of the Roman empire, especially
Tacitus, so is More's *Historia*, although until recently the nature of
More's debt was more easily intuited than demonstrated. Whereas
Jonson in *Sejanus* carefully documented his many borrowings
from Tacitus and other Roman writers, it was not until publication
of Richard Sylvester's commentary in the Yale edition that the
extent of More's similar debt was equally clear. Sylvester shows
that More borrowed eclectically from a number of the same writers that Jonson also admired, including Sallust, Livy, Suetonius,
and especially Tacitus.[11] The "highly assimilative" method that
Sylvester attributes to More (lxxxiv) was also Jonson's, and perhaps the poet viewed More's work as a model of how much could
be done (and how well) through creative imitation.[12]

More seems to have known Sallust (Jonson's major source for
Catiline) "almost by heart" (lxxxvii), but his debt to Tacitus—the
chief source of *Sejanus*—is more immediately interesting. According to Sylvester, More may have helped introduce the study

of Tacitus into England (xci), a circumstance that would further help to explain Jonson's regard for More and his interest in the *Historia*. Tacitus provided More not only with descriptions of personalities and events that paralleled the facts of Richard's life, but even more importantly with a structure by which those data could be organized and emphasized (Sylvester xcii). More's debts to Tacitus included the major contrast between an old ruler and his less scrupulous successor; quick introductions of the cast of relevant characters; the description of those characters' groupings; a strongly psychological portrait of the central figure; an emphasis on the theme and techniques of dissimulation; and the murderously unnatural nature of a villainous ruler (xciii–xcv). In addition, from Tacitus More seems largely to have borrowed what Sylvester calls the "common atmosphere which broods over both narratives," with their similar uncertainties, sudden deaths, deceptions, and stress on "omens, prognostications, and sorcery" (xcv–xcvi). If these characteristics resemble those of Jonson's *Sejanus*, the immediate successor to *Richard Crookback*, the resemblance may spring as much from his recent reading of More as from his personal study of Tacitus.

Yet despite More's heavy reliance on Tacitus and other historians, many recent writers resist viewing his own work as chiefly or simply a work of history. Other genres, particularly literary ones, have been suggested as more appropriate contexts for understanding More's achievement and purposes. Judith P. Jones, surveying several possible generic contexts, including the genre of biography, ends by suggesting that "it may be most accurate to call [the work] our first historical novel."[13] Alison Hanham not only calls attention to its dramatic aspects but also argues that More "allowed his satiric instincts full play," so that "in some important respects it forms a Lucianic, and so irreverent, comment on the whole craft of history." More, she suggests, did not take the *Historia* as seriously as some readers; in fact, "it is more profitable to regard it as literature than as a work of scholarship embodying the results of historical research. The authenticity of More's material was of minor importance to him."[14] Meanwhile, Leonard F. Dean sees More's *Historia* as "an intermediate stage" in "the movement from allegory to realism" and stresses the crucial importance of More's irony. "The ironical method is the one which chiefly distinguishes *Richard III*," and, thanks to its use, More's "characters seem to condemn themselves, and we seem to form our own judgment of them."[15] More recently, Elizabeth S. Donno, in an extremely valuable article that surveys most of the important issues relating to More's work, argues that More "was composing a historical narrative in the epideictic vein—a display piece with the object either of praise or blame, designed primarily to delight by means of its ingenuity and artifice, though Roman usage gave it a more pragmatic basis." More precisely, she sees the work "as an example of a *vituperatio*" and lists many relevant similarities.[16]

Thus, although most recent commentators acknowledge the historical basis of More's account, few seem willing to view the *Historia* as simply a work of history, even in the broader sense current in the Renaissance. Yet however one decides to describe the *Historia* generically, the comments of More's modern critics are very helpful in calling attention to various aspects of his work that would probably have made the book additionally appealing to Jonson. The satire, irony, and vituperation just mentioned as characteristics of More's work were, of course, also characteristic of Jonson's; in the years preceding his work on *Richard Crookback* he had been writing his "comical satyres" and composing plays and poems full of satire and invective. *Sejanus* itself would soon display satire, irony, and vituperation in abundance, while some of Jonson's most recent works—particularly *Cynthia's Revels*—had also demonstrated an intriguing mixture of the allegorical and the realistic. This tendency to write dramas combining both impulses typifies much of his best work (especially *Volpone*). Of course, Jonson's reading of More was certainly not responsible for these characteristics of his own writing, but when Jonson read the *Historia*, he must have recognized a style, techniques, and a temperament he probably found congenial. All the distinctive generic nuances of More's work may have made it an even more useful and suggestive source for a tragical-ironical-satirical-vituperative-allegorical-realistic drama by Jonson—precisely the sort of thing that *Sejanus* shows he could write.

However, of all the subsidiary generic qualities detected in More's *Historia*, the most important by far—and the most obviously useful to Jonson—is drama itself. Hardly a single commentator can resist describing the work as "dramatic," often in the fullest sense.[17] Various features make the *Historia* a natural source for a playwright. These include its precise focus on a limited subject and central figure, thus giving it compactness, coherence, and unity (Harris 146); its use of debate to enhance dramatic conflict (Harris 154); its "utterly natural" use of dialogue (Harris 169); the "objectivity" of its presentation—its emphasis on showing rather than telling, so that usually it simply presents behavior for our judgment, rather than making overt judgments of its own

(Harris 164); its emphasis not only on speeches but on speeches suited to particular characters and situations (Kincaid 376); its emphasis on visual details (Harris 163) and on physical description of characters (Kincaid 376); its use of dialogue and orations to develop character and present ideas (Kincaid 381); its presentation of multiple audiences (Kincaid 380) and of self-consciously theatrical scenes within the main narrative (similar to plays within plays), so that we cannot help noticing the histrionic nature of much of the action; and, as Arthur Kincaid has noted, the presentation of Richard himself as a kind of actor—a presentation that makes even his inconsistencies reflect a consistent character (378). Although many have noted the numerous resemblances between Richard and the stage Vice (Harris 156–58), Kincaid valuably emphasizes Richard's transcendence of any particular stereotype, the ways his character is both coherent and complex (378). More's relentless focus on this character was his major contribution to Richard's legend (Harris 122), and it is easy to see why and how a dramatist might have found his presentation suggestive. Kincaid stresses that More was at his best when recording action or writing dialogue (376), and several critics have argued that the *Historia* is the most powerful example of dramatic writing in England before the rise of the great Elizabethan playwrights. Little wonder, then, that Jonson turned to More when he decided to write *Richard Crookback*.[18]

What might seem at first surprising is that he turned to the Latin version of More's work rather than to the more widely known and more frequently reprinted English text—the one on which Shakespeare seems to have relied. Possibly Jonson read both versions; we know that he read the English text at some point, because he cites it frequently in his *English Grammar* (H&S 8:531–53). However, the unfinished *Grammar* is almost certainly a project of his final years and thus far distant from his work on *Richard Crookback* (H&S 11:165). In any case, there were any number of reasons why he may have chosen the Latin text, perhaps including the possibility of displaying his sophisticated learning (one recalls, for instance, his much later reference to Shakespeare's own "small *Latine*" [H&S 8:391]). Neither text was a simple "translation" of the other; their relations are extremely complicated, and More seems to have worked on both versions simultaneously, giving each a certain distinctness that makes the *History* a work different in scope and detail from the *Historia* (Sylvester l-lix). The Latin version is more coherent and complete than the unfinished English text (Harris 17), and for these reasons it also seems more thematically integrated. In fact, Hanham has argued that events in the Latin text fall into a "five act" structure (174–86, esp. 185–86), so that the Latin version might seem to lend itself more readily to dramatic treatment. Because it ends with Richard's accession, the Latin version gives greater emphasis to the usurper's rise and character than to the results of his tyranny, elaborating more fully on his evil (Harris 18). The Latin version not only stresses the fearfulness of tyrants (Harris 18), but is also more full of classical allusions and conforms more closely to the patterns of classical historiography (Harris 24). To Jonson, who would soon attempt to "english" an episode of Roman history, both of these aspects of the *Historia* may have seemed appealing. Moreover, the Latin version places less stress on providential explanations, highlighting instead the all-too-human motives behind political events (Harris 62). And the Latin version also expects readers to draw more of their own inferences and to notice more ironies for themselves (Harris 25). It might thus seem a more sophisticated, subtle, and demanding text, and these factors, combined with the others just listed and with the fact that this was the version More composed for a learned, international audience, all suggest why the *Historia* may have had greater appeal to Jonson (as a classicist and intellectual) than did the simpler, less finished *History*.

Having now surveyed the various reasons why More's account of Richard might have interested Jonson, we are in a better position to notice what, precisely, did interest him. Examining his marks will also allow us to speculate (with at least some confidence) about why he marked what he did. Certainly he seems to have shown quite an enthusiasm for marking this text. Of the roughly 3000 total lines of print (124 lines on most of the double-columned pages), more than half (about 1600) are marked with pencilled vertical lines, with Jonson's distinctive flowers, with his pointing hands, and with other marks whose shapes are less easily described. At one point (from I to I^v) the markings shift in color from the grey of a normal pencil to a reddish-brown hue, but, since this shift coincides with no obviously similar alteration in the narrative, it seems to lack special significance.

The sheer profusion of Jonson's marks makes it difficult to say for sure why he marked what he did; in some ways his marks would be easier to interpret if they were fewer in number. In addition, his markings are sometimes particularly ambiguous; it is often difficult to say, for instance, to what, precisely, the pointing hands point and thus what significance they may have.

Nonetheless, while keeping these difficulties and uncertainties in mind, it still seems possible to describe the marks so as to get some sense of what Jonson's experience of reading More may have been like and to speculate with some assurance about some of his reasons for reading. The nature of his markings hardly seems surprising in view of his interests as a dramatist and as a man concerned with promoting political and civic virtue.

Characterizing or describing Jonson's marks is not an easy task, since such a description could be organized in various ways. Merely moving through the text, passage by passage, would involve long plot summaries and inevitable repetition, since the same points can be made about a variety of individual passages. Yet it seems unwise merely to pick interesting passages out from the details in which they are embedded, discussing them out of context. The most sensible procedure may be first to characterize Jonson's markings in general terms, then to discuss an extended passage at length (thus illustrating the nature of his markings more precisely), and then to cite a few other particularly noteworthy instances. Finally, an appendix can provide a more comprehensive listing of the annotations not otherwise discussed.[19]

Jonson's markings can be divided into two large categories— those concerned with themes (or "matter") and those concerned with techniques or style ("manner"). Of course, in the *Historia* itself, these categories are thoroughly blended, but it seems useful and convenient to distinguish them here for purely analytical purposes.

Many passages marked by Jonson would have recommended themselves to a dramatist interested in dramatic techniques and in literary style, and many of these same passages would have lent themselves easily to dramatic treatment. For instance, a great number of the passages serve to introduce new characters or to characterize figures already introduced. Many of the markings seem to focus on memorable actions, gestures, or other potential "stage business," and in reading the *Historia*, Jonson seems to have kept an eye open for descriptions of memorably dramatic moments (especially confrontations or arguments), for memorable phrasing, and for strikingly vivid or effective imagery. His markings often seem to call attention to phrasing that is particularly pithy and concise and to moments when an action or a character's arguments are effectively summarized or epitomized. In fact, many of his marks seem to focus on extended arguments that not only develop the book's themes but also help to characterize the speakers involved. Many marks, like much of the *Historia* itself, are given over to quotations or to less direct reports of speech, while others (particularly some of the pointing hands) seem to indicate the beginnings and conclusions of speeches. This must have been especially useful since More's text as printed lacks any quotation marks or indications of paragraph breaks. Some of the marks highlight reactions, while others focus on moments of reasoning or reflection—moments particularly valuable to a dramatist interested in delineating character. Indeed, many of the marks seem to focus on motives, but perhaps the most frequent kind of marking (as one might have expected) deals with noting simple plot developments. Jonson clearly seems to have been interested (for obvious reasons) in keeping a firm grasp on "what happened next." Many marks focus on moments of humor, while others highlight striking examples of clever irony. In fact, Jonson's interest in irony seems to have involved both verbal and behavioral examples. Somewhat surprisingly, he marks relatively few instances of moralization, of explicit ethical assessments of characters and events. Some such passages *are* marked, but there are fewer such markings (and indeed fewer such passages) than one might have expected. All in all, the nature of the markings just described suggests that Jonson was at least as interested in the style and techniques of More's work as in its substance or themes.

In addition to these more important or more frequent indicators of Jonson's interest in More's techniques or style, various other examples of such interest seem suggested by his markings. Thus, some of the marked passages seem to focus on More's use of various rhetorical devices or his engagement in clever wordplay, while other markings seem to highlight significant narrative turning points; moments of shifting emphasis; changes in tone, atmosphere, or mood; moments of decision; conclusions of characters' speeches; poignant or touching details; particular historical events, circumstances, and explanations; and moments of behavioral or motivational complexity. Various such markings suggest that Jonson was concerned with the manner as well as the matter of More's historical writing.

Of course, distinguishing between style and substance is always artificial, and there seems little doubt that many markings were designed to call attention to important ideas or issues that help lend the *Historia* much of its intellectual interest and coherence. These include (but are hardly limited to) such themes as deceit, hypocrisy, selfishness, factionalism, the nature of women and relations between the sexes, tyranny, excessive taxation, the supernatural, abuses of the law, abuses of language in general (and flattery in particular), liberty, love, marriage, luxury, merit versus birth, appearance versus reality, patriotism, the importance of concord, and the nature of playacting. In addition, Jonson's markings strongly suggest (just as More's book strongly emphasizes) an interest in the heated issue of the rights to sanctuary. Moreover, More sometimes pauses to assert (and Jonson sometimes pauses to mark) political, psychological, or historical generalizations—truisms that seem to apply as much to his readers and their times as to the characters and events he describes. Singling out such themes as those just mentioned may involve, no doubt, neglecting others, but the themes mentioned are among the ones that most obviously help to give the *Historia* its unity and seriousness of purpose. Although it is impossible to tell from Jonson's markings precisely what may have been going on in his mind as he read, his marks do reveal just *what* he read and what he found literally noteworthy.

More's *Historia* opens with the death of Richard's predecessor, King Edward IV, briefly describing each of his surviving children. Jonson's only reaction is to draw a characteristic flower next to the brief reference to Prince Edward, the heir apparent and Richard's rival. The reference not only introduces a significant character but also reports his age (thirteen years). Jonson may have been interested in this both as an historical fact and as a fact important for presenting an accurate image of Edward on stage. In any case, no more marks occur until the very top of the next column, which has a long line drawn down its length and halfway down the next ("Henrici / set Quippe"; H ij^v.2-H iij.1). This passage, dealing with King Edward's character and with the nature of his reign, stresses his virtues while not neglecting his defects and emphasizes the stability and concord that existed during his rule. Perhaps the passage's balanced tone and implied political ideals appealed to Jonson. Certainly, as many commentators have noted, the passage serves as an extremely effective and ironic preparation for the description of Richard and his activities; Richard's personal and political defects are highlighted by this opening account of the stability he helped destroy.

Several details seem particularly to have caught Jonson's attention. Thus, he draws an odd symbol (shaped like a "p") next to praise of King Edward's boldness ("lau- / erat"; H ij^v.2). Later, in his first marking of a political generalization, he draws a flower next to the claim that Edward had ceased exacting money from his people, which is almost the only thing that alienates the minds of the English from a prince ("exigen- / molie"; H ij^v.2). The mark anticipates a later passage in Jonson's *Discoveries* that similarly warns princes against excessive taxation (H&S 8:602). Next, another flower marks another generalization, this time the claim that long rule often makes princes turn to pride ("gressio / multis"; H iij.1). It hardly seems surprising that Jonson, with his keen interest in varieties of egotism and his deep sense of the dangers of tyranny, would highlight this remark. Shortly thereafter, two brief diagonal lines (next to "natoribus"; H iij.1) call attention to Edward's generosity in inviting some city officials to hunt with him—a detail interesting not only as an historical anecdote but as an illustration of Edward's character and of the nature of his successful rule. This latter possibility is suggested by Jonson's next marking—another flower signalling another psychological and political generalization, namely that the people often value a small courtesy as a greater sign of a prince's love than they do a large favor ("quem res / ris"; H iij.1). Small wonder that Jonson, with his acute interest in the etiquette of benefits and in generosity as a token of affection, found this observation noteworthy. No other extra marks appear until the end of the marginal line, when a large (and completely typical) Jonsonian hand appears, pointing either to the end of the marked passage or (more likely) to More's first reference to Richard (the finger points between "stibus" and "set"; H iij.1). The marked passage ends with heavy moralizing about Richard's ingratitude to the dead king, but if this passage interested Jonson, he bypassed an opportunity to highlight the similar moralization that follows Richard's first appearance.

The marks just described are typical of many Jonson made in his *Historia*, reflecting his interest in historical details, in characterization, in political and psychological maxims, and in the specific and overall structure of More's account. Subsequent marks illustrate many of these same concerns. For instance, a flower singles out the start of a reference to the ambitions of Richard, Duke of York, father of Richard III ("Richardus / stiliter"; H iij.1). The reference summarizes his actions and character, and perhaps this is why it interested Jonson. Similarly, a marginal line is drawn next to a thumbnail sketch of the Duke's ambitious sons, Edward IV and his brothers George and Richard ("nati / mortem"; H iij.2). Ambition ran in the king's family, and Jonson seems keenly interested in such disruptive self-assertion. Perhaps he was also struck by this darker side of Edward, whose later life (at least) More had only recently been praising. The next mark, a hand, points to the beginning of a description of George, Duke of Clarence ("Georgius Cla-"; H iij.2)—an important sketch of an important figure.

Later, another marginal flower signals another generalization, this one claiming that women tend by nature, not by malice, to hate those whom their husbands love ("inui- / mari-"; H iij.2). This is one of several marked passages that characterize women's motives.

Jonson's fondness for odd details (perhaps as potential bits of memorable stage business) is suggested by the line next to a passage describing how King Edward, as a merciful punishment for his brother George's treason, had him drowned in a barrel of Cretan wine ("poe- / Cu-"; H iij.2). Perhaps Jonson was struck by the sardonic irony of this, or by the witty Latin wordplay (see Sylvester 165). The passage may also have helped deepen and complicate his sense of Edward's character.

Whatever the explanations for this mark, the next—another pointing hand—clearly seems designed to call attention to Richard's reemergence as the story's central focus ("Richardus, hic de"; H iij.2). A small diagonal line highlights More's brief description of Richard, focusing on his intelligence and fortitude ("atque / forma"; H iij.2). Interestingly, Jonson does not mark the entire description; perhaps the hand signals the whole section's importance, or perhaps Richard's character and appearance were so familiar that the ensuing description told Jonson little that seemed new. A brief vertical line singles out the claim that Richard had been born an "Agrippa"—feet first ("etiam / Prae-"; H iij.2). More's precise phrasing and his allusion to a classical parallel may have interested Jonson, and certainly he must have noted this partly as the first indication among many of Richard's unnaturalness (a recurrent theme in the *Historia*). Yet Jonson seems not to mark the equally striking claim that Richard may have been born with teeth—perhaps because More speculates that this was merely a rumor or perhaps because it seemed implausible to a playwright interested in constructing a credible account. In any case, Jonson does mark the charge that Richard frequently behaved unnaturally ("vo- / naturae"; H iij.2)—one of his few instances of singling out moral comment, perhaps because it suggested such an essential and basic insight into Richard's character.

Later marks further highlight Richard's nature and experiences. A flower marks out his warlike character and fortunes in battle, indicating his victories but stressing that even his rivals never attributed his defeats to cowardice or inexperience ("saepe vi- / ipsius aut"; H iij.2). Here Jonson seems interested both in Richard's disposition and in giving him his due. Three linked lines (running from "supra" to "ambi-"; H iij.2) highlight Richard's prodigality, his use of money to buy unstable friendships, his consequent need to extract money from others (thus winning their hatred), his secretiveness, his dissimulation, the skillful shiftings of his self-presentations, his flattery, and his murderous treachery. The passages not only contrast strongly with the long initial description of Edward, but they also exhibit clever wordplay ("amicitiam instabilem stabile odium"), emphasize important themes, pronounce moral judgments, and suggest that one function of the historian (as perhaps also of the playwright) is to expose the reality beneath carefully cultivated appearances.

Jonson's marginal lines (in a strangely jumbled form) resume at the top of the next page (from "tionis / terum"; H iij^v.1), emphasizing Richard's unscrupulous ambition and rumors of his involvements in the stabbing death of Henry VI and in the execution of his own brother George. The markings here suggest Jonson's interest in every possible aspect of Richard's character and behavior. Yet a later mark implies an equal interest in accuracy and a distrust of rumors: Jonson draws an s-shaped squiggle next to More's own warning that rumors and mere suspicions, although true sometimes, often prove misleading ("tus / verum"; H iij^v.1). Given Jonson's own expressed interest in accuracy in the preface to *Sejanus*, this marking takes on even more significance; it may suggest something about the historiographical principles he tried to respect.

The next marked passage (set off with a small horizontal line, a long line ["ipse iam / tionis"], and a very large hand [pointing toward "cto ad"]; H iij^v.1) recounts an ostensibly credible report that at King Edward's death a certain Mistlebrook ran to tell Potter, one of Richard's servants, who exclaimed that now Richard would be king. More notes that he heard this conversation reported to his own father, remarking that it occurred even before anyone suspected Richard's treason. Jonson's reasons for marking this highly interesting passage may have been several. Certainly this vignette would have been easy to dramatize, and its roots in More's personal testimony may have given it a credibility other passages lacked. This scene would have made a memorable moment on stage and would have helped underscore More's major contribution to the indictment of Richard—the charge that his usurpation sprang not simply from historical opportunities but had been plotted before Edward died. Yet a line also marks More's immediately following insistence that even if Richard simply did seize an opportunity—for opportunity often impels even the lazy and peaceful to crime—certainly he plotted the destruction of his young nephews and the seizure of royal power ("potum / adempta"; H iij^v.1). This fascinating passage not only combines moral and psychological generalization but also introduces a main theme (Richard's dealings with the boys) and offers an interpretation of his motives and actions as certain and unequivocal as any claim More has previously made. Indeed, his caution and carefulness in the passages preceding this one may have made his charges here seem all the more credible to Jonson.

Jonson's next marking consists of a vertical line supplemented by a long-stemmed flower ("Eduardi cog / alterius ad"; H iij^v.2). This line is followed by another ("commodum / opprime-"; H iij^v.2), and this whole section discusses Richard's efforts to encourage and exploit factional differences between relatives of the aging King and those of his queen. The dangers of factional strife were ones in which Jonson himself took a keen interest (H&S 8:579), and the kind of Machiavellian maneuvering described here was soon to be a major focus of *Sejanus.* The next marked passage, set off by two vertical lines crossed horizontally, seems relevant to More's depiction of King Edward, indicating the King's confidence in his ability to control both factions ("vtramq / po-"; H iij^v.2).

There soon follows, however, the longest marginal line Jonson has used so far ("mul- / apparauit ani-"; H iij^v.2–H iiij.2). This is the first important oration of the *Historia,* delivered by the bedridden Edward to warn his courtiers and relatives about the dangers of factionalism and to urge them, in the name of religion and the national interest, to put their differences aside. Once again Jonson's marking suggests his concern with factionalism as a theme, but it is also easy to imagine how readily this speech might have been adapted for presentation in a play. Edward's appeals to religious principles may have interested Jonson, but the first two passages he singles out with additional marks stress wisdom that seems more narrowly secular. Thus, a short vertical line marks a sentence ("Etenim / rata"; H iiij.1) in which Edward stresses the need for good relations among counselors if the prince is to receive good advice. Another passage, marked with a flower, warns that, when factions compete to influence the prince, his favor, more than truth and usefulness, dictates the kind of advice he receives ("dare / ra, quàm"; H iiij.1). Jonson's lifelong distaste for flattery and his support of good counsel both seem reflected in these markings. Later, another sentence may also be singled out (although here the added line is not as clearly distinct from the main line that runs the length of the page). The passage notes that often the deadliest hatreds exist between those who should be most deterred from them by nature or by law ("fiat vt / re. Adeo"; H iiij.1). Whether Jonson intended to single this out is uncertain, but there seems no doubt, thanks to another short but distinct marginal line, that he meant to draw special attention to Edward's witty protestation that if he could only have foreseen the discord that pride and ambition would unleash, he would never—to cite More's equally clever English version— "haue wonne the courtesye of mennes knees, with the loss of so many heades" ("poplitibus / quae sunt"; H iiij.2).[20] This is the sort of striking, pithy rhetoric likely to appeal to any reader, but perhaps especially to a playwright on the lookout for memorable phrasing.

Jonson's long marginal line continues slightly beyond the end of Edward's speech itself, paralleling a passage that describes the deceptive response of his listeners, who join in a pretended truce. Immediately following the line, a large hand (pointing to "rege fi-"; H iiij.2) singles out More's reference to Edward's death (a significant plot development) and the resumption of the regular narrative. More now describes the beginning of Prince Edward's journey from Wales to London. A short bracket highlights a new character—Anthony Woodville ("pueritiae da- / adhibiti in"; H iiij.2)—but lengthy marking resumes only at H iiij^v, almost all of which is marked in some way. A line runs nearly the length of the whole first column ("tam eius / ficum"), beside a passage describing Richard's efforts to stir up resentment against the influence over the young prince exercised by the Queen and her relatives. A hand (pointing at "eos euertendos"; H iiij^v.1), singles out an epitome of Richard's motives, which the rest of the passage merely elaborates. Another hand (pointing at "tot annis"; H iiij^v) signals the end of the account of Richard's arguments and machinations and the resumption of the regular narrative. An added line calls attention to the hypocrisy of Richard's appeals to God and his rejection of the recently concluded truce ("vestra / cordem"; H iiij^v.1). As Jonson must have realized, Richard's language here seems all the more ironic in light of Edward's deathbed appeals, while his assessments of others' motives reflect very ironically on his own.

The continuing line parallels the entrance of two new characters, the Duke of Buckingham and Richard Hastings, while a flower highlights their uneasy cooperation ("quam / vt suorum"; H iiij^v.1) and additional lines signal their plans for dealing with the Queen and her allies ("rebus inter / Itaq; cu-"; H iiij^v.2). Jonson's interest in these plot developments and factional maneuverings continues. Three closely spaced lines mark out the arguments used by Richard and his followers to dissuade the Queen from protecting her son with too many of her own followers ("excipie*ndum* / sin con-"; H iiij^v.2) Another flower marks a concise summary of the Queen's acquiescence—an important twist in the plot ("prae / Hampto-"; H iiij^v.2). Later, a short horizontal line (between "voca-" and "digressus est"; H iiij^v.2) seems to signal a transition from background explanation (about the town of Hampton) to resumption of the regular narrative. Another flower marks another notable development—Woodville's courteous welcoming of Richard and Buckingham and their friendly treatment of him ("occurrens / sermone"; H iiij^v.2), and then the final mark on this page (a curved line) signals the appearance of a new character (Sir Richard Radcliff) and highlights the start of his ironic plotting with Richard and Buckingham against the hapless and unsuspecting Woodville ("sece- / suis in-"; H iiij^v.2).

Having now discussed every mark on the first five pages of the *Historia*, we are in a good position to sum up their characteristics. Many marks simply highlight plot developments; some note new characters; others set off memorable speeches, actions, or events, while some emphasize themes. Some indicate noteworthy generalizations or moralizing comments, while others call attention to useful summaries, to character descriptions, to striking phrasing, or to conflicting interpretations of motives or conduct. Most of the marks on the remaining twenty pages seem to serve similar purposes, so that rather than discussing each and every one of them, it seems sensible instead to focus on the most interesting while listing the others in an appendix.

Several particularly interesting marks occur on the following page. In an ironic passage marked by a line, Richard and Buckingham hypocritically accuse Woodville of plotting treason ("Qui vt / orationem"; [H v.1]). In a moment of stunning physical irony set off by a flower, the scheming dukes kneel before the young prince ("de*n*te se /-trà porrecta"; [H v.1]), who extends his hand, raises them from the ground, and embraces them, not suspecting their perfidy. Jonson marks the prince's response with a large hand (pointing toward "trà"; [H v.1]); surely his marking indicates an awareness of the irony of this moment, and surely this whole vignette would have made for some very effective stage business. Similarly effective would have been the moment, a little later, when Richard lays his hands on two of the men he is accusing and one of them, Richard Grey, reaches for his sword and then relents. Jonson marks this bit of memorable business (which contrasts nicely with the recently reported embracings) with a pointing hand and a vertical line ("Thomam / dedit"; [H v.2]). If the playwright had been reading simply for facts, why would he have shown such keen interest in such obviously dramatic moments? Another such moment follows shortly when the captured Prince weeps, a detail Jonson marks with a line, which then extends to include a description of Richard's hospitality to several of his prisoners ("graui- / Caete-"; [H v.2]). Shortly thereafter, in an ironic twist, a flower highlights their executions ("post in / plectebantur"; [H v.2]).

The Queen's reaction to news of her son's capture is memorably dramatic, and Jonson highlights it with a vertical line and with a hand pointing directly at her self-recriminations ("aduersarij / asylum il-"; [H v.2]). Just as dramatic is the reaction of the Archbishop of York, whose darkly pessimistic words are noted with a marginal flower ("bi pollicetur / dimisso"; [H v^v.1]). More's vivid description of the frenetic activity at the Queen's residence is set off with a vertical line ("ac renuntia / quo magis"; [Hv^v.1]), while the Queen's angry denunciation of Hastings, the Lord Chamberlain, is marked with a flower ("suae nuntio / incumbit"; [Hv^v.1]). Jonson's interest in memorable speech, actions, and reactions is shown throughout his markings here, as when he singles out with a line the Archbishop's attempt to console the Queen and his gesture of handing her the royal seal ("incumbit / bites"; [H v^v.1]). All of this would have lent itself very readily to the stage. Equally stageworthy is the later ironic moment when the dukes' servants display captured weapons supposedly intended for treasonous use by the Queen's followers. Jonson marks this passage with a vertical line drawn between two flowers ("Caeterum / tam-"; [Hv^v.2]) and notes with a line the easy credulity of the common people ("mirum / Quum"; [H v^v.2]).

Not all of Jonson's markings focus on memorable actions. One passage, for instance, highlights memorable language—the comparison of Richard's "protection" of the young king to a wolf's being entrusted with a lamb ("ciaretur / tus est"; [H vi.1]). This passage, marked both with a vertical line and with a hand (pointing between "to" and "tus"), not only sums up an important action but moralizes about it. A little later, marked by a vertical line, a passage focusing on Richard's character also uses striking language, citing his efforts to drive his "prey" into a "snare" ("Igitur / liquam"; [H vi.1]). The frequent vividness of More's rhetoric would have been as useful to the playwright as his focus on striking behavior. Yet Jonson's interest in the book's rhetoric seems to have gone beyond isolated words or images. His next marking, for instance, consists mainly of a long, disjointed line (suggesting breaks in the annotating process), preceded by an unusually large pointing hand ("Britanniam / cuiuis ve"; [H vi.1–2]; the hand points toward "asylo" [H vi.1]). Whether the hand points to the beginning of the lined passsage or to the unlined passage that comes immediately before it is unclear, although the line's length suggests Jonson's strong interest.

The passage consists mainly of a report, with extended quotation, of Richard's accusations against the Queen; this is one of the major speeches of the *Historia*, and it would have made for a memorable speech in Jonson's play. Richard's brazenness and hypocrisy are particularly striking, and Jonson may have realized that the Protector's attacks on the Queen reflected quite ironically on himself, revealing much about his own character even as he impugned the character of others. The broken, almost sentence-by-sentence nature of some of Jonson's lining here suggests a fascinated interest in Richard's tactics, as each of his charges is ticked off one by one. Richard's words show him as a master of subtle intimidation and persuasion, and to the writer who would soon depict Sejanus and Tiberius this speech may have exercised a special appeal.

Another long speech in which Jonson seems to have taken a very strong interest is the one the Duke of Buckingham delivers, attacking abuses of the privilege of religious sanctuary ([H vi^v]–I.1). Since the Queen has moved her remaining son into a church adjacent to the palace and invoked the privilege, thus preventing Buckingham and Richard from getting hold of the boy, the Duke's words here are hardly disinterested. The right of sanctuary was a burning issue at the time More wrote, which helps account for the attention he gives it, but Jonson's detailed markings are less easy to explain. Having once taken advantage himself of the right of clergy to escape criminal punishment, he may have had some personal interest in this issue, but perhaps he also intended to use the Duke's speech as the basis of a set-piece in his own play. Certainly there are memorable moments in the speech, as when Buckingham wishes that some of the men in the Queen's family were women ("lum sibi / profecto"; CT; [H vi.^v.1]), or his ironic protestation that the boy's most excellent uncle and his cohorts are simply concerned with the prince's health and well-being ("salutem / Postremo"; I.2; marked with a reddish-brown vertical line). Other markings suggest an interest in the details of Buckingham's argument and in the technicalities of sanctuary as a legal privilege.

In a work so full of long speeches, it seems inevitable that Jonson's marks should frequently have singled out particular moments of oratory. Yet his markings also often indicate an interest in moments of speech that are also moments of conflict, as when he highlights passages of the dispute between the Queen and Cardinal Bourchier, the Archbishop of Canterbury, over the prince's custody. A striking instance of such conflict is marked with a short vertical line, a short curved line, and a large pointing hand, all in reddish-brown ink ("rus memini / nunc infirma"; I^v.1). When the Cardinal recalls a time when the Queen herself agreed that the then Prince of Wales should live apart from her, she quickly disputes not only the claim but its present relevance. Jonson's markings capture the heart of their conflict and focus on a particularly dramatic moment.

More's forceful presentation of this forceful queen would have given Jonson the makings of a memorable female character; this is a woman capable of giving as good as she gets. Her pathetic invocation of her rights as a mother and her protest against being harrassed in sanctuary, where even thieves are safe, are moving and memorable ("vbiuis /quid"; CT; I^v.2). When the Cardinal attempts to reassure her, she again disputes him with a memorable series of clipped, abrupt questions, and once again Jonson highlights their dramatic confrontation ("quicquam / illorum ini-"; I^v.2; marked with a reddish-brown y-shaped mark). Similarly, he singles out her pithy and ironic question: why should Richard fear for the prince's safety in sanctuary, of all places ("ad hanc / vbi ego"; CT; I ij.1)? In one of several marked allusions to Saint Peter, the Queen expresses assurance that the apostle will punish anyone who violates his sanctuary—a memorable warning, and part of a pattern of similar markings ("est ta$m$ / olim"; VL; I ij.1). It is easy to imagine how such a motif or pattern of echoes could have been woven into Jonson's play, each reference to the saint recalling the previous one, perhaps for ironic effect. The Queen's next marked argument invokes a claim Jonson himself often made— that protection would be unnecessary if innocence alone could assure one's safety ("recepit / ctor"; VL; I ij.1), and the mark here is followed immediately by a pointing hand (next to "ctor") that perhaps calls attention to the Queen's sardonic wordplay on Richard's title of "Protector." Yet she depends not simply on sarcasm or emotional appeals to make her points; as Jonson notes, she also is capable of citing her legal rights ("xium / quisqua*m*"; FL; I ij.1). Her long self-defense effectively counterpoints Buckingham's long speech on sanctuary, providing two memorably contrasting set pieces. All in all she is a complex and fascinating figure; one wonders what the playwright might have made of her.

The Queen's protracted resistance to the Cardinal's persuasions makes her eventual capitulation all the more poignant and dramatic, and Jonson is careful to mark with several long lines the lengthy reflections that lead up to her decision ("fide*m* pro- / niq; si"; I ij.2–I ij^v.1). Of course, if Jonson chose to dramatize this scene he would have had to find a way to articulate what the Queen simply ponders. A flower highlights her notion that although the Cardinal and his men are capable of being deceived by Richard, she is sure they are not corruptible ("qui simul / corrumpi"; I ij^v.1). Her speech, as she turns the boy over to them, is a potent mixture of plangency and sarcasm, and Jonson marks it with a long line ("adeo impudens / didicimus"; I ij^v.1). Even as she relinquishes her son she expresses powerful reasons for refusing, and Jonson marks her hesitations with a short flower ("alter / ridiculosius") and then with a longer line ("alter / vtrumq'"; I ij^v.1). Then, in perhaps the most poignant moment in More's narrative— which could easily have been the basis of a striking moment in Jonson's play—the Queen addresses her son, commends him to the saints, kisses him, makes the sign of the cross, then turns tearfully away, leaving the weeping boy behind. Jonson marks all of this ("curi sitis / nalis"; VL; 50v.1). The next mark also focuses on memorable action, particularly ironic in light of the actions just highlighted: Jonson marks Richard's lifting of his nephew and his fulsome welcoming of the boy ("subuehens / gratissi-"; CT; I ij^v.2). A few lines later, a curved mark signals the boys' entrance into the Tower—from which they never again emerge ("clamantiu*m* / vnde nun-"; I ij^v.2). The ironic juxtaposition of these two events is underlined by Jonson's juxtaposed markings.

The Tacitean atmosphere of the *Historia*, with its emphasis on deceit and scheming, is emphasized through More's extended descriptions of the nefarious activities of William Catesby— descriptions that Jonson very thoroughly marks (I iij.1–2; see Appendix). But if Catesby is More's Macro, Richard is his Sejanus or Tiberius, and it is to the markings of one of his most vivid depictions of Richard that we should now turn. The start of this episode is highlighted by an unusual mark—a small bracket similar in appearance to one of the marks made in the *Utopia*. Oddly, it appears between the two columns of print; all the other marks in the *Historia* occur in the outer margin. Whether the mark is Jonson's thus seems a bit uncertain; in any case, it focuses on only a minor detail of Richard's behavior—his apology for his tardiness in attending the famous meeting in the Tower ("cucauerat / uosat"; I iij.2).

Jonson's interest in this memorable meeting seems clear from his marks. A short line focuses on the Bishop of Ely's ingratiating response to Richard's request for strawberries ("maius / necessariae"; I iij.2). A large hand (pointing between "proceribus" and "quan-") notes the lords' delight, during Richard's momentary absence, at his unusual cheerfulness (I iij.2). Two long lines then focus on his startling transformation—his gruesome visage and enraged insinuations of treason ("similq / impijs"; I iij.2). A flower notes the ironic moment when Hastings—whom Richard intends to crush—suggests that traitors should be killed ("praesumptus / fecit"; I iij.2). A very long line notes Hastings' pleasure when he presumes that Richard intends to move against the Queen, but also his worry when he wonders why the Protector did not include him in the planning ("bantur / inquit"; I iij^v.1). Two lines— the first capped by a circle—highlight the moment when Richard lifts his sleeve, reveals his deformed arm (withered since birth), and accuses Shore's wife (Hastings' mistress) of conniving with the Queen to injure him through sorcery ("magicis / regi in"; I iij^v.1). A flower singles out Hastings' nervous comment that if the women are indeed guilty they deserve punishment ("rae commemoratione / sunt"; I iij^v.1). This is followed shortly by a wavy line with a loop on top that signals the moment when Richard accuses Hastings of treason ("cum complêuere / (inquit)"; I iij^v.1), an accusation emphasized by a large hand (pointing at "(inquit)"). Subsequent marks focus on the imprisonment of Hastings and various nobles and bishops and on Richard's advice to Hastings to prepare for death ("bat; Iamq / iussit"; CT; I iij^v.1), as well as on Richard's ironic vow by Saint Paul not to eat until Hastings has been executed and then on his impatience to see the deed done so that he can dine ("propitium ha- / praeci-"; VL, VL; I iij^v.2).

Few episodes of More's *Historia* are more dramatic. The suspense, the verbal and behavioral irony, and the stunning "stage business" would all have made this scene a perfect source for a playwright. And in fact, few scenes suggest the atmosphere of Jonson's own *Sejanus* more graphically than this. The scheming, the deception, the uncertainty, the sudden shifts of tone and fortune, the sardonic words and calculated behavior—all anticipate his depiction of the nightmare world of Tiberian Rome. Other markings also suggest such similarities, particularly Jonson's focus on the literal nightmares that forecast Hastings' fall ("insons / rerum euen-"; VL; I iijᵛ.2). Jonson's interest in such portents looks forward to the last act of *Sejanus*, when the favorite's demise is forecast by strange occurrences. A large hand (pointing to "futu"; I iijᵛ.2) marks Lord Stanley's warning, based on his dream, that he and Hastings should flee, but the playwright also marks Hastings' confident but ironic skepticism about the warning and his certainty that such dreams are merely superstitious ("inquit Ha- / si re-"; VL; I iijᵛ.2). All of this strikingly anticipates Sejanus's similar confidence in the face of omens implying his own destruction. Additional markings further emphasize Jonson's interest in such ironic portents (e.g., the three lines at I iiij.1 from "neglecto" to "aliquod," from "vt eius" to "cerdote," and from "arcis" to "animum"), while still another suggests a more basic interest in irony in general ("manendum / discessit"; VL; I iijᵛ.2).

Jonson's marks over the next few pages show his interest in such topics as Richard's playacting and the failures of some of his performances; in the famous digression on Shore's wife; in Richard's ability to exploit opportunities as well as underlings; and in a lively digressive debate on the topic of marriage (I iiij.1— [I vi.1]). Many of the episodes marked could easily have been dramatized, particularly the marriage debate and the section on Shore's wife. However, another moment that seems to have caught the playwright's attention (and perhaps inspired his pen) is the lengthy recounting of Doctor Shaw's infamous sermon on Richard's behalf. Intended to impugn the legitimacy of Richard's rivals, this is one of the more cynical and ironic orations in the whole *Historia*. Jonson, who later expressed strong contempt for preachers who stooped to flattery (H&S 1:141–42), must have felt special disdain for a man who could proclaim allegiance to the truth, compare himself to John the Baptist, yet lie so brazenly from a pulpit ("igna- / admo-"; VL; [I vi.2]). Similarly, he must have scorned Shaw's unctuous praise of Richard's appearance ("quosdam / conuene-"; VL; [I vi.2]), while enjoying the embarrassing and humorous upshot of Shaw's inept performance ("protector / tam longé"; VL; [I vi.2—I viᵛ.1]. Perhaps he took some satisfaction in the report that Shaw soon died of shame ("Cuius / audacter"; VL; [I viᵛ.1]), and surely he must have sensed the entire episode's dramatic potential. In any case, his lines next to all the passages just cited testify to his interest in Shaw's motives, words, and fate.

Jonson shows similar interest in the next major speech by one of Richard's lackeys—Buckingham's address at the Guildhall ([I vi^v.1–K.2; see Appendix]). One particularly memorable and ironic moment is highlighted by a particularly unusual mark, a curly figure looped at each end ("erat etia*m* / potuit"; K.1). This occurs next to an egregiously cynical attack on the late King Edward—the charge that anyone who could turn on his brother or fail to win his brother's love is dangerous and unlovable. The irony of this, coming from one of Richard's co-conspirators, is riveting; perhaps that is why Jonson drew special attention to it. Perhaps he sensed a similar irony and hypocrisy in Buckingham's ensuing indictment of the immorality of Shore's wife ("vile / quoad"; VL; K.1). In fact, much of Buckingham's speech boomerangs, as when he accuses the dead king of insufficient fear of God ("videtur / cipes fuistes"; CT; K.1). A long line marks Buckingham's flattery of his audience ("Et tamen / demu*m*"; K.1), but a large hand (pointing toward "attendite"; K.1) notes his ironic need to appeal for their continued attention. The hand suggests Jonson's interest in the interaction between speaker and listeners, although it also signals, perhaps, the start of the speech's next major section. The irony of its praise of Doctor Shaw as a man of God could not have escaped Jonson; certainly it did not escape his notice, since he distinguishes it with several vertical marks ("ge facundior / didicistis, hu-;" K.1–2). Similarly ironic is another passage marked with marginal lines ("supersit / quicquam"; K.2), in which Buckingham, as part of Richard's plot, blackens the reputation of the Protector's own mother while pretending concern for her good name. His claim that Richard will be reluctant to accept the power rightfully his is almost funny ("nec tam / admittet"; VL; K.2). Similarly, a flower marks the moment when Buckingham, invoking Solomon, urges the citizens to thank heaven for Richard ("idque / prouisum"; K.2). On the page, his speech is perversely fascinating; on the stage, it might have been even more so. Jonson's markings of its comic aftermath and of the citizens' baffled reactions suggest an interest in more than the simple substance of Buckingham's arguments (K^v.1–2; see Appendix). This whole set piece—the speech and the response—could easily have been dramatized.

So, too, could the cynical and ironic theatrics with which the *Historia* culminates. More describes how Buckingham and others converge on Richard's residence to declare their dissatisfaction with the prince and to appeal to the Protector to assume the throne (K^v.2; see Appendix). In one of the work's more absurd scenes, Richard humbly agrees to hear them, and Buckingham launches into an appeal so overblown and grandiloquent that it becomes funnier with each slop of images he ladles on ("nihil in / plus honoris"; K ij.1). Jonson marks it all with a line, then draws a huge hand (pointing toward "quanto") to set off the ironic conclusion—the claim that no king ruled more eager subjects than Richard will (K ij.1). The hand may also signal the start of Richard's reply, in which he feigns devotion to his dead brother's memory and affection for his nephews, magnanimously disclaiming any interest in the throne and professing instead his loyalty to the prince and his thanks to God ("ciret / eo praecipuè"; VL; K ij.1). But Buckingham will not be so easily dissuaded, and he soon reiterates the people's determination not to be ruled by bastards ("nus iterum / non aspernetur"; VL; K ij.1). A large g-shaped mark highlights Richard's reluctant agreement that no king can or should rule unwilling subjects ("decretum / me atti"). Then a curved line marks his decision to follow popular choice rather than the forms of law ("pluris ta- / facio:"; K ij.2), while a flower slashed by a line seems to single out his reference to their solid consensus and his consequent decision to serve ("facio: / fortis vi-"; K ij.2). The shameless theatricality of this entire episode would be worthy of Mosca and Volpone, and several marks indicate Jonson's focus on just this aspect of the scene. A deformed flower highlights the audience's awareness that the whole business has been stage-managed, although some excuse the performance as simply a concession to custom ("dubitarent / humanis"; K ij.2). Another marked passage notes that, when someone plays an emperor in a tragedy, the people are not ignorant that the actor is really a craftsman ("Pontificis / est illic"; CT; K ij.2). It seems apt that a work so much concerned with theatricality and its abuses should culminate in such a self-conscious discussion of this topic. Jonson's marks indicate awareness of one of the many senses in which the *Historia* is itself indeed a work of drama.

Even so, the note stressed by Jonson's very last marks has more to do with irony and political cynicism than with drama per se. A hooked line marks Richard's perverse profession of allegiance to the law ("ne rursus / administrare"; K ij^v.1), while a long line marks his self-serving proclamation of clemency ("ciliat / se offensas"; K ij^v). Finally, a wrinkled line capped by a loop marks one last memorable moment ("ode- / habuere"; K ij^v.2). In the words of More's own English version,

And to the entente y^t he might shew a proofe [of his clemency] . . .
he commaunded that one Fogge whom he had long deadly hated,
should be brought than before him. Who being brought oute of the
saintuary by (for thither had he fled, for fere of hym) in the sight of
the people, he tooke him by the hand. Whiche thyng the common
people reioysed at and praised, but wise men tooke it for a vanitye.[21]

Although fortuitous, it also seems appropriate that this passage
is the subject of Jonson's final mark. Many of the features suggested by many of his earlier markings are represented here. Richard's play-acting; his penchant for the dramatic gesture; More's
focus on the literal gesture of Richard's hand; the disparity between the actor's intention and the reactions of his more discerning observers—all these features of the scene recall many earlier,
similar passages marked by Jonson. Moreover, the whole vignette
also looks forward strikingly to moments of equal hypocrisy (in
every sense of the word) in his *Sejanus*, the immediate successor
to *Richard Crookback*.

The resemblances between More's history and Jonson's Roman
tragedy are numerous, and they suggest that Jonson's work on
that play could not help but be informed by his reading about
Richard. His marks in the *Historia*, then, are important for what
they can suggest not only about his lost drama but also about
how his labors on that play may have helped to shape *Sejanus*.
That tragedy and More's *Historia* share similar themes, characters,
situations, styles, and atmospheres; while many of the resemblances are no doubt coincidental, surely Jonson must have perceived that his Roman play in English was indebted to More's
Romanized English history. Both works, for instance, share strong
concerns with play-acting, mutual deception, dissimulation, and
verbal and situational ironies. Both deal with corrupt rhetoric,
corrupt sexuality, and corrupt courtiers and citizens, and both
feature immoral protagonists who delight in their own wicked
cleverness. Both works show how debased pairs of schemers
(Richard and Buckingham; Tiberius and Sejanus) manipulate a
gullible but not entirely ignorant populace, and both works focus
on impotent nobles whose opposition is usually ineffective despite its frequent eloquence. The protagonists of both works are
ambitious and unnatural in relatively simplistic and uncomplicated ways, so that they sometimes seem melodramatic villains
rather than complex tragic figures. Both works emphasize the
corruption of public rituals and of public institutions (such as the
church and the senate), and both stress the power of spies and

communicate atmospheres of uncertainty and general insecurity. Portents are highlighted in both works, and both show deceivers deceived. Both depict instances of mutual plotting (between Richard and his followers; between Sejanus and Tiberius), yet both also show the unstable nature of such alliances. Both the play and the history focus on murders within noble families, and both indicate how the death of a virtuous and powerful figure opens the door to scheming and intrigue. Both deal with plots against young, legitimate successors, and both show the corruption of important secondary figures. The protagonists in both works display a nauseatingly false humility, but also a talent for cynicism in dealing with the public. Both Richard and Tiberius pay lip service to admirable values, even as they make a mockery of their culture's most cherished ideals. *Sejanus*, it is true, shows both the rise and the fall of its titular figure; but the play also ends— like More's *Historia*—with the power of its most sinister character freshly confirmed.

Jonson's markings in the *Historia* imply a great deal about the nature of his lost play, about the possible connections between that play and *Sejanus*, and about the poet's political attitudes and his responses to one of the most important works of one of his most significant predecessors. Yet, just as important, the marks also show his mind at work, as he reads, ponders, notes insights, and makes discriminations. His literally marked interest in the *Historia*, then, is as full of clues about Jonson the man as it is about any of his own creations.

Appendix

Abbreviations used—AR: focus on arguments; CH: characterization; CT: circle with attached tail; FL: flower (trefoil); GN: generalization; HD: pointing hand; HM: humor; ID: important detail; IR: irony; MA: memorable action; MJ: moral judgment; MN: manner of action; MP: memorable phrasing; MT: focus on motives; PD: plot development; RB: reddish-brown colored marks; RF: reflection, reasoning; SM: summary; SP: speech; TH: important theme(s) TP: turning point; UM: unusual mark; VL: vertical line; WP: wordplay

[H v.1]: VL; "vt oppidum / patorum" (MT, PD)
[H v.1]: VL; "riti presentiam / regis aerario" (IR)
[H v.1–2]: VL; "Quid fecerit / latere iam" (PD; SP)
[H v.2]: VL; "captum à / incertum quo:" (PD; SM)
[H v.2]: FL, VL; "eadem esse mo-" (PD)

[H v^v.1]: UM; "spectus erat / uium" (MA; PD)
[H v^v.1]: VL; "alij / diuinabant" (MA; PD)
[H v^v.2]: VL; "huius / exmiani re-" (CH; PD; SP)
[H v^v.2]: FL, VL; "cognitam / reuerenter ha-" (MN, PD)
[H v^v.2]: VL; "progressi ob- / est inue-" (MN; PD)
[H vi.1]: FL; "eodem'que /-tis opinion*em*" (MN; PD; TP)
[H vi.1]: VL; "tus est / literis" (CH; PD)
[H vi.2]: FL, VL; "auden- / etiam ne-" (AR; PD; SP; TH; sanctuary)
[H vi^v.1]: VL; "spes / se. Miliebrem" (SP; TH; womanly fear)
[H vi^v.1]: UM; "si quid / non minus" (CH; SP)
[H vi^v.1]: VL; "tur sequi / met*us* sui" (AR; SP)
[H vi^v.1]: FL, VL; "ne asylo / nu*m* esse" (AR; IR; SP; TH; sanctuary)
[H vi^v.1]: FL; "Quae / institue*n*dam" (AR; SP; TH; sanctuary)
[H vi^v.2]: VL; "quod / victoria" (AR; SP; TH; sanctuary)
[H vi^v.2]: VL; "aliquis / perditorum" (AR; SP; TH; sanctuary)
[H vi^v.2]: FL, VL, FL, VL; "incom*m*oda / Illuc" (AR; SP; TH; sanctuary)
I.1: VL; "facile / tia" (AR; MP; SP)
I.1: VL; "no producere / ac natiuu*m*" (AR; SP; WP)
I.1: VL (RB); "lege / legio" (AR; SP; TH; abuse of law)
I.1: VL (RB); "tur, ipse" (AR; SP; TH; sanctuary)
I.1: VL (RB); "cto non / ei suadere*nt*" (AR; SP)
I.1: VL (RB); "dio / qui" (AR; SP; MP; TH; sanctuary; women)
I.2: VL (RB); "no*n* est / prope" (AR; SP; TH; sanctuary)
I.2: VL (RB); "spa- / efferum, vt" (AR; SM; PD; SP; IR)
I.2: UM (RB); "simul / huic" (SP)
I^v.1: VL (RB); "nos / dere" (AR; SP; ID)
I^v.1: VL; "periculo / eo frequens" (this mark is perhaps just a smudge)
I^v.1: VL (RB); "ru*m* / ci posses" (AR; SM; SP)
I^v.2: VL (RB); "fuerit / vit*a*e ver" (AR; MT; SP; SM)
I^v.2: VL (RB); "vicisim / disti-" (AR; MT; SP)
I ij.1: VL; "temus / periti" (AR; MP; SP; TH; sanctuary)
I ij.2: VL; "in quo / qua*m* hic" (ID; MP; SP; TH; sanctuary)
I ij.2: VL; "excu / vana me" (SP; MP; MT; TH; maternal privilege)
I ij.2: VL; "fide*m* pro- / ilico nec" (PD; MT; SP)
I ij^v.2: VL; "vltro / confecis-" (CH; ID; MT)
I ij^v.2: VL; "animoru*m* / vertere" (CH; ID; MT; TH; distrust; deceit)
I iij.1: VL; "gni parte*m* / rat"; FL from "qua*n*quam to "mansioris" (PD; MP)
I iij.1: VL; "rat, prouide*n*ter / earum"; HD points to "simpliciter" (CH; PD)
I iij.2: VL; "ad suas / suae fi-" (CH; PD)
I iij.2: VL; "proficerent / quia fle-" (MT; MP; PD)
I iij.2: VL; "ambitio / sceleris so" (CH; MJ; MT)
I iiij.1: UM; "ta, quae / ostendimus" (IR; SP)
I iiij.1–2: VL; "ferè. Vir / cumulauit" (CH; a large HD points to "cha-")
I iiij.2: VL; "praetexeret, prae / qualiacunque" (MA; MN; PD)

I iiij.2: VL; "Ad haec / abomina-" (CH; IR; MT; RF; SP)
I iiij.2: VL, FL; "& pro- / temporis" (ID; IR)
I iiij.2: UM; "rei poe- / maleficij magici" (SM; PD; MA; MT)
I iiij^v.1: VL; "tate Senatu / rum praecederet" (MA; MN; PD)
I iiij^v.1: UM; "rubedine*m* / quàm animo" (CH; IR; MP; TH; hypocrisy)
I iiij^v.1: VL; "dignam / lier Londini" (RF; MT)
I iiij^v.1: VL; "ab eo / rem habuisse" (CH; MT)
I iiij^v.1: FL, VL; "rem habuisse / cessit" (MA; MT)
I iiij^v.1: VL; "cebr*ae* / Nam bella" (CH; ID)
I iiij^v.1: UM; "festiuo / rustico" (CH; MN)
I iiij^v.2: UM; "abfuit / & of" (CH)
I iiij^v.2: VL; "vel prae / quantae" (CH; MT; TH; pride)
I iiij^v.2: VL; "eo / amicis"; HD points beneath "bene-" (GN; MP)
I iiij^v.2: VL; "Sed vti / productos ac" (CH; PD; TH; tyranny)
I iiij^v.2: VL; "celeriter / his, &" (MN; PD; SM)
I iiij^v.2: FL, UM; "reliquis fe- / occasione*m*" (MT; RF; SM; TP)
[I v.1]: UM; "haerebatur / facilé" (MJ; MT; PD; SM; TH; deceit)
[I v.1]: VL, FL; "thoritas / bres" (CH; ID)
[I v.1]: UM; "tionis cursu / conspectus" (ID; MA; MJ; PD; TH; sacrilege)
[I v.1]: VL; "praecipua / gitimum" (MT; PD; SM; TH; deceit)
[I v.1]: FL; "gitimum / do commune" (IR; SM)
[I v.1–2]: VL; "illud alterum / bellive gra-" (CH; historical background)
[I v.2]: VL; "vt dixi, / serua-" (MA; SP; historical background)
[I v.2]: HD; pointing to "supplicem" (MP; PD; TP)
[I v.2]: VL; "gratificare- / circumspectè" (CH; MN; MT)
[I v.2]: VL; "inhonesta / quàm le-" (CH; MJ; MT)
[I v.2—I v^v.1]: FL, VL; "pr*ae*tenda*nt*, / bant" (CH; MN; MT; PD)
[I v^v.1]: UM; "ciam / minum" (GN; MP; SP)
[I v^v.1]: VL; "pra conditionem / Graij filijs" (AR; MP; SP; TH; marriage)
[I v^v.1]: VL; "conuenit / gius progressus" (AR; MP; SP; TH; marriage)
[I v^v.1]: VL; "legato / rerum" (AR; ID; SP)
[I v^v.1]: VL; "ta serio / sese materna" (MN; MT; SP)
[I v^v.1–2]: VL; "coniugibus / mearum" (AR; SP; HM; MP; TH; marriage)
[I v^v.2]: UM; "verò ne- / eum in-" (AR; MT; SP; TH; foreign marriages)
[I v^v.2]: VL; "ducere / pr*ae*stant s*ae*-" (AR; MT; SP)
[I v^v.2]: VL; "Varnici / mihi alie-" (AR; MP; SP; MT; TH; marriage)
[I v^v.2]: VL; "officit. De- / nuptias no-" (AR; HM; IR; SP)
[I v^v.2]: FL; "cedat fau- / co*n*ciliet" (AR; HM; IR; SP)
[I v^v.2-I vi.1]: "Erat Eli- / bitu" (AR; CH; MA; SP; PD)
[I vi.1]: VL; "re conspergi / obsequium" (MA; PD; SP)
[I vi.1]: UM; "sius ope / nare. Sed" (CH; MP; WP)
[I vi.1]: UM; "tur Eduardi / ad regnum ius" (CH; MJ; PD; TH; slander)
[I vi.1]: HD; points to "Pauli" (ID; PD; marks beginning of Shaw's
  speech)
[I vi.2]: VL; "occuparint / succes-" (AR; SM; SP; IR; TH; usurpation)
[I vi.2]: VL; "subinde / consummato" (AR; SM; SP)

[I vi.2]: VL; "nullam eius" (AR; SM; SP)

[I vi^v.1]: HD; points to "monem" (ID; MA; PD)

[I vi^v.1]: VL; "literatus / cognoscitus" (CH; SP; start of oration)

[I vi^v.1]: VL; "nunc vltro / bos. Quae" (AR; IR; SP; TH; unfair taxation)

[I vi^v.1]: UM; "tatem / tulisset" (AR; SP; the tax of "benevolence")

[I vi^v.1–2]: UM, VL; "Sic minimus / gessit" (AR; SP; TH; abuse of law)

[I vi^v.2]: VL; "ex hac / nulla aut" (AR; SM; SP; TH; abuse of law)

[I vi^v.2]: VL; "bello / sui effe-" (AR; SM; SP; TH; abuse of power)

[I vi^v.2]: VL; "gere- / imminutus" (AR; SM; SP; MP; TH; civil war)

[I vi^v.2]: FL; "imminutus / poten-" (AR; SM; SP; TH; uncertainty)

K^v.1: FL; "hic habitus / tea eadem" (HM; IR; SP; PD)

K^v.1: VL; "vultu / terum" (MP; WP)

K^v.1: VL; "munus / sus vllum" (CH; ID; HM; IR; MN; MP; SP)

K^v.1: UM; "pissent / ses, inquit" (PD; MN; SP; Richard's frustration)

K^v.1: VL; "vestrarum / stis" (CH; SP; MP; Richard's anger)

K^v.2: VL; "quàm ver- / qua se" (MN; MP; PD)

K^v.2: UM; "ingemi- / adiungunt se-" (MA; PD; SP)

K^v.2: VL; "clamorem, di- / tam exi-" (IR; MA; SP)

K^v.2: VL; "caeteri / dum ani" (MA; MN; MP; MT; PD)

K^v.2: VL; "magna / ab hu-" (CH; IR; MT; PD; SP)

6

Praise and Blame in Jonson's Reading
of More and Lipsius

Issues of praise and blame were central to Jonson's poetic thinking, as indeed they were central to much Renaissance thinking
about poetry. Jonson inherited a long intellectual tradition which
taught that the poet's chief obligation was to encourage virtue
and discourage vice, either by praising the one or condemning
the other or by mixing praise with blame. By depicting positive
or negative ethical examples, a poet could help promote goodness
and deter unethical conduct, and this was especially important
in his dealings with superiors. In a hierarchical society the virtue
or vice of powerful people could enormously affect the well-being
of the commonwealth, and one of the chief functions of poetic
praise was to encourage rulers to emulate good examples and
thus serve as worthy examples for others. This function was especially relevant to the genre of panegyric, which involved formal
and somewhat lofty public praise, often of rulers or other powerful persons. Much of Jonson's writing is devoted to just such
praise, and nearly all of his praise was meant to exhort rather
than to flatter.[1]

Jonson's professional concern with poetic praise makes it all the
more interesting that he had apparently read closely another text
by Thomas More—the latter's panegyric celebrating Henry VIII's
succession. His response to More's poem seems intriguing for a
number of reasons. In the first place, his markings imply a great
deal about the political and social assumptions he seems to have
shared with More, especially their ideals of proper kingship. In
the light of Jonson's own significance as an observer, celebrant,
and critic of royal power, his markings in More's poem have an
inherent fascination. Moreover, because we can say with some
precision when Jonson was reading More, his markings provide
important evidence about his political ideals during a crucial time

in his career—the late Elizabethan or early Jacobean periods. Yet his markings also suggest the principles he seems to have found continually relevant; the marks resonate with attitudes he expressed and works he composed throughout his life as an observer and participant in the political scene. For instance, the markings suggest a disdain for spies reminiscent of such poems as "Inviting a Friend to Supper," and they also cast a provocative glow on such works as *Sejanus* and the *Discoveries*. Finally, the strong possibility exists that Jonson had More's work in mind when he wrote his own works dealing with King James's accession. Yet the relation between those writings and More's panegyric is not one of simple imitation; Jonson's poetic response to More's poem seems significantly complex and ambivalent. Thus, for all these reasons and in all these ways, the markings in More's panegyric provide valuable new data about the general political principles and specific political conduct that Jonson found appealing.[2]

It hardly seems surprising that Jonson, as a writer of celebratory verse himself, might turn to More's poem on Henry for instruction and inspiration. As James D. Garrison emphasizes in his discussion of Renaissance panegyric, More's poem was crucial in the development of this prestigious genre in England. "Although it is no doubt true," he argues, "that roughly similar poems had been written on English soil in earlier times, More's poem can be taken to mark the beginning of the panegyrical tradition in England that leads finally to Dryden."[3] Garrison suggests that More helped Christianize this important classical genre (72); in presenting his survey of English developments he stresses that "More's poem deserves particular attention because there is solid evidence that this panegyric continued to be read with pleasure over a century after it was written" (78). He cites, for instance, Henry Peacham's question, "What can be more loftie then [More's] gratulatorie verse to King *Henrie* upon his Coronation day" (78). Garrison's evidence can now be supplemented, for Jonson's markings of the panegyric indicate that one of the most important early Stuart poets had read More's work with interest and with care.

More composed his Latin "Carmen Gratulatorium" to celebrate Henry's accession to the English throne in 1509. The poem opens by exhorting England's thanks for the day it celebrates, a day that marks a decisive turning point. Henry's succession means the end of servitude and the beginning of liberty; he will end sadness and distress, replacing them with glory and with joy. The people and the nobles both rejoice in his accession, and all those who were oppressed and persecuted under the old regime of Henry's father now have cause for happiness. The coronation brings together the entire people, who strain to witness and celebrate their new ruler. Henry himself is physically powerful and attractive, but his virtues and his qualities of mind and character are equally impressive. He has already begun to correct the injustices of the old regime; he places his country before his father. The well educated Henry is loved by his people and feared by his foes. He unites his country as well as the virtues of his various ancestors, and his distinguished queen is an exemplar of morality and manners who helps unite two powerful nations. The poem ends by beseeching that Henry remain devoted to heaven and that heaven continue to bless Henry, his queen, and the offspring who will inherit their crowns.[4]

Many of the passages Jonson marks in More's poem are ones he might have been expected to highlight, but other markings seem less predictable. He seems to have shown a particular interest, for example, in the reaction of the nobility to Henry's acccession. His first marking, a long vertical line, occurs next to a passage in which More first summarizes the response of the populace in general to the monarch and then turns to the their superiors: "'The King' is all that any mouth can say. The nobility, long since at the mercy of the dregs of the population, the nobility, whose title has too long been without meaning, now lifts its head, now rejoices in such a king" (25–28; "sonat / triumphat"). Now, More proclaims, "each man happily does not hesitate to show the possessions" that in the past were hidden out of fear (37; "opes"; CT). No longer are people secretive, "for no one has secrets either to keep or to whisper. Now it is a delight to ignore informers" (43–44; "habet / nemo"; CT).

As Henry makes his way through the city, "On all sides there arises a shout of new good will. Nor are all the people satisfied to see the king just once; they change their vantage points time and time again in the hope that, from one place or another, they may see him again" (53–55; "nouo / queant"; CT). And no wonder: "There is a fiery power in his eyes, beauty in his face, and such color in his cheeks as is typical of twin roses. In fact, that face, admirable for its animated strength"—but at this point Jonson's marking abruptly stops (64–66; "Ignea / Illa"; VL). He neglects to mark the words that finish More's sentence, words declaring that Henry's face "could belong to either a young girl or a man" (67). Interestingly enough, however, he does mark the line that immediately follows: "Thus Achilles looked when he pretended to be a maiden" (68; "Talis"; CT). Typically, Jonson ignores the general phrasing and focuses instead on the specific classical allusion. As later markings will indicate, his interest in such allusions may have been part of what attracted him to More's poem. For the moment, however, his interest in Henry's appearance continues; More says that the King's "countenance bears the open message of a good heart" (73; "Est"; HL). His appearance even reveals "how great [is] his care for modest chastity" (77; "Quanta"; HL). If Jonson found this last claim retrospectively ironic, he does not indicate it through his marking.

When marking resumes, Jonson's focus has now shifted to the benefits Henry brings: "In that we are treated thus and are gaining our liberty, in that fear, harm, danger, grief have vanished, while peace, ease, joy, and laughter have returned" (86–88; "Quod / Quod"; CT, VL)—in that such things are happening, we have evidence of Henry's excellence. Whoever was once an informer is now imprisoned, "so that he himself suffers the woes which he imposed on many" (99; "Vt mala"; CT). Once again, Jonson returns to his concern with oppressed aristocrats: "And the long-scorned nobility recovered on our prince's first day the ancient rights of nobles" (102–3; "Despectusq / Obtinuit"; UM). Henry is a prince "whose natural gifts have been enhanced by a liberal education, a prince bathed by the nine sisters in the Castalian fount" (117–18; "est? / sorores"; CT). He "has forgiven the debts of all, and rendered all secure, removing all the evil of distressing fear" (124–25; "omnes / metus"; VL). "Hence it is that, while other kings have been feared by their subjects, this king is loved, since now through his action they have no cause for fear" (126–27; "istum / amant"; CT). Addressing Henry, More declares that both "your subjects' love and your enemies' fear will hedge you round" (133; "timor"; CT). "And internal strife there will not be, for what cause, what reason, is there to provoke it?" (136–37; "namq[uae] / habent?"; VL). Besides, "the fact that both your parents were high-born disposes of this problem" (141; "parens"; CR).

In addition, Henry is fortunate in his queen. The celestial powers "distinguish her and honor her by marriage with you. She it is who could vanquish the ancient Sabine women with devotion, and in dignity the holy . . . heroines of Greece" (165–67; "tuis / heroidas"; CT). "She could equal the unselfish love of Alcestis or, in her unfailing judgment, outdo Tanaquil" (168–69; "Illa / Vel"; CT). Jonson skips praise of Catherine's beauty as well as a comparison of her eloquence to that of Cornelia, but marking resumes when More claims that "she is like Penelope in loyalty to a husband" (173; "Inq"; CT). Much later Jonson marks one of More's concluding comments to Henry about his queen: "Great advantage is yours because of her, and similarly is hers because of you" (188–89; "Proueniunt / Ex"; VL). Finally, his last mark appears next to More's call for a popular offering that will prove even more potent than "incense—loyal hearts and innocent hands" (193; "Thure"; CT).

Jonson's familiarity with More's poem is demonstrated conclusively by his marginal markings, but it might have been assumed simply from the parallels that exist between More's work and Jonson's own "Panegyre" of 1604, written to commemorate James I's opening of parliament. James Garrison already has noted several of the similarities between the two poems; from the parallels he cites and from other echoes he does not discuss, it seems very likely that Jonson had More's work in mind when he composed his own. Moreover, other similarities between More's panegyric and the separate speeches that Jonson also published in 1604 as *Part of the Kings Entertainment in Passing to His Coronation* likewise suggest that Jonson may have been reading and reacting to More's work during this period. This is not to say that either Jonson's speeches or his "Panegyre" closely imitate More's poem, and in fact the differences between the two panegyrics are in some ways as interesting as their similarities. Jonson seems to have read More, as he read most things, with a mind of his own.[5]

Nonetheless, the possible echoes of More's poem in Jonson's two works of early 1604 are worth remarking. For instance, More's poem opens by stressing the joy of the "day," the "happy day" of Henry's coronation and urges the English to "give thanks to those above" for such a day (1–3). Similarly, the first of Jonson's coronation speeches opens by declaring that "TIme, Fate, and Fortune haue at length conspir'd, / To giue our Age the day so much desir'd" (270–71; H&S 7:91). A little later, More's poem describes how "the people, freed, run before their king with bright faces" (22). Similarly, in a parallel that Garrison notes as part of the "processional topos" (85), Jonson describes how some of the people, in responding to James, "on ground runne gazing by his side, / All, as vnwearied, as vnsatisfied" (43–44; H&S 7:114). More mentions that the people's "joy is almost beyond their own comprehension" (23). Similarly, Jonson describes the popular reaction to James: "some amazed stood, / As if they felt, but had not knowne their good" (35–36; H&S 7:114). In More's poem, in a passage Jonson marks, "'The King' is all that any mouth can say" (25). In Jonson's panegyric, when the people's "speech so poore a help affords / Vnto their zeales expression; they are mute" (38–39; H&S 7:114).

Yet the relationship between the two works is not merely one of imitation; Jonson's poem also sometimes departs, in interesting ways, from the passages it echoes. For instance, in More's panegyric, in a section Jonson marks, "The nobility, long since at the mercy of the dregs of the population, . . . now rejoices in such a king" (26–28). However, Jonson's poem stresses a kind of competition between the social orders that is also, paradoxically, a kind of cooperation: "the peoples loue . . . did striue / [with] The Nobles zeale, yet either kept aliue / The others flame, as doth the wike and waxe, / That friendly temper'd, one pure taper makes" (69–72; H&S 7:115). More's poem emphasizes real conflict between social classes (as well as gritty political issues in general) much more strongly than Jonson's does: interestingly enough, the poem by Jonson, who is often regarded as an elitist, tends to present the common people in a more uniformly favorable light than More's does. Jonson's panegyric is more general in its moralism and less tied to specific problems of the day.

This is less true, however, of his coronation speeches, several passages of which recall concerns dealt with by More. Yet even here there is a difference. For instance, in the second of those speeches, Jonson proclaims that because of James, "Now innocence shall cease to be the spoyle / Of rauenous greatnesse, or to steepe the soyle / Of raysed pesantrie with teares, and bloud" (602–3; H&S 7:102). Jonson's speech emphasizes the oppression of the poor far more emphatically than More's panegyric. Yet Jonson's speech also echoes More's concern with the victimization of the powerful. In a passage Jonson marked, More had declared, "Now each man happily does not hesitate to show his possessions," which in the past he had hidden because of fear (37). Similarly, Jonson's speech expresses confidence (perhaps in ambiguous language) that "No more shall rich men (for their little good) / Suspect to be guiltie" (604–5; H&S 7:102–3). More, in another passage marked by Jonson, declares that thanks to Henry, "no one has secrets either to keep or to whisper. Now it is a delight to ignore informers" (43–44). In the same fashion, Jonson's second coronation speech proclaims that now no longer will "vile spies / Enioy the lust of their so murdring eyes" (605–6; H&S 7:103). The same speech declares that the Stuart accession "hath brought / Sweet peace to sit in that bright state shee ought, /

Vnbloudie, or vntroubled" (594–96; H&S 7:102). A marginal note speaks of the blessings James brings: "Peace, Rest, Liberties, Safetie, &c." (H&S 7:102). By the same token, More's poem, in a passage Jonson marks, speaks of the "liberty" and the "peace, ease, joy, and laughter" that have returned and of the "fear, harm, danger, [and] grief" that now are vanquished (86–88). In addition, Jonson's first coronation speech commends Queen Anne (354–61; H&S 7:94) in terms recalling More's praise of Queen Catherine—praise that Jonson had heavily marked (162 ff.).

While these last examples illustrate fairly distinct parallels, another interesting example of a similarity-with-a-difference between the two works concerns the issue of tyranny and the abuse of law. More's poem proclaims that with Henry's accession, "Laws, heretofore powerless—yes, even laws put to unjust ends—now happily have regained their proper authority" (32–33). Similarly, in Jonson's poem, the goddess Themis condemns past times in which " 'lawes were made to serue the tyran' will" (99; H&S 7:115). However, this is soon followed by what seems to be an implied denunciation of the reign of Henry VIII himself; the then-Catholic Jonson speaks of times when "acts gaue licence to impetuous lust / 'To bury churches, in forgotten dust, / 'And with their ruines raise the panders bowers: / 'When, publique iustice borrow'd all her powers / 'From priuate chambers; that could then create / 'Lawes, iudges, co<u>nsellors, yea prince, and state" (101–6; H&S 7:116). Ironically, just as More had urged Henry not to follow the example of his own father, so Jonson implies that James should reject the bad examples set by Henry. Jonson's poem seems to provide a retrospective and somewhat critical assessment of Henry's performance—a performance that More's poem could only predict, and one to which its author himself eventually fell victim. When Jonson read More's celebration of Henry, he must have been struck (it is hard not to be) by the historical irony of the poem's words. Jonson seems to have incorporated some of that irony into his own panegyric, implying that Henry was guilty to some extent of the very faults that More had praised him for rejecting. Jonson's poem thus exists in a very complex relation to More's, and perhaps the later Catholic poet pondered the irony of his predecessor's role as celebrant of a king who would one day order his death. Annabel Patterson has argued that in arranging the individual works of his *Under-wood* volume, Jonson was highly aware of historical ironies and of the ways they complicated the meaning of works he had written years earlier. Perhaps the same is true of the relations between his own panegyric and More's.[6]

Other connections between More's poem and Jonson's works of 1604 seem more straightforward, and a number of these have been cited by James Garrison. He notes, for instance, how Jonson develops "the idea of national reconciliation" that had been "given formulaic statement by Thomas More" (88). More's poem describes how "The people gather together, every age, both sexes, and all ranks" (46). Similarly, Jonson notes that there was "No age, nor sex, so weake, or strongly dull, / That did not beare a part in this consent / Of hearts and voices" (58–60; H&S 7:114). Again, More says that as Henry passes, "The houses are filled to overflowing, the rooftops strain to support the weight of spectators" (52). Similarly, Jonson reports that for James's procession, "Walls, windores, roofes, towers, steeples, all were set / With seuerall eyes, that in this obiect met" (63–64; H&S 7:114). In More's poem, in a passage Jonson marks, "On all sides there arises a shout of new good will. Nor are the people satisfied to see the king just once; they change their vantage points time and time again in the hope that, from one place or another, they may see him again" (53–55). Similarly, in a passage already cited in part, Jonson reports how, in response to James,

> Some cry from tops of houses; thinking noise
> The fittest herald to proclaime true ioyes:
> Others on ground runne gazing by his side,
> All, as vnwearied, as vnsatisfied:
> And euery windore grieu'd it could not moue
> Along with him, and the same trouble proue.
> (41–46; H&S 7:114)

Perhaps Jonson still had More's poem in mind when he came to write another work of early 1604, his *Entertainment at Highgate*. In the final words of that work, Mercury hopes that James will "for euer liue safe in the loue, rather then the feare of your subiects" (274–75; H&S 7:144). One recalls that More, in a passage marked by Jonson, had proclaimed of Henry that "while other kings have been feared by their subjects, this king is loved, since now through his action they have no cause for fear" (126–27).

It is possible, of course, that this parallel and some of the others mentioned are simply coincidental or conventional; certainly Jonson did not need to read More's poem to learn how to celebrate or admonish a king. Yet his markings prove that Jonson did read More, and they corroborate Garrison's intuition that More's poem influenced Jonson's 1604 panegyric. Moreover, his markings help call attention to previously unnoted resemblances between More's panegyric and Jonson's 1604 coronation speeches. It seems unlikely, however, that reading More would have had the impact it did if Jonson had not already shared so many of More's ideas, concerns, and values. His reading of More probably did not so much influence his thinking as confirm it. Many of the preoccupations, ideas, and ideals expressed by More find expression as well in many of Jonson's own writings.

His tragedy *Sejanus*, for example, is an interesting case in point. Probably written sometime in 1603, this play would have been on Jonson's mind either shortly before, shortly after, or perhaps even during the period when he was probably reading More's panegyric. Although no evidence allows us to argue that reading More's poem influenced the writing of Jonson's play and although there is likewise no proof that work on *Sejanus* may have influenced Jonson's marking of More's panegyric, thematic links between the two works do exist and are worth noting. Such parallels suggest the general parallels between Jonson's early political concerns and the ideas expressed almost a century earlier by More. Both works, for instance, deal with the problems posed by political informers. Both are much concerned with the recovery of lost liberty. Both deal with abuses of power that enslave people previously free. Both suggest that a well motivated prince can serve as one of the chief guardians of freedom. Both deal with the corruption of laws and the debasement of legal procedures. Both express concerns about the abuses of corrupt royal servants. Both allude to a noble class that has been stripped of its old power and prestige. And both works offer unblinking views of the motives and behavior of the common people. *Sejanus* can almost be seen as a kind of antipanegyric—a work that derives much of its satiric force and effectiveness from our recognition of the many ways Tiberius and Sejanus violate the ideals of proper political conduct.[7]

Many of the same concerns and ideals shared by More's work and by Jonson's play are shared as well by a number of the poems Jonson eventually published as parts of his *Epigrammes* volume. Since most of these poems were probably written before 1612, they give us still further insights into the nature of Jonson's political values and responses during the first decade of the Jacobean reign—at the beginning of which he seems to have been reading More's panegyric. *Ep.* 4, for instance, is addressed to James and praises him for his own poetic talent, just as More had praised Henry for having been "bathed by the nine sisters in the Castalian fount" (118). Similarly, *Ep.* 35, also addressed to James, commends him for his moderate exercise of princely power. *Ep.* 59 condemns spies and also indicates—as does More's poem—that eventually they get their comeuppance. *Ep.* 64, to Robert Cecil, praises the King for rewarding virtuous servants, while *Ep.* 74, to Lord Chancellor Egerton, commends him for properly administering the law. *Ep.* 101, "Inviting a Friend to Supper," celebrates an evening of relaxed and convivial "libertie" (42) free of worry about spies and informers. Finally, *Ep.* 109, to Sir Henry Neville, extols altruistic public service, the pursuit of power motivated by the love of virtue. What such poems suggest is how many of the values articulated by More were also important to Jonson. In both cases one finds the same stress on moderation, on legality, on liberty, and on the ideal union of people and king.[8]

Similar values pervade Jonson's writings throughout his career, but they find their most explicit articulation in the important prose work of his final years, the *Discoveries*. More is listed there as one of a number of English writers who "were for their times admirable: and the more, because they began Eloquence with us" (8: 591). Such a comment suggests again Jonson's familiarity with More as a stylist, but the parallels between the political ideas expressed in the *Discoveries* and those expressed in More's poem are also worth noting.[9] Both works, for instance, stress the importance of princely clemency (78; H&S 8:597; 599–600), and both extol the union of sovereignty and learning (118; H&S 8:565; 592). Both condemn tyranny (90–91, 120–25; H&S 8:598), excessive taxation (30, 100–101; H&S 8:602), and corrupt officials (38–39, 104–5; H&S 8:603–4). Both express misgivings about the multitude (26; H&S 8:593), and both commend proper regard for justice and the laws (32–33, 108–9; H&S 8:603). Both excoriate spies (44–45, 98–99; H&S 8:613), and both support harsh punishment for blatant crimes (32–33; H&S 8:602). Both express regard for properly motivated nobles (102–3; H&S 8:598), and both view the king as a responsible servant of his people (82–83; H&S 8:594). Both express profound affection for princes who take their responsibilities seriously (128–30; H&S 8:594, 601). Both indicate that the king who rules well is loved, not feared (126–27; H&S 8:600), and both condemn princely pride (79; H&S 8:600–601).

All these parallels (and others that could be cited) are, of course, largely traditional and conventional; they are among the most widely accepted ideals of the period. Jonson's reading of More's panegyric probably did not affect at all the ideas expressed in the *Discoveries*, and yet Jonson's work and More's poem are clearly part of the same value system, part of the same broad intellectual legacy. More's poem helped articulate and pass on that legacy, and Jonson's works of 1604, like many of his other writings (including *Sejanus* and the *Discoveries*), helped give it new life, new force, and new expression. Jonson's responsiveness to More's panegyric is reflected, then, not only in his marginal markings and not only in several of his own texts, but also in the more general texture of his thinking.

* * *

If Jonson's reading of More's poem to Henry reflects his own necessary concern with the issue of addressing the powerful, then evidence of his reading of another work by another influential sixteenth century thinker seems to reflect his concern with yet another important segment of his audience—the segment comprised of rivals, antagonists, or hostile superiors. As I have argued elsewhere at length, these two groups—powerful for different reasons—composed two of the most significant portions of Jonson's audience; they were portions he could ignore only at his peril.[10] Of course, the literary tradition he had inherited had taught him the importance (indeed the obligation) of addressing and attempting to influence superiors, but familiarity with that tradition would also have reminded him of the many risks involved. By attempting to discharge his public responsibilities, a poet could arouse anger and disdain of all sorts, including the envy of rivals, the hostility of superiors, and the suspicions of official authorities. If praise and blame were the poet's chief purpose, calumny was one risk that purpose entailed.

The issue of calumny—of malicious accusations or slander—was always an important one in Jonson's works and career. He often considered himself a victim of calumny, while others charged that it was Jonson who was guilty of libel. Satire he regarded as morally justified seemed malicious to some of his readers, while numerous charges leveled against the poet struck him as envious, spiteful, or unfair. Although the problem of distinguishing justified criticism from malevolent detraction has always proven difficult, it seems to have been particularly troublesome for Renaissance satirists and their readers.[11] The problem of calumny blurs neat theoretical distinctions between praise and blame by suggesting that not all praise was disinterested, that not all blame was morally objective or impersonal, and that not all readers would agree about how to interpret a writer's ethical intentions. From the start of his career until its end, a concern with calumny was a constant feature of Jonson's life and writings. He often felt himself the victim of calumny or was accused of it by others.[12]

Examples abound. An early play, *The Isle of Dogs*, led to the poet's imprisonment for writing "sclandrous matter" (H&S 1: 15), while similar charges against *Eastward Ho* would later lead to a similar imprisonment (H&S 1:38). Jonson was also suspected of detraction both in *Epicoene* (H&S 5:143–47) and in *Volpone*, and he spends much of the latter play's dedication insisting that its satire is impersonal.[13] His dramas frequently feature insult-slinging "railers," and gossip and false accusations figure prominently in the plots of such works as *Cynthia's Revels*, *Sejanus*, *Volpone*, and *Poetaster*.[14] The last play, of course, was merely one salvo in the so-called "poetomachia," Jonson's theatrical dogfight with John Marston and Thomas Dekker. Dekker's ferocious assault in *Satiromastix* depicts Jonson as guilty (among many other things) of hypocritical calumny, although Jonson of course viewed Dekker's attack itself as the epitome of slander.[15] The Countess of Bedford became annoyed when a poem by Jonson surreptitiously branded her cousin a whore, while calumny is one of Jonson's usual charges against his archrival, Inigo Jones, who in turn accused Jonson of libel and railing (H&S 11:385–86).[16] George Chapman also irritably assaulted Jonson for being petulant (H&S 11:406–12), while, in his oft-quoted celebration of Shakespeare, Jonson famously disavowed any "envy" of his great contemporary (whose writings he nonetheless subsequently mocked).[17] At various times Jonson was officially charged with seducing youths to papistry (an accusation he denied [H&S 1:41–43]); with supporting the assassination of the royal favorite (another charge he confuted [H&S 1:94]); and with using offensive language in his play *The Magnetic Lady* (still another allegation he successfully repulsed [H&S 2:203]). In his "Tribe of Ben" epistle he censures a "Covey of Witts" for censuring others (H&S 8:218–20). In the masque *Time Vindicated*, he whips carping critics (H&S 7:655–73), while in *Love Restored* he satirizes satirists of masquing (H&S 7:377–85). The notorious "Ode to Himselfe" doggedly defends the poet against detractors while also taking a slap at his one-time servant, Richard Brome (H&S 6:492–94). And in the prose *Discoveries* he relishes the thought of backbiters being cudgeled. He sniped at Alexander Gill the elder, was later attacked by Gill's son, and then responded to the latter's satire with stinging sarcasm of his own (H&S 11:158–59). The list could go on and on. At one point, for instance, Jonson suspected that John Taylor had set out to scorn him (H&S 1:149), but after Jonson died it was Taylor who published the first of several poems defending him against posthumous attacks. Even death, it seems, did not exempt the poet from calumny.[18]

Given Jonson's lifelong preoccupation (whether as accuser or accused) with malediction and satire, it hardly seems surprising that he shows such a strong interest in the oration *De Culumnia* by Justus Lipsius, the widely influential Flemish intellectual.[19] Jonson's personal copy of this work, included in his eight-volume set of Lipsius's writings now on deposit at Emmanuel College in Cambridge, is marked throughout with the poet's characteristic marginalia. The markings are clearly his, and they just as clearly indicate his keen interest in Lipsius's thoughts on this important subject.[20] Like other markings in the Emmanuel College Lipsius and in other books once owned by Jonson, the marginalia and underlining in *De Calumnia* were made with a soft pencil, so that sometimes a mark from one page has "bled" onto the page it faces. Examining the book *in situ* makes it easy to distinguish the "original" marks (which are usually darker) from their pale "reflections," and so it becomes possible to say with some assurance precisely which passages the poet singled out.[21] However, why he emphasized the ones he did is a far more interesting problem. Jonson's markings in his copy of *De Calumnia* provide new evidence of his fascination with a topic that evidently haunted him all his life.

One indication of his conscious concern with calumny is the frequency with which he deals with the topic in his commonplace book of prose *Discoveries*, where slander and its effects are mentioned repeatedly and at length. One of the very first entries, for instance, notes that "*A Fame* that is wounded to the world, would bee better cured by anothers *Apologie*, then its owne: . . . the man that is once hated, both his *good*, and his *evill* deeds oppresse him: Hee is not easily *emergent*" (H&S 8:563–64). A tarnished reputation is not easily repaired, and this fact alone would immediately magnify the damage of any libel. As Jonson indicates later, innocence itself is no protection against attack, but this early passage also makes clear that even exemplary behavior following a slander can do little to repair the damage. Ironically, only the slanderer himself has the power to undo its ill effects, but he also, perhaps, has the least motivation to do so, since his own reputation is at stake. From the start of the *Discoveries*, then, one senses that libel is difficult to ignore or dismiss, no matter how much one might like to do so.

A later passage indicates how Jonson could try to make the best of a bad situation. "I am beholden to *Calumny*," he notes, "that she hath so endeavor'd, and taken paines to bely mee. It shall make mee set a surer Guard on my selfe, and keepe a better watch upon my *Actions*" (H&S 8:569). Calumny, in other words, encourages self-policing, a self-concern rooted in a concern with others' reactions, a self-consciousness involving an acute consciousness of one's fellows. Precisely because it is impossible to control the behavior of others, control of oneself must be that much more intense. The virtue that calumny can ironically help inculcate is nonetheless felt, in part, not so much as freedom but as a kind of constraint. Thus, even one's best behavior—the behavior in which one can take most pride—is partly a response to fear and is a practical result of relative social impotence. Such are the paradoxes of a goodness nurtured by a need to avoid attack.

Of course, the self-restraint that could help minimize the chances of being slandered (but that could never immunize one entirely) could also help prevent one from victimizing others: "A *wise tounge* should not be licentious, and wandring; . . . it was excellently said of that Philosopher; that there was a Wall, or Parapet of teeth set in our mouth, to restraine the petulancy of our words" (H&S 8:573). The impulse that leads to calumny is difficult to curb, whether we are its targets or its perpetrators. The price of freedom, both from libel and from libelling, is a kind of eternal vigilance. Elsewhere Jonson indicates that not even benevolence is an effective safeguard against ill-will, and it is only a scant comfort to console oneself with the thought that a slanderer's attacks may be rooted in a kind of self-contempt: "*Some* Actions be they never so beautifull, and generous, are often obscur'd by base, and vile mis-constructions; either out of envy, or ill nature, that judgeth of others, as of it selfe" (H&S 8:579). Thus, only the victim (and perhaps the attacker) is sure to feel that a libel tarnishes the libeller, and such knowledge cannot, in any case, undo the damage done.

Given the tenor of these passages and of others from the *Discoveries* to be examined later, it hardly seems surprising that Jonson responded as he did to *De Calumnia*. Yet his curiosity about the work and its subject matter was evidently shared by many contemporaries. One indication of the oration's interest for other readers in England is the fact that it was one of only a few Latin works by Lipsius to be issued separately from a British press, and it was also one of only several of his works to be translated into English. The translator, Anthony Stafford, may have had his own reasons for curiosity about this topic: his brother had been executed for homosexual misconduct, and Stafford apparently had suffered ridicule as a result.[22] Despite his claim not to have "always closely followed the Authors steppes," and notwithstanding his modest opinion that the work had been "ill translated," in fact his version is usually quite faithful to its source. Jonson, of course, read the work in the original Latin, although the precise period in which he read and marked his copy is impossible to specify.[23]

Lipsius begins his oration by asserting that, of all the vices, calumny is the greatest enemy to God (103/134). He emphasizes the guile and lying it involves; its purposes are to hurt and to deceive, and Lipsius stresses its frequency in the present age. Nonetheless, few previous writers (he claims) have dealt with the topic. He intends first to show how filthy it is, then how pernicious, and then how to avoid it. In the first passage marked by Jonson, Lipsius pronounces that both calumny and those guilty of it are filthy; such persons are "base, idle, [and] prattling" ([Viles, Ignauas, Loquaces]; 103/134). Jonson underlines most of this and draws a marginal flower apparently designed to highlight the emphatic adjectives ("foedissimas / adeò"). His interest in these specific traits of calumniators is interesting in its own right. Perhaps it indicates, among other possibilities, behavior from which Jonson might wish to distance himself, or signs of potential calumny he might look for in others, or features he could ascribe to calumniators in his own creative works. At the very least, his markings seem to indicate an interest in Lipsius's neatly methodical division of the discussion—an interest literally underscored when he underlines again the word "Viles" (103/134), which begins the next sentence and which initiates the author's elaboration on this particular trait.

According to Lipsius, no good person was ever guilty of calumny. Instead (in a passage Jonson underlines), those who "haue beene prone to this vice" have been

> onely sad, and maligne natures, envying others and distrusting themselues; whom . . . *Saturne* hath blasted with his starre. Did you neuer see little, cowardly dogs barke at guests, that durst not bite beasts? Why, such are these worser sort of men; who are borne onely to hurt and vexe the harmelesse. ("bis / re. Nati"; 104/135)

A marginal flower trailing a curving stem singles out the first sentence of this passage; perhaps Jonson found the classical allu-

sion ("quas sidere suo Saturnus afflauit") particularly worth noting. In his markings throughout the oration, striking imagery
often seems to have caught his attention; the highlighted reference here to the cowardly dogs, for instance, is another example
of such interest, and it accords well with the disdainful tone that
Jonson himself so often adopts toward his antagonists. The poet's
abiding and reiterated conviction of his own "harmelesse" innocence would only have increased his dismissive contempt for such
"minutos illos canes & degeneres," yet Lipsius's contention that
these curs are relatively powerless is nonetheless combined with
a sense that they can also vex and hurt. The ambivalent tone that
characterizes Jonson's own pronouncements about his enemies is
also reflected in this passage marked in Lipsius.[24]

In closing his discussion of the baseness of calumniators, Lipsius concludes that such persons are never at rest until they have
brought disquiet to others. Jonson's interest in Lipsius's methodical development of his ideas is indicated again by his next underlining, which picks out the orator's reference to idleness
("Ignauos"; 104/136), the second trait he had ascribed to detractors. Jonson underscores Lipsius's claim that "the first sparke,
and tinder of Calumny, is Sloth [otium]; for, no man will haue
leasure to enquire into other mens affaires, who is deteined by his
owne" ("Ignauos / quirere"; 104/136). In an especially intriguing
passage, Lipsius suggests that if anyone doubts this,

> let him but a little frequent the Palaces of Princes, and places of
> Pleading [Forum & Basilicas nostras paullisper adeat]; in which, occa-
> sion and matter of Calumny is daily, and aboundantly, sowen by
> those, who make this their only businesse, *To walke and talke.* What-
> soeuer is publikely, or priuately done, is there censured, and scourged
> [vapulant]. The Prince, & his Counsellours [administri] are said to
> doe amisse: one man is said to haue done this; another man to haue
> spoken that. To conclude; no report of any man can stand with them
> vnblemisht, and vnslandred [denique nulla de quoquam fabula est,
> que*m* apud eos stet, vt cum poëtâ dicam, talo recto]. ("piam / apud";
> 104/137–38)

Jonson underlines all of this, and a marginal flower seems to
single out the same word play italicized in the Stafford translation
("Ambulare and Fabulari"). However, perhaps what is particularly interesting about Jonson's marking here is the sympathy it
may suggest for those in prominent positions—particularly the
King—who were easy targets of public censure. A number of
Jonson's own works suggest a similar sympathy, which was per-

haps more akin to empathy since the poet's lofty status in the literary hierarchy gave him an unusual appreciation of how prominence could expose a person to gossip and attack. On more than one occasion Jonson seems to have felt that he had been targeted for abuse largely because of the eminence of his position.[25]

In an unmarked passage, Lipsius objects to the idea that ignorant persons should presume to attack what they do not understand, like a passenger on a ship who criticizes the sailors without offering them help. Jonson's underlining resumes when Lipsius continues that "vnto vs, these emptie vessels must needs be molestfull, which sound most, and haue least liquor in them" ("uere / bent"; 104/138–39). A marginal flower also marks these words, which may have been interesting to the poet primarily for their imagery and phrasing. Immediately following this marking, Jonson emphasizes through underlining the third adjective—prattling ("Loquaces")—that Lipsius had ascribed to calumniators. A flower is drawn in the margin next to the line in which this word appears, and then the flower's stem drops down for another seven lines.

In the passage highlighted in this fashion, Lipsius asks, "And, indeede, how should they be other? since" (and here Jonson's underlining resumes) "it is proper to these babblers [lingulacis insitum], not only to speak much, but much euill" ("turâ / mala"; 104/139). Underlining ceases briefly as Lipsius asks, "Haue any of you at any time ranked your selues with those head-strong vntamed people" (and now underlining begins), "who haue, as *Pindar* saith, vncurbed mouthes? [Siquis vestrûm adfuit indomitis istis, & quibus, vt Pindarus ait, os sine fraeno]" (104/139). Underlining ceases for a while as Lipsius continues:

If you haue; tell me, was not the greatest part of their talke not onely of some body, but against some body? surely, it was. For, they vent things, both heard and unheard; mingling, things true and certaine, with things vaine [que vera, que vana]. And, as in a lake of *Iudea,* call'd *Asphaltes,* nothing sinks; [and now Jonson's underlining resumes] but whatsoeuer is cast-in, swimmes vpon the surface of the water [sed supernatant omnia iniecta]: so, nothing goes to the bottome of their bosomes; all things keepe the toppe, and flote ouer. ("solùm / pectore"; 104/139–40)

At this point the underlining ceases, and the stem of the marginal flower ends as well. Surely one thing that must have interested the poet about all the underlined sections of this flowered passage was the vivid language Lipsius uses, but the denigration of compulsive talk also reminds one of the already quoted passage from the *Discoveries* referring to the teeth as a "Parapet . . . set in our mouth, to restraine the petulancy of our words" (H&S 8: 573). In fact, Jonson's general disdain for empty verbiage may have been rooted partly in a desire to distinguish himself from the sort of unrestrained prattling that Lipsius condemns.

Lipsius continues by remarking that when such prattlers lack any other targets, they turn upon themselves. With this observation, the first section of his oration concludes. In the next part, he promises, he will deal not so much with calumniators but with Calumny herself. Here again his penchant for dividing his topic into threes manifests itself: he reports that Calumny has two parents, "Lying and Enuy" ("Mendacium & Inuidia"), and he notes that "Curiositie" is "her Nurse" (105/142). A marginal flower highlights this passage, and the quoted words are underlined, as is the second part of the following sentence, which asks how attractive such an offspring can be born "from three such foule vices" ("à bellâ hac vitiorum trigâ"; 105/142). Here as throughout, Jonson tends to mark memorable phrasing and summary passages that capture the key points and moments of transition in Lipsius's developing argument.

Lipsius argues that lying is the father of Calumny, since without it she has neither life nor vigor. In a question most of which is underlined by Jonson, Lipsius asks, "What Backbiter was euer yet content with the naked truth [simplici vero] only?" ("contentus vin-"; 105/141). A calumniator is forced to lie, since he can do no damage if he sticks to the truth. Therefore he exaggerates, embroidering simple facts with his own inventions. A long-stemmed marginal flower emphasizes the sentence suggesting that "As Spiders, with a woonderfull Art, bring-forth threds and cobwebs out of their bodies: so, hee begets, and weaues subtle snares with his wit." This sentence, with its striking imagery, is underlined, as is the immediately following transition: "I haue truly & sufficiently shewed, that Lying is the Father of Calumny: it now resteth that I proue Envy to be her Mother, who in the malignant womb of her wit, conceiues, beares, and at last brings forth this . . . infant [concipit, gestat, parit denique hanc infantem]" ("mi- / ca-"; 105/145–46). The stem of the marginal flower ends here, and so, momentarily, does Jonson's underlining. It resumes when Lipsius notes that calumniators usually attack "those whom they see to excell others in vertue, in learning, or in some other thing worthy of admiration" ("virtute / cur"; 105/146). In short (in another underlined assertion), "Calumny pursues the better sort" ("are"; 105/147). Paradoxically, then, attacks meant to degrade could actually be seen as signs of worth, and certainly Jonson often seems to have tried to view them this way. Lipsius remarks that, just as bulls are stirred by the color red, so calumniators are provoked by virtue.

A long-stemmed flower marks the transition to the third part of this section, in which Lipsius reminds us that "Last of all, I added, that Curiositie was the Nurse of Calumny. . . . sith she feeds and fosters this Damsell [puellam] with the long sought-for meat [cibo] of speeches and rumors. Take her from Calumny, and what can she doe? She will straight wex weak, faint, & em-ptie; hauing no more will, than power to hurt" ("cas / quàm"; 106/147–48). The stem of Jonson's marginal flower extends nearly to the end of this passage, and all the quoted sentences are under-lined. Once again, an interest in memorable language and sum-mary argument seems to have prompted the poet's marking. Curiosity (Lipsius continues) ranges widely, seeking out news concerning the court and foreign countries and never resting sat-isfied. Rather, "as a putrid and scabbed limb delights to be scratcht, and rubb'd: so she itcheth for sharpe and opprobrious speeches [sic ista sermonibus, & presertim asperis malisque, as-siduè scabi]" ("pit / sertim"; 106/149). Jonson underlines this strik-ing passage and marks it with a flower. Lipsius elaborates at length upon the characteristics of Curiosity, then concludes his whole second section by reiterating that Calumny is "begotte<n> by Lying, brought forth by Envy, & brought up by Curiosity" ("quae / Inuidia"; 106/154). Jonson underlines this all and sets it off with a flower. Few markings reveal more clearly than this one his architectonic interest in the orderly structure and develop-ment of Lipsius's oration.

In the next section, Lipsius deals with the mischief calumny causes. Jonson flowers and underlines the assertion that calumny "wounds deeply, & priuily" ("Variam"; 107/153), a claim Lipsius proceeds to develop. Also underlined is the response of the Spar-tan soldier who, when asked whether his sword was sharp enough, replied that it was keener than calumny ("*Satisne acutus esset? Acutior,* inquit, *Calumniá*" [107/154]). A marginal flower and more underlining highlight Lipsius's explanation that by this the soldier meant that "no edge of iron and steele, could compare in keenenesse with the edge of the tongue" ("aut / Quid"; 107/154). The historical anecdote and memorable imagery must have ap-pealed to Jonson, but perhaps he also reflected that the same verbal potency that made calumniators so fearsome (and so feared) could also prove a powerful weapon in the hands of satirists like himself. What finally distinguished satirists from detractors was not their instruments but their underlying motives.

Nothing, Lipsius continues, is exempt from the power of calumny, whose effectiveness depends partly on its secrecy ("efficaciùs, quoniam Occultè"; UL; [107/155]). "How can a weapon bee avoided, that is not seene? The clowds forewarne vs of the ensuing tempest; smoake of the ensuing fire; a Spy, of the approach of the Enemy: but, the mischiefe that comes from a Calumniator, is sudden, and vnexpected" ("Tempesta- / calumniante"; UL, FL; 107/155). Remarks like this one may help to explain the often quite public nature of Jonson's beligerence, particularly in his attacks on rivals. If the fault of calumny was associated with secrecy and hypocrisy, Jonson may have believed that there was more honor in being open about one's anger than in expressing it covertly. The very vehemence that has sometimes made him seem somewhat unattractive may have been viewed by him as greatly preferable to (and more courageous than) surreptitious backbiting or dissembling flattery, the latter of which Lipsius now proceeds to excoriate. Jonson underlines an italicized quotation from an unnamed historian asserting that "A mans greatest enemies are his greatest praisers [Pessimum inimicorum genus, laudantes]" (107/156–57). Although Lipsius expresses further contempt for such hypocrisy, Jonson's markings cease for the rest of this page.

His marking resumes briefly at the top of the next page, where underlining and a marginal flower emphasize the suggestion that calumny is a "publique calamity, and the Phaeton (if I may so say) of the Earth's circle" ("ordinem / dam"; 108/159). What is interesting about this marking is that Jonson breaks into the middle of Lipsius's sentence; the mythological allusion seems to have caught his attention. Nothing else, however, is marked on the rest of this page, in which Lipsius emphasizes the particular dangers calumny poses for eminent men and how calumny focuses on what people value most, especially fame. Although calumny cannot hurt true virtue, it can cloud virtuous acts. God, heaven, motives, character—none of these are exempt from her reach. Jonson's markings begin again only when Lipsius quotes a passage from Homer describing Ate as "A mischieuous Goddesse . . . which offendeth all: / Which toucheth not the earth, but, walks upon the heads of men, / And hath hurt Iupiter himselfe" ("omnes / laesit"; 109/165–66). Jonson both underlines and flowers this quotation, whose significance Lipsius now discusses in frankly allegorical terms. Jonson himself had alluded to Ate in *Catiline* (H&S 5:503), and so he may have taken a particular interest in Lipsius's thoughts on this subject. Not surprisingly, Lipsius sees Ate as signifying calumny: she offends all and seldom attacks base (or "earthy") men. Jonson fails to mark these interpretations, but a marginal line does single out the suggestion that she attacks "the highest matters, and most eminent persons [summa petit, & summates]" ("id / laedit"; 109/167). Moreover, he underlines the final quote ("In conclusion; *shee hurts* Iupiter *himselfe*" ["Denique *Jouem ipsum laedit*"]) as well as the explanatory comment that such injury consists partly in "not suffering Religion herselfe to goe free and vntoucht of her venomed tooth" ("im- / ad-"; 109/167–68). Jonson's own disdain for religious polemicists—whom he called "*Controverters* in Divinity" and "*Fencers* in Religion" (H&S 8:595–96)—may have made such a passage seem worth marking.

Of particular interest, given Jonson's status and circumstances, is his next marking, which shifts attention toward the calumny that is practiced "in the Courts of Princes. For here is her proper and true throne: heere shee plaies the wanton, and curuets within her circle [Hîc enim ei sedes: hîc admissis equis lasciuit & currit, vt in suo circo]" (109/168; UL, FL). Such a marking helps explain Jonson's oft-expressed contempt for the court and courtiers he knew so well. His own connections at court would have made him quite familiar (especially as an occasional victim) with the calumny practiced there, and they would also have made him eager to distance himself (if only in his own mind) from a practice connected with courtly corruption. Although Jonson mostly by-passes the opportunity to mark Lipsius's detailed elaboration on the evils of such court calumny, underlining and a marginal flower do emphasize the summary assertion that "we neuer see, or haue seene, any wickednesse whatsoeuer, but . . . diffused from this . . . Fountaine [quod non ab hac scaturigine diffusum]. Subiects against their Princes, Princes against their subiects, are first stirred-vp, kindled, prouoked, & enflamed" by calumny at court ("vidimus / quam"; 109/171). What makes such a charge especially intriguing is its emphasis on the public and political fallout of private vice. Like a number of other marked passages, this one suggests Jonson's fear of the social disorder that calumny could help unleash.

Unfortunately, Jonson leaves all of the next page (110) unmarked. Here Lipsius elaborates on the public consequences of calumny, notes that early Christians associated this vice with the devil, and wonders why no civilized nation has seen fit to make calumny a crime. He concludes that they despaired of attempting to punish a vice so incurable and widespread. In introducing the third and final section of his oration, which deals with avoiding calumny, Lipsius cautions once more that anyone who thinks himself immune from its effects is deceived. However, he does suggest two shields—innocence and patience. Concerning the innocent he asks (in a sentence Jonson underlines and flowers), "and indeed they, which liue in integritie of life, warines of speech, modestie of actions, why should they fear her [Calumny]?" ("cauti / politis"; 111/175). According to Cicero (whose words Lipsius italicizes and Jonson underlines), *"as fire cast into water, is in an instant extinguished; so, a false accusation on a chast life [Vt ignis in acquam coniectus continuòr estinguitur: sic falsum crimen in castam vitam]"* (111/178). Interestingly, although Jonson marks this optimistic assessment (with its possible word play on *"falsum"* and *"castam"*), he fails to single out Lipsius's gloomy qualifications, which precede and follow it. Lipsius stresses that even the purest persons can be wounded, "For, Calumny (as I said before) supports her selfe by Lying. And she may doe it safely" ("docui"; 111/179), thanks to gullibility. Jonson underlines the words just quoted and then flowers and underlines the quoted claim that *"nothing was to bee spoken against any man; for . . . though the wound may be healed, the scarre will remain. A shrewd speech; [but] . . . very wittie [Pestilens, (sed) . . . ingeniosum dictum]"* ("qui / origo"; 111/179–80). The stem of Jonson's flower takes in the words he underscores as well as the immediately subsequent passage (not underlined), which argues that this "speech"

> takes his original, and credite from our owne natures. For, it is grafted in the dispositions of many men, not onely to giue open, but credulous eare, to al whispering reports [delationibus]; and the more willinglie, if they treat of any wrong done, or to be done. Hee, whose chance it is to be spotted, will hardly wash himselfe cleane again [Et cùm semel aspersus sis, vix est vt plenè eluas hanc labem]

For (at this point the stem of the flower ends and underlining resumes), "the suspicion will remaine, though the crime doe not" ("Suspicio inquam manet, vbi non crimen"; 111/180–81). This whole section, stressing the long-lasting effects of calumny, must have enhanced Jonson's sense of slander's dangers and of the need to avoid them. Of course, calumny's effects would be even more indelible in the relatively circumscribed arena in which Jonson had to operate. For an English writer of his day and type, there were few alternatives to London and the court. A poet with Jonson's ambitions could not easily flourish in another place; the risks of losing face in London were compounded by the fact that there were so few other places to succeed, or even fail. The poet's sense of the dangers of losing his reputation can be glimpsed, for instance, in his epigram "TO MY MUSE" (*Ep.* 65), in which he hopes that she will help some other wretch "Get . . . the times long grudge, the courts ill will; / And, reconcil'd, keepe him suspected still" (H&S 8:48; 7–8). Calumny in general was bad enough, but calumny in the closed circles in which Jonson moved could be far more difficult to escape, undo, or counteract.

Thus, according to Lipsius, calumny had to be borne with patience and courage. As a brave soldier scorns weak darts, so should a wise man respond to attacks. "For, what can they take from him? His good name? That will euer be good, amongst good men" ("Quid enim tibi tollunt? Famam? bona ea semper erit apud bonos"; UL; 111/182). Jonson's underlining of this brief passage is typical of many of his markings throughout the oration. Perhaps the passage appealed to him because of its word play ("bona . . . apud bonos"), its sententiousness, and its effective summary of points elsewhere developed at length. But the passage also suggests another possible function of Jonson's reading of this treatise: the consolation it might provide. Although Lipsius repeatedly emphasizes calumny's pervasiveness, his final section (especially) also offers glimmers of hope and practical suggestions for dealing with a problem that both he and Jonson seem to have felt was inescapable. Jonson probably turned to Lipsius less out of scholarly curiosity about an academic topic than out of a genuine and personal interest in the real problems the oration confronts. Even the more depressing of Lipsius's arguments had their consoling features: it was especially the good, for instance, who were likely to be calumny's targets. In a sense, then, the more one was unfairly attacked, the more evidence there was of one's moral stature. Besides, such attacks could not touch one's virtue, which is (after all) all that really matters. Lipsius italicizes (and Jonson flowers and underlines) the proclamation that "*All that is mine I carry with mee*" ("*Omnia mea mecum porto*"; 111/183). The ideal of self-possession, so central to Jonson's life and writings, affects his markings, too.

The stem of the flower just mentioned drops to take in some sentences that immediately follow the italicized phrase. These sentences, also underlined, anticipate objections: "But, thou wilt reply, that the meere . . . appearance of Infamie is to be feared [Quòd si infamiae tamen specie moueris]. If thou be guilty, feare it: if not, why fearest thou? [benè, si verâ; sin autem falsâ, quid ad te?] Apply it not to thy selfe; and all is well [non eam habes]. *Diogenes*, the Cinicke (a man of a towring wisedome . . . [here the stem of Jonson's flower ends, at the bottom of page 111]) was wont to say, when the people mockt him; *They deride me: yet, I am not derided [Illi me rident? ego non rideor]*" ("si / illa"; 111–12/183). This ideal of calm indifference to attack—so appealing to the poet and yet so difficult to practice—motivates a number of Jonson's markings, as when he underlines the admonition that "Calumniators neuer lightly contemne or scorn any man, that hath not first contemnd himselfe [Nemo ab istis conteritur aut contemnitur, nisi qui antè se contempsit]" (112/184). Similarly, he underlines the italicized response of Cato to a man who had attacked him and then sought his pardon: "*I assure thee, I remember no such matter [Non hercules*, inquit, *animaduerteram]*" (112/184). Such attacks, after all, are merely words.

A final marginal symbol (trident-shaped, with a long curving stem) at last brings Jonson's markings to a close. The trident's prongs help emphasize a sentence that the poet also underlines. Referring to malicious attacks, Lipsius advises: "Refuse to vnderstand them; and, withall, the scoffer hath lost the whole purpose and fruit of his contumely [Noli ea intelligere, perijt conuiciatori contumelie suae fructus]." Although the underlining momentarily ceases, the trident's stem encloses the immediately following sentence: "These (. . . Auditours) are the safest [solida] weapons against Calumny: not those, which the vulgar fight withall [vsurpat]; Memory, and Reuenge [reponere & vindicare]." Then the underlining resumes: "As in trauelling, if a dogge, or horse dash mee [luto me adspergat], I am nothing mov'd at him; but rather, rubbe it offe [non excandesco statim & viccissim in illum regero, sed potiùs me purgo]," so, Lipsius concludes (as Jonson's underlining ceases), "so should wee doe here; accounting of them as of Curres, and Iades [caniculis aut equuleis]: whose iniuries proceede not from iudgement; but, from froward passion [sed impetu & proteruiâ laedunt]" ("gae / petu"; 112/185–86). At this point the trident's stem curves into the end of Lipsius's paragraph, causing Jonson to underline the last three and a half words (from "petu" to "laedunt"). The oration itself continues for another few sentences, in which Lipsius urges his listeners to banish the plague of calumny as offensive to God. It is impossible to handle hot iron without being burned. Calumniators are poisonous asps. The oration ends with an imprecation borrowed from the biblical David, beseeching God to confound the deceitful lips of those who speak against the just.

Jonson's interest in calumny—and in Lipsius's thoughts and advice—hardly seems academic. Obviously the subject resonated with concerns that touched him deeply throughout his life. The passages cited earlier from his *Discoveries* indicate his conscious preoccupation with the topic, and numerous similar passages could easily be quoted. The markings in *De Calumnia*, then, are just some of many data indicating Jonson's abiding concern with the damage that could be wreaked by calumny and calumniators.

Such damage could be especially hurtful in the rigidly hierarchical society in which Jonson had to compete and survive. Being attacked was bad enough, but being attacked before a superior, reported to an authority figure, or gossiped about in the presence of a patron, lord, or master could feel—and could be—infinitely more hurtful and threatening. In a democracy, in which equality of status is officially presumed, slander cannot in theory undermine the roots of one's social power. But in a society like Jonson's, in which real power so often had to be solicited (and could suddenly be withdrawn), the impulse to attack competitors and the consequences of being slandered might both be felt more deeply. Perhaps this explains the poet's violent reaction in the *Discoveries* to what (in another context) he once called "houshold spyes" (H&S 8:102):

> They are an odious, and vile kind of creatures, that fly about the house all day; and picking up filth of the house, like Pies or Swallowes, carry it to their nest (the Lords eares) and oftentimes report the lyes they have fain'd, for what they have seene and heard. . . . How often have I seene, (and worthily) these Censors of the family, undertaken by some honest *Rustick*, and cudgel'd thriftily? These are commonly the off-scowring, and dregs of men, that doe these things, or culumniate others: Yet I know not truly which is worse; hee that malignes all, or that praises all. There is as great a vice in praising, and as frequent, as in detracting. (H&S 8:613)

Jonson's own experiences of being attacked before (or reported to) his superiors are suggested in a memorable passage (based on Apuleius) that conveys a full sense of his practical insecurity and of his personal interest in the problem of calumny:

> It is true, I have been accus'd to the Lords, to the *King;* and by great ones: but it hap'ned my accusers had not thought of the Accusations

with themselves; and were so driven, for want of crimes, to use invention, which was found slander: or too late, (being entred so farre) to
seeke starting-holes for their rashnesse, which were not given
them. . . . which though from their hired, and mercenary impudence, I might have past by, as granted to a Nation of Barkers, that
let out their tongues to lick others sores; yet I durst not leave myself
undefended, having a paire of eares unskilfull to heare lyes; or have
those things said of me, which I could truly prove of them. . . . Nay,
they would offer to urge mine owne Writings against me; but by
pieces (which was an excellent way of malice) as if any mans Context,
might not seeme dangerous, and offensive, if that which was knit, to
what went before, were defrauded of his beginning; or that things,
by themselves utter'd, might not seeme subject to Calumnie, which
read entire, would appeare most free. (H&S 8:604–5).

Many previously discussed strands of Jonson's thinking about
calumny come together here. To the danger of being accused before superiors is added the danger of being accused by them.
Having a detractor would be reason enough to worry, but being
attacked by a detractor with superior social status must have
seemed even more seriously threatening. The impulse to ignore
attacks and to rest merely upon one's innocence often proves
weaker, in Jonson's case, than the impulse to exonerate himself,
while the phrase suggesting that he "durst not" fail to respond
implies the risks involved in the very attempt to ignore attacks.
Indeed, the passage describing his predicament becomes part of
his self-defense. Moreover, the passage also indicates that slanderers could be motivated not simply by personal vice but by
payment (presumably from malevolent superiors wealthier than
themselves), and it also indicates that accusations could be turned
against the accusers in a process that would inevitably collapse
any clear distinctions between innocence and blame.

Jonson's fascination with calumny, then, is indicated not only
by his markings in Lipsius but by numerous examples from his
own life and works, including the passages just quoted from the
Discoveries. The locus classicus of such passages, although much
too extensive to transcribe in full, illustrates by its very length
his interest in this topic. Borrowed from J. J. Scaliger's Confutatio
Stultissimae Burdonum Fabulae (another text the poet owned and
marked), this passage begins by noting that "Envy is no new
thing, nor was it borne onely in our times. The Ages past have
brought it forth, and the comming Ages will." Yet (the passage
later continues),

It is a new, but a foolish way you have found out, that whom you cannot equall, or come neere in doing, you would destroy, or ruine with evill speaking: As if you had bound both your wits, and natures prentises to slander, and then came forth the best Artificers, when you could forme the foulest calumnies.

Indeed, nothing is of more credit, or request now, then a petulant paper, or scoffing verses; . . . Hee is upbraydingly call'd a *Poet*, as if it were a most contemptible *Nick-name*. But the *Professors* (indeed) have made the learning cheape. Rayling, and tinckling *Rimers*, whose Writings the vulgar more greedily reade; as being taken with scurrility, and petulancie of such wits. Hee shall not have a Reader now, unlesse hee jeere and lye. It is the food of mens natures: the diet of the times! *Gallants* cannot sleepe else. The Writer must lye, and the gentle Reader rests happy, to heare the worthiest workes misinterpreted; the clearest actions obscured; the innocent'st life traduc'd; And in such a licence of lying, a field so fruitfull of slanders, how can there be matter wanting to his laughter? Hence comes the *Epidemicall* Infection. For how can they escape the contagion of the Writings, whom the virulency of the calumnies hath not stav'd off from reading?

Nothing doth more invite a greedy Reader, then an unlook'd-for *subject*. And what more unlook'd-for, then to see a person of an unblam'd life, made ridiculous, or odious, by the Artifice of lying.

As this passage indicates, the very popularity of calumny could make it tempting to a poet seeking to build a reputation—and Jonson himself, of course, had often been accused precisely of slandering others to promote to his own interests. Perhaps part of the reason that he showed such a recurring fascination with calumny and that he so strongly and repeatedly indicated his personal revulsion at it was his felt need to distinguish his own works and motives from the vice he attacked. His persistent sense of being subject to abuse; his contempt for "trivial" antagonists whom he nonetheless could not bring himself to ignore; his paradoxical sense of threatened superiority—these and other motives seem to have prompted not only his interest in calumny but also his markings in *De Calumnia*. His responses to Lipsius's oration, far from being merely bookish, instead speak volumes about some of Jonson's deepest hopes and fears.

7

Jonson Reading Edmondes Reading Caesar

Jonson's marked personal copy of Clement Edmondes's *Observations upon Caesar's Commentaries* is only one of several books from his library that suggest his dual interest in history and in military affairs.[1] Yet his copy of Edmondes's massive work is of special interest for a number of reasons. For one thing, Edmondes not only comments on Caesar's commentaries but also translates them. Although Jonson could easily have read Caesar in the original Latin and no doubt did, no personal copy of a Latin version has been reported to survive. Edmondes's book thus shows, if nothing else, that Jonson did have access to Caesar's important narratives of the Gallic and Civil wars. For another thing, however, Edmondes's work is neither so derivative nor so focused as its title might imply. The size of his book is massive, and its scope is wide-ranging. Edmondes labored over his project for years, adding to it as time went by and expanding it in successive editions. The resulting tome testifies not only to his careful reading of Caesar but to his easy familiarity with the numerous classical and modern authors he cites in support of his observations. Moreover, Edmondes is not at all narrowly concerned simply with interpreting Caesar or with commenting on the technicalities of warfare. His range is encyclopedic, and he seems to have felt that the subject of his work was neither arcane nor antiquarian. For Edmondes and for Jonson, the book seemed variously relevant to problems of contemporary life. This is suggested not only by Jonson's markings—which highlight a broad gamut of topics—but also by two commendatory epigrams the poet wrote to preface Edmondes's book. The poems, combined with the markings, provide valuable evidence not only of Jonson's interest in the work but also of his detailed reactions to it.

Clement Edmondes might have seemed an unlikely person to offer such voluminous opinions about the art of warfare. Although he served in 1600 as "the bearer of a despatch from Sir

Francis Vere with news of the battle of Nieuport,"[2] he seems to have earned his living chiefly as a bureaucrat or public servant, and he opens his *Observations* by defending the practical relevance of military theory. Born perhaps in 1564, Edmondes entered Oxford in 1586 as "a yeoman's son" and received B.A. and M.A. degrees in 1589 and 1593 respectively. "It is probable that Edmondes owed his political advancement in great part to his marriage with a lady of the court" named "Mary Clerk, described as an attendant upon the Lady Stafford." In 1601 he became an assistant to Giles Fletcher as remembrancer of the city of London, and in 1605, when Fletcher resigned, Edmondes succeeded him, earning an annual salary of £100. "As the official mouthpiece of the city he was in constant communication with the court, and made such good use of his opportunities as to obtain, 13 Aug. 1609, the grant of the office of clerk of the council for life." He subsequently resigned as remembrancer and spent most of the rest of his career in the orbit of the court. "Between 1610 and 1612 Edmondes benefited largely from the forfeiture of recusants' estates," and during the following decade he received a number of appointments and was knighted in 1617. "His final promotion was to the office of secretary of state, but he was prevented from entering upon its duties by his death, from apoplexy, which took place on 13 Oct. 1622."

This sketch of Edmondes's life makes his connections with Jonson seem all the more interesting. Edmondes was hardly an obscure and penurious author, toiling away on recondite topics. He was a significant and well connected official whose influence continually grew. Moreover, the volume of his *Commentaries* in which Jonson's commendatory poems were first printed probably appeared in 1609, a time when Edmondes was achieving new prominence at court.[3] In addition, this publication coincided with the growing power of Prince Henry, to whom Edmondes dedicated the book and who seems to have known Edmondes and to have taken a personal interest in his completion of the project.[4] In fact, the work's dedication declares that it was at Henry's own initiative that the book was finished: "*HAuing ended this taske of Obseruations, and according to your gratious pleasure & command, supplied such parts as were wanting to make vp the Totall of these Commentaries: it doth return again, by the lowest steps of humblenesse, to implore the high patronage of your Princely fauour*" (sig. Aij). Henry's martial temperament and interest in national self-assertion had already made him a magnet for those who favored a more aggressive foreign policy than the one pursued by King James. Many looked forward to the day when Henry might spearhead an anti-Catholic, anti-Spanish crusade. By the time Edmondes dedicated his work on warfare to the Prince, the latter had increasingly begun to assume and assert power independent of his father's, and the Prince's influence seemed likely only to grow.[5]

Therefore, Edmondes's connections with the Prince might have been expected to make Edmondes himself seem more significant. Certainly the militarists in Henry's camp would have welcomed the kind of advice that Edmondes had to offer. Yet Edmondes's dedication is also careful to pay homage to James and to Jacobean pacificism. Caesar is called *"the same Author: which, in the deepe Iudgement of his most excellent Maiesty, is preferd aboue all other profane histories; and so, commended, by his sacred Authoritie, to your reading, as a cheefe paterne and Maister-peece of the Art of warre"* (Aij). If Edmondes worried that he might seem to be encouraging tendencies on which Henry's father frowned, he could thus justify himself by pointing to James's own advice to his son in *Basilikon Doron*.[6] Yet Edmondes also stresses that knowledge of warfare *"is not altogether vnproper for these happie dayes,"* since *"Warre is neuer so well handled, as when it is made an Argument of discourse in times of sweete and plentious peace. The blessings whereof, may euer crowne your yeares; as the soueraigne good of this temporarie life, and the chiefest ornaments of Princely condition"* (Aij-Aij[v]). As his book itself suggests, Edmondes seems to have shared Jonson's own attractions toward peace and his ambivalence concerning war.[7]

Jonson's varied responses to Edmondes's book are implied by his markings, but some of them are also spelled out in his two commendatory poems preceding the work. These poems are interesting not only as biographical data but as works of art, although neither they nor Jonson's commendatory poems in general have received much sustained attention. For the insights these works can provide about Jonson's reactions to Edmondes, they may be worth scrutinizing in some detail before we turn to his marks themselves. The fact that the poems were printed with Edmondes's commentaries suggests interesting things about Jonson's relationship with Edmondes, about his own status in Jacobean society, and about the usefulness of commendatory poems for personal self-display. The poems reveal at least as much about Jonson as they do about Edmondes or his book.

The skill of the first poem to Edmondes (*Ep.* 110) suggests that Jonson took seriously his task of commendation:

> NOt CAESARS deeds, nor all his honours wonne,
>   In these west-parts, nor when that warre was done,

The name of POMPEY for an enemie,
  CATO'S to boote, *Rome,* and her libertie,
All yeelding to his fortune, nor, the while,
  To haue engrau'd these acts, with his own stile,
And that so strong and deepe, as 't might be thought,
  He wrote, with the same spirit that he fought,
Nor that his worke liu'd in the hands of foes,
  Vn-argued then, and yet hath fame from those;
Not all these, EDMONDS, or what else put too,
  Can so speake CAESAR, as thy labours doe.
For, where his person liu'd scarce one iust age,
  And that, midst enuy' and parts; then fell by rage:
His deedes too dying, but in bookes (whose good
  How few haue read! how fewer vnderstood!)
Thy learned hand, and true *Promethean* art
  (As by a new creation) part by part,
In euery counsell, stratageme, designe,
  Action, or engine, worth a note of thine,
T<o>'all future time, not onely doth restore
  His life, but makes, that he can dye no more.[8]

Like a number of Jonson's other epigrams, this one opens with
negation, with suspended syntax, and with an increasingly elaborate set of distinctions ending in a judgment establishing its subject's unique merit. The fact that Jonson delays the opening
sentence's main verb until the sentence is nearly complete (in 12)
gives the first part of his poem both narrative and syntactical
suspense, so that the concluding judgment comes with a finality
all the more powerful for having been postponed. The poem's
opening line emphasizes actions and their consequences, and it
also immediately suggests uncomplicated praise, which the poem
will soon proceed to complicate. Although the poem's subject
might at first seem literally distant from the concerns of Jonson's
readers, the second line brings "CAESARS deeds" literally home
to them, reminding them of his military involvement in early
Britain ("these west-parts"). A similar shift in perspective can be
seen in the transition from 2 to 3, from a concern with external
conflict to a focus on civil war—a transition, by the way, that
neatly encapsulates both major sections of Edmondes's book.
  Progression of a different sort can be seen in 3–4, which detail
Caesar's enemies. The first is highly personal—"POMPEY," a single man who (as Edmondes stresses) had flaws and failings of
his own. The second name (Cato) is less ambiguous, more clearly
associated with uncompromising virtue. The shift from Pompey
to Cato suggests already a shift from personal conflict to a conflict

rooted in contrasting values. When the focus shifts again, this time to "*Rome*," the antagonist is suddenly even less personal than before; Caesar's "enemie" is now the entire city, and the conflict implied is more obviously political, fraticidal, and unattractive. Finally, the last "enemie" named is neither a single person nor an aggregate of people but an impersonal ideal—"libertie," a transnational, transhistorical principle. (The emphatic irony of rhyming "enemie" and "libertie" was surely deliberate.) Just as Jonson earlier reminded his British readers of the implications of Caesar's deeds for their own place and past, so he reminds them here of the relevance of this story to larger issues of political philosophy. In two lines the poem radiates outward from a focus on private feuding to a concern with a cherished but threatened value.

Line 5 describes how Caesar's enemies "yeeld[ed] to his fortune," and yet that final word is disturbingly ambiguous, suggesting already what the poem later makes clear—that Caesar was also subject to powers greater than he. His foes yielded not so much to him as to his "fortune," a word already implying the instability of his triumph. Caesar has "engrau'd" his acts "with his own stile" in a double sense (6): he has made them seem grave and imposing through his manner of performing them, and he has also recorded them in writing with his own stilus. Words and deeds, spirit and acts, literature and war: Caesar unites them all. His "worke liu'd in the hands of foes" (9) in the sense that his writings survived and were valued by descendants of the very peoples he conquered, and also in the sense that his enemies could not forget their physical combat with the forces he led. Even now the line is not exhausted, for the phrasing can also suggest that his deeds were written down and celebrated by the descendants of his former enemies—including men such as Edmondes. Caesar's work was "Vn-argued then, and yet hath fame from those" (10): once again he bridges contrasts, in this case between past and present. Caesar's literary style—"strong and deepe" (7)—reflects his character, and perhaps these adjectives also suggest the kind of effect Jonson hoped to achieve through the phrasing of his own poem.

Certainly the sheer length and complexity of the opening catalogue convey an impression of literary mastery: the lines illustrate not only Edmondes's comprehensive knowledge but also Jonson's poetic ability to keep the poem expanding but controlled. His praise of Edmondes displays the same knowledge and judiciousness it commends. Line 11 situates the name "EDMONDS" between a summary reference to everything that has gone before ("all these") and everything that Jonson could further mention if he chose ("what else . . . too"). The opening catalogue, he suggests, could easily have been expanded further. Edmondes's capitalized name is juxtaposed with Caesar's (11–12), the emphatic placement suggesting the close identification between the scholar and his subject, just as the reference to Edmondes's "labours" (12) recalls the earlier references to Caesar's "deeds" (1) and "worke" (9). Caesar wins fame in part through his writing, while Edmondes—through his own work and through Jonson's poem— wins fame for and through his writing about Caesar.

The repetition of Caesar's capitalized name in 12 ends the catalogue that began with the first appearance of that name in 1, and with 12 both the opening sentence and the first part of the poem conclude. The transition from 12 to 13 inaugurates the epigram's second sentence and section, the word "For" suggesting logical connection between the two halves and logical development from the first. The second part will now explain the assertion that consumed the poem's opening section. Caesar's "person," Jonson contends, barely lived a normal life-span, and even the time he did live was spent "midst enuy' and parts" (or factions), after which he "fell by rage" (14). The phrasing here can seem ambiguous: Caesar was surrounded by envy and factions, but he also participated in them. The final reference to "rage," however, reminds us of the manner in which he died and thus makes him seem more an innocent victim than he has seemed so far. The already complicated depiction of Caesar in this poem is thus complicated even further. Moreover, the poetic complexity of Jonson's phrasing is neatly illustrated in 14–16, with their alliteration and assonance ("deeds . . . dying"; "bookes . . . good") and with their progression from Caesar's death to the death of his deeds, then to the survival of those deeds in books, then to the paucity of the books' readers, and then to the incomplete understanding even among those few who have read them. The effect of these lines is to complicate immensely the poem's earlier confident assertions about the survival of Caesar's writings and reputation and thus to highlight the significance of the restorative and interpretative work of such men as Edmondes (and Jonson).

The reference to Edmondes's "learned hand" (17), for instance, thus recalls the earlier reference to Caesar "liu[ing] in the hands of foes" (9). And, just as Caesar combines various qualities, so does Edmondes unite learning and "art" (17). His commentaries on commentaries are no more derivative than Jonson's own poem commending them: Edmondes's work, like Jonson's, is generative in its own way (18). Jonson sees Edmondes's project of translation and commentary not as parasitical or secondary but as truly creative and restorative. Line 18 inaugurates a final catalogue that answers the one with which the poem opened. Line 19 emphasizes various sorts of thought, while line 20 stresses various kinds of actions and instruments—a double emphasis typical of Caesar's life, Edmondes's work, and Jonson's entire poem. What impresses Jonson about Edmondes's reading and response to Caesar is obviously, in part, their thoroughness, and Jonson's own closing catalogue seeks to do thorough justice to Edmondes's own accomplishment.

Jonson's epigram is a complex and sophisticated poem. It deals with Caesar as a reader (and writer) of himself, with Edmondes as a reader of Caesar, with Jonson as a reader of Edmondes (but also of Caesar), with us as readers of Jonson reading Edmondes and Caesar, and thus with our own readings of these two as colored by our reading of Jonson. Just as Edmondes has studied Caesar carefully, part by part, so does Jonson's epigram indicate that he has carefully scrutinized and evaluated Edmondes's book. Edmondes himself provides a model for Jonson's own reading of Edmondes, just as Jonson's scrutiny of Edmondes provides a model for our own confrontation with Jonson's poem. Edmondes helps perpetuate Caesar's fame, just as Jonson helps promote and perpetuate both Edmondes and his subject. Caesar's military "deeds" have become his literary "worke," just as Edmondes's scholarly "labours" are now embodied in the book Jonson extols. In these ways and in its closing lines, the poem continually works to resolve contradictions, to make but also to harmonize distinctions. Thus, the final couplet describes how Edmondes's work "T<o>'all future time, not only doth restore / [Caesar's] life, but makes, that he can dye no more" (21–22). Past, present, and future are here conjoined, as they were earlier in the poem (for example, in line 10), thus linking the poem's present with its own past. Edmondes's efforts as a reader and writer, far from being parasitical, are life-giving: he has restored not, of course, Caesar's literal "life" (22), but rather the full meaning and vitality of his writings. In the same way, Jonson as a reader and writer helps unfold the rich significance of the very book he praises.

The theme of past and present emphasized so strongly at the conclusion of Jonson's first commendatory poem is also emphasized at the beginning of his second (*Ep.* 111), entitled "TO THE SAME, ON THE SAME":

WHo EDMONDS, reades thy booke, and doth not see
  What th'antique souldiers were, the moderne bee?
Wherein thou shew'st, how much the latter are
  Beholding, to this master of the warre;
And that, in action, there is nothing new,
  More, then to varie what our elders knew:
Which all, but ignorant Captaynes, will confesse:
  Nor to giue CAESAR this, makes ours the lesse.
Yet thou, perhaps, shalt meet some tongues will grutch,
  That to the world thou should'st reueale so much,
And thence, depraue thee, and thy worke. To those
  CAESAR stands vp, as from his vrne late rose,
By thy great helpe: and doth proclaime by mee,
  They murder him againe, that enuie thee.

In a typical move, the opening lines ascribe to readers of Jonson's own poem the poet's understanding of Edmondes: the initial question makes his positive reaction to the book seem merely a matter of common sense. At the same time, however, the poet feels a need to unfold this reading, thus acting as our spokesman while also calling attention to the qualities (and quality) of his personal response. Once again syntax is exploited in interesting ways: each of the first four couplets makes a separate and discrete assertion, yet all are linked by connective phrases, and each builds on the one before it. Caesar here is commended simply as a "master of the warre" (4)—praise that involves none of the uncomfortable moral and political questions implied by the widening description of his "enemie[s]" in the first poem. The praise here is more neutral and less equivocal than before.

Both poems deal with debts. Just as Caesar himself was pictured in the previous epigram as indebted to Edmondes for the sustenance of his reputation, so modern soldiers are depicted here as "Beholding" to Caesar for his cultivation of military skills (4). In the first poem, past depends on present; in the second, the reverse is true. Moreover, both poems are concerned with the links between knowledge and action; in the second poem, acts of warfare, which might seem quintessentially authentic, are depicted as secondary and derivative: "in action, there is nothing new, / More, then to varie what our elders knew" (5–6). Jonson thus turns one of the potential charges against Edmondes's book—that it was parasitic upon the writings and acts it described—back against potential accusers, particularly military men who might doubt Edmondes's ability to comment intelligently on matters of warfare. Jonson's poem increases the prestige

of those, like Edmondes and himself, who can impart true knowledge, since right action depends on proper understanding. Moreover, to give Caesar and Edmondes their due is not to discredit
modern soldiers, as the best such soldiers realize (7–8).

Jonson's eloquent praise of both men distances him from the
very ignorance he condemns. Just as the first poem makes clear
that Caesar was surrounded by "enuy" (14), so the present poem
indicates, also in line 14, that Edmondes faces the prospect of
"enuie," too. This parallel may be coincidental, although it seems
worth noting that in both poems the name "CAESAR" is highlighted in the lines that begin the works' respective second halves.
Such similarites suggest that Jonson may have intended the two
poems to be compared and contrasted; their publication side by
side could only have encouraged this response. In any case, Jonson's own generous response to Caesar and to Edmondes sets a
standard by which the "enuie" of others can be judged. Edmondes must anticipate that "some tongues" (unlike Jonson's) "will
grutch, / That to the world thou should'st reueale so much" (9–
10)—"so much" suggesting either the mysteries and intricacies
of military tactics or perhaps simply the bare fact that modern
soldiers are not completely original. Such readers, unlike the generous Jonson, will "depraue" Edmondes and his "worke" (11)—
a word associated with Caesar in the first poem (9). In subtle
ways like these, Jonson implicitly compares Edmondes himself
with his subject.

The links and parallels between Caesar, Edmondes, and Jonson
are emphasized again at the poem's conclusion. There Jonson
imagines that Caesar "stands vp" to condemn Edmondes's
antagonists (12–13), but Caesar is able to stand only because of
Edmondes's own "great helpe" (13). Similarly, Caesar's condemnation of Edmondes's enemies is "proclaime[d] by mee" (13)—
that is, by Jonson. These lines describe the mutual dependence
of Caesar and Edmondes, and of both on Jonson, a dependence
suggested as well by the final rhyme ("mee / thee"). Whereas it
is Caesar who metaphorically and imaginatively "stands vp" to
Edmondes's enemies, one cannot help but notice that it is Jonson
who does this in fact. His praise of Caesar also reflects well on
himself, both on his intent and on his act. To envy Edmondes,
Jonson makes clear, is once more to "murder" Caesar—a verb
that again presents the Roman as a more unequivocally sympathetic figure than he had seemed in the first poem. Both works
conclude with references to death, but whereas the first ends
hopefully (thanks to Edmondes, Caesar "can dye no more" [22]),

the ending of the second seems more contingent, and emphasizes more emphatically the poet's crucial role as defender of the book he values.

That Jonson did value the book seems clear not only from the poems he wrote to commend it but also from an elaborate inscription he wrote inside his personal copy when he later presented the volume to his friend Henry Theobald. Edmondes himself, in giving the book to Jonson, had inscribed the following note: "Clement Edmondes commendeth himself to Ben. Johnson and dedicateth this booke to his vertues and his love to Clement Edmondes." Jonson, when he in turn presented the book to Theobald, emphasized the learning and erudition of the commentaries and their worthiness as a pledge of love or friendship to someone he considered an excellent soldier and a very dear friend ("Optimum Belli Magistrum, etiam Auctorem cum doctissimis commentariis Amici eruditiss. quem ipse mihi, & Musaeo meo dono concesserit, & dignatus sit, In aeternum pignus amoris, amicissimo, sive potius amicitiae ipsi D. Hen. Theobaldo Ben. Ionsonius aeternem amicus, vouet"). Yet Jonson's regard for the book is indicated not simply by such words and by his prefatory poems but also by his scores of markings, which suggest that he read the volume with very careful attention.

Like the book itself, the passages Jonson marked are wide-ranging and diverse. Nonetheless, the markings seem completely typical of the man who made them, not only in their appearance but also in the interests and concerns they suggest. Many marks imply a curiosity about precise historical details, and a surprising number concern the acts and career of Hannibal. Some marks highlight passages dealing with issues of language, including battlefield rhetoric and technical terminology. Others call attention to Latin *sententiae*, and many emphasize general psychological insights. Some of the marked passages offer moral evaluation, make moral distinctions, or deal with other issues of morality, while other highlighted passages are more narrowly concerned with specific military tactics. Some markings suggest an interest in early British history and in contemporary parallels to historical events, and one of the most interesting set of markings focuses on duelling, a controversial topic in Jonson's day. The marked passages frequently suggest a concern with the larger social implications of military matters, but they also imply a poet's eye for specific examples and details of all sorts. Finally, some of the markings suggest Edmondes's value to Jonson not only as a writer but as a reader himself, for some marks call attention to ideas and phrasing derived from a host of secondary sources. In one sense, in fact, everything that Jonson highlights is secondary, since his marks are entirely restricted to Edmondes's observations. Not once does he mark a passage from Edmondes's full translations of Caesar.

The first of Jonson's markings occurs in an observation Edmondes makes on book 1, chapter 7 of Caesar's commentary on the Gallic wars. Coincidentally, the marked passage follows hard upon a reference to Justus Lipsius, whose book on the Roman military Jonson also owned.[9] Speaking of a tactic described by Caesar, Edmondes notes that soldiers of the modern age "neuer imitateth this triple battell, but onely in a march: for, then commonly they make three companies; a vanguard, a battell, and a rereward: but in imbattelling, they draw these three Companies all in front, making two cornets and the battell, without any other troops to second them" (GW 1.7. 21; CR).[10] This marking is typical of a number that suggest Jonson's detailed interest in military tactics. As a former soldier himself who often boasted of his martial prowess, he must have had a personal fascination with the more specifically military observations that Edmondes frequently offers.

His next marking, however, concerns a topic of more obvious interest to a poet: the power of words. Edmondes stresses the importance of battlefield rhetoric, "for, if at any time that saying be true, that *Oratio plus potest quam pecunia* [eloquence can do more than money], it is here more powerfull and of greater effect. For, a donatiue or liberanca, can but procure a mercenarie indeauour, euer yielding to a better offer, and doe oftentimes breed a suspicion of wrong, euen amongst those that are willingly inriched with them . . ." (GW 1.8. 23; CR). Like many of Jonson's marks, this one does not emcompass Edmondes's entire sentence; Jonson seems to pick out only what interests him. It seems odd, for instance, that he highlights none of Edmondes's ensuing elaboration on the power of rhetoric, nor does he mark the passage condemning the modern age for its scoffing and derisive reaction to grave speeches during battle. He does, however, mark the observation that the modern "discontinuance of so necessarie a part, hath bred at length such an *inutilem pudorem* [unprofitable modesty] in our chief Commanders, that they had rather lose the gaine of a great aduantage, then buy it with words to be deliuered in publique" (GW 1.8, 23; CR). This and other marked passages imply Jonson's agreement that the power of the word could enhance the power of the sword.

Jonson's next two markings are particularly fascinating for what they imply about his interest in strict military discipline. Edmondes observes that breaches of such discipline, "in the rigour of Camp-policie, could not passe without due punishment: for, what can more contradict the fortunate successe of an expedition, then to suffer to bee measured with the vulgar conceit? or weighed in the balance of such false iudgments? especially, when those weake Censors are to be Actors, and Executioners of the designe: for, then, euery man will sute the nature of the action according to his owne humour . . ." (GW 1.16. 43; CR). The wise and prudent captain must balance "the losse of many particulars, with the health and safetie of the publique good. For, if euery man should prescribe; who should obay? *Tam nescire quaedam milites, quàm scire oportet* ['It is as proper that soldiers should not know certain things as that they should know them'], saith Otho in Tacitus, vpon the like disorder: and againe, *Parendo potiùs quam imperia ducum sciscitando, res militares continentur* ['It is rather by obedience . . . than by questioning the commands of the leaders, that success in war is obtained']. Which proueth, that the greatest vertue which is required in a souldier, is obedience . . ." (GW 1.16. 43; CR). Such markings suggest Jonson's concern, at least in military affairs, with proper hierarchy and with strict chains of command.[11]

His interest in specific historical details is implied by his next mark, which highlights Scipio's argument, in a debate with Fabius about how to defeat Carthage, that the best defense was a good offense ("Scipio / flicted"; GW 1.16. 42 [44]; CR). An ensuing marked passage endorses this view, noting that "There was a great difference in the nature of the action, betweene the spoile and waste of a strangers Country, and to see their owne natiue Countrey wasted with sword and destruction: *Plus animi est inferenti periculum, quàm propulsanti* [inflicting danger is a thing of greater spirit than repelling it]. For, he that inuadeth anothers kingdom, easily discouereth both the aduantage which may be taken against the enemy . . ." (GW 1.16. 42 [44]; VL). Once again Jonson's mark breaks off before Edmondes's syntax ends, but his mark captures the gist of the passage, with its Latin tag and its emphasis on the advantages of aggression. This emphasis is touched on again in the passage Jonson highlights next, which stresses the dispiriting effect of a Carthaginian invasion: "For, when Hanniball was come into Italie, and had defeated Sempronius the Consull at Trebeas, the Romaines were driuen into such an extasie of terrour, that they belieued verily, that the enemie

was then comming to assault the Citty; neither had they any hope
or aide in themselues, to keep or defend the same" (*GW.* 1.16.
45; CR). This is the first of numerous marks that focus squarely
on the doings of Hannibal. In fact, such marks are among the
most frequent Jonson made in his copy of Edmondes's book. Why
he should have shown such a fascination with the Carthaginian
general is a matter I will discuss later at greater length, but his
interest is all the more intriguing since not every passage dealing
with Hannibal is marked. His interest, in other words, seems to
have been intense but not exhaustive. Hannibal is touched on
once more, for example, in the next marked observation dealing
with 1.16. which notes that, when the Romans attacked Carthage,
the Carthaginians with all "speed . . . sent for Hanniball out of
Italy, to be their Champion against young Scipio. If therefore other
things bee correspondent (as there are many other particularities
concerning the power and strength of either Nation to be considered) I take it much better for a Prince to inuade an enemy in his
own country, then to attend him at home in his owne kingdome"
(*GW* 1.16. 46; CR). Once again Jonson marks a passage advocating
an offensive strategy, but this passage, in its sensible balancing
of general precept and specific contingencies, is also typical of
many of Edmondes's observations and suggests one reason Jonson may have valued his opinions.[12]

Later markings highlight a wide range of topics. For instance,
Edmondes at one point notes that such cities as yielded "to the
[Roman] Empire, and became tributarie to their treasury (how-
soeuer they were otherwise combined by confederacy) seldome
or neuer repented them of their facte, in regard of the noble patronage which they found in that state, and of the due respect
obserued towards them" (*GW* 2.1. 60; CR). What is interesting
about this marking is not so much the acceptance of imperialism
it may suggest, but rather its stress on the imperial power's obligations to treat its dependents fairly. Markings such as this imply
much about the larger political principles that may have guided
Jonson's thinking. Other markings suggest Jonson's recognition of
Caesar's ability as a leader. At one point, for instance, he marks
the observation that Caesar never encountered an enemy without
sufficient "power either in number or in valour to make head
against them: which equality of strength, being first laide as a
sure foundation, howsed his owne industrie and skill, and the
discipline wherein his men were trained, as aduantages to ouer-
sway his aduersarie: and so drew victorie maugre fortune vnto
himselfe, and seldome failed in any of his battels" (*GW* 2.3. 62,

CR). At the same time, however, Jonson's persistent interest in another commander—Hannibal—is reflected in a marked passage stressing a general's need to know the details of the territory through which he passes. If he does, he "hath all these particularities as maine aduantages, to giue meanes of so many seuerall attempts vpon an enemy: And in this point Hannibal had a singular dexterity, and excelled all the commanders of his time in making vse of the way, by which he was to passe. But he that leadeth an army, by an vnknown and vndiscouered way, and marcheth blindfold vpon vncertaine aduentures," is subject to casualties and disadvantages (*GW* 2.4. 71; CR). Both Caesar and Hannibal illustrated a leader's need to combine native skills with careful prudence.[13]

The importance of a prudent leader is suggested in another of the many marked passages dealing with Hannibal. Edmondes observes that Roman losses to the Carthaginian were "neither to be imputed to the defect of their Armes, or disposition of their Armies; but to the dexteritie and industrie of Hanniball: but wee haue entreated therof when we made mention of the battels themselues, and the end it selfe of that warre doth especially confirme this our opinion" (*GW* 2.10. 91; CR). This last comment alludes to Edmondes's ensuing argument that when the Romans found in Scipio a commander equal to Hannibal, the latter's victories vanished. Yet, despite his obvious interest in Hannibal, Jonson fails to mark a number of very long discussions of him, such as an observation on book 3, chapter 10 of the *Gallic Wars* (125). After a long gap in which no marks appear, Jonson does highlight the following general advice to exploit advantages as they arise: "Let a souldiour therefore take such holde of occasions, and opportunities that are offered vnto him, that in time of battaile hee may seeme to cast necessitie vpon his own cause, and retaine it in his paie: considering how the power therof altereth the workes of nature, and changeth their effects into contrary operations, being neuer subiect to any ordinance or lawe; and yet making that lawful which proceedeth from it" (*GW* 4.3. 138; CR).

Jonson's next marking is one of the most interesting in the entire book. Edmondes, in discussing whether or not princes and other commanders must always abide by strict principles of integrity, cites conflicting opinions. Although he begins by seeming to condemn contemporary "Polititians" who would justify the necessity of deceit, he proceeds to report their arguments in a neutral and objective tone. One of these arguments is marked by Jonson. Distinguishing the falsehood of private persons from the deception sometimes practiced by rulers, Edmondes reports the view that rulers "deriue their conclusions from other principles, whereof inferiour subiects are no more capable, then men are able to vnderstande the workes of the Godes: and therefore they are called *arcana imperij*, to bee reuerenced rather, then lookt into" (GW 4.4. 140; CR). Whether Jonson endorsed this opinion or rejected it is of course unclear from his markings alone, and external evidence can point either way.[14] Significantly, perhaps, he fails to mark any of the ensuing summarized views of those who "affirme vertue to be the same both in prince and people" (140), nor does he highlight Edmondes's warning that deception can come back to haunt the deceivers (140). At the very least, however, his marking indicates his real interest in the complicated issue the passage discusses.

The first reference to British history marked by Jonson also illustrates once more Caesar's prudence as a leader. Edmondes notes that, according to Suetonius, Caesar "neuer vndertooke any expedition, but he first receiued true intelligence of the particular site, and nature of the country, as also of the maners and qualitie of the people; and that he would not vndertake the voiage into Britanie, vntill he had made perfect discouerie by himselfe, of the magnitude and situation of the Iland" (GW 4.8. 146; CR). Jonson's markings of Edmondes often reflect this sort of interest in practical matters; they frequently highlight passages concerning military skill rather than larger political principles. He bypasses, for instance, the opportunity to mark a brief disquisition on liberty (GW 4.11. 156–57), nor does he highlight the reference to Caesar as the first who imposed on the British "the heauie name of a subdued people" (GW 5.7. 174). In marking Edmondes's book, he seems more often to have been interested in more immediately pragmatic concerns. One such case involves the issue of rhetoric, a recurrent theme of his markings. Thus when Terentius was arraigned for his friendship with Sejanus, the fallen favorite of the emperor Tiberius (and the subject of one of Jonson's tragedies), he defended himself by claiming that specific treasons should be punished, but as for friendships, "dueties, pleasures and good turnes, the same ende shall discharge and quit thee, O Caesar, and vs! The constancie of this Oration preuailed so much, that his Accusers were punished with exile. And thus we see howe particularities decide the controuersie, and make the waie plaine to good direction" (GW 5.10. 185; CR). Once again Edmondes observes, and Jonson marks, the power of the spoken word.[15] A poet who was compelled to defend himself as frequently as

Jonson was must have found Terentius's behavior and its results both inspiring and instructive.

The obverse of Edmondes's frequent emphasis on the importance of good leadership is his occasional discussion of bad examples, as in a passage Jonson marks that suggests how one coward can subvert the sound deliberations "of the rest of the leaders: for his timerousnesse flieth alwaies to extremities, making him rash in consultation, peremptorie in opinion, and base in case of perill" (GW 5.14. 191; CR). Such observations about human character seem always to have interested Jonson, and so it is not surprising that he marks at length the conclusions Edmondes draws from Caesar's story about two Roman soldiers whose personal rivalry provoked them to compete (but also to help each other) during combat with the enemy:

> For these *Simultates* [rivalries], which desire of honor had cast between them, brought forth emulation which is the spur of vertue, far from enmitie or hatefull contention: for the difference betweene these two qualities is, that enmitie hunteth after destruction, and onely reioiceth in that which bringeth to our aduersary vtter ruine, dishonour or ill atchieuement: but emulation contendeth only by well deseruing, to gaine the aduantage of an other mans fame, that vseth the same meanes to attaine to the like end; and is alwaies mixed with loue, in regard of the affinity of their affections, and the sympathie of their desires. (GW 5.19. 197)

This is one of the longest passages that Jonson marks, and his interest in it is not surprising since the style and sentiments it expresses are so obviously his own.[16] The careful distinctions, the moral emphasis, the stress on virtuous competition for public honor—all these notes are recognizably Jonsonian. The next marked passage also seems unsurprising, for in it Edmondes ponders the causes of contemporary moral decline. He wonders whether it was the ancients' discipline "which brought forth such honest effects of vertue, to their glory and our ignominy, hauing learned better rules then were known vnto them; or whether the world weakened with age, want[s] strength in these times to bring foorth her creatures in that perfection, as it did in those daies" (GW 5.19. 197). Such questions could just as easily have been asked by Jonson as by Edmondes. Both men apparently shared a strong sense of the moral degeneration of their own times.[17]

The particular "Observation" in which these questions are raised is one of the most heavily marked sections of the entire book, and its focus soon shifts from general issues to the highly specific and controversial topic of duelling. Duelling had evidently become popular enough to be the target of government efforts to suppress it, and King James himself would soon take a personal interest in condemning the activity.[18] Jonson alludes to duelling satirically in several of his plays,[19] and his markings of Edmondes's comments can perhaps shed further light on his own thinking about private combat. The first marked passage notes that in the early monarchies such combat was permitted only with foreigners; these were considered the only objects of the justice "which the priuate sworde should execute: for they well perceiued that these single battels were, as sparkles of ciuill discorde, and intestine warres; although not so apparent in the generall viewe of their state, yet as odious in particular, and as dishonourable to good gouernment" (GW 5.19. 198; CR). Nonetheless, Edmondes argues that no law, no matter how rigorous, can relieve this disorder without producing enormities just as great and just as intolerable to good government. Edmondes mentions one king who prohibited duelling and then had to withdraw his decree. "The like dict was published in France by Philip the Faire, but was within two yeeres reuoked againe, at the instante request of his subiectes, in regarde of the murthers and assassinats committed in that kingdome. The onlie remedie, that I finde to take effect in this case, was that of late time, which the Prince of Melphe in Piemont, inuented to preuent this euill" (GW 5.19. 198; CR). Oddly enough, however, Jonson does not mark this recommended remedy, which involved slaying the loser of any duel and ignominiously disposing of his body.

Jonson's next marking highlights the claim that what is "yet worst of all, is that custome hath now made it [duelling] so familiar, that euery trifle seemeth sufficient to call the matter to a priuate combate; a crosse looke calleth an other mans honour in question; but the word lye is of as great consequence, as any stabbe or villanie whatsoeuer. Whereat we may well wonder howe it happeneth, that wee feele our selues so much exasperated at the reproch of that vice, which we so ordinarilie commit" (GW 5.19. 198; CR). One could hardly ask for a comment more Jonsonian in tone and spirit; the poet had a strong sense of human resistance to moral correction.[20] Edmondes soon makes clear that he does not mean to mitigate the seriousness of the charge of lying; rather, his point is to emphasize human hypocrisy, "to shew the crookednesse of our disposition in disdaining to acknowledge that fault, which wee so commonlie commit. But I would faine learne when honor first came to be measured with words, for from the beginning it was not so. Caesar was often called to his face theefe, and dronkard, without any further matter; and libertie of inuectiues" between great persons ended simply with words (GW 5.19. 198; CR). Perhaps Jonson was intrigued by this evidence that past rulers were less sensitive to criticism than their latter-day successors. In any case, a mark not entirely uncharacteristic of the kinds most often made in this book and thus probably but not certainly Jonson's, signals the conclusion of this "Observation." Edmondes believes the person who simply returns the lie in a challenge, "and so letteth it rest, vntill further proofe, to haue as great aduantage in the reputation of honour, as the former, that first gaue the disgrace" (GW 5.19. 199; CT). Jonson's interest in social order and in personal self-control seems reflected in his markings here. He always seems to have been concerned with the social implications of individual behavior and with how such behavior affected social custom.[21]

The connection between a society's customs and its martial vigor is in turn the subject of some later passages by Edmondes marked by Jonson. Thus he incompletely highlights a section contrasting the vitality of the Germans and the relative impotence of their neighbors. The latter enjoyed "a more plentifull manner of life, which by litle and litle had weakened their strength, and made them far inferiour to the *Germaines*. Which bringeth to our consideration that which is often attributed to a ciuill life, that such as tast of the sweetnesse of ease, and are qualified with the complements of ciuilitie . . ." (GW 6.10.31; CR). A printed marginal summary left no room for extending the mark, but Edmondes proceeds to claim that those who enjoy such an easy life are indisposed to warlike practices. A subsequent marked passage notes that "*Marcellus* was blamed for being the first that corrupted *Rome* with the delicate and curious workes of *Greece:* for before that he brought from the sacking of *Syracusa* the wel wrought tables of pictures and imagery, *Rome* neuer knew any such delicacie, but stood ful fraught with armor & weapons of barbarous people" (GW 6.10.31; CR). Such thinking jibes with suspicions of luxury that Jonson himself frequently expressed, perhaps most memorably in his "*Epistle to a Friend, to Perswade Him to the Warres*" (*Und.* 15).[22]

That poem, like many of Jonson's writings, emphasizes the importance of integrity—a value reflected as well in a marked passage in which Edmondes describes how, in dealing with an ally, "*Caesar* chose rather to aduenture the armie vpon the casualities of hard prouision, then to blemish the *Romaine* name with the infamie of disloyaltie. Which was lesse daungerous also in regard of the effect: for where the bond is of valew, there the forfeiture is great" (GW 7.5. 56; CR). Jonson's emphasis on the importance of keeping personal commitments is well known,[23] but his marking here suggests that he similarly valued the importance of upholding trust between nations. Yet if a leader must be careful in dealing with his allies, he must take equal care in the treatment of his foes. Unusual double markings highlight a passage describing how

> At the siege of *Carthage* the *Romaines* hauing taken away their armes, they notwithstanding finding store of mettall within the towne, caused workemen to make euery day a hundred targets [shields] and three hundred swords, besides arrowes and casting slings, vsing womens haire for want of hempe, and pulling downe their houses for timber to build shipping. Whereby we may perceiue, that a General cannot be too carefull to depriue an enemie of all such helpes as may any way strengthen his hand, or make way to resistance. (GW 7.6.58–59; CR, CR)

Perhaps Jonson found the resourcefulness of the Carthaginians as noteworthy as the conclusion Edmondes drew from it.

Sometimes memorable phrasing seems to have prompted Jonson's marks. One such case, surely, must include the passage in which Edmondes comments on a Gallic strategem to escape the Romans by sneaking from a surrounded town at nightfall. When their women perceived that they might thus be abandoned to the Romans, they alerted the enemy to the planned escape. Edmondes observes that at first the Gauls seemed valorous in their conflict with Rome. "But being a litle spent in the action, like a pot that hath a mouth as bigge as the belly, and powreth out all the liquor at an instant, they fell at length to that basenesse, as shewed lesse spirit then the women did, who chose rather to betray their husbands purposes to the enemie" (GW 7.13, 75; CR). The striking image may have provoked Jonson to mark a moral assessment with which he probably concurred.

If the passage just cited deals with a loss of courage, Jonson's next marking highlights its recovery; in both cases the marks imply the poet's interest in the psychology of warfare. Edmondes notes that during the Roman conflict "with *Annibal,* in all the fights they made, they continued their first losse vnto the battel at *Nola,* at what time by *Marcellus* good directions, they gaue him an ouerthrow, which was the first time that euer *Annibals* souldiers began to giue place to the *Romaines,* and repaired the *Ro-*

maines valour againe, after so many battels as they lost: for then they were perswaded that they fought not with an enemie altogether inuincible, but that he was subiect to losse and ouerthrow" (*GW* 7.24. 99; CR). Yet sometimes the appearance of cowardice was a price worth paying to achieve a tactical advantage. Fabius the Roman was called a coward by the people of Rome "while he gaue place to the furie of the *Carthaginian,* and refused to receiue a third ouerthrow. And thus he altered the course of the *Romaine* warfare according to the time, and ouerthrew that enemie by shunning to encounter him, which in a battel would haue hazarded the conquest of *Rome.* In like maner *Cu. Sulpitius* the Dictator did imitate this wisdome of *Fabius* against the *Gaules,* by lingring out the warre" (*GW* 7.26. 102; CR).

The two passages just cited help prepare for a later one that Jonson also marks, in which Edmondes juxtaposes Fabius's caution with the impulsiveness of Marcellus. "The *Romaines* finding *Fabius Maximus* to be full of doubts and delay, good to defend, but not to offend, and *Marcellus* of a stirring spirit, neither quiet with good nor ill fortune, (as *Anniball* truly said of him) they thought to ioyne *Marcellus* youthfull courage with *Fabius* feare and wisdome, and so make a temperature fit for a Generall; whereupon they called *Marcellus* the sword, and *Fabius* the buckler: wherein *Caesar* of himself was excellent, of whom *Suetonius* reporteth, *Dubium cautior, an audentior* ['it is a question whether he was more cautious or more daring'] (*GW* 7.27. 106; CR).[24] Surely the imagery here must have caught Jonson's eye, but the passage's emphasis on a balance between extremes probably appealed to him as well. Nonetheless, he marks Edmonde's closing comment that Marcellus "kept his youthfull resolution to his old dayes, for being threescore yeares of age, he neuer longed for any thing more then to fight with *Annibal* hand to hand" (*GW* 7.27. 106; CR). Jonson, who was proud of his own courage and would declare in middle age his willingness to fight for his king, must have found appealing the notion of such physical courage in the service of a greater cause.[25]

It seems appropriate that one of the very last passages Jonson marked in his copy of Edmondes's *Commentaries* on the Gallic Wars should again mention Hannibal. As noted, Hannibal had been an object of prime interest for Jonson in his reading of Edmondes's book, and in fact it seems particularly striking that so much of his focus, when reading an account of warfare with the Gauls, should have fallen so squarely on this major figure from Rome's second Punic War with Carthage. Edmondes's occasional

digressions about Hannibal seem to have been of special interest
to Jonson, and part of the reason, perhaps, may be suggested by
a comment he made in the winter of 1618/19 to William Drummond. While visiting Scotland, Jonson told his host that "The
best wits of England" had been "Employed for making" Sir Walter
Ralegh's *History of the World*, a massive if incomplete volume published in 1614 with a prefatory poem by Jonson. Jonson told
Drummond that he "himself had written a peice to him of ye
punick warre which he [Ralegh] altered and set in his booke."
Perhaps this was one reason the poet also told Drummond that
"Raughlye esteemed more of fame than conscience" (H&S 1:138).
If Jonson had been reading Edmondes as part of his research
about the Punic War, his keen interest in the doings of Hannibal,
Fabius, Marcellus, and other actors in that famous conflict sud-
denly seems more explicable.

Jonson's comment to Drummond suggests that he had composed a set "peice" for Ralegh—which is to say, a passage of some
length with a concentrated focus. Ralegh's decision to "alter" the
piece complicates any effort to determine which portion of the
History may have been composed by Jonson; we have no way of
knowing how, or how extensively, Ralegh may have tampered
with Jonson's original work. C. H. Firth has suggested that Jonson
may have been responsible for a section of book 5 dealing with a
revolt by mercenaries,[26] but, if this were in fact the case, the passages Jonson marked in Edmondes's *Commentaries* seem not to
have contributed to his work. Jonson marked many of Edmondes's
comments on duelling, and duelling is, of course, the topic of one
of Ralegh's most famous and lengthy digressions in the *History*.
However, no obvious parallels exist between this digression and
the passages on duelling marked by Jonson; and besides, Jonson
seems to have been quite explicit in telling Drummond that his
contribution to the *History* dealt with the conflict between Rome
and Carthage.

A number of passages in Edmondes's book that were marked
by Jonson do in fact have parallels in Ralegh's *History*, but, because
these links are scattered over scores of pages, they do not hang
together as the sort of concentrated "peice" Drummond mentions. In addition, the parallels are often brief, and there are few
obvious echoes of Edmondes's exact phrasing. Moreover, many
of the same details mentioned in Edmondes would have been
available in other sources, and so the mere fact that Ralegh's *History* touches on matters also discussed by Edmondes (and marked

by Jonson) does not necessarily provide evidence that Edmondes was a source, via Jonson, for Ralegh's work.

Nevertheless, it seems worth noting the parallels that do exist, one of the most obvious of which involves the last quoted passage from Edmondes, where Marcellus was called the sword and Fabius the buckler (*GW* 8.27. 106; CR). A sentence in Ralegh's *History* similarly notes that "Fabius was called *the shield,* and Marcellus *the Roman sword.*"[27] Another similarity between Edmondes's book and Ralegh's *History* concerns Hannibal's defeat at Nola, which (in words by Edmondes marked by Jonson) "was the first time that euer *Annibals* souldiers began to giue place to the *Romaines,* and repaired the *Romaines* valour againe, after so many battels as they lost" (7.24. 99; CR). Ralegh recounts the same incident in comparable fashion, noting that this event was "reputed one of the bravest acts performed in all that war; forasmuch as hereby it was first proved, that Hannibal might be overcome."[28] By the same token, Jonson marks a passage in Edmondes dealing with a debate between Scipio and Fabius about whether or not to attack the Carthaginians in Africa. Edmondes notes (and Jonson marks) Scipio's opinion that "There was a great difference in the nature of the action, betweene the spoile and waste of a strangers Countrey, and to see their own natiue Countrey wasted with sword and destruction" (1.16. 42 [44]). In arguing with his opponent, "Scipio, on the other side, caried on with the honour of so glorious an exercise, wanted neither reasons nor examples to impugn Fabius his authoritie" (1.16. 42 [44]). Similarly, Ralegh's *History* notes that

> Scipio, on the other side, insisted upon this point, that it was better to make an offensive than a defensive war; . . . So promising to draw Hannibal into Afric for defence of his own home, and taxing as civilly as he could the envy of Fabius, which withstood such a gallant enterprise, he proposed the matter again unto the senate.[29]

This passage would seem to be the closest Ralegh's *History* comes to echoing the actual phrasing of passages marked by Jonson in Edmondes's book. The possibility that the echoes were influenced by Jonson's reading seems remote, but what does seem undenible is that Jonson's reading of Edmondes, as well as his contribution to Ralegh's work of a "peice" dealing with the Punic War, demonstrate his interest not only in that particular conflict but in military matters in general.

In fact, his only remaining mark in Edmondes's observations

on the *Gallic Wars* is typical in emphasizing a passage dealing with the advantages of military discipline and unity. Citing Tacitus, Edmondes declares that "as one bodie requireth but one head, so one businesse would haue but one director, forasmuch as *AE-mulation inter pares & ex eo impedimentum* [hinderance results from rivalry between equals]" (*GW* 7.35. 122; CR). While Jonson always valued virtuous competition, rivalry rooted in personal pride was a motive he often disdained, and nowhere were the potential dangers of such rivalry better illustrated than in the work that is the subject of his next set of marks and of Edmondes's next set of observations, Caesar's *Commentary on the Civil War*. Jonson's markings in this work are less numerous and less extensive than the marks he made in its companion piece, and in this and in another way the marks are somewhat disappointing. They offer little insight into Jonson's thinking about the "larger" political principles associated with Caesar's conflict with Pompey; instead, the marks usually reflect the same concerns with practical conduct, tactical maneuvers, and personal ethics that seem to have prompted many of his markings in the earlier *Observations*. This very fact, however, suggests what it was that interested Jonson when he read Edmondes's book, and in so doing it also suggests interesting things about his general intellectual orientation and habits of mind.

The purpose of Jonson's first mark dealing with the Civil War is not entirely clear. It flanks a passage flanked in turn by a printed Latin tag; thus it is uncertain whether Jonson's mark was meant to emphasize the note itself or the passage next to it. The note, derived from Tacitus, reads as follows: "*Vt gratia oneri, sic vltio in quaestu habetur* [as gratitude is considered a burden, so revenge is held an advantage]." The passage annotated by this claim asserts that, once human nature has committed itself, it cannot "easilie be reclaimed by motiues of reason, but is rather incited thereby (*per Antiperistasin* [through contrariness]) to persist in wilfulnesse, then to harken to that which is more conuenient; especially, when either iealousie or reuenge doe implie an aduantage: for, then partialitie keepeth no measure; but to iustifie an errour, runnes headlong into all extremities" (*CW* 1.2. 7; CR). Whether Jonson meant to highlight the passage itself, its accompanying note, or both, what does seem clear from his marking is his abiding interest in human psychology, particularly in the ways perversions of thought can lead to perverse behavior.[30]

Jonson's use of Edmondes's book as a source of information deriving from Edmondes's own reading is clear from his next marking, which singles out a quotation from the poet Ennius that describes Fabius Maximus (the subject of a number of Jonson's markings in the observations on the *Gallic Wars*):

> *Vnus homo nobis cunctando restituit rem:*
> *Non ponebat enim rumores ante salutem.*
> *Ergo póstque magisque viri nunc gloria claret.*
> One man restored things to us by delaying:
> For he did not value common opinion more than well being.
> And therefore now he is a great and renowned man.
> (CW, 1.2. 8; CR)[31]

Jonson seems to have shared Edmondes's admiration for Fabius, not simply because of his tactical intelligence but also because of his self-assurance, his determination, and his indifference to external opinion. Ironically, what others saw as his weakness was actually a sign of his strength, both of character and of mind. This was a paradox that Jonson could undoubtedly value.[32]

The range of Jonson's interests is suggested by his next few markings, which highlight a variety of topics. One mark occurs next to the observation that "great Empires [are] as easily disturbed, as the states of pettie Princes" (CW 1.7. 25; CR)—a claim that, in its emphasis on the risks of political instability, helps illuminate other marks emphasizing the need for unity and discipline. Jonson's next mark, however, focuses not on grand concerns with the fate of empires but on the importance of individual responsibility. We must be careful, Edmondes asserts, not to jeopardize well laid plans by "negligent or inconsiderate cariage; but rather, to make good any want or defect, by serious and warie prosecution of the same" (CW 1.16. 54; CR). This advice, as its context makes clear, applies not only to military matters but to life in general. Finally, a pair of ensuing marks shifts the focus yet again, this time stressing the kind of definition and discrimination to which Jonson felt so attracted. Edmondes emphasizes "the difference betweene true valour and foole-hardy rashnesse; beeing but one and the same thing, if they were not distinguished by the subiect wherein they are shewed. For, to runne headlong into strange adventures, vpon no iust occasion, were to shew more leuitie then discretion: And againe, to vse the like boldnesse in cases of extreamitie, deserueth the opinion of vertuous endeuor" (CW 1.16. 55; CR). It was this distinction which prompted Diomedes to censure Glaucus for exposing himself to the fury of the Greeks; either Diomedes was a god, he said, "or else but a lost and forlorne man. Which may serue to learne vs the true vse of courage; that ordinarily is neuer more shewed then in misimployment" (*CW* 1.16. 56; CR). Jonson's marking of comments such as these suggests his interest in how moral distinctions could both reflect and promote distinct behaviors.[33]

The concern with the uses of speech that prompted some of the poet's markings of earlier observations also prompted the marking here of a passage interesting for what it implies about Jonson's stylistic ideals. At one point Edmondes asserts that, "As in matter of Geometry, *Rectum est Index sui, et obliqui* [straightness is the measure of itself and of what is crooked], beeing equall to all the parts of rectitude, and vnequall to obliquity: so is it in reason and discourse. For, a direct and well grounded speech, carieth such a natiue equalitie with all its parts" (*CW* 2.13. 117; CR). As in other instances, Jonson's marking here does not encompass the entire thought, but Edmondes continues that such a speech shows not only what is fit but also what is crooked in the matter it deals with. Jonson would undoubtedly have agreed,[34] but the fact that his mark stops before the idea is finished may imply that he was as interested in Edmondes's geometrical analogy as in the thought it was meant to illuminate.

Jonson's next mark requires some explaining. It highlights part of Edmondes's discussion of the rashness of Curio, a Roman commander who was defeated after having recently been victorious himself. In attempting to make sense of this reversal, Edmondes mentions three factors that contributed to Curio's defeat. The first two were his youthful ardor and his recent good fortune, but it is the third—presumption—that seems to have provoked Jonson's mark. Edmondes notes that "Presumption, beeing euer accompanied with Negligence, is subiect to as many casualties, as those that goe vnarmed vpon extreamitie of danger. And these were the three things that miscaried Curio. Out of which we may obserue with Xenophon, that *Ingens et arduum opus est rectè imperare* [it is a remarkable and arduous task to command correctly]" (*CW* 2.15. 125; CR). However, the last half of this passage is flanked by a marginal tag, noting, "*Incauta semper nimia praesumptio et sui negliligens* [sic]. *Egesip.* [presumption is always too incautious and negligent of itself]." The fact that Jonson's mark begins before the tag starts suggests that it was chiefly the passage itself that interested him, but the thought expressed in the tag is, in any case, obviously relevant to the section's main message. Once again Jonson picks out a passage illustrating the larger public consequences of personal traits.

The book's next marking was probably not made by Jonson. Its appearance is uncharacteristic, and it is drawn in ink rather than in the pencil used for the other marks that are recognizably his. It occurs next to a passage arguing that women can prove a burden during times of war (*CW* 3.3. 138). Although Jonson may well have shared the sentiment, he seems not to have highlighted it.[35] The next mark that is almost certainly his occurs many pages later, and it is also his last. It falls next to a passage stressing the dangers of delay in wartime. This was a fault Caesar avoided, as Edmondes makes clear. Protraction, he observes, "is oftentimes the interrupter of absolute victorie, and the onely supplanter of that which is desired. *Vincere scis Haniball, sed victoria vti nescis* [you know how to conquer, Hannibal, but you do not know how to take advantage of victory], was a common by-word, and happened then well for the state of Rome. But now it fell out otherwise; hauing met with one that knew how to conquer, and how to follow victorie to purpose" (*CW* 3.23. 205). Caesar's skills and foresight were one thing, but it was his ability to exploit fast-developing circumstances that gave him his clear advantage as a leader.

The neutral tone of this passage is typical of the ones Jonson marked in Edmondes's *Observations.* When he picks out acts that Edmondes praises or condemns, the praise or condemnation is usually framed in ethical or tactical terms rather than in terms of strictly political principles or competing ideological ideals. Partly this is due, no doubt, to the practical and moral tendency of Edmondes's own comments, but it seems also to reflect the nature of Jonson's interests during his reading of the combined *Observations.* Edmondes does make comments of a more narrowly political nature, but Jonson usually ignores them. What he seems to have valued most were his friend's thoughts on military matters, on practical behavior, and on issues of ethical significance. The frequency and range of his marks suggest his genuine interest in Edmondes's opinions, his genuine respect for the latter's *Observations.* His markings imply that he read the volume from beginning to end, and they suggest that the praise he offered in his commendatory poems was not formulaic but was rooted in a real regard for Edmondes's efforts and accomplishment. In his poems as in his markings, in reading this book and in dealing with all the others I have examined, Jonson shows himself discharging a role he greatly admired—the role of thoughtful and discerning reader, of one who both reads *and* understands.

APPENDIX

GW 1.17. 50: "fore they / stead of"; CR; choice and arms of Roman infantry

GW. 1.19. 57: "battell / inclosed"; CR; how Hannibal entrapped the Romans

GW. 2.4. 73: "slingers / short ar-"; CR; the force and types of slings

GW. 2.9. 88: "if my / cularities"; CR; battlefield slogans, now neglected

GW. 5.6. 170: "heauy / Polybius"; CR; the Roman infantry's arms and armor

GW. 5.10. 184: "they / The enemie"; CR; Italian advantages in war with French

GW. 5.12. 188–89: "Commanders / the same"; CR; Hannibal, Scipio prove the decisive importance of leaders in determining which side is victorious

GW. 5.12. 190: "I Haue / altogether"; CR; the manner of the Roman fight

GW. 5.16. 193: "to haue / commended the"; CR; M. Cicero the orator would have celebrated his brother's exploits if he himself had done them

GW. 5.17. 194: "former / a place"; CR; Ambiorix's assault on a Roman camp

GW. 6.5. 14: "hazard the / or more"; UM; Sir Francis Vere's sound advice not to abandon a superior position in the Battle of Newport (1600)

GW. 6.11. 34: "*Nocuit* / otherwise"; CR; Lucan quoted to support speedy execution of directions or decisions

GW. 6.13. 38: "wes of / place"; CR; covert warfare vs. open encounter

GW. 6.14. 40: "and diuert / *bello*"; CR; Hannibal's complaint about war

GW. 6.16. 43: "wherein / known"; CR; inexperienced men will fail even under another Hannibal

GW. 7.7. 60: "the counsell / the worse"; CR; how Hannibal used his superior cavalry

Notes

PREFACE

1. See the standard edition, *Ben Jonson*, ed. C. H. Herford and Percy and Evelyn Simpson, 11 vols. (Oxford: Clarendon Press, 1925–52), 1:139. All subsequent references to Jonson's works will refer in parentheses to this edition, abbreviated as "H&S," and will cite appropriate volume and page numbers. When referring to collections of Jonson's poetry, I will use the following abbreviations: "*Ep.*" (*Epigrammes*); "*For.*" (*The Forrest*); "*Und.*" (*Under-wood*); "*U.V.*" (*Ungathered Verse*).

2. For the Latin text, see H&S 1:219–20; for the English translation cited here, see Jesse Franklin Bradley and Joseph Quincy Adams, *The Jonson Allusion-Book: A Collection of Allusions to Ben Jonson from 1597 to 1700* (New Haven: Yale University Press, 1922), 4. Subsequent quotations from the indictment will derive from this translation.

3. See David Riggs, *Ben Jonson: A Life* (Cambridge: Harvard University Press, 1989), 52.

CHAPTER 1. INTRODUCTION

1. The two most important previous discussions of Jonson's reading are those in the standard edition, *Ben Jonson*, ed. C. H. Herford and Percy and Evelyn Simpson, 1:250–71 and 11:593–603, and David McPherson's invaluable "Ben Jonson's Library and Marginalia: An Annotated Catalogue," *Studies in Philology* 71.5 (1974), *Texts and Studies* series. McPherson's "Introduction" (3–22) is particularly helpful. See also James A. Riddell and Stanley Stewart, "Jonson Reads 'The Ruines of Time,'" *Studies in Philology* 87 (1990): 427–55.

2. A new catalogue of Jonson's library is being prepared by Professor Henry Woudhuysen.

3. On this point, see Achsah Guibbory, "A Sense of the Future: Projected Audiences of Donne and Jonson," *John Donne Journal* 2 (1983): 11–21.

4. On literacy in Jonson's culture see, for example, David Cressy, *Literacy and the Social Order: Reading and Writing in Tudor and Stuart England* (Cambridge: Cambridge University Press, 1980).

5. See W. H. Herendeen, "A New Way to Pay Old Debts: Pretexts to the 1616 Folio," in *Ben Jonson's 1616 Folio*, ed. Jennifer Brady and W. H. Herendeen (Newark: University of Delaware Press, 1991), 38–63, esp. 54.

6. The Latin tag is translated by the phrase that immediately precedes it.

7. On this effort see, for instance, George E. Rowe, *Distinguishing Jonson: Imitation, Rivalry, and the Direction of a Dramatic Career* (Lincoln: University of Nebraska Press, 1988).

8. On Jonson's reading of writers in the classical tradition see, for instance,

two articles by Stella P. Revard: "Pindar and Jonson's Cary-Morison Ode," in *Classic and Cavalier: Essays on Jonson and the Sons of Ben*, ed. Claude J. Summers and Ted-Larry Pebworth (Pittsburgh: University of Pittsburgh Press, 1982), 17–30, and "Classicism and Neo-Classicism in Jonson's *Epigrammes*," in *Ben Jonson's 1616 Folio*, 138–67.

9. On this point see, for instance, George E. Rowe, Jr., "Ben Jonson's Quarrel with Audience and Its Renaissance Context," *Studies in Philology* 81 (1984): 438–60.

10. Recent studies of Jonson's use of numerology suggest another sense in which he may have expected his readers to look beneath the surface of texts. See, for instance, Sibyl Lutz Severance, "'To Shine in Union': Measure, Number, and Harmony in Ben Jonson's *'Poems* of Devotion,'" *Studies in Philology* 80 (1983): 183–99, and Richard Harp, "Jonson's 'To Penshurst': The Country House as Church," *John Donne Journal* 7 (1988): 73–89.

11. For Jonson's comments on the reading of some specific contemporary authors, see H&S 8:582.

12. For specific discussions of Jonson's own independence as a reader see, for instance, Philip J. Ayres, "The Nature of Jonson's Roman History," *English Literary Renaissance* 16 (1986): 166–81, and A. Richard Dutton, "The Sources, Text, and Readers of *Sejanus*: Jonson's 'Integrity in the Story,'" *Philological Quarterly* 75 (1978): 181–98. John Ferns challenges Jonas Barish's conclusions about Jonson's reading in "Ovid, Juvenal, and 'The Silent Woman': A Reconsideration," *Modern Language Review* 65 (1970): 248–53. Almost any discussion of Jonson's view of ancient Rome inevitably involves discussion of his reading; see, for instance, William Blissett, "Roman Ben Jonson," in *Ben Jonson's 1616 Folio*, 90–110. See also Katharine Eisaman Maus, *Ben Jonson and the Roman Frame of Mind* (Princeton: Princeton University Press, 1984).

13. One of the most valuable discussions of these issues is Stanley Fish's "Authors-Readers: Jonson's Community of the Same," *Representations* no. 7 (1984): 26–58.

14. See, for instance, Guibbory, "A Sense of the Future."

15. For a discussion of reading as a stimulus see, for instance, Kurt R. Niland and Robert C. Evans, "Jonson and Quintilian on the Deaths of Sons" (forthcoming). For valuable discussions of Jonson's practice of *imitatio*, see Richard S. Peterson, *Imitation and Praise in the Poems of Ben Jonson* (New Haven: Yale University Press, 1981) and the chapter on Jonson in Thomas M. Greene, *The Light in Troy: Imitation and Discovery in Renaissance Poetry* (New Haven: Yale University Press, 1982).

16. On this point see, for instance, Joseph Loewenstein, *Responsive Readings: Versions of Echo in Pastoral, Epic, and the Jonsonian Masque* (New Haven: Yale University Press, 1984).

17. See particularly the recent work of Leah S. Marcus, especially *The Politics of Mirth: Jonson, Herrick, Milton, Marvell and the Defense of Old Holiday Pastimes* (Chicago: University of Chicago Press, 1986).

18. See, for instance, Joseph Loewenstein, "Printing and 'The Multitudinous Presse'": The Contentious Texts of Jonson's Masques," in *Ben Jonson's 1616 Folio*, 168–91. In the same volume, see Kevin J. Donovan, "Jonson's Texts in the First Folio," 23–37.

19. For useful discussions of this issue see, for instance, Joseph Loewenstein, "The Script in the Marketplace," *Representations* no. 12 (1985): 101–14 and Timo-

thy Murray, "From Foul Sheets to Legitimate Model: Antitheater, Text, Ben Jonson," *New Literary History* 14 (1983): 641–64.

20. Issues at stake in recent readings of Jonson are surveyed in the final chapter of Jongsook Lee's *Ben Jonson's Poesis: A Literary Dialectic of Ideal and History* (Charlottesville: University Press of Virginia, 1989).

21. On the significance of judgment in Jonson's thinking see, for instance, Gabrielle Bernhard Jackson, *Vision and Judgment in Ben Jonson's Drama* (New Haven: Yale University Press, 1968).

22. On this issue see, for instance, Jack D. Winner, "Ben Jonson's Epigrams and the Conventions of Formal Verse Satire," *Studies in English Literature* 23 (1983): 61–76.

23. On the issue of self-promotion in Jonson's poetry, see my earlier study *Ben Jonson and the Poetics of Patronage* (Lewisburg, Pa.: Bucknell University Press, 1989). *Ep.* 49, "TO PLAY-WRIGHT," also presents reading as a means of public self-definition. The poem implies that what one expects of a book says a great deal about oneself, and it suggests the dangers of approaching a book with preconceived expectations. Here and elsewhere, Jonson seems to assume that a book reflects upon the manners of both its author and its reader. On this point, see also *Ep.* 67, "TO THOMAS EARLE OF SVFFOLKE."

24. *Ep.* 58, "TO GROOME IDEOT," also presents both public reading and public listening as forms of self-display; ironically, Ideot becomes the object of the very sarcasm he shows himself incapable of properly appreciating. The poem exposes his ostensibly generous response to Jonson's poetry as essentially self-interested; he attempts to bask in the glow of the poet's wit. Public reading is also implied in *Ep.* 72, "TO COVRT-LING," which describes a critic who derives his power from his place in the circle of an influential lady.

25. *Ep.* 81, "TO PROVLE THE PLAGIARY," is also obviously concerned with literary theft. Here Jonson depicts the misappropriation of a text not simply (as in other poems) as the result of misunderstanding or misinterpretation but as the consequence of deliberate stealing.

26. On this association see, for instance, Joseph Loewenstein, "The Jonsonian Corpulence: Or, The Poet as Mouthpiece," *ELH* 53 (1986): 491–518, and also Bruce Thomas Boehrer, "Renaissance Overeating: The Sad Case of Ben Jonson," *PMLA* 105 (1990): 1071–82.

27. Sara van den Berg also sees this phrasing as "perhaps a reference to the Bible"; see *The Action of Ben Jonson's Poetry* (Newark: University of Delaware Press, 1987), 56.

28. Jonson told William Drummond that "his father Losed all his estate under Queen Marie, having been cast in prison and forfaitted, at last turn'd Minister So he was a Ministers son" (H&S 1:139). As Herford and the Simpsons explain, "It is hardly doubtful that the father adopted the Reform doctrines under Edward, suffered for them under [the Catholic] Mary, and took orders, finally, under Elizabeth. 'A grave minister of the gospel' was the tradition of him current in [Anthony] Wood's time" (H&S 1:2).

29. He may have been converted to Catholicism by the famous Father Thomas Wright, one of whose books Jonson publicly praised; see H&S 11:128–29. Other Catholics whose works Jonson praised in print included Thomas Palmer (H&S 11:124–25) and Hugh Holland (H&S 11:126–27). Not long before the Gunpowder Plot, Jonson dined at a party given by Robert Catesby, one of the Catholic conspirators (H&S 11:578), yet his Catholic connections were also useful to the government in the immediate aftermath of the Plot's discovery (H&S 1:40–41).

On Jonson's friendship with William Dakins, an Anglican minister and one of the translators of the authorized version of the Bible, see chapter 5, below. And, of course, most of Jonson's important patrons were Protestants (including Robert Cecil; William, Earl of Pembroke; and Lucy, Countess of Bedford).

30. The "Execration" reports that the fire destroyed "twice-twelve-yeares stor'd up humanitie, / With humble Gleanings in Divinitie, / After the Fathers, and those wiser Guides / Whom Faction had not drawne to studie sides" (101–4; H&S 8:207).

31. For the location of the Anglo-Saxon gospels, I am indebted to Professor Henry Woudhuysen. For the information on the Psalms, see McPherson, 31. On the "spurious" copy of Ecclesiasticus, see McPherson, 104.

32. McPherson, 31. The book is *Biblia sacra* . . . . (Antwerp: Apud I. Moretum, 1599). McPherson also notes that the book, untypically, has "no motto or sig[nature] on title page" (31). However, this may be because there was not enough room. The book's authenticity is bolstered by inscriptions in Jonson's hand that appear on the verso of the title page: "'Ex dono D. Thomae Strange, 1605, Beniamin Jonsonius me tenet' [From the gift of Sir Thomas Strange, 1605, Ben Jonson owns me]. 'Benedicam Dominum in omni tempore, semper laus eius in ore meo.—Ps[alms]: xxxiii. [1]"; see McPherson, 31.

33. See chapter 5, below.

34. For English translations of the relevant biblical passages, I have relied on *The Holy Bible: Douay Version* . . . (London: Catholic Truth Society, 1963). In reporting the passages that Jonson marks, I will not only provide chapter and verse but will also cite parenthetically the first and final words or word parts that occur along the margin closest to the mark; this will give readers a very precise idea of where, exactly, the marks appear in Jonson's text. Thus, the verse cited here appears as follows in Jonson's text:

*Ap-
pellauitque lucem Diem, & tenebras
Noctem: factumq; est vespere, & ma-
ne, dies vnus. *Dixit quoque Deus:

The circle with the curvy tail occurs in the left margin next to the first two full lines; the numeral "1" appears between the second and third full lines.

35. On Jonson's strong interest in princely clemency, see H&S 8:599–600. I discuss this aspect of Jonson's thinking at length in my book *Jonson, Lipsius, and the Politics of Renaissance Stoicism* (Wakefield, N.H.: Longwood, 1992).

36. Flowers flanked by dots also appear, for instance, in Jonson's 1619 edition of Martial's epigrams; see McPherson, 68–70.

CHAPTER 2: JONSON'S SENECA

1. Elisabeth Henry, "Seneca the Younger," in *Ancient Writers: Greece and Rome*, ed. T. James Luce, 2 vols. (New York: Scribner's, 1982), 2:807–32; for the cited passage, see 2:808.

2. See the works indexed in H&S 11:659–60. However, my own work with the Herford and Simpson edition suggests that even this listing is incomplete.

3. See McPherson, 22.

4. For information about the anthology, *Chorus Poetarum* . . . , see McPherson, 36. Pencil underlining occurs in Seneca's play *Hippolytus*, printed in this

volume, but whether the lining is Jonson's is uncertain. Thus I have chosen not to discuss his markings in this work. Jonson also owned an annotated edition of Seneca's tragedies; see McPherson, 82.

5. *L. Annaei Senecae Philosophi Scripta qvae extant . . .* (Paris: Apud Marcum Orry, 1599). Jonson's signature has been partly inked over. Unless otherwise indicated, Jonson's markings in this book are in pencil. The Glasgow University Library copy of the book is bound with an edition of the writings of Seneca's father entitled *Rhetoris Controversar. Lib. X. . . .* (Paris: Apud Marcum Orry, 1599). The title page of this work bears neither Jonson's motto nor his signature, and the scattered markings in the volume (mainly various kinds of crosses drawn in ink) bear little resemblance to Jonson's characteristic marginalia. For all these reasons I have chosen not to discuss this book.

6. See Katherine Eisaman Maus, *Ben Jonson and the Roman Frame of Mind* (Princeton: Princeton University Press, 1984). Maus's book is one of the best studies of Jonson's general debt to classical habits of thought. Much of what she says about his relation to the "Roman moralists" is relevant to the subject of this chapter.

7. For a good brief survey of Seneca's life and times, see Anna Lydia Motto, *Seneca* (New York: Twayne, 1973), esp. 15–41. For insights into how Seneca's life was interpreted in the Renaissance, see the brief biography written by the Flemish scholar Justus Lipsius. This is reprinted, for instance, in Seneca, *On Benefits,* trans. Thomas Lodge (London: Dent, 1899), ix–xli.

8. On this point as it applies to Seneca, see Richard Mott Gummere, *Seneca the Philosopher and His Modern Message* (New York: Cooper Square, 1963), 45. In drawing parallels and distinctions between Jonson and Seneca, I will document only claims that relate to the latter. Most of what I will say about Jonson is widely acknowledged; however, for fuller treatment of some of these issues see, for instance, David Riggs, *Ben Jonson: A Life* and my own *Ben Jonson and the Poetics of Patronage.*

9. See Miriam T. Griffin, *Seneca: A Philosopher in Politics* (Oxford: Clarendon Press, 1976), 9. Griffin's is one of the most thorough and helpful discussions of Seneca's political views and circumstances. Also exceptionally valuable are the comments on Seneca in J. P. Sullivan, *Literature and Politics in the Age of Nero* (Ithaca: Cornell University Press, 1985); see esp. 115–43.

10. See Gordon Braden, *Renaissance Tragedy and the Senecan Tradition: Anger's Privilege* (New Haven: Yale University Press, 1985), 16.

11. Villy Sørenson, *Seneca: The Humanist at the Court of Nero,* trans. W. Glyn Jones (Chicago: University of Chicago Press, 1984), 129.

12. For the source of both quotations, see the Loeb Classical Library edition of Seneca's *Moral Essays,* trans. John W. Basore, 3 vols. (Cambridge: Harvard University Press, 1975), 3:vii. Volume 3 is entirely devoted to *De Beneficiis.*

In referring to marked passages in Jonson's copy of Seneca, I will give in parentheses the first and final words or word parts that occur along the margin closest to the mark; this will give readers a very precise idea of where the marks appear in Jonson's text. After reporting this information, I will then indicate through abbreviations the kind of mark Jonson has made, unless this information is spelled out in my text itself. Finally, following the abbreviation(s), I will give two page numbers separated by a slash mark. The first number will refer to the page on which the relevant passage appears in Jonson's copy; the second number will indicate the page on which a translation of this passage appears in the relevant volume of the Loeb Classical Library. Providing the Loeb page references will make it easy for readers without access to Jonson's edition to place his markings in a larger context.

Although for the most part I have tried to offer fairly literal paraphrases of the passages Jonson marks, when I occasionally also quote from the Loeb renderings, these are set off by quotation marks or indentations. I have also found it helpful to consult Thomas Lodge's translation of *The Workes of L. A. Seneca Both Morall and Naturall*, enlarged edition (London, 1620).

Some of the marks mentioned in my discussion of this book—particularly the "circle-tails" (CT)—have not been emphasized in previous descriptions of Jonson's library, but I have found them in many of his surviving books, including several not previously reported. They are present, for instance, in the Pierpont Morgan Library's copy of Jonson's Bible (McPherson #25), and they are also present in his newly discovered copy of the works of Sir Thomas More (see chapters 1 and 5 of this book) and in his newly reported copy of *Daphnis and Chloë* (see my article in *English Language Notes* 27 [1990]: 28–32). They are also present in his copies of the works of Athenaeus and Claudian at the Bodleian Library (McPherson #14 and #42), in his copy of Pythagoras at Emmanuel College, Cambridge (McPherson #148), and in his copy of the works of Juvenal and Persius (McPherson #92), now located in the library of Lincoln's Inn. I will be discussing much of this new evidence more fully in several forthcoming publications.

13. Any passages quoted or indented will be from the Loeb Classical Library edition of Seneca's *Ad Lucilium Epistulae Morales*, trans. R. M. Gummere, 3 vols. (Cambridge: Harvard University Press: 1970–71).

14. The most famous example, of course, is the memorable note, "*Language most shewes a man: speake that I may see thee*" (H&S 8:625). For a listing of Jonson's allusions to Seneca's *Epistles*, see H&S 11:660. Although Jonson's works often allude to many of the same epistles he marked in his copy of Seneca, the passages marked are not the precise passages alluded to.

15. Any passages quoted or indented are from Basore's translation in the Loeb edition of the *Moral Essays*, 1:106–355.

16. Any passages quoted or indented are from Basore's translation in the Loeb edition of the *Moral Essays*, 1:356–449.

17. Here and in the passages that follow, the underlining in Jonson's text is represented by italic print.

18. Any passages quoted or indented are are from Basore's translation in the Loeb edition of the *Moral Essays*, 2:98–179.

19. Any passages quoted or indented are from Basore's translation in the Loeb edition of the *Moral Essays*, 2:202–85.

20. On this ambivalence see, for instance, Robert C. Jones, "The Satirist's Retirement in Jonson's 'Apologetical Dialogue,'" *ELH* 34 (1967): 447–67.

21. On this point see, for instance, chapter 5 of Evans, *Ben Jonson and the Poetics of Patronage*. See also such poems as *For.* 12, *U.V.* 30, and especially *Und.* 76.

22. Any passages quoted or indented are from Basore's translation in the Loeb edition of the *Moral Essays*, 2:2–97.

23. Any passages quoted or indented are from Basore's translation in the Loeb edition of the *Moral Essays*, 2:416–89.

24. Lodge translates this passage as follows: "thou camest backe againe vnto me, not to enioy any pleasure or contentment by thy sonne, but to the end thou mightest not lose the good to conuerse and communicate with him" (754).

25. See, for instance, Clarence Beverly Hilberry, *Ben Jonson's Ethics in Relation to Stoic and Humanistic Ethical Thought* (Norwood, Pa.: Folcroft Library Editions, 1973). See also my study *Jonson, Lipsius, and the Politics of Renaissance Stoicism*.

CHAPTER 3: JONSON'S APULEIUS:
THE *APOLOGY* AND *FLORIDA*

1. See Elizabeth Hazelton Haight, *Apuleius and His Influence* (New York: Longmans, Green, 1927), 26.
2. See Moses Hadas, *A History of Latin Literature* (New York: Columbia University Press, 1952), 340.
3. See *The Confessions and Letters of St. Augustin*, vol. 1 of *A Select Library of the Nicene and Post-Nicene Fathers of the Christian Church*, ed. Philip Scaff, 14 vols. (New York: Charles Scribner's, 1886), 487.
4. In the "Execration upon Vulcan" (*Und.* 43), Jonson mentions the loss by fire of "twice-twelve-yeares stor'd up humanitie, / With humble Gleanings in Divinitie, / After the Fathers, and those wiser Guides / Whom Faction had not drawne to studie sides" (101–4).
5. See *The City of God*, trans. Marcus Dods (New York: Modern Library, 1950), 259.
6. "The Progress of Renaissance Latin Prose: The Case of Apuleianism," *Renaissance Quarterly* 37 (1984): 351–94.
7. Jonson owned *L. Apuleii . . . Opera omnia . . . .* 2 parts. Leyden: Ex officina Plantiniana, apud F. Raphelengium, 1588. This is presently housed in the Bodleian Library. For further information, see McPherson, 25.
8. See James F. Tatum, *Apuleius and the "Golden Ass"* (Ithaca: Cornell University Press, 1979), 109.
9. See P. G. Walsh, "Apuleius," in the second volume of *The Cambridge History of Classical Literature: Latin Literature*, ed. E. J. Kenney and W. V. Clausen (Cambridge: Cambridge University Press, 1982), 2:775.
10. *Apuleius and the "Golden Ass"*, 114.
11. See George Kennedy, *The Art of Rhetoric in the Roman World: 300 B.C.–A.D. 300* (Princeton: Princeton University Press, 1972), 605.
12. Tatum, in *Apuleius and the "Golden Ass"*, suggests that the published text would take four hours to deliver orally (114).
13. On this point see Tatum, *Apuleius and the "Golden Ass"*, 112. See also my discussion of Jonson's reactions to *De Calumnia* by Justus Lipsius in chapter 6 below.
14. On the rhetorical structure of the *Apology*, see Walsh, 775.
15. See *Apuleius and the "Golden Ass"*, 112.
16. In citing the passages Jonson marked in his copy of Apuleius, I will give in parentheses the first and last words or word parts that occur along the margin closest to the mark; this will give readers a very precise idea of where the marks appear in Jonson's text. After reporting this information, I will then indicate through abbreviations the kind of mark Jonson has made, unless this information is spelled out in my text itself. Finally, following the abbreviation(s), I will give two page numbers separated by a slash mark. The first number will refer to the page on which the relevant passage appears in Jonson's copy; the second page number will indicate the page on which a translation of this passage appears in *The Works of Apuleius* (London: George Bell, 1889). No translator's name

is provided, but this translation is quite literal. However, I have also consulted *The Apologia and Florida of Apuleius of Madura*, trans. H. E. Butler (Oxford: Clarendon Press, 1909). To conserve space, when referring to Apuleius in the Appendix, I will cite the abbreviation "A."

17. On the ambivalence of Jonson's attitude toward self-defense see, for instance, Robert C. Jones, "The Satirist's Retirement in Jonson's 'Apologetical Dialogue.'"

18. On tensions in Jonson's attitudes toward his rivals see, for instance, my article "Strategic Debris: Ben Jonson's Satires on Inigo Jones," *Renaissance Papers* (1986): 69–82.

19. For discussions of Jonson's interest in the absurd see, for instance, Jackson I. Cope, "*Bartholomew Fair* as Blasphemy," *Renaissance Drama* 8 (1965): 127–52 and John S. Weld, "Christian Comedy: Volpone," *Studies in Philology* 51 (1954): 172–93.

20. For a useful discussion of this issue see, for instance, H. Jennifer Brady, "Ben Jonson's 'Works of Judgment': A Study of Rhetorical Strategies in the 'Epigrammes'" (Ph.D. diss., Princeton University, 1980).

21. On this issue see, for instance, Lawrence Venuti, "Why Jonson Wrote Not of Love," *Journal of Medieval and Renaissance Studies* 12 (1982): 195–220.

22. On this issue see, for instance, McPherson, 11–12 and 68–70.

23. For further discussion of Jonson's distinction between lust and love, see, for instance, the conclusion of my remarks dealing with his copy of Chaucer's works (chapter 4, below).

24. I discuss this poem at length in a forthcoming book entitled *Jonson and the Contexts of His Time.*

25. On mirror imagery in Jonson's poems, see William E. Cain, "Mirrors, Intentions, and Texts in Ben Jonson," *Essays in Literature* 8 (1981): 11–24.

26. For a discussion of Jonson's own finances see, for instance, Frances Teague, "Ben Jonson's Poverty," *Biography* 2 (1979): 260–65. Jonson himself told Drummond of Hawthornden (perhaps somewhat facetiously) that poetry "had beggered him, when he might have been a rich lawer, Physitian or Marchant" (H&S 1:149).

27. On the importance of worth over birth in Jonson's thinking see, for instance, the final chapter of Don E. Wayne, *Penshurst: The Semiotics of Place and the Poetics of History* (Madison: University of Wisconsin Press, 1984).

28. On this point see, for instance, the comments in Jonson's *Discoveries* on the popularity of "writh'd, and tortur'd" language (H&S 8:581).

29. On the latter point, see the comments in the *Discoveries* on the idea that "Truth lyes open to all" and on the importance of "Stand[ing] for *Truth*" (H&S 8:567–68). Jonson's interest in science is discussed by, for instance, Lawrence Babb, "Scientific Theories of Grief in Some Elizabethan Plays," *Studies in Philology* 40 (1943): 502–19 and by Marjorie Nicolson, "The 'New Astronomy' and English Literary Imagination," *Studies in Philology* 32 (1935): 428–62.

30. Many critics have noted that Jonson's tragedy *Catiline* focuses on a triumphant intellectual in the figure of Cicero; for a good recent discussion see, for instance, Richard Dutton, *Ben Jonson: To the First Folio* (Cambridge: Cambridge University Press, 1983), 124.

31. On Jonson and science see, for instance, James V. Holleran, "Character Transmutation in *The Alchemist*," *College Language Association Journal* 11 (1968): 221–27 and especially John S. Mebane, *Renaissance Magic and the Return of the Golden Age* (Lincoln: University of Nebraska Press, 1989), 156–73. On Jonson

and women see, for instance, my discussion of his copy of Chaucer (chapter 4, below) and the chapter on Jonson in Kathleen McLuskie, *Renaissance Dramatists* (Atlantic Highlands, N.J.: Humanities, 1989).

32. On this issue see, for instance, my article " 'Making Just Approaches': Ben Jonson's Poems to the Earl of Newcastle," *Renaissance Papers* (1988): 63–76.

33. On these matters see, for instance, the closing lines of the famous poem "To Penshurst" (*For.* 2), and also Douglas Lanier, "Brainchildren: Self-representation and Patriarchy in Ben Jonson's Early Works," *Renaissance Papers* (1986): 53–68.

34. See, for instance, *Ep.* 7, 25, 26, 39, 57, 62, 118. Numerous other poems might be cited. See also the introduction to Jonas Barish's edition of *Volpone* (New York: Appleton-Century-Crofts, 1958).

35. Jonson uses the same tactic in the letters he wrote while imprisoned because of *Eastward Ho;* see H&S 1:193–200.

36. On the self-conviction of innocence, see H&S 8:604–5. Earlier Jonson notes, "*A Fame* that is wounded to the world, would bee better cured by anothers *Apologie,* then its owne: For few can apply medicines well themselves" (H&S 8:563); and yet, of course, Jonson was always ready to defend himself and attack his foes.

37. For discussion of these matters see, for instance, my book *Ben Jonson and the Poetics of Patronage,* esp. chapters 1–4.

38. Walsh, 775–76.

39. J. Tatum, "Apuleius," in *Ancient Writers: Greece and Rome,* ed. T. James Luce, 2 vols. (New York: Scribner's, 1982), 2:1099–1116; for the quoted passage, see 1113.

40. Tatum, *Apuleius and the "Golden Ass",* 125.

41. Tatum, *Apuleius and the "Golden Ass",* 123.

42. Tatum, *Apuleius and the "Golden Ass",* 124.

43. On this topic see, for instance, Mary Livingstone, "Ben Jonson: The Poet to the Painter," *Texas Studies in Literature and Language* 18 (1977): 381–92. See also John Lemly, "Masks and Self-Portraits in Jonson's Late Poetry," *ELH* 44 (1977): 248–66. I discuss this matter in a long note in "Poetry and Power: Ben Jonson and the Poetics of Patronage" (Ph.D. diss., Princeton University, 1984), 507–08.

44. I discuss this matter at length in *Jonson, Lipsius, and the Politics of Renaissance Stoicism.*

45. Jonson's own self-consciousness is suggested by numerous data, many of them discussed in my book *Ben Jonson and the Poetics of Patronage.* However, see also Steven C. Young, "A Check List of Tudor and Stuart Induction Plays," *Philological Quarterly* 48 (1969): 131–34. Young shows that Jonson used inductions far more frequently than any other dramatist of his time.

46. On Jonson's political ideals see, for instance, Joseph John Kelly, "Ben Jonson's Politics," *Renaissance and Reformation,* n.s. 7 (1983): 192–215. See also my own *Jonson, Lipsius, and the Politics of Renaissance Stoicism.*

47. Jonson owned a copy of writings by Pythagoras (see McPherson, 80), and the markings this book contains are almost certainly his.

48. On Jonson's thinking about benefits and gratitude, see my discussion of his copy of Seneca (chapter 2, above). See also the opening chapter of my forthcoming book *Jonson and the Contexts of His Time,* which discusses at length the important epistle to Sir Edward Sackville (*Und.* 13). For another example of Jonson's view of proper gratitude see his epigram to Lord Aubigny (*Ep.* 127).

49. On this issue see, for instance, Roger B. Rollin, "The Anxiety of Identifica-

tion: Jonson and the Rival Poets," in *Classic and Cavalier: Essays on Jonson and the Sons of Ben*, ed. Claude J. Summers and Ted-Larry Pebworth (Pittsburgh: University of Pittsburgh Press, 1982), 139–56. See also George E. Rowe, *Distinguishing Jonson: Imitation, Rivalry, and the Direction of a Dramatic Career* (Lincoln: University of Nebraska Press, 1988).

50. H. E. Butler translates the last clause (perhaps more clearly) as "as though I were his equal" (193).

51. A note to the translation I have cited reports that the phrase translated as "fascination apart" ("*praefiscine dixerim*") "was a common form of speech for averting the ill luck which was supposed to be imminent where a man was excessively praised by himself or others" (394n). H. E. Butler translates the phrase as "pardon my vanity" (195).

52. One of the best discussions of this issue remains the chapter on Jonson in Richard Helgerson, *Self-Crowned Laureates: Spenser, Jonson, Milton and the Literary System* (Berkeley: University of California Press, 1983).

53. On Jonson's ideals of friendship see, for instance, Richard Finkelstein, "Ben Jonson's Ciceronian Rhetoric of Friendship," *Journal of Medieval and Renaissance Studies* 16 (1986): 103–24.

54. On this point see, for instance, George E. Rowe, "Ben Jonson's Quarrel with Audience and Its Renaissance Context," *Studies in Philology* 81 (1984): 438–60. See also John Gordon Sweeney III, *Jonson and the Psychology of Public Theater* (Princeton: Princeton University Press, 1985).

55. The depth of Jonson's interest in fame is suggested by the fact that the word is one of the most frequently cited terms in all of his nondramatic poetry; see Steven L. Bates and Sidney D. Orr, *A Concordance to the Poems of Ben Jonson* (Athens: Ohio University Press, 1978), 239–40 and 848. Yet Jonson is careful to insist that only a worthy or "legitimate fame" is valuable; see, for example, *Ep.* 17. He rejects mere notoriety, praising Sir Thomas Roe for studying "conscience, more then thou would'st fame" (*Ep.* 98, l. 10).

56. Similarly, in the dedication to *Volpone*, Jonson says that the poet "*is able to informe yong-men to all good disciplines, inflame growne-men to all great vertues, keepe old-men in their best and supreme state, or as they decline to child-hood, recouer them to their first strength*" (H&S 5:17).

57. On this distinction see, for instance, Katharine Eisaman Maus, "Facts of the Matter: Satiric and Ideal Economies in the Jonsonian Imagination," in *Ben Jonson's 1616 Folio* (Newark: University of Delaware Press, 1991), 64–89.

CHAPTER 4: JONSON'S CHAUCER

1. See, for instance, Alice S. Miskimin, *The Renaissance Chaucer* (New Haven and London: Yale University Press, 1975); E. Talbot Donaldson and Judith J. Kollmann, eds., *Chaucerian Shakespeare: Adaptation and Transformation*, Medieval and Renaissance Monograph Series 2 (Detroit: Michigan Consortium for Medieval and Early Modern Studies, 1983); E. Talbot Donaldson, *The Swan at the Well: Shakespeare Reading Chaucer* (New Haven and London: Yale University Press, 1985); and Ann Thomson, *Shakespeare's Chaucer: A Study in Literary Origins* (Liverpool: Liverpool University Press, 1978). C. G. Thayer briefly discusses Jonson and Chaucer at a number of points in his book *Ben Jonson: Studies in the Plays* (Norman: University of Oklahoma Press, 1963).

2. For a thorough listing and discussion of echoes of Chaucer's works in the

Renaissance generally and in Jonson specifically, see Otto Ballmann, "Chaucers einfluss auf das englische drama im zeitalter der königin Elisabeth und der beiden ersten Stuart-könige," *Anglia* 25 (1902): 1–85; on Jonson in particular, see 14–28.

3. See Richard Helgerson, *Self-Crowned Laureates: Spenser, Jonson, Milton, and the Literary System*. The recent reappearance on the market of Jonson's heavily annotated copy of the 1617 edition of Spenser's works, which was for many years unavailable to scholars, should enrich our understanding of Jonson's attitudes toward Spenser, especially in the latter stage of Jonson's career, when he was himself reportedly at work on a heroic poem. I am grateful to James Riddell for showing me several photocopies he was able to make of Jonson's annotations in *The Faerie Queene*. See also the article by Riddell and Stanley Stewart cited in chapter 1, note 1 above.

4. *The Workes of Our Ancient and Learned English Poet, Geffrey Chaucer*, ed. Thomas Speght (London: Impensis Geor. Bishop, 1602). The introductory pages of the volume list signatures, although in some cases even these marks are lacking; the pages of the book proper are identified both by signature markings (at the bottom) and by numbers in the upper corners of each folio page. In citing from the book throughout this chapter, I use the folio numbering whenever possible.

5. McPherson, 36.

6. See John R. Hetherington, *Chaucer, 1532–1602: Notes and Facsimile Texts* (Birmingham, England: John R. Hetherington, 1964), 5. See also [Derek Brewer, ed.,] *Geoffrey Chaucer: The Works 1532; with Supplementary Material from the Editions of 1542, 1561, 1598, and 1602* (Menston, England: The Scolar Press, 1969). A very full discussion of the edition is offered by Derek Pearsall in his article "Thomas Speght," in *Editing Chaucer: The Great Tradition*, ed. Paul G. Ruggiers (Norman, Okla.: Pilgrim Books, 1984), 71–92 and 266–69.

7. Walter W. Skeat, in *The Chaucer Canon* (Oxford: Clarendon Press, 1900), several times suggests that Chaucer's sixteenth-century editors, at least, and perhaps even some readers, were aware that certain of the poems included in the printed texts were not by Chaucer but were included because they were written by contemporaries of Chaucer or were in the Chaucerian style; see 99, 113, and 127. Skeat's argument, however, seems to be colored by his exasperation with some of his contemporaries who still believed that the mere inclusion of a poem in an early printed edition was sound evidence of its authenticity. Francis Thynne, whose father had compiled the first printed edition of Chaucer, prepared an exhaustive manuscript critique of Speght's 1598 edition (which Speght apparently consulted in putting together his edition of 1602). At one point Thynne writes: "One other thinge ys, that yt wolde be good that Chaucers proper woorkes were distinguyshed from the adulterat, and suche as were not his, as the testamente of Cressyde, The Letter of Cupide, and the ballade begynnynge 'I haue a ladye, where so she bee,' &c. which Chaucer neuer composed, as may suffycientlye be proued by the thinges them selues." (See Thynne's *Chaucer. Animaduersions vppon the Annotacions and Corrections of Some Imperfections of Impressiones of Chaucers Workes [Sett Downe before Tyme, and Nowe] Reprinted in the Yere of Oure Lord 1598*, ed. G. H. Kingsley (London: Early English Text Society, 1865; revised by F. J. Furnivall, 1875). Thynne's comments suggest that at least some contemporaries were aware, at least to some extent, that some of the works included in contemporary editions of "Chaucer's Works" were not by Chaucer. However, it seems clear that many readers did assume that most of the works

so included were indeed by Chaucer. Even Skeat offers evidence to support this assumption (99), and it is significant that Thynne himself mentions only a few titles from among the many apocryphal works the contemporary editions included. For good discussions of this complicated matter, see chapter 8 ("The Renaissance Chaucer: From Manuscript to Print") of Miskimin's book (226–61; esp. 230–38); Francis W. Bonner, "The Genesis of the Chaucer Apocrypha," *Studies in Philology*, 48 (1951): 461–81; and Russell Hope Robbins, "The Chaucerian Apocrypha," in *A Manual of the Writings in Middle English, 1050–1500*, 3 vols. (New Haven: Connecticut Academy of Arts and Sciences, 1973) 3:1061–1104.

8. For a penetrating discussion of the importance of print to Jonson's works and self-understanding, see Richard Newton, "Jonson and the (Re-) Invention of the Book," in *Classic and Cavalier: Essays on Jonson and the Sons of Ben*, ed. Claude J. Summers and Ted-Larry Pebworth (Pittsburgh: University of Pittsburgh Press, 1982), 31–58.

9. The original version of Beaumont's letter, printed in the 1598 edition, contains substantially the same assertions. Interestingly, Beaumont also writes that Chaucer's "Canterbury tales conteine in them almost the same Argument, that is handled in Comedies," and, although the specific examples he mentions are all from the classical period, the basic point of similarity would not have been lost on Jonson ("To his very louing and assured good friend M. *Thomas Speght*"). Pearsall notes that this Francis Beaumont was *not* the famous dramatist of the same name (266, n. 6). Jonson's *Every Man in His Humour* was first acted in September 1598; *Every Man Out of His Humour* followed sometime in 1599.

10. In the ensuing biographical summary, I report the "facts" of Chaucer's life as Speght (and presumably Jonson) understood them, even if Speght's assertions have since been challenged by later scholars.

11. Coincidentally, Jonson's own connections with the Inns of Court and his own efforts to attract aristocratic patronage were particularly intense in the years immediately preceding 1602. His famous "Epistle to Elizabeth Countesse of Rutland" (*Forrest* 12) was a New Year's gift for 1600. The original version of *Every Man Out of His Humour* created controversy through its fulsome and somewhat indecorous concluding praise of the Queen (H&S 3:599–604), while *Cynthias Revels* defended in passing her dealings with the Earl of Essex (see William Matchett, *The Phoenix and the Turtle: Shakespeare's Poem and Chester's "Loues Martyr"* [The Hague: Mouton, 1965], 134–86). Jonson later dedicated *Every Man Out* to the Inns of Court, saying that "When I wrote this *Poeme* I had friendship with diuers in your Societies; who, as they were great Names in learning, so they were no lesse Examples of liuing" (H&S 1:22n). One of the best treatments of this period in Jonson's life remains W. David Kay's "The Shaping of Ben Jonson's Career: A Reexamination of Facts and Problems," *Modern Philology* 67 (1970): 224–37.

12. Even Jonson's warning (cited in the first paragraph of this chapter) against exposing the young too soon to Chaucer's archaic style nonetheless implies the "weight" of Chaucer's matter. It was not that Jonson distrusted Chaucer's influence per se; rather, he distrusted the inability of the young to separate the superficial from the substantial when they read Chaucer.

13. See Greene's chapter on Jonson in *The Light in Troy: Imitation and Discovery in Renaissance Poetry*. See also Peterson, *Imitation and Praise in the Poems of Ben Jonson*, and Maus, *Ben Jonson and the Roman Frame of Mind*. For a discussion of

Jonson's appropriation of Chaucer's House of Fame, see Loewenstein, *Responsive Readings: Versions of Echo in Pastoral, Epic, and the Jonsonian Masque,* 116–17.

14. It is possible, of course, that Jonson's notes on Chaucer's most important works were transcribed in a commonplace book lost either to time or to the famous fire of 1623. His surviving *Discoveries* volume, for instance, betrays an intense response to his reading.

15. Among John Aubrey's notes on Jonson is this one: "'Twas an ingeniose remarque of my Lady Hoskins, that B. J. never writes of Love. or if he does, does it not naturally" (H&S 1:180).

16. "Why Jonson Wrote Not of Love," 195. I am a little uncomfortable with Venuti's contention that "Jonson's neglect of love results from his view that the poet's task is to represent reality truly in order to give his reader moral instruction. The subject of love does not present opportunities for such instruction because of its resistance to language, but erotic conventions are even more problematic because they can misrepresent experience" (197). Perhaps this argument neglects the poet's ability to instruct by treating erotic emotions and erotic conventions with poetic irony.

17. Cupid, of course, appears frequently as a character in Jonson's works, especially the masques; for details, see D. Heywood Brock, *A Ben Jonson Companion* (Bloomington: Indiana University Press, 1983), 60.

For a modern text and helpful discussion of this poem, see *The Works of Sir John Clanvowe,* ed. V. J. Scattergood (Totowa, N.J.: Rowman and Littlefield, 1975).

18. For an intriguing discussion of the role of debate in English Renaissance drama, see Joel Altman, *The Tudor Play of Mind: Rhetorical Inquiry and the Development of Elizabethan Drama* (Berkeley: University of California Press, 1978). Altman suggests that some plays may have "functioned as media of intellectual and emotional exploration for minds that were accustomed to examine the many sides of a given theme, to entertain opposing ideals, and by so exercising the understanding, to move toward some fuller apprehension of truth that could be discerned only through the total action of the drama" (6). Perhaps "Of the Cuckow and the Nightingale" appealed to Jonson for similar reasons, as indeed I partly suggest in my next paragraph. I would argue, however, that for a reader attuned to the poem's comic ironies, the cuckow ultimately has the better argument. Much of what the nightingale says (e.g., about the ennobling effects of love) seems commendable, but some of her other remarks (e.g., about the mental anguish lovers suffer) seem to contradict these passages. Her and the narrator's meanness of spirit, combined with her flustered emotionalism and his unquestioning obeisance, make the poem seem not only more moral in its implications, but funnier as well.

I take comfort from V. J. Scattergood's opinion that "if either bird can be said to win the argument, it is the cuckoo" (13). He notes that "it was the rule of medieval school's debate that whoever argued his adversary into silence was the victor" (84). Scattergood considers the poem "a wryly self-mocking treatment of the touching irrational folly that love is capable of producing in those old enough and wise enough to know better" (13–14).

19. Robert Knoll offers a provocative discussion of Jonson's possible exploitation of the Parable of the Talents in *The Alchemist;* see his book *Ben Jonson's Plays: An Introduction* (Lincoln: University of Nebraska Press, 1964), 134–35.

20. For discussion of the impact of native dramatic traditions on Jonson's works, see Alan C. Dessen, *Jonson's Moral Comedy* (Evanston, Ill.: Northwestern University Press, 1971).

CHAPTER 5: MORE'S *RICHARD III* AND JONSON'S
RICHARD CROOKBACK AND *SEJANUS*

1. For this record, see H&S 11:308.

2. On some of the possibilities just mentioned, as well as for the few general discussions of the work, see H&S 1:33; Marchette Chute, *Ben Jonson of Westminster* (New York: Dutton, 1953), 105; Anne Barton, *Ben Jonson, Dramatist* (Cambridge: Cambridge University Press, 1984), 9, 13–14; Rosalind Miles, *Ben Jonson: His Life and Work* (London: Routledge and Kegan Paul, 1986), 65; David Riggs, *Ben Jonson: A Life*, 87, 91, 98–99; J. Payne Collier, ed., *The Ghost of Richard the Third: A Poem* . . . (London: The Shakespeare Society, 1844), xii–xiii.

3. *Thomae Mori Angli, viri eruditionis pariter ac virtvtis nomine clarissimi, Angliaeqve olim cancellarii, Omnia . . . Latina Opera . . .* (Lovanii: Apud Ioannem Bogardum, 1566).

4. On Dakins, see the *Dictionary of National Biography*.

5. Several possible meanings of "D.D.D." exist. These include "Datum decreto decurionum," "Dat, donat, dedicat," "Domini tres," "Dono dedit, dedicavit," and "Deo donum dedit." See Adriano Cappelli, *Lexicon Abbreviaturarum: Dizionario di Abbreviature Latine ed Italiane*, 6th ed. (Milan: Editore Ulrico Hoepli, 1985), 447.

6. The lines appear in book 2 of the *Utopia*, in the section marked "De Servis", on fol. C of Jonson's copy. They occur in the left margin. As one reads down the edge of the first column, the lines begin with "lantur" and extend to just beyond "piter." This passage deals with voluntary suicide, or sanctioned euthanasia. The fact that the marks coincide so precisely with this passage suggests that they may have been drawn, although it is also possible that they are simply accidental.

In describing the marks in this book, I will (as in this case) report the words or word parts that occur at the extreme edge of either the left margin (in the case of columns on the left side of the page) or the right margin (in the case of columns on the right side of the page). This will allow me to give a very precise sense of where the markings begin and where they end, so that readers without access to the Canterbury volume may nonetheless check my reports against other copies of the 1566 Louvain edition. Since almost all of Jonson's marks are marginal, mentioning the words or word parts closest to the margins avoids the danger of making assumptions about where, precisely, Jonson intended his marks to intervene in the regular syntax. In the case of the marks just reported, for instance, it seems fairly clear that the markings (if deliberate and intentional) were meant to single out the passage that begins not with "lantur" but with the word that follows it ("Caeterum"), which is the start of a new sentence. Similarly, the marks seem intended to end not with "piter" but with "abijcitur," which ends a sentence. However, in the case of many other marks the precise beginnings and endings are not always obvious; thus, rather than making personal assumptions about what, exactly, such marks include and exclude, I have decided to report where, exactly, they begin and end in the margins. A reader can thus reconstruct for himself a fairly precise idea of how Jonson's marks appear in the original.

A final note on methodology: in reporting the marks, I will cite not only the beginning and concluding words or word parts but also the number of the folio page on which such marks appear and whether they appear in the first or second columns on that page. According to this system, the markings reported above would be cited as follows: "'lantur / piter'; C.1" (i.e., the mark extends along the left margin from "lantur" to "piter" on fol. C, in column 1).

7. This is one of the few marks in this volume that occurs not only in one of the large outer margins but also within the narrow, inner margin. In this case, two brackets single out fairly precisely the following sentence from book 2: "Quo sit, vti interimentum citra cuiusquam sensum accidat" (C ij ᵛ). This alludes to the Utopian strategy for preventing loss to private individuals during war.

8. See Philp J. Ayres, "The Nature of Jonson's Roman History," 166–81.

9. Richard Marius, *Thomas More: A Biography* (New York: Alfred A. Knopf, 1985), 101.

10. By Harry Elmer Barnes, as quoted in Muriel Sheila Harris, "Sir Thomas More's *History of Richard III* as Humanist Historiography" (Ph.D. diss., Columbia University, 1972), 189. Harris's work is particularly helpful since it is one of the few discussions of More's *History* that compares and contrasts the Latin and English versions in detail.

11. See *The History of King Richard III*, ed. Richard S. Sylvester, vol. 2 of *The Complete Works of St. Thomas More* (New Haven: Yale University Press), 1963, esp. lxxx-ci. Throughout this chapter, my debt to Sylvester's scholarship is very great.

12. Valuable discussions of Jonson's own debts to Roman writers include the section on Jonson in Greene, *The Light in Troy;* Maus, *Ben Jonson and the Roman Frame of Mind;* and especially Peterson, *Imitation and Praise in the Poems of Ben Jonson.*

13. See *Thomas More* (Boston: Twayne, 1979), 30. For a discussion of the work as an inverted saint's life, see Robert E. Reiter, "On the Genre of Thomas More's *Richard III*," *Moreana* 7, no. 25 (1970): 5–16.

14. See *Richard III and His Early Historians, 1483–1535* (Oxford: Clarendon Press, 1975), 155. For an assault on Hanham's view, see Damian Grace, "More's *Richard III*: A 'Satirical Drama?'", *Moreana* 15, no. 57 (1978): 31–37. For fuller discussion of the "literary" aspects of the work, see Patrick Grant, "Thomas More's *Richard III*: Moral Narration and Humanist Method," *Renaissance and Reformation* 19 (1983): 157–72.

15. See "Literary Problems in More's *Richard III*," in *Essential Articles for the Study of Thomas More,* ed. R. S. Sylvester and G. P. Marćhadour (Hamden, Conn.: Archon Books, 1977), 324; 317.

16. See "Thomas More and *Richard III*," *Renaissance Quarterly* 35 (1982): 401–47; for the argument cited, see 422–23.

17. Harris provides a very valuable discussion of the work's dramatic elements, as does Arthur Noel Kincaid, "The Dramatic Structure of Sir Thomas More's *History of King Richard III*," in *Essential Articles*, ed. Sylvester and Marc'hadour, 375–87 (see note 15 above).

18. Other work by Kincaid may possibly suggest still another reason that Jonson may have decided not to publish his play. In his edition of Sir George Buck's *History of King Richard the Third* (London: Alan Sutton, 1979), Kincaid not only shows Buck's importance in arguing for a more favorable view of Richard's character and reign, but also suggests that such a view was beginning to gain acceptance among other historians in the early decades of the seventeenth century. According to Kincaid, these included even Jonson's friend and mentor William Camden; he notes positive changes in Camden's presentation of Richard between the 1600 and 1607 versions of his account in the *Britannia* (xlv; ciii). In researching his history of Richard, Buck used books from the libraries of a

number of figures with whom Jonson was also associated (xliv–xlvii), and his position as Master of the Revels makes it likely that he and Jonson would have known each other. Moreover, Kincaid's edition of *The Encomium of Richard III*, by Sir William Cornwallis the Younger (London: Turner and Devereux, 1977), prints dedications of that work to John Donne (1) and to Sir Henry Neville (33)—two men with whom Jonson had friendly relations. What these data may suggest, then, is that by the time he came to assemble the 1616 folio edition of his *Workes*, Jonson may have become increasingly dubious about the accuracy or justice of More's account of Richard. Certainly he could easily have heard about the projects of Buck and Cornwallis from their mutual friends. I mention this simply as another possibility among many.

19. For help in making sense of the Latin of the 1566 text (whose meaning is often unclear) I have consulted the English version printed on facing pages in Sylvester's Yale edition (3–93). However, since the English is not always a parallel or literal translation (see Sylvester liv–lix), I also have relied on Sylvester's very valuable commentary (153–276) as well as on the translation of another Latin version recently offered by Daniel Kinney (*In Defense of Humanism*, vol. 15 of *The Complete Works of St. Thomas More* [New Haven: Yale University Press, 1986]). Kinney notes that the Louvain version is "replete with opaque, ungrammatical phrases which give the misleading impression that More left his Latin history not merely unpolished but half-formed" (cxxxiii). Although he makes a strong case for regarding his newly discovered text as superior to the Louvain version, it is of course the Louvain version that Jonson read and marked and thus it is the one that must be examined here.

20. For the English, see Sylvester's Yale edition, 13.

Chapter 6: Praise and Blame in Jonson's Reading of More and Lipsius

1. On such matters see, for instance, W. H. Herendeen, "Like a Circle Bounded in Itself: Jonson, Camden, and the Strategies of Praise," *Journal of Medieval and Renaissance Studies* 11, no. 2 (1981): 137–67, or Jennifer Brady, "Jonson's 'To King James': Plain Speaking in the *Epigrammes* and the *Conversations*," *Studies in Philology* 82 (1985): 380–98.

2. For a fuller discussion of Jonson's political principles, see my book *Jonson, Lipsius, and the Politics of Renaissance Stoicism*. For further discussion of Jonson and More, see chapter 5, above. Jonson's copy of More, presently housed at the Library of the Canterbury Cathedral, is *Thomae Mori Angli, viri eruditionis pariter ac virtutis nomine clarissimi, Angliaeqve olim cancellarii, Omnia . . . Latina Opera . . .* (Louvain: Apud Ioannem Bogardum, 1566). For the text of More's panegyric, see sigs. Dii^v—Diij^v (pp. 20^v- 21^v). Although More's poem is printed in italics, when citing it I have not italicized.

3. *Dryden and the Tradition of Panegyric* (Berkeley: University of California Press, 1975), 69–70.

4. For convenient access to More's poem, see the text and translation printed in volume 3, part 2 of *The Complete Works of St. Thomas More* (New Haven: Yale University Press, 1984), 100–113. This volume is edited by Clarence H. Miller, Leicester Bradner, Charles A. Lynch, and Revilo P. Oliver; More's poem is translated by Bradner and Lynch.

A few words about my citation methods may be helpful. The differences between the Latin text printed in the Yale edition and the one Jonson owned are negligible. Since the Yale text is much more accessible than the 1566 Louvain edition, and since the latter provides no line numbers, in referring to More's poem I will cite the Yale line numbers. When Jonson marks a cited passage, I will also provide the initial or final words (depending upon which are closest to the mark) of the first and last lines Jonson highlights. This will give a very precise idea of exactly where the marks appear in the Canterbury text. For instance, the first highlighted passage reads as follows:

> Nec quicquam nisi rex quolibet ore sonat.
> Nobilitas, vulgi iamdudum obnoxia feci,
> Nobilitas, nimium nomen inane diu,
> Nunc caput attollit, nunc tali rege triumphat.

Just to the right of this, Jonson has drawn a vertical line. These are lines 25–28 of the Yale text. Thus, my parenthetical citation will read as follows: (25–28; "sonat / triumphat"; VL). If the vertical line were drawn to the left of this passage, I would cite the passage as follows: (25–28; "Nec / Nunc"; VL).

    5. It seems worth noting that both Jonson's "Panegyre" and his *Part of the King's Entertainment* were written for ceremonies that occurred in March 1604 (modern-style dating). The original title page of the *Entertainment* indicates that the poem was written to commemorate events of 15 March 1603 (H&S 7:81), while the original title page of the "Panegyre" alludes to events of 19 March 1603. In fact, of course, Queen Elizabeth did not even die until 24 March 1603, and, because of an outbreak of plague, James's coronation and the opening of his first parliament were delayed until the following March. It is with these events of 1604 that Jonson's works are associated. All of this seems worth mentioning, since modern editions, reference works, and critical discussions do not always report these data clearly.

    6. See Annabel Patterson, *Censorship and Interpretation: The Conditions of Writing and Reading in Early Modern England* (Madison: University of Wisconsin Press, 1984), 120–44.

    7. An especially memorable moment in Jonson's play involves Tiberius's initial appearance before the Senate, when he voices many of the values he has already trampled on; see act 1, 374–505 (H&S 6:367–71). As the virtuous Silius remarks during this performance, "If this man / Had but a minde allied vnto his words, / How blest a fate it were to vs, and *Rome?*" (440–42; H&S 6:368).

    8. I discuss Jonson's political ideas much more fully in *Jonson, Lipsius, and the Politics of Renaissance Stoicism*. See also Joseph John Kelly, "Ben Jonson's Politics," *Renaissance and Reformation*, n.s. 7 (1983): 192–215, as well as his "Ben Jonson's Political Identity" (Ph.D. diss., Temple University, 1980). A good overview of Jonson's politics is offered by Isabel Rivers in *The Poetry of Conservatism, 1600–1745: A Study of Poets and Public Affairs from Jonson to Pope* (Cambridge: Rivers Press, 1973).

    9. In the parenthetical references that follow, the line numbers are those of the Yale edition of More's poem; the volume and page numbers refer to the Herford and Simpson edition of Jonson's works.

    10. See *Ben Jonson and the Poetics of Patronage*.

    11. On this problem see, for instance, Alvin Kernan, *The Cankered Muse* (New Haven: Yale University Press, 1959).

    12. See, for instance, the evidence presented in chapters 3 and 5 of my book *Ben Jonson and the Poetics of Patronage*.

13. For details see Robert C. Evans, "Thomas Sutton: Ben Jonson's Volpone?" in *Philological Quarterly* 68 (1989): 295–314.

14. On Jonson's "railers" see, for instance, Judd Arnold, *A Grace Peculiar: Ben Jonson's Cavalier Heroes* (University Park: Pennsylvania State University Press, 1972).

15. On Jonson's rivalries with Dekker and others, see the sources cited in note 12, above, as well as several chapters in my forthcoming book *Jonson and the Contexts of His Time*.

16. On the whole episode involving Cecilia Bulstrode, Lady Bedford's cousin, see Evans, *Ben Jonson and the Poetics of Patronage*, 75–80. This book also discusses in detail Jonson's relations with Jones; see 158–78.

17. For the poem to Shakespeare (which incidentally contains an allusive attack on the poet William Basse), see H&S 8:390–92. In the 1629 "Ode to Himselfe," appended to his failed play *The New Inn*, Jonson attacks the public for preferring "some mouldy tale, / Like *Pericles*" (H&S 6:492; 21–22).

18. On the defensive nature of many of the eulogies written about Jonson, see Evans, *Ben Jonson and the Poetics of Patronage*, 185–91.

19. On Lipsius's life see, for instance, Jason Lewis Saunders, *Justus Lipsius: The Philosophy of Renaissance Stoicism* (New York: Liberal Arts Press, 1955). For a more recent overview, see Anthony Grafton, "Portrait of Justus Lipsius," *American Scholar* 56 (1987): 382–90. More generally, see Leonard Forster, "Lipsius and Renaissance Neostoicism," in *Festschrift for Ralph Farrell*, ed. Anthony Stephens et al. (Bern: Peter Lang, 1977), 201–20. I discuss the impact of Lipsius on Jonson's political thinking, as implied by the poet's markings in Lipsius's *Politicorum, sive civilis doctrinae libri sex*, in my book *Jonson, Lipsius, and the Politics of Renaissance Stoicism*. That book also goes into much greater detail about Lipsius's career and influence and about Jonson's responses to him.

20. *Iusti Lipsii V. C. opera omnia . . . .* 8 vol. (Antwerp: Ex Officina Plantiniana, apud Viduam & Filios J Moreti, 1614). On Jonson's habits as a book collector and on his characteristic marginal markings, see McPherson, *Ben Jonson's Library and Marginalia: An Annotated Catalogue*, esp. 3–19. For McPherson's thumbnail descriptions of the Emmanuel College Lipsius set, see 59–60. His brief comments on volume 2 of the set, which contains *De Calumnia* (on pages 103–12), do not make it entirely clear that the oration itself is marked.

21. On the phenomenon of "bleeding," which is very common in surviving copies of Jonson's books, see my article "Ben Jonson Reads *Daphnis and Chloë*," *English Language Notes* 27 (1990): 28–32. See also the "Introduction" to my book *Jonson, Lipsius, and the Politics of Renaissance Stoicism*. This discusses the "bleeding" in the Lipsius volume (and methods for coping with it) in great detail.

22. *Iusti LipsI oratio in calumniam* was issued in 1615 by F. Kyngston. For this and the other publication data mentioned, see the entry on Lipsius in the Pollard and Redgrave *Short Title Catalogue*. On Stafford's circumstances, see Giles D. Monsarrat, *Light from the Porch: Stoicism and English Renaissance Literature* (Paris: Didier-Érudition, 1984), 117–25. Jonson, incidentally, may have been the author of commendatory verses praising a religious work by Stafford; see H&S 8:412–14 and 11:159–60. Stafford's translation of "An Oration of Iustus Lipsius, *Against Calumny*" is appended to his own *Meditations, and Resolutions, Moral, Divine, Political* (London, 1612), 127–88.

23. For Stafford's modest comments, see page 128 of the "Aduertisement" that precedes his translation. In fact, the opening words of this preface warn "Whosoeuer shall come to the reading of this Oration . . . that it is not translated

like *Quae genus*, to teach any man to construe" (127). Because Stafford's renderings occasionally depart from the strict sense of Lipsius's Latin, when citing from his work I have sometimes inserted the Latin phrasing in parentheses, especially when the quoted matter is particularly interesting. (To have given full Latin and English versions of all the matter quoted in this chapter would have made it excessively long.) In addition, when Stafford sometimes exuberantly adds an adjective or some other term not found in the original, I have occasionally used elipses (. . .) to delete such excrescences and bring the translation more in line with the original phrasing. Finally, in referring to or quoting from *De Calumnia*, I have cited the relevant page numbers, first of the original, then of the translation. Thus, "103/134" indicates that the relevant passage appears on page 103 of the original and on page 134 of Stafford's translation.

24. On such ambivalence, see Evans, *Ben Jonson and the Poetics of Patronage*, 149–51.

25. *Und.* 73 (subtitled *"To the Envious"*) celebrates Lord Treasurer Weston in the face of detraction directed against that royal favorite (H&S 8:250). In a poem addressed "To my Detractor" (*U.V.* 37), Jonson responds to John Eliot, who had criticized the poet for taking money from Weston. Jonson torments Eliot by accusing him of having made "cheape, the Lord, the lines, the price," and in true Lipsian fashion he repeatedly compares Eliot to a barking dog. Similarly, *Under-wood* 76 mentions that Jonson's royal pension had provoked "from the times, / All the envie of the *Rymes*, / And the ratling pit-pat-noyse, / Of the lesse-*Poëtique* boyes" (17–20). In asking Charles to raise his pension, Jonson relishes the discomfort this would cause his detractors: "This would all their envie burst" (30).

CHAPTER 7: JONSON READING EDMONDES READING CAESAR

1. For full information about the copy of Edmondes's work owned by Jonson, see McPherson, *Ben Jonson's Library and Marginalia*, 42–43. Although Professor McPherson claims that the "pencil marks in margin throughout are not especially characteristic of Jonson," the markings in fact correspond to ones found in many other books once owned by the poet. For other examples of books he owned dealing with military matters, see, for instance, McPherson's listings #1 and 100.

2. For this and the other information about Edmondes cited in this paragraph, see the relevant article in the *Dictionary of National Biography*.

3. On the publication date of Jonson's poems, see Brock, *A Ben Jonson Companion*, 81.

4. In a dedicatory poem prefacing the *Commentaries*, Joshua Sylvester refers to "*HENRY*, thy Patron," whom he considers a prospective "*CAESAR* of our owne."

5. On Henry's career see especially Roy Strong, *Henry, Prince of Wales, and England's Lost Renaissance* (London: Thames and Hudson, 1986).

6. James himself cites Caesar in his advice to Henry concerning "the forme of making warres"; see *The Political Works of James I*, ed. Charles Howard McIlwain (Cambridge: Harvard University Press, 1918), 28–29.

7. On Jonson's "pacifism," see, for instance, Joseph John Kelly, "Ben Jonson's Political Identity," 131–35.

8. For the texts of the poems, see H&S 8:71–72.

9. Actually, Jonson owned at least two copies of this work; see McPherson, *Ben Jonson's Library and Marginalia*, 60–61.

10. In citing Edmondes's works, I will list first an abbreviated title (*GW* = his commentary on Casear's *Gallic Wars*; *CW* = his commentary on Caesar's *Civil Wars*). Then I will use Roman numerals to indicate Edmondes's own book and chapter numbers. These will be followed by arabic numerals indicating the precise page(s) on which the marks occur. Finally, abbreviations will indicate the kinds of marks Jonson drew in the margin. Most of the marks in the Edmondes volume are his distinctive cross-marks (CR), drawn in pencil. In reporting some marks in the Appendix, I will again cite the beginning and ending word or word-parts that occur along the margin closest to the particular marking.

11. On these matters see my book *Jonson, Lipsius, and the Politics of Renaissance Stoicism*, 43–45, and the notes cited there. For the translated quotations, see Tacitus, *The Histories* and *The Annals*, trans. Clifford H. Moore and John Jackson, 4 vols., Loeb Classical Library (Cambridge: Harvard University Press, 1962), 1:141–42.

12. On the general importance of pragmatic balance in Jonson's thinking, see my book *Jonson, Lipsius, and the Politics of Renaissance Stoicism*.

13. In *Und.* 78, Jonson celebrates Sir Kenelm Digby for being "prudent, valiant, just, and temperate" (5), and implies the usefulness of such qualities in a famous military engagement that Digby directed (13).

14. On the issue of Jonson's attitude toward royal authority see, for instance, chapter 2 of my book *Jonson, Lipsius, and the Politics of Renaissance Stoicism*. One of the fullest and most explicit poetic statements of Jonson's political attitudes is contained in his "Panegyre" for James; see H&S 7:113–17. There James is reminded "That princes, since they know it is their fate, / Oft-times, to haue the secrets of their state / Betraid to fame, should take more care, and feare / In publique acts what face and form they beare" (85–88). In *Und.* 47, Jonson disclaims any interest in detailed knowledge of current affairs, declaring simply, "I wish all well, and pray high heaven conspire / My Princes safetie, and my Kings desire" (37–38). *Ep.* 92, "THE NEW CRIE," mocks those who pretend to secret knowledge: "The councels, proiects, practises they know, / And what each prince doth for intelligence owe, / And vnto whom" (11–13). Jonson himself professes a more "modest" (but more accurate) knowledge (40). A passage in the *Discoveries* attacks the "beastly natures of the multitude; especially when they come to that iniquity, to censure their *Soveraign's* actions" (H&S 8:593). On the other hand, *Ep.* 95 claims that "We need a man, can speake of the intents, / The councells, actions, orders, and euents / Of state, and censure them" (31–33).

15. Self-defense is, of course, a constant theme in Jonson's writings, particularly in the prologues and epilogues to some of his plays. For his typical stance, indebted in this case to Apuleius, see H&S 8:604–5.

16. On Jonson's attitudes toward emulation see, for instance, George E. Rowe, *Distinguishing Jonson*, 10–19.

17. *Ep.* 66, for instance, speaks of "the sloth of this our time" (5), while *Und.* 64, echoing Cicero, exclaims, "O Times! O Manners! Surfet bred of ease, / The truly Epidemicall disease!" (16–17). Similarly, *Und.* 15 urges a "Friend" to "flie" from his corrupt "times" (161–62).

18. See, for instance, G. P. V. Akrigg, *Jacobean Pageant: or The Court of King James I* (Cambridge: Harvard University Press, 1962), 251, 258; and also S. R. Gardiner, *History of England from the Accession of James I to the Outbreak of Civil War*, 10 vols. (London: Longmans, Green, 1883–84), 2:212–13.

19. See, for instance, *The Devil Is an Ass* and also *Ep.* 48, which mentions "our Duéllists" (l. 3). *Ep.* 115 chides its target for being able to "Doe all, that longs to the *anarchy* of drinke, / Except the *duell*" (12–13).

20. See, for instance, *Ep.* 94, which claims that most people dislike satires because "the most of mankind bee / Their vn-auoided subiect." For this reason, "none ere tooke that pleasure in sinnes sense, / But, when they heard it tax'd, tooke more offence" (7–10). Similarly, the prologue to *Every Man in His Humour* claims that the purpose of comedy is to "shew an Image of the times, / And sport with humane follies, not with crimes. / Except, we make 'hem such, by louing still / Our popular errors, when we know th'are ill" (23–26; H&S 3:303). In addition, Jonson claims in the prologue to *The Alchemist* that his "pen / Did neuer aime to grieue, but better men; How e'er the age, he liues in, doth endure / The vices that shee breeds, aboue their cure" (11–14; H&S 5:294).

21. See, for instance, his praise of James, who, "entring with the power of a king, / The temp'rance of a priuate man did bring, / That wan affections, ere his steps wan ground" (139–41; H&S 7:117). Similarly, James is later praised in *The Haddington Masque* because he "dares esteeme it the first fortitude, / To haue his passions, foes at home, subdued" (222–23; H&S 7:256). Moreover, a character in *Sejanus* describes how the Romans originally "were borne / Free, and equall lords of the triumphed world, / And knew no masters, but affections, / To which betraying first our liberties, / We since became the slaues to one mans lusts" (1.1.59–63; H&S 4:357).

22. There, while listing other corruptions, Jonson claims that "Our Delicacies are growne capitall, / And even our sports are dangers!" (37–38). Later he refers to the corrupting influence of "our ill-us'd freedome, and soft peace" (121).

23. He told Drummond, for instance, that "of all stiles he loved most to be named honest, and hath of that ane hundreth letters so naming him" (H&S 1:150). Similarly, in *Und.* 17 he criticizes "some greater names [who] have broke with me, / And their words too" (8–9).

24. On this point see chapter 2 of my book *Jonson, Lipsius, and the Politics of Renaissance Stoicism*. For the translated quotation, see the Loeb Classical Library edition of *Suetonius*, trans. J. C. Rolfe, 2 vols. (Cambridge: Harvard University Press, 1964), 1:81.

25. In the "Tribe of Ben" epistle (*Und.* 47), Jonson declares that "if for honour, we must draw the Sword, / And force back that, which will not be restor'd, / I have a body, yet, that spirit drawes / To live, or fall a Carkasse in the cause" (39–42).

26. See his article, "Sir Walter Raleigh's 'History of the World,'" in *Essays Historical and Literary* (Oxford: Clarendon Press, 1938), 37–38. Interestingly enough, C. A. Patrides, in his abridged edition of the *History of the World* (Philadelphia: Temple University Press, 1971), calls attention to an allusion to Edmondes's *Commentaries* in book 5, chapter 1 of Ralegh's work. See the footnote on page 345 of the Patrides edition.

27. Sir Walter Ralegh, *Works*, 8 vols. (1829; rpt. New York: Burt Franklin, 1964), 7:356.

28. Ralegh, *Works*, 8:298.

29. Ralegh, *Works*, 8:472–73.

30. The obvious examples are Jonson's "humours" plays and the characters in other plays who are controlled by such humors or obsessions. On this point see, for instance, Robert N. Watson, *Ben Jonson's Parodic Strategy*, which shows how Jonson's characters often ludicrously attempt to mimic literary stereotypes.

31. For a slightly different text and translation of this passage, see Cicero, *De Officiis*, trans. Walter Miller (Cambridge: Harvard University Press, 1961), 87.

32. See, for instance, *Ep.* 2, in which Jonson takes pleasure in deceiving popular expectations about the style of epigrams, or the prologue to *Every Man in His Humour*, in which he similarly attacks popular expectations about the drama. However, perhaps the best example of Jonson's avowed willingness to flout popular conceptions occurs in the "apologeticall Dialogue" appended to *Poetaster*, where "The Author" is confronted with the charge that "the Multitude . . . / . . . thinke you hit, and hurt: and dare giue out / Your silence argues it, in not reioyning / To this, or that, late libell." To which The Author responds by beginning, "'Lasse, good rout! / I can affoord them leaue, to erre so still: / And, like the barking students of Beares-Colledge, / To swallow vp the garbadge of the time / With greedy gullets, whilst my selfe sit by, / Pleas'd, and yet tortur'd, with their beastly feeding" (40–48; H&S 4:318).

33. See, for example, *For.* 3, in which Jonson censures "guiltie armes" and condemns the "furie of a rash command" (67–68), or *Und.* 59, in which he proclaims that "daring not to doe a wrong, is true / Valour! to sleight it, being done to you! To know the heads of danger! where 'tis fit / To bend, to breake, provoke, or suffer it!" (15–18). Here and elsewhere Jonson's concern is less with behavior per se than with the motives by which behavior is dictated.

34. See the famous passage from the *Discoveries*: "*There* cannot be one colour of the mind; an other of the wit. If the mind be staid, grave, and compos'd, the wit is so; that vitiated, the other is blowne, and deflowr'd. Doe we not see, if the mind languish, the members are dull? . . . Wheresoever, manners, and fashions are corrupted, Language is. It imitates the publicke riot. The excesse of Feasts, and apparell, are the notes of a sick State; and the wantonnesse of language, of a sick mind" (H&S 8:592–93).

35. On Jonson's possible misogyny, see my discussion in *Jonson, Lipsius, and the Politics of Renaissance Stoicism*, 47.

Bibliography

Primary Sources

Apuleius, Lucius. *L. Apuleii . . . Opera Omnia . . . .* 2 parts. Leyden: Ex officina Plantiniana, apud F. Raphelengium, 1588. Bodleian Library, Oxford University.

Biblia sacra . . . . Antwerp: Apud I. Moretum, 1599. Pierpont Morgan Library.

Chaucer, Geoffrey. *The Workes of Our Ancient and Learned English Poet, Geffrey Chaucer.* Edited by Thomas Speght. London: Impensis Geor. Bishop, 1602. Folger Shakespeare Library.

Edmondes, Sir Clement. *Observations upon Ceasars Commentaries, by C. Edmondes.* London: 1609? British Library.

The Holy Bible: Douay Version. London: Catholic Truth Society, 1963.

Lipsius, Justus. *Iusti Lipsii V. C. opera omnia . . . .* Antwerp: Ex officina Plantiniana, apud Viduam & Filios J. Moreti, 1614. Library of Emmanuel College, Cambridge University.

More, Thomas. *Thomae Mori Angli, viri eruditionis pariter ac virtvtis nomine clarissimi, Angliaeqve olim cancellarii, Omnia . . . Latin opera . . . .* Louvain: Apud Ioannem Bogardem, 1566. Library of Canterbury Cathedral.

Seneca, Lucius Annaeus. *L. Annaei Senecae Philosophi Scripta qvae extant . . . .* Paris: Apud Marcum Orry, 1599. Glasgow University Library.

Secondary Sources

Akrigg, G. P. V. *Jacobean Pageant: or The Court of King James I.* Cambridge: Harvard University Press, 1962.

Altman, Joel. *The Tudor Play of Mind: Rhetorical Inquiry and the Development of Elizabethan Drama.* Berkeley: University of California Press, 1978.

Apuleius, Lucius. *The Apologia and Florida of Apuleius of Madura.* Translated by H. E. Butler. Oxford: Clarendon Press, 1909.

———. *The Works of Apuleius.* London: George Bell, 1889.

Arnold, Judd. *A Grace Peculiar: Ben Jonson's Cavalier Heroes.* University Park: Pennsylvania State University Press, 1972.

Augustine, Saint. *The City of God.* Translated by Marcus Dods. New York: Modern Library, 1950.

———. *The Confessions and Letters of St. Augustin.* Vol. 1 of *A Select Library of the Nicene and Post-Nicene Fathers of the Christian Church.* Edited by Philip Scaff. 14 vols. New York: Charles Scribner's, 1886.

Ayres, Philip J. "The Nature of Jonson's Roman History." *English Literary Renaissance* 16 (1986): 166–81.

Babb, Lawrence. "Scientific Theories of Grief in Some Elizabethan Plays." *Studies in Philology* 40 (1943): 502–19.

Ballmann, Otto. "Chaucers einfluss auf das englische drama im zeitalter der königin Elisabeth und der beiden ersten Stuart-könige." *Anglia* 25 (1902): 1–85.

Barton, Anne. *Ben Jonson, Dramatist.* Cambridge: Cambridge University Press, 1984.

Bates, Steven L., and Sidney D. Orr. *A Concordance to the Poems of Ben Jonson.* Athens: Ohio University Press, 1978.

Blisset, William. "Roman Ben Jonson." In *Ben Jonson's 1616 Folio,* edited by Jennifer Brady and W. H. Herendeen, 90–110. Newark: University of Delaware Press, 1991.

Boehrer, Bruce Thomas. "Renaissance Overeating: The Sad Case of Ben Jonson." *PMLA* 105 (1990): 1071–82.

Bonner, Francis W. "The Genesis of the Chaucer Apocrypha." *Studies in Philology* 48 (1951): 461–81.

Braden, Gordon. *Renaissance Tragedy and the Senecan Tradition: Anger's Privilege.* New Haven: Yale University Press, 1985.

Bradley, Jesse Franklin, and Joseph Quincy Adams. *The Jonson Allusion-Book: A Collection of Allusions to Ben Jonson from 1597–1700.* New Haven: Yale University Press, 1922.

Brady, H. Jennifer. "Ben Jonson's 'Works of Judgment': A Study of Rhetorical Strategies in the 'Epigrammes.'" Ph.D. dissertation, Princeton University, 1980.

———. "Jonson's 'To King James': Plain Speaking in the *Epigrammes* and the *Conversations.*" *Studies in Philology* 82 (1985): 380–98.

Brock, D. Heyward. *A Ben Jonson Companion.* Bloomington: Indiana University Press, 1983.

Buck, Sir George. *History of King Richard the Third.* Edited by Arthur Noel Kincaid. London: Alan Sutton, 1979.

Cain, William E. "Mirrors, Intentions, and Texts in Ben Jonson." *Essays in Literature* 8 (1981): 11–24.

Cappelli, Adriano. *Lexicon Abbreviaturarum: Dizionario di Abbreviature Latine ed Italiane.* 6th ed. Milan: Editore Ulrico Hoepli, 1985.

Chaucer, Geoffrey. *Geoffrey Chaucer: The Works 1532; with Supplementary Material from the Editions of 1542, 1561, 1598, and 1602.* Edited by Derek Brewer. Menston, England: The Scolar Press, 1969.

Chute, Marchette. *Ben Jonson of Westminster.* New York: Dutton, 1953.

Cicero, Marcus Tullius. *De Officiis.* Translated by Walter Miller. Cambridge: Harvard University Press, 1961.

Clanvowe, Sir John. *The Works of Sir John Clanvowe.* Edited by V. J. Scattergood. Totowa, N.J.: Rowman and Littlefield, 1975.

Collier, J. Payne. *The Ghost of Richard the Third: A Poem . . . .* London: The Shakespeare Society, 1844.

Cope, Jackson I. "*Bartholomew Fair* as Blasphemy." *Renaissance Drama* 8 (1965): 127–52.

Cornwallis, Sir William the Younger. *The Encomium of Richard III.* Edited by Arthur Noel Kincaid. London: Turner and Devereux, 1977.

Cressy, David. *Literacy and the Social Order: Reading and Writing in Tudor and Stuart England.* Cambridge: Cambridge University Press, 1980.

D'Amico, John F. "The Progress of Renaissance Latin Prose: The Case of Apuleianism." *Renaissance Quarterly* 37 (1984): 351–94.

Dean, Leonard F. "Literary Problems in More's *Richard III.*" In *Essential Articles for the Study of Thomas More,* edited by R. S. Sylvester and G. P. Marc'hadour, 315–25. Hamden, Conn. Archon Books, 1977.

Dessen, Alan C. *Jonson's Moral Comedy.* Evanston, Ill.: Northwestern University Press, 1971.

Donaldson, E. Talbot, and Judith J. Kollmann, eds. *Chaucerian Shakespeare: Adaptation and Transformation.* Medieval and Renaissance Monograph Series 2. Detroit: Michigan Consortium for Medieval and Early Modern Studies, 1983.

Donaldson, E. Talbot. *The Swan at the Well: Shakespeare Reading Chaucer.* New Haven: Yale University Press, 1985.

Donno, Elizabeth S. "Thomas More and *Richard III.*" *Renaissance Quarterly* 35 (1982): 401–47.

Donovan, Kevin J. "Jonson's Texts in the First Folio." In *Ben Jonson's 1616 Folio,* edited by Jennifer Brady and W. H. Herendeen, 23–37. Newark: University of Delaware Press, 1991.

Dutton, Richard. *Ben Jonson: To the First Folio.* Cambridge: Cambridge University Press, 1983.

———. "The Sources, Text, and Readers of *Sejanus:* Jonson's 'Integrity in the Story.'" *Philological Quarterly* 75 (1978): 181–98.

Evans, Robert C. *Ben Jonson and the Poetics of Patronage.* Lewisburg, Pa.: Bucknell University Press, 1989.

———. "Ben Jonson Reads *Daphnis and Chloë.*" *English Language Notes* 27 (1990): 28–32.

———. *Jonson and the Contexts of His Time.* Lewisburg, Pa.: Bucknell University Press, 1994.

———. *Jonson, Lipsius, and the Politics of Renaissance Stoicism.* Wakefield, N.H.: Longwood Academic, 1992.

———. "'Making Just Approaches': Ben Jonson's Poems to the Earl of Newcastle.'" *Renaissance Papers* (1988): 63–76.

———. "Poetry and Power: Ben Jonson and the Poetics of Patronage." Ph.D. dissertation, Princeton University, 1984.

———. "Strategic Debris: Ben Jonson's Satires on Inigo Jones." *Renaissance Papers* (1986): 69–82.

———. "Thomas Sutton: Ben Jonson's Volpone?" *Philological Quarterly* 68 (1989): 295–314.

Ferns, John. "Ovid, Juvenal, and 'The Silent Woman': A Reconsideration." *Modern Language Review* 65 (1970): 248–53.

Finkelstein, Richard. "Ben Jonson's Ciceronian Rhetoric of Friendship." *Journal of Medieval and Renaissance Studies* 16 (1986): 103–24.

Firth, C. H. *Essays Historical and Literary.* Oxford: Clarendon Press, 1938.

Fish, Stanley. "Authors-Readers: Jonson's Community of the Same." *Representations* no. 7 (1984): 36–58.

Forster, Leonard. "Lipsius and Renaissance Neostoicism." *Festscrift for Ralph Farrell,* edited by Anthony Stephens et al., 201–20. Bern: Peter Lang, 1977.

Gardiner, S. R. *History of England from the Accession of James I to the Outbreak of Civil War*. 10 vols. London: Longmans, Green, 1883–84.

Garrison, James D. *Dryden and the Tradition of Panegyric*. Berkeley: University of California Press, 1975.

Grace, Damian. "More's *Richard III*: A 'Satirical Drama'?" *Moreana* 15, no. 57 (1978): 31–37.

Grafton, Anthony. "Portrait of Justus Lipsius." *American Scholar* 56 (1987): 382–90.

Grant, Patrick. "Thomas More's *Richard III:* Moral Narration and Humanist Method." *Renaissance and Reformation* 19 (1983): 157–72.

Greene, Thomas M. *The Light in Troy: Imitation and Discovery in Renaissance Poetry*. New Haven: Yale University Press, 1982.

Griffin, Miriam T. *Seneca: A Philosopher in Politics*. Oxford: Clarendon Press, 1976.

Guibbory, Achsah. "A Sense of the Future: Projected Audiences of Donne and Jonson." *John Donne Journal* 2 (1983): 11–21.

Gummere, Richard Mott. *Seneca the Philosopher and His Modern Message*. New York: Cooper Square, 1963.

Hadas, Moses. *A History of Latin Literature*. New York: Columbia University Press, 1952.

Haight, Elizabeth Hazelton. *Apuleius and His Influence*. New York: Longmans, Green, 1927.

Hanham, Alison. *Richard III and His Early Historians, 1483–1535*. Oxford: Clarendon Press, 1975.

Harp, Richard. "Jonson's 'To Penshurst': The Country House as Church." *John Donne Journal* 7 (1988): 73–89.

Harris, Muriel Sheila. "Sir Thomas More's *History of Richard III* as Humanist Historiography." Ph.D. dissertation, Columbia University, 1972.

Helgerson, Richard. *Self-Crowned Laureates: Spenser, Jonson, Milton and the Literary System*. Berkeley: University of California Press, 1983.

Henry, Elisabeth. "Seneca the Younger." In *Ancient Writers : Greece and Rome*, edited by T. James Luce, 2:807–32. New York: Scribner's, 1982.

Herendeen, W. H. "Like a Circle Bounded in Itself: Jonson, Camden, and the Strategies of Praise." *Journal of Medieval and Renaissance Studies* 11, no. 2 (1981): 137–67.

———. "A New Way to Pay Old Debts: Pretexts to the 1616 Folio." In *Ben Jonson's 1616 Folio*, edited by Jennifer Brady and W. H. Herendeen, 38–63. Newark: University of Delaware Press, 1991.

Hetherington, John R. *Chaucer, 1532–1602: Notes and Facsimile Texts*. Birmingham, England: John R. Hetherington, 1964.

Hilberry, Clarence Beverly. *Ben Jonson's Ethics in Relation to Stoic and Humanistic Ethical Thought*. Norwood, Pa.: Folcroft Library Editions, 1973.

Holleran, James V. "Character Transmutation in *The Alchemist*." *CLAJ* 11 (1968): 221–27.

Jackson, Gabrielle Bernhard. *Vision and Judgment in Ben Jonson's Drama*. New Haven: Yale University Press, 1968.

James I, King. *The Political Works of James I*. Edited by Charles Howard McIlwain. Cambridge: Harvard University Press, 1918.

Jones, Judith P. *Thomas More*. Boston: Twayne, 1979.

Jones, Robert C. "The Satirist's Retirement in Jonson's 'Apologetical Dialogue.'" *ELH* 34 (1967): 447–67.

Jonson, Ben. *Ben Jonson*. Edited by C. H. Herford, Percy Simpson, and Evelyn Simpson. 11 vols. Oxford: Clarendon Press, 1925–52.

———. *Volpone*. Edited by Jonas Barish. New York: Appleton-Century-Crofts, 1958.

Kay, W. David. "The Shaping of Ben Jonson's Career: A Reexamination of Facts and Problems." *Modern Philology* 67 (1970): 224–37.

Kelly, Joseph John. "Ben Jonson's Political Identity." Ph.D. dissertation, Temple University, 1980.

———. "Ben Jonson's Politics." *Renaissance and Reformation*, n.s. 7 (1983): 192–215.

Kennedy, George. *The Art of Rhetoric in the Roman World: 300 B.C.–A.D. 300*. Princeton: Princeton University Press, 1972.

Kernan, Alvin. *The Cankered Muse*. New Haven: Yale University Press, 1959.

Kincaid, Arthur Noel. "The Dramatic Structure of Sir Thomas More's *History of King Richard III*." In *Essential Articles for the Study of Thomas More*, edited by R. S. Sylvester and G. P. Marćhadour, 375–87. Hamden, Conn.: Archon Books, 1977.

Knoll, Robert. *Ben Jonson's Plays: An Introduction*. Lincoln: University of Nebraska Press, 1964.

Lanier, Douglas. "Brainchildren: Self-representation and Patriarchy in Ben Jonson's Early Works." *Renaissance Papers* (1986): 53–68.

Lee, Jongsook. *Ben Jonson's Poesis: A Literary Dialectic of Ideal and History*. Charlottesville: University Press of Virginia, 1989.

Lemly, John. "Masks and Self-Portraits in Jonson's Late Poetry." *ELH* 44 (1977): 248–66.

Livingstone, Mary. "Ben Jonson: The Poet to the Painter." *Texas Studies in Literature and Language* 18 (1977): 381–92.

Loewenstein, Joseph. "The Jonsonian Corpulence: Or, The Poet as Mouthpiece." *ELH* 53 (1986): 491–518.

———. "Printing and 'The Multitudinous Presse': The Contentious Texts of Jonson's Masques." In *Ben Jonson's 1616 Folio*, edited by Jennifer Brady and W. H. Herendeen, 168–91. Newark: University of Delaware Press, 1991.

———. *Responsive Readings: Versions of Echo in Pastoral, Epic, and the Jonsonian Masque*. New Haven: Yale University Press, 1984.

———. "The Script in the Marketplace." *Representations* no. 12 (1985): 101–14.

McLuskie, Kathleen. *Renaissance Dramatists*. Atlantic Highlands, N.J.: Humanities, 1989.

McPherson, David. "Ben Jonson's Library and Marginalia: An Annotated Catalogue." *Studies in Philology* 71.5 [Texts and Studies Series] (1974), 1–106.

Marcus, Leah S. *The Politics of Mirth: Jonson, Herrick, Milton, Marvell and the Defense of Old Holiday Pastimes*. Chicago: University of Chicago Press, 1986.

Marius, Richard. *Thomas More: A Biography*. New York: Alfred A. Knopf, 1985.

Matchett, William. *The Phoenix and the Turtle: Shakespeare's Poem and Chester's "Loues Martyr."* The Hague: Mouton, 1965.

Maus, Katherine Eisaman. *Ben Jonson and the Roman Frame of Mind*. Princeton: Princeton University Press, 1984.

————. "Facts of the Matter: Satiric and Ideal Economies in the Jonsonian Imagination." In *Ben Jonson's 1616 Folio*, edited by Jennifer Brady and W. H. Herendeen, 64–89. Newark: University of Delaware Press, 1991.

Mebane, John S. *Renaissance Magic and the Return of the Golden Age*. Lincoln: University of Nebraska Press, 1989.

Miles, Rosalind. *Ben Jonson: His Life and Work*. London: Routledge and Kegan Paul, 1986.

Miskimin, Alice S. *The Renaissance Chaucer*. New Haven: Yale University Press, 1975.

Monsarrat, Giles D. *Light from the Porch: Stoicism and English Renaissance Literature*. Paris: Didier-Érudition, 1984.

More, Thomas. *The History of King Richard III*. Edited by Richard Sylvester. Vol. 2 of *The Complete Works of St. Thomas More*. New Haven: Yale University Press, 1963.

————. *In Defense of Humanism*. Edited by Daniel Kinney. Vol. 15 of *The Complete Works of St. Thomas More*. New Haven: Yale University Press, 1986.

————. *The Latin Epigrams*. Edited by Clarence H. Miller, Leicester Bradner, Charles A. Lynch, and Revilo P. Oliver. Vol. 3, part 2 of *The Complete Works of St. Thomas More*. New Haven: Yale University Press, 1984.

Motto, Anna Lydia. *Seneca*. New York: Twayne, 1973.

Murray, Timothy. "From Foul Sheets to Legitimate Model: Antitheater, Text, Ben Jonson." *New Literary History* 14 (1983): 641–64.

Newton, Richard. "Jonson and the (Re-) Invention of the Book." In *Classic and Cavalier: Essays on Jonson and the Sons of Ben*, edited by Claude J. Summers and Ted-Larry Pebworth, 31–58. Pittsburgh: University of Pittsburgh Press, 1982.

Nicholson, Marjorie. "The 'New Astronomy' and English Literary Imagination." *Studies in Philology* 32 (1935): 428–62.

Niland, Kurt R., and Robert C. Evans. "Jonson and Quintilian on the Deaths of Sons" (forthcoming).

Patterson, Annabel. *Censorship and Interpretation: The Conditions of Writing and Reading in Early Modern England*. Madison: University of Wisconsin Press, 1984.

Pearsall, Derek. "Thomas Speght." In *Editing Chaucer: The Great Tradition*, edited by Paul G. Ruggiers, 71–92. Norman, Okla.: Pilgrim Books, 1984.

Peterson, Richard S. *Imitation and Praise in the Poems of Ben Jonson*. New Haven: Yale University Press, 1981.

Pollard, A. W., and G. R. Redgrave. *A Short-Title Catalogue of Books Printed in England, Scotland, and Ireland . . . 1475–1640*. London: Bernard Quaritch, 1926.

Ralegh, Sir Walter. *History of the World*. Edited by C. A. Patrides. Philadelphia: Temple University Press, 1971.

————. *Works*. 8 vols. 1829. Reprint. New York: Burt Franklin, 1964.

Reiter, Robert E. "On the Genre of Thomas More's *Richard III*." *Moreana* 7, no. 25 (1970): 5–16.

Revard, Stella P. "Classicism and Neo-Classicism in Jonson's *Epigrammes*." In *Ben Jonson's 1616 Folio*, edited by Jennifer Brady and W. H. Herendeen, 138–67. Newark: University of Delaware Press, 1991.

―――. "Pindar and Jonson's Cary-Morison Ode." In *Classic and Cavalier: Essays on Jonson and the Sons of Ben,* edited by Claude J. Summers and Ted-Larry Pebworth, 17–30. Pittsburgh: University of Pittsburgh Press, 1982.

Riddell, James A., and Stanley Stewart. "Jonson Reads 'The Ruines of Time.'" *Studies in Philology* 87 (1990): 427–55.

Riggs, David. *Ben Jonson: A Life.* Cambridge: Harvard University Press, 1989.

Rivers, Isabel. *The Poetry of Conservatism, 1600–1745: A Study of Poets and Public Affairs from Jonson to Pope.* Cambridge: Rivers Press, 1973.

Robbins, Russell Hope. "The Chaucerian Apocrypha." In *A Manual of the Writings in Middle English, 1050–1500,* 3:1061–1104. New Haven: Connecticut Academy of Arts and Sciences, 1973.

Rollin, Roger B. "The Anxiety of Identification: Jonson and the Rival Poets." In *Classic and Cavalier: Essays on Jonson and the Sons of Ben,* edited by Claude J. Summers and Ted-Larry Pebworth, 139–56. Pittsburgh: University of Pittsburgh Press, 1982.

Rowe, George E. "Ben Jonson's Quarrel with Audience and Its Renaissance Context." *Studies in Philology* 81 (1984): 438–60.

―――. *Distinguishing Jonson: Imitation, Rivalry, and the Direction of a Dramatic Career.* Lincoln: University of Nebraska Press, 1988.

Saunders, Jason Lewis. *Justus Lipsius: The Philosophy of Renaissance Stoicism.* New York: Liberal Arts Press, 1955.

Seneca, Lucius Annaeus. *Ad Lucilium Epistulae Morales.* Translated by R. M. Gummere. 3 vols. Loeb Classical Library. Cambridge: Harvard University Press, 1970–71.

―――. *Moral Essays.* Translated by John W. Basore. 3 vols. Loeb Classical Library. Cambridge: Harvard University Press, 1975.

―――. *On Benefits.* Translated by Thomas Lodge. London: Dent, 1899.

―――. *The Works of L. A. Seneca Both Morall and Naturall.* Translated by Thomas Lodge. London: 1620.

Suetonius. *Suetonius.* Translated by J. C. Rolfe. 2 vols. Loeb Classical Library. Cambridge: Harvard University Press, 1964.

Severance, Sibyl Lutz. "'To Shine in Union': Measure, Number, and Harmony in Ben Jonson's 'Poems of Devotion.'" *Studies in Philology* 80 (1983): 183–99.

Skeat, Walter W. *The Chaucer Canon.* Oxford: Clarendon Press, 1900.

Sørenson, Villy. *Seneca: The Humanist at the Court of Nero.* Translated by W. Glyn Jones. Chicago: University of Chicago Press, 1984.

Stafford, Anthony. *Meditations, and Resolutions, Moral, Divine, Political.* London, 1612.

Strong, Roy. *Henry, Prince of Wales, and England's Lost Renaissance.* London: Thames and Hudson, 1986.

Sullivan, J. P. *Literature and Politics in the Age of Nero.* Ithaca: Cornell University Press, 1985.

Sweeney, John Gordon III. *Jonson and the Psychology of Public Theater.* Princeton: Princeton University Press, 1985.

Tacitus, Publius Cornelius. *The Histories* and *The Annals.* Translated by Clifford H. Moore and John Jackson. 4 vols. Loeb Classical Library. Cambridge: Harvard University Press, 1962.

Tatum, James F. "Apuleius." In *Ancient Writers: Greece and Rome*, edited by T. James Luce, 2:1099–1116. New York: Scribner's, 1982.

———. *Apuleius and the "Golden Ass."* Ithaca: Cornell University Press, 1979.

Teague, Frances. "Ben Jonson's Poverty." *Biography* 2 (1979): 260–65.

Thayer, C. G. *Ben Jonson: Studies in the Plays.* Norman: University of Oklahoma Press, 1963.

Thomson, Ann. *Shakespeare's Chaucer: A Study of Literary Origins.* Liverpool: Liverpool University Press, 1978.

Thynne, Francis. *Chaucer. Animaduersions vppon the Annotacions and Corrections of Some Imperfections of Impressiones of Chaucers Workes [Sett Downe before Tyme, and Nowe] Reprinted in the Yere of Oure Lord 1598.* Edited by G. H. Kingsley. London: Early English Text Society, 1865. Revised by F. J. Furnivall, 1875.

van den Berg, Sara. *The Action of Ben Jonson's Poetry.* Newark: University of Delaware Press, 1987.

Venuti, Lawrence. "Why Jonson Wrote Not of Love." *Journal of Medieval and Renaissance Studies* 12 (1982): 195–220.

Walsh, P. G. "Apuleius." In *The Cambridge History of Classical Literature: Latin Literature*, edited by E. J. Kenney and W. V. Clausen, 2:774–86. Cambridge: Cambridge University Press, 1982.

Wayne, Don E. *Penshurst: The Semiotics of Place and the Poetics of History.* Madison: University of Wisconsin Press, 1984.

Weld, John S. "Christian Comedy: *Volpone.*" *Studies in Philology* 51 (1954): 172–93.

Winner, Jack D. "Ben Jonson's Epigrams and the Conventions of Formal Verse Satire." *Studies in English Literature* 23 (1983): 61–76.

Young, Steven C. "A Check List of Tudor and Stuart Induction Plays." *Philological Quarterly* 48 (1969): 131–34.

Topical Index

Index of Names, Places, and Titles